MEXICO
IN
INTERNATIONAL FINANCE AND DIPLOMACY

Prepared under the auspices of

COLUMBIA UNIVERSITY COUNCIL FOR RESEARCH
IN THE SOCIAL SCIENCES

VOLUME I

MEXICO AND HER FOREIGN CREDITORS

BY
EDGAR TURLINGTON

MEXICO AND HER FOREIGN CREDITORS

BY

EDGAR TURLINGTON

NEW YORK

COLUMBIA UNIVERSITY PRESS

1930

Published October, 1930

PRINTED IN THE UNITED STATES OF AMERICA
BY THE PLIMPTON PRESS · NORWOOD · MASS.

PREFACE

This is not a conventional treatise on the financial status of a debtor country, nor is it simply a political history of diplomatic negotiations between Mexico and her creditors. It is something more than either of these things. Combining financial and diplomatic history, it throws new light on both. Diplomatic archives, loan contracts, financial reports, and political history alike have been drawn upon during five years of coöperative research to provide materials for a more comprehensive synthesis than would ordinarily be possible for an individual scholar to undertake single-handed.

The subject was selected partly because of the possibilities it seemed to offer for an experimental demonstration of the value of this type of scholarship in the field of international relations, but more particularly for its intrinsic interest. The Mexican debt problem has recurrently claimed conspicuous notice in the news columns during the past decade, and just as this volume goes to press the signature of a new agreement is being announced. But whatever the news of the day, a study such as this will have lasting value, it is hoped, as a scholarly and dispassionate exhibit of the facts respecting one of the most important instances of international borrowing with all its interesting diplomatic accompaniments and repercussions. A thorough analysis of the Mexican experience in this domain may perhaps throw light, not only upon the contacts between the United States and Latin America, but also upon the wider problem of relations between debtor countries and their creditors.

The present volume is one of a series of studies on "Mexico in International Finance and Diplomacy" representing the product of researches conducted under the auspices of the Columbia University Council for Research in the Social Sciences and made possible through the grant of funds to that body by the Laura Spelman Rockefeller Memorial. The project was planned and directed by a committee of the Columbia faculty, namely, Professors James W. Angell, Joseph P. Chamberlain, Edward M. Earle, Carlton J. H. Hayes, Philip C. Jessup (secretary), William R. Shepherd, and Parker Thomas Moon (chairman).

Work was begun in 1925. The investigation of legal and diplomatic aspects of Mexican foreign loans was confided to Mr. Edgar Turlington, whose experience in the State Department in matters of pecuniary claims proved to be peculiarly useful in affording a perspective for the present inquiry. Miss Georgia Baxter left her research work at the Chase National Bank to undertake, with specialized competence, the study of the financial materials on the subject. In so far as it pertained to the foreign loans issued by the Mexican Government, the information obtained by Mr. Turlington, Miss Baxter, and their assistants was utilized by Mr. Turlington in the preparation of the present volume. For whatever merit the book may have, credit is due to his fine discrimination and able authorship.

In addition to Mr. Turlington's work, two other volumes are in preparation for this series. The analysis of the diplomatic policies and legal questions relative to the protection of American lives and property in Mexico has been entrusted to Mr. Frederick S. Dunn. Mr. Herbert Feis has assumed responsibility for the third volume, which is to deal with the foreign financing of railroads in Mexico.

For this first volume, dealing with Mexico's foreign debt and her relations with her creditors, a considerable mass of financial and economic material was accessible in the *Memorias* and *Informes* of the Mexican Ministry of Finance, in the annual reports of the London Corporation of Foreign Bondholders, and in various economic journals such as *The Commercial and Financial Chronicle*, of New York, and *The Economist*, of London. On the political side much was to be found in published diplomatic correspondence, particularly that of Great Britain and that of the United States. The manuscript despatches and instructions in the archives of the Department of State at Washington were also available for the period up to and including the year 1906. For the period subsequent to 1906 it was necessary to supplement the published materials by making private inquiries in informed quarters.

Numerous books which touch at greater or less length upon the subject of Mexican finance were, of course, also used. Among these may be mentioned *México y sus Cuestiones Financieras con la Inglaterra, la España, y la Francia* (Mexico, 1862) by Manuel Payno y Flores; *La Deuda contraida en Londres* (Mexico, 1885) by Joaquin D. Casasús; *Apuntes para la Liquidación de la Deuda contraida en Londres* (Mexico, 1886) by Mariano Ortíz de Montellano; *Tres Monografías que dan Idea de Una Parte de la Evolución Económica de México* (Mexico, 1905) by Pablo Macedo; *The Public Debt of Mexico* (New York, 1919) by Thomas R. Lill; and *The Public Finances of Mexico* (New York and London, 1921) by Walter F. McCaleb.

Grateful acknowledgments for courtesies and for assistance in the collection of pertinent data are made to the Honorable Dwight W. Morrow, American Ambassador to Mexico; to the Honorable Luis Montes de Oca, Minister of Finance of Mexico; to Captain Lewis B. McBride, United States Naval Attaché at Mexico City; to Dr. Eyler N. Simpson, representative in Mexico of the Institute of Current World Affairs; to Dr. Tyler Dennett, Historical Adviser, Mr. Arthur Bliss Lane, Chief of the Division of Mexican Affairs, and other officials of the Department of State at Washington; and to the staffs of the New York Public Library, the Library of Congress, the Library of the Carnegie Endowment for International Peace, and the Library of the Mexican Ministry of Finance. It will of course be realized that none of the persons named is in any sense responsible for any part of the present volume.

The committee owes gratitude to the Laura Spelman Rockefeller Memorial, which made this enterprise possible; to the Columbia Council for Research in the Social Sciences, which sponsored it; to Mr. Turlington and his associates, who have so competently carried the project to fruition; and to Mr. Frederick Coykendall and the other Trustees of Columbia University, thanks to whose kindness this series is published by the Columbia University Press.

Finally, this preface, written at a time when the members of the committee are too widely scattered for consultation, may conclude with an expression of the chairman's warm thanks for the wise counsel and patient effort which his colleagues have devoted to an otherwise thankless but, it is hoped, not a barren task.

PARKER THOMAS MOON

CONTENTS

PREFACE BY PARKER THOMAS MOON v

I. THE MEXICAN DEBT AS AN INTERNATIONAL PROBLEM . 1
II. FIRST STEPS IN FOREIGN FINANCING (1822–1825) . . 16
III. A GENERATION OF FINANCIAL CONFUSION (1826–1845) . 49
IV. "CONFUSION WORSE CONFOUNDED" (1846–1860) . . 91
V. A EUROPEAN INTERLUDE (1861–1867). 126
VI. THE REËSTABLISHMENT OF MEXICAN CREDIT (1867–1887) 171
VII. GROWTH OF THE FOREIGN DEBT (1888–1914) 212
VIII. "A VIA CRUCIS OF PENURY" (1915–1929) 263
IX. THE FOREIGN DEBT IN 1929 318

APPENDICES

I. TABLE: THE BURDEN OF THE EXTERNAL DEBT OF MEXICO AT VARIOUS EPOCHS 345
II. PRINCIPAL PROVISIONS OF CONTRACT OF FEBRUARY 7, 1824, AS AMENDED 347
III. PRINCIPAL PROVISIONS OF CONTRACT OF AUGUST 25, 1824, FOR THE LOAN OF 1825 351
IV. THE DOYLE CONVENTION OF DECEMBER 4, 1851 . . 353
V. THE CARBAJAL-CORLIES CONTRACT 356
VI. CONTRACT FOR MEXICAN EXTERNAL FOUR PER CENT GOLD DEBT OF 1910 364
VII. AGREEMENT BETWEEN THE MEXICAN GOVERNMENT AND THE INTERNATIONAL COMMITTEE OF BANKERS ON MEXICO 379

VIII. Deposit Agreement for Bonds, Notes and Other Securities included in Plan and Agreement Dated June 16, 1922 387

IX. Agreement between the Mexican Government and the International Committee of Bankers on Mexico Modifying and Supplementing the Agreement Dated June 16, 1922 421

X. The Law of January 25, 1929 436

Index 441

CHAPTER I

THE MEXICAN DEBT AS AN INTERNATIONAL PROBLEM

THE total bonded indebtedness of Mexico, including arrears of interest, is approximately $575,000,000. Of this amount about $545,000,000 is due to foreigners. The distribution of the obligations of the bonded debt in foreign countries is roughly as follows:

(In millions of dollars)

COUNTRIES	DIRECT DEBT[a]	GUARANTEED RAILWAY DEBT[a]	TOTAL
France	144	40	184
Great Britain	88	39	127
United States	102	14	116
Netherlands	27	11	38
Germany	30	—	30
Belgium	26	2	28
Switzerland	18	3	21
Totals	435	109	544

[a] The Direct Debt includes the Tehuantepec Railway loans and the state and municipal loans for which responsibility has been assumed by the federal government.

The totals here given are not staggering. Even the addition of $450,000,000 — the estimated amount of the so-called floating debt, comprising unliquidated accounts, claims of Mexicans and foreigners for loss of life, personal injuries, damage to property, seizure of funds, expropriation of lands, and the like — would bring the debt of Mexico to but little more than $1,000,000,000. This is unquestionably a large debt for a country of 15,000,000 inhabitants, the majority of whom have no taxable property. The potential wealth of Mexico is, however, known to be enormous, and it can undoubtedly be developed to the point of being adequate for the service of the existing debt, *upon one condition.* That condition is the maintenance of peace and order.

Two generations ago the attempt of Napoleon III to establish a stable government in Mexico was brought to an end, largely by the insistence of the United States upon the withdrawal of the French troops which had kept Maximilian on the throne at Mexico City. To Napoleon's argument that the French intervention was justified by the "prevalence of anarchy" in Mexico, Secretary Seward replied, in part:

> The Mexican population have, and their situation has, some peculiarities which are doubtless well understood by France. Early in the present century they were forced, by convictions which mankind cannot but respect, to cast off a foreign monarchical rule which they deemed incompatible with their welfare and aggrandizement. They were forced at the same time, by convictions which the world must respect, to attempt the establishment of republican institutions, without the full experience and practical education and habits which would render those institutions all at once firm and satisfactory. Mexico was a theatre of conflict between European commercial, ecclesiastical, and political institutions and dogmas and novel American institutions and ideas. . . . We cannot deny that all the anarchy in Mexico . . . was necessarily, and even wisely, endured in the attempts to lay sure foundations of broad republican liberty.

During the forty years preceding this American apologia for the prevalence of anarchy in Mexico, the foreign creditors of our neighbor to the south had received but a small part of the interest due on their bonds. With untold natural wealth lying untouched because of incessant political strife, the young republic had been forced to seek compositions with her foreign creditors in 1830, 1837, 1846, and 1850. The armed intervention of France, Great Britain, and Spain at the end of 1861 — an intervention from which Spain and Great Britain almost immediately withdrew — had, moreover, been due very largely to the failure of Mexico (because of political disturbances) to comply with her obligations to her foreign creditors.

The work of laying the "sure foundations of broad republican liberty" continued, with the usual accompaniment of civil strife, for more than a decade after the withdrawal of the French troops from Mexico. The long dictatorship of Díaz, which began in

1876, was in itself the antithesis of broad republican liberty. By improving the facilities for communication, however, by encouraging the development of natural resources, and by maintaining peace and order, at any cost, Díaz contributed very greatly to the integration of the nation, in fact and in the consciousness of its inhabitants. A further contribution of the dictator to the foundations of broad republican liberty was the development of efficient administrative officers, for lack of whom the republic had suffered severely at its inception. The most efficient of these officers were probably in the Department of Finance, to which the foreign holders of Mexican bonds had occasion to be grateful for the reëstablishment and maintenance of the regular service on the debt.

The revolution which began in 1910 and which is regarded by many Mexicans as still in the process of consolidation appears to have been motivated to a large extent by consideration for the welfare of the great mass of the Mexican people — Indians and mestizos without property and without education. If these Indians and mestizos are given a valuable "stake in the country" and if they are educated to the point of taking an intelligent interest in politics, the "foundations of broad republican liberty," to which Secretary Seward referred, will apparently at last have been securely laid. Meanwhile, the government of the United States, whose nationals own far more Mexican bonds and other Mexican property than they did in 1866, considers it no longer necessary to justify the prevalence of anarchy as a stage in the development of republican institutions in Mexico. In connection with the revolt of 1929, indeed, as well as in connection with the revolt of 1923, our government has done all that it could do, short of armed intervention, to aid the existing Mexican government in restoring peace and order.

During the last fifteen years Mexico has paid less than $40,000,000 on account of the interest on her bonded debt. Approximately one-third of that debt, accordingly, represents interest due and unpaid. Under agreements made in 1922 and 1925 with the International Committee of Bankers on Mexico, the arrears of interest to the end of 1922 and a part of the interest for the ensuing five years were to be paid over a period of forty years, beginning on January 1, 1928. The agreements of 1922 and 1925 were declared by the Mexican government in 1927 to be impossible of further execution. Negotiations for a new agreement with the International Committee were in progress at the outbreak of the revolt in March, 1929, and will probably be resumed at some time in the near future. The new agreement, it has been declared, must be made on the basis of Mexico's capacity to pay. This is the same basis on which the agreements of 1922 and 1925 were ostensibly made, but these agreements are considered to have been made without accurate information as to the economic and fiscal condition of the country.

The determination of the extent to which Mexico will be able to pay her acknowledged foreign debt under the conditions that may prevail during the period of the new agreement will present obvious difficulties. Of these difficulties no detailed examination will be made in this volume. Concerning a less obvious difficulty, which lies at the root of the Mexican demand for a reduction of the foreign debt, some comment may, however, be appropriate at this point. This difficulty is a conviction, in the minds of responsible Mexican statesmen, that Mexico has been exploited by foreign capitalists, with respect to her debt as well as with respect to her natural resources. This conviction was expressed by a President of Mexico some years ago in the following words:

> We have always paid our debts. We always will pay our debts. We have seen a loan of $20,000,000 received in 1824, changed magically into a debt of more than $100,000,000. We have seen Maximilian sign an obligation for $40,000,000 in return for a loan of $20,000,000. We have seen Miramón, the counter-revolutionist, sign a note for $15,000,000 in return for a loan of $750,000. Yet not once, even under these outrageous burdens, have we ever advanced the idea of repudiation.

The statement here quoted is inaccurate in several details. The two loans received in 1824 and 1825, in the amount of approximately $20,000,000, in return for bonds of a face value of $32,000,000, did indeed change into a debt of even more than $100,000,000. The transformation was, however, not magical; it was the natural effect of the accumulation of simple interest due and unpaid. Maximilian's bonds totaled some $150,000,000; but except for an issue of $25,000,000 for the funding of interest in arrears for ten years before the unfortunate puppet of Napoleon III ascended the throne of Mexico, all of these bonds were repudiated in their entirety; and the bonds which were not entirely repudiated were eventually redeemed, after an intermediate operation of conversion, at only one-fifth of their face value. Miramón's obligation of $15,000,000 was liquidated at one-sixth of its face value.

In connection with the statement that Mexico has always paid her debts, it may be noted that during the first sixty-seven years of Mexican independence, most of them years of continuous civil disturbance, all of the money actually received by Mexico on account of the loans of 1824 and 1825 was in fact repaid with interest averaging about 2 per cent per annum. The loans of 1824 and 1825 were the only external loans floated by Mexico prior to 1888 with the exception of the Juárez loan of 1865, which was eventually repaid at not much less than its face value, and the Maximilian loans of 1864 and 1865, which were repudiated, as already shown, upon considerations of some moral, if not legal, weight. The net proceeds of the loans of 1824 and 1825, which had a face value of $32,000,000, were $21,000,000. Approximately $5,000,000 (face value) of the bonds of 1824 were redeemed in 1825, at an average price of 63 (after payment of interest at 5 per cent for one year), as against the price of 50 at which the Mexican government had sold them. On account of the remaining bonds of the face value of $27,000,000 — for which Mexico had received $18,500,000 — there were paid in cash up to the end of the year 1888 sums aggregating nearly $40,000,000. The first $2,500,000 received by Mexico on account of a foreign loan was thus repaid in full with interest at about 36 per cent for one year. Upon the remainder of the first two loans Mexico, besides returning the capital received, paid interest at the rate of nearly 2 per cent per annum.

The return to the investor who purchased the bonds of 1824 and 1825 at their original market price, and who held the bonds until 1888, was somewhat less than the amount indicated by the foregoing figures. The obvious reason for the disparity is the fact that the amount paid for the bonds by the public in 1824 and 1825 was considerably above that received by Mexico.

The investor who bought the bonds immediately after their issue was able, despite numerous defaults and partial repudiations in the meantime, to recover the whole of his capital in 1888 with interest averaging 2.3 per cent a year on the bond of 1824 and 1.1 per cent a year on the bond of 1825.

On the other side of the ledger should, of course, be put the amounts which were due and not paid. The payments which should have been made to the purchaser of a £1,000 bond up to the end of 1888, according to the contracts for the loans of 1824 and 1825, were £1,000 (the principal) plus £3,250 (for interest) in the first case and £1,000 (the principal) plus £3,840 (for interest) in the second case. There were thus, apart from various modifications of the original contracts, a sacrifice of £2,800 of the amount due on the first bond and a sacrifice of £3,360 of the amount due on the second bond.

Sacrifices similar to those of the holders of the bonds of the London debt, which was finally liquidated with the proceeds of the loan of 1888, have been imposed upon the holders of the bonds of two other debts, known as the diplomatic convention debts.[1] Since 1914, moreover, the holders of the bonds issued in 1886 and in later years have received but a small fraction of the interest due, and there were notable sacrifices in connection with the revisions of 1922 and 1925.[2]

It is true that under the spur of necessity Mexico has frequently borrowed money abroad at very high rates. Upon a survey of the entire financial history of Mexico, however, it appears that foreign capitalists, in their dealings with the Mexican government, have had no advantage except such as may have resulted from their possession of funds which the government was eager to borrow. In their efforts to recover the amounts advanced, with interest, foreign bondholders have generally been at a distinct disadvantage as compared with the Mexican government. A relatively unimportant class of foreign capitalists, who

[1] See p. 100 *infra*. [2] See pp. 290, 307 *infra*.

have advanced funds directly to Mexico under special arrangements, for short periods and without the issue of bonds, have, indeed, always been accorded formal diplomatic support by their own governments in their efforts to recover the sums advanced. Several diplomatic conventions embodying engagements to repay such sums with interest and stipulating security in the form of special assignments of customs duties were signed by Mexico with Great Britain, France, and Spain during the fifth and sixth decades of the last century. The British convention debt was declared by an American Minister to Mexico in 1857 to be "a rod of influence and constraint" which had been "unsparingly used" against Mexico by Great Britain. The suspension of the execution of the conventions regarding the debts on account of which Great Britain, France, and Spain had interposed diplomatically was one of the principal grounds for the military intervention of those three powers in 1861. It is interesting to note that all the convention debts taken together, with arrears of interest included, amounted in 1861 to only $12,000,000, whereas the debt represented by the bonds and unpaid coupons of the so-called London debt amounted at the same time to more than $60,000,000. Yet the British government prior to 1861 had consistently refused to follow with respect to the bonds of the London debt, almost entirely in the hands of British subjects, the course which it had followed without hesitation with respect to the bonds of the convention debt, many of which had passed into the hands of Mexicans. The demands which British naval officers made upon the authorities at Veracruz in 1859 and 1860 in behalf of the bondholders of the London debt appear to have been made without authorization from the Foreign Office and as mere incidents to the demands made by the same officers in behalf of the bondholders of the convention debt. The action of these officers was subsequently approved and the rights of the London bondholders were declared by the Foreign Office to have been given an international character by the undertakings exacted from the authorities at Veracruz. In general, however, that is, at all times prior to 1859 and after 1862, the British government has refrained from official action in behalf of investors in the public funds of Mexico. The interruption of diplomatic relations between Mexico and Great Britain, which extended from 1867 to 1884, was not terminated until after formal assurances had been given by Mexico with reference to the recognition of the British convention debt. The matter of the London debt, on the other hand, was left to be adjusted between Mexico and the bondholders.

The possibility of the increase of British commerce and of British political influence in Mexico, as an indirect consequence of the flotation of a Mexican loan in London, was doubtless appreciated by the British government when the first moves were made toward the realization of such a loan. The British consul who advanced funds to Mexico in 1823 and the British commissioner who guaranteed the advance undoubtedly believed that their action would be approved by their government. The consul and the commissioners were, however, officially reprimanded, and the representative of Mexico in London was told at the Foreign Office that His Majesty's Government could have nothing to do with the loan desired. Shortly after the first default of Mexico upon the London debt the British vice-consuls at Veracruz and Tampico were permitted to receive certain payments for the account of the bondholders, but the Foreign Office in London took pains to make it clear that the vice-consuls were in this matter acting entirely in their private capacity. During the next thirty years unofficial representations in behalf of the bondholders were frequently made by the British legation at Mexico City. The unofficial character of the representations was, however, always emphasized. Representations of an official and "authoritative" character were considered to be inappropriate for the reasons indicated by Lord Palmerston in 1848, partly as follows:

> It has hitherto been thought by the successive Governments of Great Britain undesirable that British subjects should invest their capital in loans to foreign governments instead of employing it in profitable undertakings at home; . . .
>
> For the British Government has considered that the losses of imprudent men, who have placed mistaken confidence in the good faith of foreign governments, would prove a salutary warning to others. . . .

The position of the British government, as announced by Palmerston, was reaffirmed by Granville in 1871, by Salisbury in 1880, and by Balfour in 1902. It was not substantially modified through the British participation in the Hague Convention of 1907, which binds the signatories not to resort to armed force for the recovery of contract debts in behalf of their nationals *unless* the debtor state "refuses or neglects to reply to an offer of arbitration, or, after accepting the offer, prevents any *compromis* from being agreed on, or, after the arbitration, fails to submit to the award." The obvious inference from the language here used was pointed out in 1912 by the Solicitor for the Department of State, lately Under-Secretary of State, Mr. Clark, in connection with the discussion of a projected American loan to Honduras. The government of the United States, said Mr. Clark, "would have the right, should any of those exceptions arise, to use force in behalf of the Americans making the loan."

Prior to 1864 the only substantial holdings in the foreign debt of Mexico, other than the French and Spanish convention debts, were British. Certain obligations of the London debt were held by Dutch subjects, who endeavored without success, first during the European intervention and later during the Juárez régime, to obtain satisfaction of their claims through their consul general at Mexico City. The Dutch holdings were, however, relatively unimportant. In 1864 and 1865 a large quantity of Mexican bonds was bought by French investors, with the encouragement and practical guarantee of their government. These investors were subsequently reimbursed by the French government for the greater part of their outlay.

The bonds offered for sale in New York in 1865 by a representative of Juárez were issued without objection but with no sort of positive encouragement from the government at Washington. Only 9,000 pesos of these bonds were actually sold, at sixty cents in American money to the peso, but nearly 2,000,000 pesos of them were accepted by American merchants and manufacturers, at the same rate, in payment for supplies and munitions of war. The potential advantages to the United States of loans to the Mexican government had been enthusiastically presented to the Department of State on several occasions prior to 1865. A chargé d'affaires and two ministers to Mexico had pointed out the extreme ease with which a loan to Mexico upon the security of Mexican territory might lead to the acquisition of the territory by the United States. Except in 1861, however, when it appeared to be possible to forestall the European intervention by paying the interest on the foreign debt of Mexico, the Department of State and the President declined to give serious consideration to the suggestion of an official American loan to Mexico.

The Mexican loans of the modern era, beginning in 1888, have been made in numerous markets, including, in the order of the amounts of the present holdings, those of France, Great Britain, the United States, the Netherlands, Germany, Belgium, and Switzerland. None of the governments in the countries named appears to have given official encouragement to these loans, by diplomatic action or otherwise. In each of these countries, indeed, with the exception of the United States, there has long existed some sort of device for closing the exchanges to bonds that are deemed unsound or politically undesirable. In Great Britain as long ago as 1875 a Parliamentary Commission, stirred by recent losses of British investors in the bonds of politically unstable or financially unsound foreign governments, reached the conclusion that the most effective deterrent to the repetition of such losses was full publicity as to the circumstances and conditions of every projected loan. Most of the devices of control are directed primarily toward securing such publicity. The stock exchanges are themselves extremely active toward that end, and Mexico had occasion to discover in 1874 and for several years thereafter that the exchanges in various countries are capable of reaching agreements for blocking the flotation of new loans by governments that do not maintain the service of their existing loans. Practical unanimity of the exchanges was again established with particular reference to Mexico in 1913, when various European governments followed the lead of President Wilson in favoring the "financial starvation" of Huerta. The failure of Carranza and Obregón to obtain foreign loans between 1917 and 1922 was also not unconnected with a governmentally approved unanimity of the money markets. The fact that during these years the State Department at Washington announced its desire to inspect in advance the terms of every foreign loan floated in the United States was not due to the Mexican situation. It is relevant here, however, as a further indication of the recent tendency of governments to curb rather than foster the flotation of foreign loans by their nationals.

The closing of the European exchanges to new issues of Mexican bonds between 1874 and 1886 was due primarily to representations by the Corporation of Foreign Bondholders at London, organized in 1868. A committee of Mexican bondholders had been formed at London as early as 1829, had been merged for a while in a committee of Spanish-American bondholders, had later resumed its separate existence, and had finally become a part of the Corporation of Foreign Bondholders. The Association Nationale des Porteurs Français de Valeurs Mobilières was formed in Paris in 1899, and similar bodies were organized in Belgium and the Netherlands. These voluntary associations have sometimes been accorded valuable support by the governments to which their members looked for protection. The British government, for example, has on many occasions lent its good offices and friendly aid to the Corporation of Foreign Bondholders at London. Only on rare occasions, however, have the associations of bondholders been accorded anything more than the good offices and friendly aid of their governments. The London Corporation, indeed, at the beginning of its career, declared that the interests of bondholders are generally opposed to "any measures which can place H. M. Government in simple antagonism to that of another country" and that bondholders are far from desiring "hostile interposition which must come home in disturbance of our own commerce, besides the creation of dangerous complications."

The present close association of the bondholders' organs of self-help with their governments did not begin until after the World War. The governments whose nationals held most of the foreign bonds of Mexico had meanwhile bound themselves, by the Hague Convention of 1907, to refrain from the use of force for the collection of contract debts until after recourse to arbitration had been refused or until after an arbitral award, duly decreed, had been denied execution by a debtor government. The number of holders of foreign bonds in various countries, especially in the United States, and the quantity of their holdings had, however, been rapidly increasing, and it was evident that the basis of the distinction drawn by Lord Palmerston in 1848 between holders of foreign bonds in default, on the one hand, and persons injured by the tortious action of foreign governments, on the other hand, was being undermined. It was, therefore, not at all surprising that the governments of France, Great Britain, and the United States, whose nationals held two-thirds of all the government and railway bonds of Mexico, found it possible, in 1919, to approve in advance the formation of an International Committee of Bankers on Mexico whose purpose was to study the situation in Mexico and to prepare for such action as might be feasible with a view to inducing the Mexican government to resume payments on its bonds. With both the International Committee and the governments of the leading capitalistic countries insisting on a satisfactory settlement by Mexico with respect to her outstanding obligations, it was obvious that Mexico would be obliged either to make the settlement required or to find within her own borders the funds necessary for her subsistence and development. The close association of the three governments with the International Committee gave these governments, moreover, a formidable advantage in their demands that Mexico furnish assurances with respect to vested property rights of various kinds that were deemed to be menaced by certain provisions of the new constitution of Mexico.

The apparent effectiveness of the International Committee of Bankers, as an instrument of self-help known to be favored by the governments to which the bondholders might look for eventual protection, was demonstrated in the agreement of 1922, in which Mexico assumed, for a time, the responsibility for the entire debt of the Mexican railways as well as for her own direct obligations. The agreement of 1922 was assailed by Mexican critics as laying upon their government a burden greater than it could bear. The Minister of Finance who had signed the agreement was charged with incompetence and with giving false assurances to the President in order to secure the approval of the agreement. The terms of the agreement were observed for only one year. After extensive correspondence and negotiations a new agreement was concluded in 1925, relieving the Mexican government of responsibility for the greater part of the railway debt. The agreement of 1925 was observed for only two years.

What the future may hold in store for Mexico and her foreign creditors no one can predict with confidence. The revolt of March and April, 1929, is a discouraging symptom. If public order can be maintained and if the social ideals of the revolution which began in 1910 can be reconciled, in practice, with the conditions necessary for the profitable conduct of enterprises backed by foreign as well as by domestic capital, the whole of the foreign debt can doubtless be liquidated within a reasonable period. If chaos reasserts itself, the service of the debt cannot be kept up and foreign creditors may be expected to call loudly upon their governments for diplomatic interposition or more drastic action. In view of the magnitude of the interests involved in the foreign debt of Mexico, to say nothing of the "great respectability" of the bondholders, by which Lord Aberdeen was influenced in 1830, the governments of the bondholders may not adhere indefinitely to the distinction evolved under the conditions of a century ago between losses upon bonds and losses upon other kinds of property.

There is a tendency, in certain quarters, toward the view that persons who invest in foreign bonds or in any other kind of property whose value depends on conditions in a foreign country should be required to take all the risks of their ventures. There is, however, another tendency, which for the present seems stronger, toward the view, expressed by Mr. Coolidge in 1927, that there is "a distinct and binding obligation on the part of self-respecting governments to afford protection . . . to the property of their citizens wherever they may be." Bonds are property no less than houses, mines, and crops; and in a country given to frequent revolution their value is hardly more speculative than that of more tangible holdings. A government that is able to pay indemnities for damage to houses, mines, and crops can doubtless find the money for reimbursement of investors in its bonds. In the case of foreign bonds, certainly, if not in the case of internal bonds, there appears to be no sound basis in law for a distinction between the rights of international reclamation of defrauded bondholders and those of other persons injured by the wrongful acts of a government. The right of sovereignty of the state which issues a bond has often been alleged as a bar to claims in behalf of bondholders. Sovereignty, however, it has been realized more fully in recent years, is a term which should be confined to the sphere of municipal relations, and the right of sovereignty cannot properly be invoked as a cover for injustice.[3]

This is not to say that holders of foreign bonds may in every case of default demand of their governments, as a matter of right, the exercise of pressure upon the defaulting government. The grant of protection to any complainant, whether a bondholder or the holder of any other form of property, is always discretionary. Protection is doubtless granted as a matter of course, though not as a matter of right, in many instances, and it is doubtless well to proceed with more circumspection in the case of a bondholder who may have acquired his bond in the open market at a greatly depreciated rate than in the case of a resident of a foreign country whose crops are seized by the government of that country without compensation. Careful attention should be given, as the French Minister of Foreign Affairs pointed out in 1907, not only to the circumstances of the acquisition of the bonds but also to the circumstances of their issue.

If no satisfactory arrangement is made between Mexico and the International Committee of Bankers in the near future, or if an arrangement is made and shortly afterward breaks down, it is not improbable that the governments of the United States, Great Britain, France, and other countries whose nationals hold

[3] An excellent discussion of the question of intervention in behalf of bondholders is contained in Sir John Fischer Williams' *International Law and International Obligations Arising from Contract* (Leyden, 1923).

Mexican bonds may be moved to suggest an arbitration as to how much Mexico should pay on her bonds and how the payments shall be secured. There would seem to be no insuperable difficulty in defining the terms of reference to an arbitral body.

Any international solution that may be found for the problem of the Mexican foreign debt will, of course, require an understanding of the background of that debt, not only by the experts who may be detailed to study the problem but also by the members of the public who may be called upon to approve the participation of their governments in the solution. It is primarily for this public that the following chapters have been prepared.[4]

[4] An agreement providing, *inter alia,* for the remission of a considerable part of the interest in arrears and for the resumption of the full service on the "Direct Debt" in 1935, at a uniform interest rate of five per cent, was signed at New York on behalf of Mexico and the International Committee of Bankers on July 25, 1930, just as this volume went to press. The agreement is subject to the approval of the bondholders, the authorized representation of their interests by the International Committee having ceased in 1928. For the joint announcement of the Committee and the Mexican Minister of Finance, with reference to the negotiations and the general terms of the agreement, see *The New York Times,* July 26, 1930.

CHAPTER II

FIRST STEPS IN FOREIGN FINANCING (1822–1825)

Financial Perplexities of a New Nation

The political independence of the colony of New Spain was virtually assured when General Agustín de Iturbide entered Mexico City at the end of September, 1821, with his Army of the Three Guarantees.[1] In pursuance of the treaty of peace which he had signed with the Spanish viceroy, O'Donojú, at Córdoba a month before, Iturbide immediately convoked a Provisional Assembly of thirty-six persons "prominent for their virtues, offices, fortunes, representation, and character." This Assembly, on the first day of October, elected a Regency, composed of Iturbide, O'Donojú, and three others, to constitute the executive pending the ratification of the treaty and the designation of an Emperor of Mexico by the Spanish Cortes.[2]

The Army of the Three Guarantees, which had compelled the viceroy to sign the treaty of Córdoba, could not safely be dispersed so long as there was well founded apprehension that the treaty might be repudiated by the Cortes or that the elements in Mexico which favored a republican form of government might attempt to overthrow the Regency. Large sums were therefore required for the payment of troops and the purchase of military supplies. Considerable expenditures for the promotion of commerce, industry, and agriculture, which had been almost completely paralyzed by the revolutionary struggles of eleven years, might also be legitimately expected of a government devoted to

[1] The three guarantees were Religion, Independence, and Equality.

[2] Hubert Howe Bancroft, *History of Mexico* (San Francisco, 1866), Vol. IV, pp. 729–735; Herbert Ingram Priestley, *The Mexican Nation, a History* (New York, 1926), pp. 246–251.

the welfare of the Mexican people instead of to the policy of exploitation which had been systematically followed for three centuries by Spain.[3] Less justifiable but apparently irresistible demands, moreover, were made upon the treasury for the maintenance of the dignity of the new nation and for the expression of the national gratitude to Iturbide and other heroes of the revolution.[4]

To meet its urgent financial needs, the Regency was unable to utilize the elaborate fiscal machinery by which the viceroys had been accustomed before 1810 to collect more than four times as much revenue as was required for the colonial administration.[5] This machinery had totally collapsed during the revolution, and the viceroys had been obliged to resort to forced loans and other irregular measures, as a result of which formidable pecuniary

[3] Commerce with any foreign country had been forbidden to the colony until 1778. Even the commerce with the mother country had been for many years confined to a single port. Agriculture was burdened by heavy restrictions upon the cultivation of crops which could be grown in Spain. The only industries permitted were those which would not compete with Spanish industries. Details concerning the policy of exploitation followed in New Spain may be found in Lucas Alamán, *Historia de Mejico desde los primeros movimientos que prepararon su independencia en el año de 1808 hasta la época presente* (Mexico, 1849), pp. 88–114.

[4] As President of the Regency, Iturbide was given a salary of 120,000 pesos a year. As a revolutionary hero, he was awarded a prize of 1,000,000 pesos and twenty square leagues of land. The peso was then the equivalent of the United States dollar.

[5] The annual net revenues of New Spain in the first decade of the nineteenth century were in excess of 14,000,000 pesos. Of these revenues some were known as *communes,* or ordinary, and were devoted so far as was deemed necessary to the administrative expenses of the colony. Others, known as *remisibles* and consisting chiefly of the profits of the tobacco and quicksilver monopolies, were remitted annually to the Crown. The revenues called *particulares* were used only for designated objects, chiefly ecclesiastical. With respect to the fourth division of the revenues, known as *ajenos,* the viceregal government exercised only administrative or fiduciary functions. The net yield of these revenues was usually about as follows: *communes,* 10,000,000 pesos; *remisibles,* 3,500,000 pesos; *particulares,* 500,000 pesos; *ajenos,* 200,000 pesos. *Cf.* Matías Romero, *Memoria de Hacienda y Crédito Público* (Mexico, 1871), pp. 61–64; Lorenzo de Zavala, *Ensayo Historico de las Revoluciones de México desde 1808 hasta 1830* (Vol. I., Paris, 1831; Vol. II, New York, 1832; Vols. I and II reprinted together, Mexico, 1845), pp. 23–24; José María Luis Mora, *Méjico y Sus Revoluciones* (Paris, 1836), Vol. I, pp. 242 *et seq.;* Walter F. McCaleb, *The Public Finances of Mexico* (New York and London, 1921), pp. 12–16. The sources of the ordinary revenues (*communes*) and the use made of these

claims had accumulated against the viceregal treasury.[6] The reëstablishment of the fiscal system of the viceroys was made impracticable by considerations which were in part economic and in part political. The economic obstacle was the fact that

---

revenues are conveniently shown in the following table, adapted from Romero, for the year 1789:

Revenues

	In pesos (Here designated by the symbol P)
Assay of gold	13,314
Assay of silver	1,800,546
Coinage of gold and silver	1,215,393
Gunpowder (chiefly for use in mining)	63,630
Salt and salt mines	91,118
Duty on imports and exports	600,579
Alcabala (tax on internal commerce)	3,127,572
Stamped paper	56,412
Ninth part of tithes	151,555
Tax on ecclesiastical appointments	55,176
Lottery	61,970
Pulque (fermented juice of maguey)	737,021
Tributes (from Indian tribes)	696,987
Other sources of revenue	360,917
Total revenues	P9,032,190

Expenditures

Maintenance of troops, garrisons, arsenal, etc.	3,023,304
Treasury Department	508,389
Administration of justice	124,294
Other expenses of administration	513,004
Debts of former administrations and interest on the same	98,485
Sums remitted to other Spanish possessions	3,011,664
Total expenditures	7,279,140
Surplus	1,753,050
Total	P9,032,190

[6] These claims were later recognized, by a decree of June 28, 1824, to the extent of P36,000,000. No claims were allowed except those of natives of the country who could prove that their advances to the viceregal government were made under compulsion. See Manuel Payno y Flores, *México y Sus Cuestiones Financieras con la Inglaterra, la España, y la Francia* (Mexico, 1862), Appendix, p. 108; Manuel Dublán, José María Lozano, and continuators, *Legislación Mexicana* (Mexico, 1876–1912), Vol. I, p. 709.

commerce, mining, and the tobacco industry, which had been the sources of more than 12,000,000 pesos of the annual revenues of the viceregal government, were practically at a standstill and could not be revived without considerable outlays of capital and the lapse of considerable time. Sufficient capital for an economic revival was in the possession of Spaniards in Mexico, but these Spaniards were leaving the country in great numbers in fear of private vengeance or, at the least, of unfriendly treatment at the hands of a government controlled by creoles, mestizos, and Indians.[7]

The political obstacle to the reimposition of the pre-revolutionary fiscal machinery was the opposition of elements of the population which the viceroys had been able to disregard. The Indians, in view of their services to the revolutionary cause and of the revolutionary guarantee of equality, could not again be subjected to the annual tribute of more than a million pesos which had been collected since the days of Moctezuma. Another million was sacrificed, by way of concession to the people, in the discontinuance of the tax on pulque[8] and cane alcohol. The *alcabala,* a tax on merchandise transported from one community to another, was reduced from 16 to 6 per cent in consequence of its extreme unpopularity. Upon more reasonable grounds but nevertheless largely out of pure sentiment, the tobacco monopoly, formerly described as "the precious jewel which the King has in his American dominions,"[9] was ordered to be terminated within two years, after which the cultivation, manipulation, and sale of tobacco were to be entirely free. The removal of the import duty on quicksilver, an indispensable commodity in mining operations, and the drastic reduction of the duties on the output of the mines may perhaps have been dictated by concern for the promotion of an essential industry. In general, however, there can be no doubt that one of the strongest influences upon the action of the Regency with respect to taxes was the desire to win

[7] Bancroft, *op. cit.*, Vol. IV, p. 741; Alamán, *op. cit.*, *loc. cit.;* Romero, *op. cit.*, pp. 61–66.

[8] The fermented juice of the maguey.

[9] Joaquin Maniau, *Compendio de la historia de la real hacienda de Nueva España* (Mexico, 1794), p. 51.

or hold the favor of the people.[10] The President of the Regency, it will be remembered, had still to realize his ambition to be crowned first Emperor of Mexico.[11]

Unable or unwilling to draw upon the sources of revenue which the viceroys had found most profitable, the Regency first appealed to local capitalists for voluntary loans up to 300,000 pesos a month. The appeal was ineffectual, chiefly because confidence in the permanence of the new régime was lacking. By the end of the year 1821 not quite 300,000 pesos had been supplied voluntarily. The Regency therefore sought and obtained from the Provisional Assembly authorization to levy forced loans. For the repayment of these loans the property of the extinguished Inquisition and the Pious Fund of the Californias were to be pledged.[12]

At the beginning of January, 1822, the President of the Regency was authorized to negotiate a loan of 1,500,000 pesos upon the security of such sources of revenue as he might deem advisable. Approximately one-third of this loan was obtained by a levy upon the Cathedral chapters. In February specific portions of the loan were fixed as quotas to be collected by force from designated persons. On March 16, 1822, the Constituent Congress, which had replaced the Provisional Assembly on February 24, ordered the exaction of this loan to be stopped. The Congress authorized the Regency to obtain funds by selling at auction the secular lands of religious corporations, especially the lands of the Jesuits, who had been expelled in 1767. To supplement the funds thus obtained, it invited the people in all the provinces to give or lend money voluntarily for the "necessities of the army and other needs of the State." The invitation was generally ignored.[13]

10 Romero, *op. cit.*, p. 66; Joaquin D. Casasús, *La deuda contraida en Londres* (Mexico, 1885), pp. 13–15.

11 Bancroft, *op. cit.*, Vol. IV, p. 733.

12 Romero, *op. cit.*, p. 67. The Inquisition had been suppressed at the inception of the Regency (Bancroft, *op. cit.*, Vol. IV, p. 699). The Pious Fund, composed of donations for the propagation of the Catholic faith in Upper and Lower California, had been taken over by the viceregal government upon the expulsion of the Jesuits in 1767 (*Catholic Encyclopedia*, New York, 1911, Vol. XII, p. 106).

13 Romero, *op. cit.*, p. 69.

Confidence in the Regency and in any government which might be substituted for it as a result of the deliberations of the Constituent Congress was at this time greatly shaken by the receipt of the news that the Spanish Cortes had on February 13 rejected the treaty of Córdoba. The Mexican patriots were considerably encouraged by the recognition of the independence of their country by the Congress of the United States, pursuant to President Monroe's recommendation of March 8. This recognition did not, however, notably increase the prestige of the Regency, and the popularity of Iturbide as "El Libertador" was distinctly waning at the moment when he was proclaimed Emperor of Mexico, on May 19, 1822.[14]

The elevation of Iturbide to the imperial dignity was not sufficiently gratifying to the possessors of capital to induce them to advance funds voluntarily for the needs of the government. On June 11, therefore, the Constituent Congress authorized the levy of a forced loan of 600,000 pesos upon the tribunals of commerce (*consulados*) of Mexico City, Puebla, Veracruz and Guadalajara. For the repayment of this loan a temporary charge of two per cent was placed on gold and silver coins exported through the frontier customs-houses.[15]

A Foreign Loan Authorized

Some months before the change in the form of government, the financial perplexities of the new nation had come to the attention of Francisco de Borja Migoni, a Mexican merchant who had been for several years resident in London. In a letter addressed to General Iturbide, as President of the Regency, on March 26, 1822, Migoni had declared that the necessities of the Mexican treasury could readily be met by means of a loan which he was willing to undertake to raise in England.[16]

It would be highly advantageous, said Migoni, for Mexico to establish relations with foreign countries and particularly with

[14] Bancroft, *op. cit.*, Vol. IV, pp. 761–775.

[15] Romero, *op. cit.*, p. 69.

[16] *La Diplomacia Mexicana* (Mexico, 1910, 1912, 1913), Vol. II, pp. 137–140 (hereinafter cited as *Dip. Mex.*).

England, the most influential of them. Spain, blind to her own interests, would persist as long as possible in her refusal to recognize her former colonies in America. England, on the other hand, if a loan were obtained in that country by the Mexican government, would acquire a substantial interest in the maintenance of Mexican independence.

> Any nation which lends money to another nation [he declared] acquires an interest in the continuance of the latter's independence. The English government protects the interests of its people, and if the English people have funds in Mexico, I ask you: Will not Mexico be given some slight consideration by that government? The reconquest of Venezuela by the Peninsula [Spain] would be displeasing to England today—because of the £2,000,000 which she would lose thereby.

In addition to the loan of £2,000,000 which Venezuela had recently obtained from English bankers, Migoni mentioned a loan of the same amount which had just been negotiated in London by a representative of Colombia. The latter loan was designed partly for the repayment of advances, up to £500,000, which had been made by English friends of Colombia during her struggle for independence.

The expedient suggested by Migoni was approved by the Mexican Congress on June 25, 1822. On that date the Congress authorized the imperial government to "seek among foreign powers a loan of twenty-five to thirty million pesos in such manner and under such conditions as its well known zeal may consider least onerous to the nation." As security for the repayment of the loan the government was authorized to "hypothecate the generality of the national revenue existing or to be established."[17]

Failure of the Loan Project

At the beginning of July the government considered itself fortunate in concluding a contract with a certain James Barry, a foreigner resident in Mexico City, for the raising of a loan of 10,000,000 pesos at ten per cent in London. Among the conditions of the contract was the advance to Barry of a considerable sum against bills of exchange to the amount of 1,000,000 pesos,

[17] *Legislación Mexicana*, Vol. I, p. 617.

drawn by him upon the supposititious London house of Thomas Morton Jones. Two firms at Veracruz were induced to guarantee the bills, which, it was agreed, would not be placed in circulation until the lapse of twenty days after they were drawn. Before the lapse of this period, Barry, on the point of sailing from Tampico, wrote the government that in his opinion it would be better for the national credit to keep the bills out of circulation until the receipt of a further communication from him after his arrival in London. It was only then that the government realized that Barry had no financial standing and that his sole asset was the hope of finding in London the means of fulfilling his contract.[18]

So sponsored, the first effort of the imperial government to obtain a loan in the European market could hardly have been expected to succeed. When the circumstances became known, they brought the government into ridicule and contempt.[19] The negotiations of one Dennis A. Smith, another foreigner, who had likewise concluded a contract with the government for the raising of a loan in Europe, appear to have been equally unsuccessful.[20]

Negotiations were apparently still in progress in Europe at the end of October, 1822, when Manuel Zozaya, the first Mexican Minister received in Washington, was authorized to borrow 10,000,000 pesos in the United States upon the least onerous conditions possible. Although the Minister was sure that he could have borrowed this sum, he entered into no negotiations to that end. His inactivity in the matter may have been due to the conviction, which he had acquired before the end of December, that the United States would in time be the "sworn enemies" of Mexico and ought therefore to be treated "as such from the present day."

> The haughtiness of these republicans [he informed his government on December 26] does not permit them to regard us as equals but as inferiors; their vanity in my opinion goes so far as to believe that their capital will be the capital of all the Americas.

18 Mariano Ortiz de Montellano, *Apuntes para la liquidación de la deuda contraida en Londres* (Mexico, 1886), p. 2. Several bills drawn by Barry were redeemed by the government. *Cf.* pp. 26 and 40, *infra.*

19 Casasús, *op. cit.*, p. 17.

20 See decree of May 1, 1823, *infra*, p. 26.

Five months later, after the fall of the imperial government, the Minister wrote:

> Indeed, if it can be said that I have done my country any service on this mission, that service can consist only in my having done nothing, at least so far as the foreign loan is concerned.[21]

CONTINUING FINANCIAL PERPLEXITIES

On October 28, 1822, the Minister of Finance informed the Constituent Congress that the total expenditures of the government for the year about to end would be approximately 13,500,000 pesos. The total revenues, including the proceeds of forced loans, he estimated at less than 11,000,000 pesos, leaving a deficit of nearly 3,000,000 pesos. To meet this deficit, to repay forced loans, and to maintain the imperial palace, the military and naval establishments, and the civil administration during the year 1823, more than 20,000,000 pesos would be needed. In view of the progress which had been made in the rehabilitation of the tobacco monopoly and the promotion of commerce, agriculture, and mining, the Minister believed that the ordinary revenues would amount to 14,000,000 pesos in 1823. The additional 6,000,000 pesos required would be obtained by a direct contribution levied upon the provincial governments.[22]

The probability of the realization of the contribution levied upon the provincial governments was considerably diminished by the Emperor's high-handed dissolution of the Congress on the last day of October and by his expropriation of 1,300,000 pesos in gold and silver which had been entrusted to officers of the imperial government for safe convoy to the port of Veracruz. As the convoy had been represented to be necessary to prevent the seizure of the money by robbers or by the Spanish forces which had not yet relinquished the fortress of San Juan de Ulúa, at Veracruz, the expropriation was regarded as a breach of trust. The financial situation was made worse instead of better, in January, 1823, by the issue of 2,400,000 pesos in paper money with which one-third of any tax or duty could be paid. The financial as well as the political situation was rendered untenable by the

21 *Dip. Mex.*, Vol. I, pp. 83, 103, 109.

22 Romero, *op. cit.*, p. 72.

revolution which began, under the leadership of General Antonio Lopez de Santa Anna, in December, 1822, and which ended four months later with Iturbide's departure from the country as an exile.[23]

On March 31, 1823, the reconvened Congress to which Iturbide had presented his abdication entrusted the executive power to a military triumvirate pending the eventual decision of the Congress with respect to the form of government. The members of this triumvirate were Generals Nicolás Bravo, Guadalupe Victoria, and Pedro Celestino Negrete — all well-known champions of a republican form of government. To assist them in their labors, they chose a cabinet of four persons, including Lucas Alamán, as Minister of Foreign Relations and of the Interior, and Francisco de Arrillaga, as Minister of Finance.[24]

The state of the treasury was found by Arrillaga to be

> most wretched, and its administration in the greatest disorder. All the public resources exhausted; . . . forced loans upon commerce pushed to excess; the tithes and other taxes pledged to the amount of many hundreds of thousands of dollars . . . ; public credit destroyed by the improper seizure of convoys of money belonging to private individuals, by the foolish bargain made with an adventurer [Barry], by new forced loans, by excessive and ruinous impositions, and by the issue of paper money which depreciated seventy-five per cent. These proceedings, all of them unjust and impolitic, destroyed credit and public confidence, and drove from the country capital and capitalists [chiefly Spaniards], leaving us without resources, and with scarcely a hope of a remedy.[25]

To this gloomy portrayal of the state of the treasury should be added the fact that the national debt, exclusive of sums borrowed locally since the revolution, amounted to some 45,000,000 pesos. This debt embraced not only the obligations which had been contracted by the Regency and by the Empire but also certain obligations contracted before and during the revolution. The debt incurred by the viceregal government during the revolution was, as already noted, recognized in so far as it had been

23 Bancroft, *op. cit.*, Vol. IV, pp. 784–803; Casasús, *op. cit.*, pp. 18–20.

24 Bancroft, *op. cit.*, Vol. V, pp. 2–3.

25 *Memoria que el Secretario de Estado y del Despacho de Hacienda presentó al Soberano Congreso Constituyente sobre los Ramos del Ministerio de su Cargo, leida en la Sesión del dia 12 de Noviembre de 1823*, p. 4.

imposed upon natives of Mexico against their will. All debts incurred in the cause of independence by responsible revolutionary chiefs were also recognized.[26] The greater part of the debt of 45,000,000 pesos was owed to a comparatively small number of Mexican capitalists. The claims of Spanish subjects arising from transactions prior to the achievement of Mexican independence do not appear to have been recognized until some years later.[27]

Second Approach to London

"Fully convinced of the great penury of the treasury, in consequence of which the payment of the civil and military lists is considerably in arrears, large obligations of the executive cannot be met, and the measures designed to assure public tranquillity and internal and external security cannot be opportunely taken," the Constituent Congress, on May 1, 1823, authorized the negotiation of a loan of 8,000,000 pesos for the current year. Preference was ordered to be given to "the foreign house which agrees to receive the money in Mexico [for delivery to the government] and offers help to the treasury most quickly." All the national revenues were to serve as a general pledge. A specific duty or tax was, moreover, to be assigned exclusively to the payment of interest and the formation of a sinking fund. The government was directed to endeavor to avoid fixing any term for the repayment of the loan. The authorization previously given to Iturbide and to Barry and Smith or "any others," under the act of June 25, 1822, was declared null and void for the future, and "the measures taken by the government to retire the bills of exchange drawn by the first of these foreigners and to avoid the discredit and injury which might be caused by the second" were approved. The government was most strictly enjoined to take active measures to counteract the damage which had been or might be occasioned by the unfortunate experience of the imperial government with Barry and Smith.[28]

Pursuant to this authorization, Francisco de Borja Migoni,

[26] See page 18, *supra*, and citations there given.

[27] See page 100, *infra*.

[28] *Legislación Mexicana*, Vol. IV, p. 617; *cf.* p. 23, *supra*.

the merchant who had a year earlier suggested the negotiation of a loan in London, was on May 14, 1823, given full power to

> negotiate and contract in the name of this Supreme Government . . . a loan of eight million pesos in specie, pledging for the security of the lenders the entire national revenues.[29]

In his instructions, which were issued the following day, Migoni was informed that the government had received various proposals from foreign houses established in Mexico and from representatives of London houses. Some of these proposals had provided for loans at 6 per cent which would produce 70 to 75 per cent of the face value of the bonds to be issued, but none of them had provided for the immediate advance of the sum of 500,000 pesos which was urgently needed by the government. The government had always been disposed to give Migoni the preference in negotiating a loan in London, for it believed that through his "effective agency and respectable connections" he would be able to obtain the most advantageous terms possible. He was urged to negotiate the loan as soon as possible and at the most favorable price which could be obtained in view of the political condition of Mexico. It was hoped that he would be able to obtain a loan of 5 per cent, the rate at which contracts were usually made with European nations.

With his instructions Migoni was given a circular statement regarding

> the little foresight and less circumspection with which the former Imperial Government compromised the credit of this splendid nation by pledging its name and resources at the first opportunity in foreign countries.

This statement was enclosed for use toward the vindication

> of the good name deserved by the present sober, just and equitable government, which would sooner cease to exist than be lacking in the integrity and good faith which form its essential and true character.

Concurrent Negotiations at Home

Shortly after these instructions were sent to the agent in London the government was approached by Robert P. Staples, a

[29] The appointment and instructions are printed in *Dip. Mex.*, Vol. II, pp. 144–149.

British subject residing in Mexico and representing the London house of Thomas Kinder, Jr. On June 28, 1823, Staples offered to advance a total sum of £572,400 at the rate of £20,000 a month provided that this sum should be half in cash and half in receipts for the convoys which the government had expropriated.[30] As the receipts in question could be purchased in the market at 30 per cent of their face value, the total advance would have been equivalent to considerably less than £400,000 in cash. In return for this advance the government was asked to assume the obligation to pay £1,000,000 at the end of twenty years and, meanwhile, to pay 5 per cent interest a year on the amount of the obligation. The effect of the arrangement would have been that the government would borrow at the rate of more than 20 per cent per annum. The needs of the government were so pressing, however, that the proposal would probably have been accepted but for two unexpected developments.[31]

The first of these developments was the arrival of an envoy of the British government in July, 1823, with an expression of the "ardent desire" of Great Britain "to establish relations of amity and commerce" with Mexico. This envoy, P. Mackie, M. D., a former resident of Mexico, had been chosen by Canning as having "special facilities for acquiring exact information in regard to the sentiments of animosity [*animosidad,* possibly intended for *amistad*] of that country."[32]

Immediately after his arrival Mackie communicated with General Guadalupe Victoria, who was temporarily residing at Jalapa, leaving to a substitute the discharge of his duties as one of the three respositories of the Supreme Executive Power. In informing the Minister of Foreign Affairs of the overtures made to him, General Victoria urged that he be authorized by the

[30] *Cf.* p. 24, *supra.*

[31] Casasús, *op. cit.*, p. 60; Analysis of the report of the Secretary of the Treasury to the Mexican Congress in 1825, accompanying despatch No. 12, August 5, 1825, from Mr. Poinsett, Minister of the United States to Mexico, Dept. of State, Washington, Manuscript Despatches, Mexico (hereinafter cited as MS. Desp. Mex.), Vol. 1.

[32] The documents relating to Mackie's mission are printed in *Dip. Mex.*, Vol. II, pp. 97–131.

Supreme Executive Power to enter into negotiations with the British envoy. Such negotiations, if made in due time, would, he believed, establish the prosperity and greatness of Mexico. Should they reach the point of a solemn treaty, he would not lose sight of the dignity and honor of his nation but would propose always as unalterable conditions the formal recognition of its independence, the integrity of its territory, the equality of duties on foreign commerce, and the prompt granting of the assistance which Mexico might need.

The news of Mackie's overtures was received with great enthusiasm by Minister Alamán. In communicating to General Victoria the authorization to enter upon the proposed negotiations, he stated that as the English appeared to be opening the door to lending assistance to Mexico, the General might be able to obtain an advance of £150,000 each month for one year, to begin from the date of the signature of the expected treaty of amity and commerce. He might also be able to obtain equipment for 50,000 infantry and 22,000 cavalry. The position of Mexico made such assistance necessary, and it would be advantageous to England to have a powerful friend in the Mexican nation.

Mackie appeared to have no authority to commit his government to any action with respect to the making of a loan or the furnishing of equipment to Mexico. The most definite statement that he was prepared to make was that which he made on August 7, to the effect that he had no doubt that the Mexican nation could count on every kind of aid from the English nation.

Immediate financial relief through an advance from the British government appearing to be out of the question, the Mexican government might still have been obliged to accept the proposal of Staples but for the second development above mentioned. This development was the presentation of a proposal by a local representative of the London house of Barclay, Herring, Richardson and Company, providing for a 6 per cent loan in the nominal amount of £4,000,000 from which the government would actually receive £2,500,000 at the rate of £100,000 a month. A contract accepting this proposal was signed by the Minister of Finance on August 18, 1823, and was submitted for ratification to the Constituent Congress. The Congress thereupon became the scene of a bitter contest between the agents of the two London houses concerned. The disappointed agent of Thomas Kinder, Jr., endeavored to persuade the most influential members of Congress to reject the contract which had been signed with his rival. The contest ended in the apparent triumph of the house of Barclay, the Congress authorizing a loan in the amount named in the contract with that house, in addition to the loan of 8,000,000 pesos which Migoni was trying to negotiate. In pursuance of the authorization, the Minister of Finance, on December 6, recognized the contract of August 18 as binding, subject to a minor change with respect to the sinking fund and subject to ratification by the house of Barclay before June 9, 1824.[83]

While the contest in Congress was at its height, the contract of August 18 came to the attention of Mackie, who was on the point of returning to England. Irrespective of the truth or falsity of Migoni's later statement that Mackie had sought in Mexico only his own personal advantage, there is no doubt that he was seriously concerned at learning of this contract. From Veracruz he wrote General Victoria, on August 23, that it was "beyond all measure and prejudicial to the nation." He added that he was confident that in coöperation with Migoni in London he himself could secure a loan for Mexico at as favorable a rate as 75 or 80, instead of the rate of 70 (before deduction of the 10 per cent commission) provided for in the Barclay contract.[84]

Migoni's Negotiations in London

The developments above indicated, with the exception of the submission of the Staples proposal of June 28, were unknown to Migoni on August 21, 1823, the date of his formal acceptance of the appointment as agent for the negotiation of the loan of 8,000,000 pesos. Migoni was still ignorant of the developments in connection with the Barclay proposals on October 8, 1823, when he informed his government that the bankers with whom he was negotiating had been disconcerted by the news of the

[83] Casasús, *op. cit.*, pp. 59–63.

[84] *Dip. Mex.*, Vol. II, p. 131.

negotiations with Staples. The agent's efforts in London had been further obstructed by rumors of new revolutionary movements in Mexico, some of them instigated by partisans of the exiled Iturbide and others by those who urged the immediate establishment of a federal republican form of government. The French intervention for the restoration of absolutism in Spain, pursuant to the decisions of the Congress of Vérona at the end of 1822, had, moreover, caused a marked depreciation of South American as well as Spanish bonds.[85] English capitalists, finally, had suffered considerable losses through the failure of projected loans to Colombia, Peru, and Chile. Despite all these obstacles to success, Migoni had made substantial headway in his efforts to obtain a loan for Mexico.[86]

The bankers with whom Migoni had been negotiating were of the house of B. A. Goldschmidt and Company. He continued his negotiations with them after the date of the despatch above mentioned. During the next month he received notification of his appointment as diplomatic agent of Mexico to the British government. On November 24 he had his first interview with one of the under-secretaries of the Foreign Office. Three days later he had an extended conference with Charles R. Broughton, a veteran of the Foreign Office who had served under Pitt and who was at this time confidential secretary to Canning. Broughton informed Migoni that the genius of Pitt had conceived the plan of an offensive and defensive alliance between Great Britain and Mexico, the nation which, by reason of its situation, would ultimately "hold the balance of all the Nations of America." [87]

Before the end of December, 1823, Migoni received a proposal from "reputable financiers" said to be "connected with the British government." These financiers were introduced by

[85] From June, 1822, to June, 1823, the London quotations on the bonds of Spain, Colombia, and Chile declined as follows (*The Times*, London, June 4 and 28, 1822; May 31 and June 28, 1823):

Spain	61¼ to 47
Colombia	82 to 58½
Chile	78 to 67

[86] *Dip. Mex.*, Vol. II, pp. 163–167.

[87] *Ibid.*, p. 171.

Mackie, the former British envoy to Mexico, who had been so much shocked by the unfairness of the Barclay contract. Starting from the point which Migoni had reached with Goldschmidt and Company, who were disposed to advance £1,600,000 in consideration of Mexico's assuming an obligation of twice that amount at 5 per cent interest per annum, they had first offered to lend from £3,000,000 to £10,000,000 in cash, at 10 per cent interest. Later they had reduced their offer to £3,000,000, nominal, on the same conditions which had been offered by the house of Goldschmidt. Upon being asked for a deposit they had convinced Migoni of their irresponsibility by saying that they would have to get a commercial house to take up the project.

Gradually withdrawing from Mackie's friends and resuming negotiations with the house of Goldschmidt, Migoni had been visited by Mackie and told that the British government was so eager to assist Mexico that it would itself advance funds and furnish the military supplies which, Mackie had heard from General Victoria, were urgently needed by the Mexican government. Migoni had replied that he had received no instructions confirming the alleged urgent need for military supplies, but after his conference with Mackie he had gone to the Foreign Office and learned from Broughton that the British government, however sympathetic toward the cause of Mexican independence, was not prepared to provide the new nation with military equipment nor to lend it so much as a single guinea.[38]

The British Commission and the Staples Loan

While Broughton was indicating the strictly correct attitude of his government with respect to participation in the provision of money and supplies for the former dependency still claimed by Spain, a Commission which his chief had sent to Mexico in October was proceeding with less circumspection. The members of this Commission were Lionel Hervey, H. G. Ward, and Charles O'Gorman. Their object, as later declared by Canning, was "to

[38] *Dip. Mex.*, Vol. II, pp. 181–183.

ascertain the fact of Mexican independence . . . and to form and report an opinion of the stability of the government." [39]

Migoni had had grave misgivings with respect to the Commission before its departure from England. Its members had an arrogant manner (*carácter orgulloso*) which he felt obliged to denounce in a confidential communication to his government. Although they came in the guise of those who would offer protection to Mexico, it should be borne in mind that the country which they represented had need of Mexican commerce. Mexico, it was true, needed much from England, but this should not be obtained at the sacrifice of dignity. Although it was understood that, in the event of the recognition of the new nation by Great Britain, Hervey would be appointed Minister, Ward Secretary of Legation, and O'Gorman Consul General at the capital, Migoni believed that the executive would do well "to pay no attention to this kind of people." They should be received in the manner of Caesar, who was "*generoso y reservado*," and should be given to understand that Mexico was like her northern neighbor in not stooping to any kind of baseness (*bajeza*).[40]

The Commissioners reached Mexico in the last week of December, 1823. They were received with the generosity but without the reserve of Caesar. They reciprocated with an enthusiastic report to their government within three weeks after their arrival, although at the moment of their report a formidable revolt was in progress. This revolt [41] had scarcely been put down, through stringent measures on the part of the government, when Hervey, the head of the Commission, gave his official endorsement to a new loan project put forward by the same Robert P. Staples who had offered to lend money at twenty per cent in the summer of 1823.[42]

[39] F. L. Paxson, *Independence of the South American Republics* (Philadelphia, 1903), p. 219.

[40] *Dip. Mex.*, Vol. II, pp. 163–169.

[41] Headed by General José María Lobato and aimed chiefly at the removal of all Spaniards from public office. *Cf.* de Zavala, op. cit., pp. 201–203; Joel R. Poinsett, *Notes on Mexico* (Philadelphia, 1824), p. 62.

[42] William R. Manning, *Early Diplomatic Relations between the United States and Mexico* (Baltimore, 1918), p. 62; *British and Foreign State Papers*, Vol. 28, p. 971.

Staples had meanwhile become British Consul at Mexico City. Seven years afterwards, when he sought the official intervention of his government with a view to obtaining the payment of sums still due him on account of this transaction, he was told that the instructions then recently given to the Legation at Mexico City, with respect to the support of the representations of other claimants, would be applicable to his case. "Lord Aberdeen," however, it was added, "without entering minutely into your case, cannot overlook the fact that at the time when your claim had its origin, you were expressly prohibited by your instructions, as His Majesty's Consul, from entering into transactions of this nature." What disciplinary measures may have been applied to him at the time of his offense does not appear from the data available. Presumably he was dropped from the service. Hervey, at any rate, was instantly recalled by Canning, and the part which he had been induced by Staples to take "to facilitate the loan" was "peremptorily disavowed" in July, 1824. In April, 1824, however, the attitude of the Commissioners had been thought to be that of their government, and the Mexicans had been so grateful "for the support which they felt they were receiving from England" that the executive and the Congress had seriously considered "whether the approaching birthday of the King of England should be publicly celebrated." [43]

The loan proposed by Consul Staples and guaranteed by Commissioner Hervey was approved by the Mexican Congress on the last day of January, 1824. On that day the government was authorized to contract with Staples for the raising of a loan of 1,500,000 pesos in London upon the most favorable terms possible. The evidences of indebtedness to be given to the lenders were to be redeemed out of the proceeds of the loans which had been authorized in May and August of the preceding year. The Staples loan was thus in the nature of a discount transaction upon bonds which had not yet been issued.[44]

[43] Manning, *op. cit.*, p. 63; *B. and F. State Papers*, volume and page above cited. The name of Staples does not appear in the official register of former British consuls.

[44] *Legislación Mexicana*, Vol. I, p. 697.

The available data regarding the Staples transaction are incomplete. It is clear that the obliging Consul provided the government with 1,263,701 pesos "in money, credits, and tobacco." [45] It is not clear, however, that any portion of the advance was obtained by him in London, and it cannot be ascertained how much of the advance was made in cash or what obligations it entailed upon the government. The indications are that the entire transaction took place in Mexico.

The "credits" which constituted a part of the Staples loan, it may be noted, were receipts or certificates which the government had given to individuals or corporations upon the seizure of convoys [46] or of funds, known as *minería,* formerly advanced to mining concerns by way of subsidy. These "credits," being indefinite as to term of payment and being "held by Europeans, who want confidence in the present state of things," could be purchased in the market at much less than half their face value. The tobacco which comprised another part of the loan appears to have been taken at an agreed price considerably in excess of that which had been paid for it. The government doubtless hoped to resell it later at a profit. There was apparently nothing irregular in the transaction. The government might, indeed, be applauded for the redemption of the "credits" at their face value. The fact remained, however, that the government obtained through the transaction a very small sum of ready money.[47]

The Goldschmidt Loan

The first substantial loan to Mexico was made under a contract which was signed in London on February 7, 1824, by Migoni and the house of Goldschmidt.[48] By this contract Goldschmidt and Company undertook to place at the disposal of the Mexican

[45] Analysis of the report of the Secretary of the Treasury to the Mexican Congress in 1825, *sup. cit.*

[46] *Cf.* p. 24, *supra.*

[47] Analysis of the report, *etc., sup. cit.*

[48] The principal provisions of the contract are reproduced in Appendix II. *Cf.* Casasús, *op. cit.,* pp. 36–54, and L. Alamán, *Liquidación General de la Deuda Esterior* (Mexico, 1845), pp. 4–6.

government, within fifteen months,[49] the sum of £1,600,000 (8,000,000 pesos) which Migoni had been authorized to borrow. In return for this sum, the government was obliged to issue bonds for £3,200,000 redeemable within thirty years from October 1, 1823, and bearing interest meanwhile at the rate of 5 per cent per annum. For the payment of interest and the maintenance of the redemption fund of £32,000 [50] a year, the government gave a general pledge of its entire revenues and a special pledge of one-third of the duties to be collected in the customs-houses on the Gulf of Mexico after April 1, 1825. The government undertook to refrain from contracting any further loan within one year from February 7, 1824. Moreover, if it contracted a second loan before the completion of the first operation (that is, before the marketing of the bonds, delivery of funds, etc.), one-fourth of the proceeds of the second loan must be applied to the redemption of bonds of the first.

The contract of February 7 was approved by the Mexican Congress on May 14, 1824. From the sum of £1,600,000 nominally placed at the disposal of the government, approximately £400,000 was immediately deducted for payment of interest and redemption fund for the first two years. A smaller but nevertheless considerable deduction was made for the bankers' commission of 1.5 per cent on the amounts passing through their hands for payment of interest and redemption of principal. The government's bonds for £3,200,000 were sold to the public by the house of Goldschmidt at 58 per cent of their face value,[51] leaving to that house a gross profit of approximately a quarter

[49] This period was actually fixed by the exercise of options after the date of the contract. The amount definitely agreed upon on February 7 was £600,000 (3,000,000 pesos), to be advanced within a year. On March 1 and May 6, the contracting house gave notice of its acceptance of the options which it had reserved to furnish additional amounts aggregating £1,000,000 (5,000,000 pesos) within a year from the date last mentioned. Ortiz de Montellano, *op. cit.*, p. 5.

[50] £64,000 for the first year. It was anticipated that the market price of the bonds would be sufficiently low to make it possible to redeem the entire issue out of the redemption fund within thirty years. Any bonds still outstanding at the end of that time were to be immediately redeemed.

[51] Corporation of Foreign Bondholders, London (hereinafter cited as C.F.B.), *Fifty-fifth Annual Report*, 1927, p. 290.

of a million pounds besides the assurance of substantial commissions for the debt service for ten years to come. The expected yield to investors was 8.62 per cent.

The procurement of less than 6,000,000 pesos in cash in return for the assumption of an obligation of 16,000,000 pesos would seem, at first view, to be nothing to boast of. Migoni, however, in announcing to his government the conclusion of the contract providing for this transaction, was moved to express "*una satisfacción inexplicable*" with the result of his persistence. "My satisfaction," he declared, "exceeds the great difficulties which, fortunately, I have overcome." As to the nature of these difficulties he said:

> What an example, for the Cabinets as well as the peoples of the two hemispheres, is afforded by the realization of our loan at a time when the present government of the King of Spain is unable to obtain a loan even with the moral influence of the Holy Alliance and when the organs of that Alliance are continually frightening the public with announcements of attacks intended upon our liberty.
>
> Without doubt, the apprehensions thus diffused have caused a part of the difficulties I have met in my negotiations. Our enemies, knowing the condition of our public treasury and our immediate need of additional funds, have omitted no means to prevent our obtaining them. Thus, besides inspiring the apprehensions above referred to, they have managed to frighten capitalists by reminding them of the unhappy fate of those who invested in the bonds of Spain, Colombia and Peru. . . .
>
> But what gave the greatest impetus to malevolence was the act of our own Sovereign Congress authorizing the Supreme Executive Power to contract a loan of 20,000,000 pesos at the same time as the loan which I had been directed to raise.

Refraining from extended comment on the embarrassments occasioned by the act referred to, Migoni proceeded to elaborate upon the features of his contract which he regarded as particularly advantageous. The first of these features was the provision for an interest rate of 5 per cent, which was preferred because "no European power issues securities bearing more than 5 per cent interest" and because "it would be in keeping with the dignity of our country to enter upon a career of credit without fixing a rate of interest higher than that borne by European securities." A more important achievement, in the agent's opinion, was that he had obtained terms as good as France had obtained in 1818 and better than those which had been accorded to Spain in connection with the loans of 1820 and 1821; France, it appeared, had been given but 50 per cent of the nominal value of her 5 per cent loans and Spain had been given as low as 44 per cent of the nominal value of her loan of 1821. While Chile and Colombia had apparently borrowed on more favorable terms, it should be recalled that their loans had been granted

> before confidence in American bonds had received the blow which it suffered through the French invasion of Spain, the refusal of the present government at Madrid to recognize the loans made to its constitutional predecessor, the repudiation by the Colombian Congress of the loan contracted by its agent Zea, and the difficulties of another kind encountered by the Peruvian loan.[52]

It should, moreover, be borne in mind that some of the South American loans had been remitted to a large extent in securities of various kinds instead of in cash.[53]

A wholly different view of the Goldschmidt transaction was adopted by Jose Mariano Michelena, who in June, 1824, succeeded Migoni as diplomatic representative of Mexico at London.[54] According to Michelena, Migoni had not done "the least service for the country." As early as October 1, 1823, he had "got himself entangled" with Goldschmidt, "the banker of the Holy Alliance," and after that date he had rejected "the proposals made to him without inviting others." While awaiting a definite reply from Goldschmidt, he had written to the government "lies and contradictions, speaking of measures of the Holy Alliance prejudicial to the loan." The "scandalous contract" signed on February 7, 1824, had entailed a "horrible sacrifice . . . without precedent in the history of loans."[55]

Echoes of Michelena's opinion regarding the Goldschmidt loan are still heard in discussions of the foreign debt of Mexico. It is

[52] *Cf.* p. 31 *supra*.

[53] For Migoni's communication to his government announcing the conclusion of the loan, see *Dip. Mex.*, Vol. II, pp. 185–194. Various securities, it will be recalled, had been accepted in lieu of cash in the Staples transaction, *supra*, p. 35.

[54] *Dip. Mex.*, Vol. III, p. 18.

[55] *Ibid.*, pp. 218–221.

believed, however, after a careful consideration of the circumstances in which the loan was obtained, that the terms accorded to Mexico on this foreign loan were actually more favorable than could have been expected on the basis of a dispassionate survey of the political and economic conditions prevailing in the country.[56] The revolt of General Lobato, already mentioned,[57] had been in progress during Migoni's negotiations. The elements opposed to a republican form of government were far from satisfied with the indications that the Constituent Congress was about to adopt a constitution (promulgated January 31, 1824) on the model of that of the United States. Brigands, the backwash of the revolutionary struggle, made transportation unsafe. The menace of a Spanish invasion was constantly held over the country by the continued possession of the fortress of San Juan de Ulúa, at Veracruz, by Spanish troops. This menace and the frequent outbreaks of internal disorder, more or less political in origin, caused large bodies of men formerly engaged in productive labor to be kept in arms. Such conditions inevitably resulted in a sharp reduction of the national revenue and in an enormous increase of expenditures for military purposes.[58] No one familiar with these conditions could have failed to have serious doubts as to the ability of Mexico, however jealous of her honor and credit, to provide in the near future for the payment of annual interest and amortization charges on so large a sum as 16,000,000 pesos. The fact that Goldschmidt and Company apparently expected her to begin the full service of the loan so early as the fall of 1825 and to maintain it regularly thereafter can be explained only on the assumption that the London bankers were not familiar with actual conditions in Mexico or that they shared the belief of the enthusiastic friends of Mexican independence that the country was just entering upon an era of order and prosperity. It would be uncharitable, and possibly anachronistic, to suggest that the

[56] *Cf.* Casasús, *op. cit.*, pp. 81–108.

[57] *Supra*, p. 33.

[58] The budget estimates for 1825 showed revenues of 8,452,829 pesos (exclusive of foreign loans) and expenditures of 17,986,674 pesos. Military and naval expenditures were budgeted at 14,934,533 pesos — almost twice the total amount of the ordinary revenues.

bankers had no real concern in the matter except to sell the bonds to the English public.

From the point of view of the effect of the operation on the welfare of Mexico, the terms on which the Goldschmidt loan was obtained are of less importance than the urgency of the need for the loan. One measure of the urgency of this need is found in the disposition of the funds actually obtained by the government. According to the official reports made by the Ministry of Finance in January, 1827,[59] the sum of 5,686,157 pesos which remained to the government's credit after deduction of 2,313,843 pesos for redemption fund, interest, commissions, printing, and incidental expenses, was disposed of as follows:

Purchase of military and naval equipment	P422,091
Repayment of Staples' loan and payment of Barry's drafts	930,000
Redemption of orders on customs-houses	97,177
Redemption of receipts for forced loans and for seizure of convoys	342,110
Redemption of receipts for tobacco	211,666
Purchase of tobacco	965,124
Other expenditures (chiefly for current administration and the payment of arrears of salaries and pensions)	2,717,989
Total	P5,686,157

The expenditure of more than 400,000 pesos for military and naval equipment is considered by Casasús, the official historian of the so-called London debt up to 1885, to have been extremely foolish.[60] It is true that before this expenditure was made, Monroe and Canning had announced the opposition of the United States and Great Britain to the recovery by Spain of her former colonies in the New World.[61] On the other hand, Spain, backed by the Holy Alliance, was known to cherish still the dream of

[59] *Memoria de la Hacienda*, etc., January 3 and 4, 1827; Report of Ministry of Finance, January 10, 1827, quoted in *B. and F. State Papers*, Vol. 14, p. 869.

[60] *Op. cit.*, p. 101.

[61] Manning, *op. cit.*, pp. 58–59.

reconquest.[62] Mexico could hardly be expected to leave the defense of her independence wholly to the United States and Great Britain. Some of the equipment in question was, moreover, doubtless required for the maintenance of internal order.

The urgency of the other items can hardly be questioned. The payment of bills of exchange drawn by Staples (870,000 pesos) and by Barry (60,000 pesos), under their contracts,[63] was indispensable for the maintenance of the government's credit. The redemption of the orders and receipts mentioned in the next three items (totalling 650,000 pesos) was necessary for the same purpose. The tobacco for which receipts had been given had been acquired by the government in connection with the administration of the formerly lucrative tobacco monopoly, which the government had decided to continue in force.[64] The purchase of tobacco (965,000 pesos) was declared by the Ministry of Finance to be essential to the reëstablishment of the monopoly as a profitable source of revenue.[65] The use of a large part of the remainder of the proceeds for current expenses of administration was doubtless imperative, in view of the wide margin existing between ordinary revenues and expenditures. In the difficult task of reducing this margin the government can hardly be censured for having applied so large a part of the proceeds of the loan to the maintenance of essential administrative functions.

The Barclay Loan

On February 10, 1824, three days after the conclusion of the contract for the Goldschmidt loan, the London office of Barclay, Herring, Richardson and Company addressed a com-

[62] Paxson, *op. cit.*, p. 206; Bancroft, *op. cit.*, Vol. IV, p. 749 and Vol. V, p. 55. The Liverpool *Advertiser* of Nov. 15, 1823, said: "It seems to be now seriously credited that Spain has it in contemplation, with the aid of France, to make vigorous attempts to regain mastery over South America. Spain and her colleague, France, if they pursue the purpose which is now talked of, will assuredly be visited by every moral reasoner with the deepest sentiment of reprobation."

[63] *Cf.* pp. 23, 35, *supra*.

[64] *Legislación Mexicana*, Vol. I, p. 689.

[65] Report of Ministry of Finance, January 10, 1827, quoted in *B. and F. State Papers*, Vol. 14, p. 869.

munication to the Mexican Minister of Finance approving, in principle, the contract which the representative of the firm in Mexico had signed with the Minister, in August of the preceding year. As an earnest of its intention to comply with the terms of the contract, the firm began to pay orders, amounting to 500,000 pesos, which its representative had drawn upon it in favor of the Mexican government. It did not give its definite and final ratification of the contract, however, for the reason that the text of the modification requested by the Minister on December 6 had not yet reached London. Shortly after the receipt of the text of this modification, the firm sent representatives to Mexico with authority to ratify the contract, subject to further modifications which it was believed would be readily accepted by the government. Through a combination of adverse circumstances, including unfavorable winds at sea, they were prevented from reaching the capital before the end of June.

Presenting themselves at the Ministry of Finance on June 30, three weeks after the expiration of the period which had been fixed for the ratification of the contract, the representatives of the house of Barclay were confronted with a demand for a radical revision of the arrangement. They replied that their delay was unavoidable and that inasmuch as the period allowed for ratification was stated in the contract to be subject to unexpected contingencies (*salvo el caso fortuito*), they had still the right to ratify the contract in the name of their firm. By this time, however — largely no doubt as a result of the clearing of the international political atmosphere by the declarations of Monroe and Canning with respect to the reconquest of the former Spanish colonies — the 5 per cent bonds of the Goldschmidt loan had attained a quotation of more than 70 per cent of their face value on the London market. The government, therefore, had a strong motive for insisting, as it did insist, that the contract was no longer open to ratification.

A new contract was at length signed on August 25, 1824. This contract provided for a 6 per cent loan of £3,200,000 (equivalent to 16,000,000 pesos) to be sold at the best possible price with a commission of 6 per cent of the sale price to the bankers. The loan was to be secured by a special assignment of one-third of the proceeds of the maritime customs.[66]

In pursuance of the contract of August 25, 1824, the second loan was issued in February, 1825, at the price of 86.75, yielding a total of 13,880,000 pesos. From this amount the following deductions were immediately made:[67]

Bankers' commission of 6 per cent of sale price	P832,800
Interest for 18 months	1,440,000
Redemption fund for 18 months	240,000
Bankers' commission on interest and redemption fund	24,000
Printing, etc.	9,902
Total	P2,546,702

The sum of 11,333,298 pesos, remaining after these deductions was disposed of as follows:[68]

Redemption of bonds of the Goldschmidt loan	P3,000,000
Loan to the government of Colombia	315,000
Repayment of advances made by English capitalists in Mexico	1,020,712
Interest on the Goldschmidt loan	152,774
Loss by failure of bankers while in possession of part of the proceeds of the loan	1,519,645
Purchase of tobacco and redemption of receipts for tobacco	340,000
Purchase of ships and munitions	1,390,334
Other items (expenses of administration, etc.)	3,594,833
Total	P11,333,298

The redemption of bonds of the 5 per cent loan of the preceding year was made in pursuance of a provision in the Gold-

[66] Casasús, *op. cit.*, pp. 63–69; Alamán, *Liquidación General, sup. cit.*, pp. 12–13. A more detailed summary of the contract is given in Appendix III.

[67] Casasús, *op. cit.*, pp. 110–112. [68] *Ibid.*

schmidt contract that one-fourth of the proceeds of any loan floated before the completion of the operation should be devoted to the redemption of the bonds issued in 1824. The proceeds of such a loan were doubtless understood to mean the amount placed to the credit of the government before any deduction except for such items as the bankers' commission on the sale price of the new bonds. The sum which the government should have devoted to this object was therefore approximately 3,250,000 pesos, instead of the 3,000,000 pesos actually applied in partial fulfilment of the provision of the contract. By the redemption of Goldschmidt bonds in this manner, at an average price of about 63, the government reduced the amount of its 5 per cent foreign debt by 4,749,500 pesos.

The reason for the withholding of a part of the sum which should have been applied to the redemption of Goldschmidt bonds was apparently the desire of the Mexican Minister at London to accommodate the government of Colombia, then hard pressed for funds with which to pay interest on its London debt. The Minister's generosity toward Colombia is difficult to understand in the light of what is now known regarding the financial difficulties of his own government at the time. The Minister doubtless believed that Mexico could afford to be generous to her neighbor. He had in mind, moreover, the fact that a treaty of "perpetual union, league, and confederation," which had been concluded between Colombia and Mexico in October, 1823, was expected by both its signatories to "form the basis of the true family compact, which will unite all Americans for the defense of their liberty and independence, and for the encouragement of their commerce and mutual interests."[69] The credit accruing from the loan of 315,000 pesos to Colombia, it may be noted, was sold by the Mexican government thirty years later to brokers, who paid 30,000 pesos in cash and 800,000 pesos in obligations of the internal debt.[70]

[69] Report of the Mexican Secretary of State, Nov. 8, 1823, quoted from Poinsett, *op. cit.*, p. 315. For criticisms of the loan, see Casasús, *op. cit.*, pp. 98–102.

[70] *Memoria presentada . . . por el C. Miguel Lerdo de Tejada*, 1857, pp. 39–41.

The repayment of advances of capital made in Mexico, the payment of interest due on the Goldschmidt loan, the purchase of tobacco, and the redemption of tobacco receipts were justified by considerations such as those which have been mentioned in connection with the items of expenditure of the Goldschmidt loan. The ships and munitions purchased at a cost of nearly 1,400,000 pesos had been contracted for at the end of 1823, when there was still grave apprehension of immediate Spanish attempts to reconquer Mexico. The loss of more than 1,500,000 pesos through the failure of the house of Barclay was declared by contemporary critics to have been due to lack of diligence on the part of Mexican officials, after they had been warned of the imminence of the failure. The charge of lack of diligence seems to be at least partially substantiated. The last item of the disposition of the Barclay loan is, moreover, clearly open to criticism on the ground that 3,600,000 pesos is too large a portion of the loan to have been applied to expenses of administration. It would undoubtedly have been wiser, as Casasús points out,[71] to devote a considerable part of this sum to productive works which would have improved the economic condition of the country and assured "the development of industry, agriculture and commerce in such a way as to increase the revenues." On the other hand, it should be realized that the Mexican statesmen of the first decade of their country's independence had little opportunity to weigh the relative advantages of various uses to be made of the proceeds of foreign loans. Esteva, who became Minister of Finance in August, 1824, had found

> the army and civilian employees clamorous for the arrears due to them; those who had advanced money demanding the interest; the tobacco planters, the settlement of their accounts; the merchants, the restitution of the *conductas* (convoys); . . . in short, the antechambers of the President and of the Ministry crowded with claimants.[72]

It would have required more than farsightedness, in such circumstances, to apply any large part of the proceeds of the Barclay loan to projects not yielding immediate returns.

[71] *Op. cit.*, p. 98.

[72] Report of Minister of Finance, January 10, 1827, quoted from *B. and F. State Papers*, Vol. 14, p. 856.

Mexico at the End of 1825

Although the use made of the proceeds of the Goldschmidt and Barclay loans was not in all respects that which a judicious economist would have recommended, the effect of the loans upon the general situation of the country was decidedly encouraging. According to a statement of the Mexican Minister of Foreign Affairs,[73] "immense wealth" circulated throughout Mexico at this time,

> owing to the loans contracted in London and the various companies established for the encouragement of the different branches of trade. By this powerful impulse, all the mines, the operations of which had been for a long time suspended, recommenced working; a new direction was given to commerce; internal trade revived; and, advancing onwards, the repairs and opening of roads were projected, and it was about to be undertaken to effect a communication between the two oceans across the Isthmus of Tehuantepec. These enterprises, at the same time that they gave life to the republic in the interior, secured its foreign relations by fixing the interest of thousands of foreigners towards us, not only by feelings of sympathy and speculative anticipations, but by positive engagements which identified with the fate of the republic that of the capitalists of those parts of the world.

An equally hopeful view of the situation was taken by Joel R. Poinsett, who had been received as the first Minister of the United States in June, 1825. Writing to Secretary of State Clay with respect to Mexican finances in August, Poinsett declared that

> although the receipts do not cover the expenditures, the foreign trade increases so rapidly that it is probable in another year the former will prove sufficient, notwithstanding the most wasteful and improvident extravagance.[74]

Enthusiasm for the future of Mexico was also still felt by the British Mission which had arrived in Mexico at the end of the year 1823. That Mission, now headed by James Morier, named in place of Hervey, had in fact, in April, 1825, concluded a treaty of commerce with Mexico which contained terms so favorable to the new nation that Canning was impelled to reject

[73] Made to Congress on Feb. 12, 1830, as quoted in *B. and F. State Papers*, Vol. 18, p. 1416.

[74] Despatch No. 12, Aug. 5, 1825, MS. Desp. Mex., Vol. 1.

the treaty in September, 1825, and to inform Ward, who had been made Chargé d'Affaires in Mexico City, that Great Britain would not abandon

for the sake of this new connexion, principles which we have never conceded, in our intercourse with other states, whether of the Old World or the New, either to considerations of friendship or to menaces of hostility.[75]

Negotiations for the conclusion of a new treaty were, however, begun immediately after it became known in Mexico that the treaty signed in April had been rejected. Mexican confidence in a future trade of large dimensions with Great Britain was therefore unbroken. In the course of the new negotiations, which were in progress at the end of the year, the Mexican Minister of Finance was reported to be eager for the conclusion of a treaty because of the probability that a new loan would soon be required.[76] The attitude of Mexican officials in anticipation of such a loan was believed by the American Minister to be "not very honourable to their character." [77]

Despite the "immense wealth" reported to be in circulation and the "powerful impulse" declared to have been felt by trade and industry, the balance sheet of the government at the end of 1825 was far from favorable. Despite the extraordinary income during the year from the foreign loans, expenditures were approximately 8,000,000 pesos in excess of receipts. The largest item of expenditure was again military and naval — more than 15,000,000 pesos out of a total of less than 20,000,000 pesos.[78]

The menace of Spanish invasion was no longer so imminent since the Spanish troops had at last been withdrawn from San Juan de Ulúa. Internal disturbances had, moreover, almost ceased to exist since the installation of General Victoria as first

[75] Paxson, *op. cit.*, p. 220.

[76] Poinsett's No. 32, Jan. 4, 1826, MS. Desp. Mex., Vol. I.

[77] They "court the English government," declared Poinsett. What troubled him more was that "they affect in consequence to treat very lightly the favours they have received from our hands." The favours referred to were our "decided stand" for the independence of the Spanish-American States and "the really open declaration" of President Monroe in the famous message of December, 1823. Poinsett's No. 12, August 5, 1825, MS. Desp. Mex., Vol. 1.

[78] Romero, *op. cit.*, p. 81.

President, under a federal constitution, in October of the preceding year. There were, nevertheless, some seeds of disaffection, especially among those who had preferred a centralized to a federal government. President Victoria and his advisers therefore deemed it necessary to maintain a considerable military establishment.[79]

[79] Priestley, *op. cit.*, p. 265; Bancroft, *op. cit.*, Vol. V, pp. 32–34, 64.

CHAPTER III

A GENERATION OF FINANCIAL CONFUSION
(1826–1845)

Mexican Self-Sufficiency

During the year 1826 foreign capital, chiefly British, German, and American, continued to arrive in Mexico for use in private enterprises, especially mining. The foreign investments in Mexican mines from 1825 to 1827 were calculated by a competent British observer [1] at £6,000,000. Exports of gold and silver from Mexico in 1826 amounted to 5,847,795 pesos. The next year they reached a total of 9,669,428 pesos.[2] Although the profits on the mining and other ventures of foreign investors were for the most part retained outside Mexico, the economic life of the country was considerably stimulated by these activities.

The net revenues of Mexico from normal sources for the fiscal year beginning July 1, 1826, were 12,300,000 pesos. With 1,400,000 pesos, which had been in the treasury at the beginning of the fiscal year, and with 500,000 pesos from extraordinary sources, the sum available to the government during this period was 14,200,000 pesos. The expenditures were 13,500,000 pesos.[3] The resulting surplus of 700,000 pesos was in strikingly favorable contrast to the deficit of 8,000,000 pesos which had appeared in 1825, when the revenues, on the basis of figures for eight months, were calculated at less than 12,000,000 pesos.[4] A particularly encouraging circumstance was the decline of military and naval expenditures from 15,000,000 to 10,000,000 pesos.[5]

[1] H. G. Ward (British Chargé d'Affaires at Mexico City), in his book entitled *Mexico,* published in London in 1829.

[2] Matías Romero, *Mexico and the United States* (New York, 1898), p. 155.

[3] Romero, *Memoria de Hacienda, sup. cit.*, pp. 86, 87.

[4] *Ibid.*, p. 81.

[5] *Ibid.*, pp. 86, 87.

It is not surprising that Esteva, the Minister of Finance, felt justified in saying to the Congress at the middle of the fiscal year, in January, 1827:

> It will always be a source of the highest satisfaction to me, to reflect, that during the period of my administration and direction of the public revenue, so great and rapid an improvement should have been effected, as to banish all our former wants and penury, and to enable us to provide with ease for all our burdens, at the same time that we have dried up the tears of many unfortunate individuals, to whom above 1,000,000 pesos have been paid, for arrears of salary due to them from the time of my predecessors.

Taking into account the sums due from the Mexican States, amounting to 3,000,000 pesos, the Minister was of the opinion that Mexico was able to maintain her situation in the world without foreign assistance.[6]

In the same spirit, President Victoria, in a message to Congress at the same time, declared that the government's credit, though profoundly shaken by the failure of its bankers, in August, 1826, was well on the way to restoration. Not only had sums sufficient for the payment of interest and amortization on the government's bonds been remitted to London, but " most especial precautions " had been taken to see that due provision should be made in advance for the year 1827. As a result, the bonds of the second loan, which had been quoted at 40 immediately after the failure of the bankers, had risen in September to 63.5.[7]

Default

The sanguine belief of Minister Esteva that all the " former wants and penury " of Mexico had been banished was unfortunately not to be justified by the developments which soon followed. The contribution of 3,000,000 pesos from the States, upon which he had reckoned, was not to be received. One of the most important States, Veracruz, was indeed within a few months to begin a revolution against the federal government, motivated partly by the desire to effect the expulsion of the

[6] *Memoria de la Hacienda,* January 3 and 4, 1827, p. 6.

[7] Poinsett's No. 68, January 17, 1827, MS. Desp. Mex., Vol. 2.

Spaniards remaining in the country.[8] Another State, Puebla, was to join the insurrectionary movement before the end of the year. The bitterness existing between the Masons of the Scottish rite and those of the York rite, representing, respectively, the aristocratic and the democratic tendencies among the people, was to culminate in armed conflict. In the midst of these developments all forms of productive enterprise were to be paralyzed, and the fundamental weaknesses of the fiscal system were to be pitilessly exposed.

The interest due on July 1, 1827, amounting to £221,697,[9] was paid only with the assistance of an advance of £131,154 by Baring Brothers, who had become the financial agents of Mexico in London in September of the preceding year.[10] By the first of October the situation of the republic had become such that the interest due on that date was not paid.[11] Poinsett, reporting to Washington on October 6, 1827, remarked that the subject which most immediately engaged the attention of the Mexican Congress was the state of the treasury. The government not only had not wherewithal to pay the interest on the loan for the quarter ending September 30, but it was also without means of satisfying other demands equally urgent, the neglect of which might be attended with fatal effects.[12]

Evidences of Good Faith

The remedy which was being considered by the executive at the time of Poinsett's report was an anticipation of the revenue of the following year by the sale of "orders on the customs-houses for duties and on the States for monies to become due for the purchase of tobacco — the two most important branches of their revenue." In payment for these orders, the government would accept its own past-due obligations (receipts for loans,

[8] The expulsion of all the Spaniards belonging to certain specified classes was decreed on December 20, 1827. (*Legislación Mexicana*, Vol. II, pp. 47–48).

[9] Payno, *op. cit.*, p. 45.

[10] Casasús, *op. cit.*, p. 113.

[11] *B. and F. State Papers*, Vol. 16, p. 940.

[12] Poinsett's No. 102, Oct. 6, 1827, MS. Desp. Mex., Vol. 3.

tobacco, etc.) at 56 per cent of their face value, "on condition of an equal amount of cash being paid." In this way the government hoped to raise 4,000,000 pesos.

As the past-due obligations of the government could be bought in the market at less than 20 per cent of their nominal value, the terms proposed were distinctly advantageous to the contractor.[13] Poinsett was inclined to the opinion that an outright loan of 20,000,000 pesos would be much better for the government than the proposed anticipation of resources. He believed that within a few years the mines would become more productive and that "the gradual augmentation of the class of consumers must be attended by a proportionate increase of commerce." The tax on internal trade and the old system of monopolies must also "yield shortly to more enlightened views of political economy." But, he declared,

> notwithstanding these certain causes of the increasing prosperity and resources of the country, there exists such a disposition to prodigal waste, such excessive corruption on the part of those who collect and administer the finances of the State, and such an insatiable desire for places and pensions, that no income, however great, can suffice.[14]

On November 16, 1827, a new tariff of maritime customs duties was published. In this tariff some of the import duties which had been established immediately after the inauguration of the Regency in 1821 were reduced and the number of prohibited articles was diminished. It was hoped that by these means the revenues would be increased. In the same tariff one-eighth of the net proceeds of the maritime customs was assigned for the service of the public debt.[15]

In December, 1827, the government still had in view a local loan based upon the anticipation of its resources. A law had been passed on November 21, authorizing such an operation and providing that its proceeds should be applied in part to the payment of interest and amortization on the London loans.[16] The

[13] Poinsett's No. 102, Oct. 6, 1827, MS. Desp. Mex., Vol. 3.

[14] Poinsett's No. 107, Nov. 10, 1827, MS. Desp. Mex., Vol. 3.

[15] Romero, *Memoria, sup. cit.*, pp. 91–92.

[16] *Ibid.*, p. 90.

terms specified were, however, not sufficiently attractive to local capitalists who could command from two to three per cent a month on private loans with good security, and the project had not been realized. Pending further action by the Congress, the government was subsisting upon small sums borrowed from the merchants and upon what it could get from the states in advance for tobaccos.[17]

The financial distress, continuing, was accompanied by a sensitiveness toward foreign opinion which was evidenced by the Mexican Senate's rejection of the nomination of a Minister to England on the ground that until the interest due on the loans was paid, a representative of Mexico would not be likely to be well received at the English court. With a view to obtaining funds for the payment of interest on the loans, the government contemplated a secret operation on the London market — an operation which does not appear to have been carried out — involving a large purchase of Mexican bonds at the prevailing low prices and their subsequent sale at the enhanced figure which would naturally have been induced by the purchase.[18]

In a message to Congress on May 21, 1828, President Victoria stated that the government had been punctually paying its engagements in the interior of the country and that, as it had used its utmost efforts to satisfy with fidelity and punctuality the loans made with foreign houses, it could assure the members of the Congress that its earnest desires, seconded by the indefatigable activity and zeal of the Congress, would effect the object to which they were directed. Several proposals had been made to the Congress with a view to supplementing the assignment of one-eighth of the maritime customs duties, provided for in the tariff of November 16, 1827. If these proposals were enacted into law, the government, in the President's opinion, would be able to give renewed evidence of the good faith which characterized the nation.[19]

Two days after the President's message one of the proposals

[17] Poinsett's No. 110, Dec. 8, 1827, MS. Desp. Mex., Vol. 3.

[18] Poinsett's No. 124, MS. Desp. Mex., Vol. 4.

[19] Poinsett's No. 128, June 4, 1828, MS. Desp. Mex., Vol. 4.

to which he had referred became a law. By this law the one-eighth of the maritime customs duties which had been assigned to the public debt generally, the foreign and the domestic obligations sharing the proceeds equally, was made applicable exclusively to the foreign debt. To this assignment were added all the export duties on gold and silver, whether coined, manufactured or in bars.[20]

The funds thus allocated to the service of the foreign debt were not in fact applied to that service. Since January of the preceding year, according to a statement of the Minister of Finance,[21] there had been " scarcely a single month without political incidents which disturbed the public tranquillity." The government, urgently in need of funds to maintain itself against attacks, had to make the difficult choice between political disintegration and financial default.

During the summer of 1828 the government succeeded in borrowing somewhat more than 1,000,000 pesos under the authorization of November 21, 1827.[22] No part of this sum was, however, applied to the service of the foreign debt. With a view to giving at least a measure of satisfaction to the bondholders, the Congress, on October 28, 1828, passed an act providing for the capitalization of overdue interest, subject to the prior assent of the creditors.[23] This act was considered by the financial agents in London to be inopportune, and it was not even made known to the bondholders.[24] The arrears, accordingly, continued to accumulate. The financial distress of the government was at the same time greatly aggravated by the struggle over the succession to President Victoria.[25]

[20] *Legislación Mexicana,* Vol. II, p. 74.

[21] *Memoria de Hacienda,* January, 1829, p. 2; Bancroft, *op. cit.,* Vol. V, pp. 32–41.

[22] *Memoria de Hacienda,* April, 1830, "*Estado General de los Ingresos, Egresos y Productos Liquidos.*"

[23] *Legislación Mexicana,* Vol. II, p. 86.

[24] Casasús, *op. cit.,* pp. 118–121. " I hope you will pardon me," wrote Mr. Baring, " if I say that I cannot consent to risk my name when I see no positive indication of the actual fulfilment of the promises and pledges which would be given through my intervention as agent of the government."

[25] Bancroft, *op. cit.,* Vol. V, pp. 41–44.

General Guerrero, who had taken up arms against Gómez Pedraza, the President-Elect, finally succeeded in eliminating his rival. He assumed the office of President on April 1, 1829. He immediately authorized negotiations with two English merchants in Mexico for a loan of 10,000,000 pesos at 60. For the punctual payment of the interest on this loan it was proposed to pledge the duties on liquors and paper, amounting to about 1,200,000 pesos annually. The value of the security was believed by Poinsett, who reported the matter to the State Department on April 3, 1829, to depend entirely upon the good faith and stability of the government; and this, in turn, upon the persons who might be called into the councils of the President.[26]

The Minister of Finance chosen by President Guerrero was Lorenzo de Zavala, whose attitude toward his task was indicated in an "exposition" submitted to the Mexican House of Representatives shortly after his assumption of office on April 18, 1829. He was convinced, he said, that without credit Mexico could do nothing. He was equally persuaded that the preservation of credit depended solely upon an exact compliance with engagements and the most sacred punctuality in payments. How, he asked, could the Executive fail to tremble on pronouncing the word *credit*, when the most solemn engagements made within and without the Republic had been violated? The government could not justify itself by pleading the bad faith of one or two of the contractors or the bankruptcy of others. The engagements of a government were independent of the faults of its agents. The revolutionary disturbances of the latter part of the year 1828 had left consequences which must long be felt. They had been described in exaggerated terms in the public prints of Mexico interested in casting discredit upon the government. Letters in the same spirit "from Spaniards and from foreigners, unfriendly to the new order of things" had produced in foreign countries an impression fatal to Mexican credit and even to the opinion which might have been entertained regarding the stability of Mexican institutions. The value of Mexican bonds had in consequence considerably diminished, and a public functionary had not been

[26] Poinsett's No. 167, MS. Desp. Mex., Vol. 4.

wanting who had ventured to say that they were not worth the paper on which they were printed.

In the opinion of the Minister, the most solemn promises to pay the public debt would inspire no confidence whatever unless there were a radical change in the method of handling the debts. It was of no avail to hypothecate duties if the government laid hands upon such duties for current expenses. It was necessary to form a separate department for the sole purpose of administering the funds destined to the payment of the principal and interest of the public debt. The misapplication of the revenues set apart for this purpose would thus be rendered impossible. It was of the utmost necessity to take measures to cover a deficiency of more than 3,000,000 pesos annually. The national honor required that the creditors have clear and satisfactory security and that agreements be made with them which would enable them to know their fate. Finally, it was absolutely necessary to adopt such measures as would dissipate all causes destructive of public confidence and establish it on a solid basis.[27]

War and Revolution

The immediate realization of the reforms projected by Lorenzo de Zavala was prevented by the landing of Spanish troops near Tampico in July, 1829. The ensuing campaign, in which Spain was decisively beaten, reflected glory upon the national arms but seriously embarrassed the national treasury. Forced loans, the seizure of all private property of Spanish subjects, and the other extraordinary measures which were employed at this critical time did not produce revenues sufficient for the needs of the government. Before the end of the war, "all the proceeds of the maritime customs duties, which constituted the most lucrative sources of the national revenues, had been pledged to money-lenders." [28]

At the end of the year 1829 the financial distress of the government was rendered even more acute by the outbreak of a revolution led by General Bustamante, the Vice-President, who had resigned his office and denounced the President on the ground

[27] Poinsett's No. 170, May 15, 1829, MS. Desp. Mex., Vol. 4.

[28] Romero, *Memoria, sup. cit.*, pp. 101–103.

that the latter was unduly tenacious of the dictatorial powers accorded to him during the invasion.[29]

Action of the British Government

Shortly before the Spanish invasion British holders of the bonds issued by Mexico in 1824 and 1825 had appealed to their government for assistance in inducing the Mexican government to fulfil its engagements. The Foreign Office at London had replied that the grievances of the bondholders on account of the non-payment of interest arose out of speculations of a purely private nature for the success of which His Majesty's Government was in no way responsible and upon which it could not, as a matter of right, claim to exercise any authoritative interference. The chargé d'affaires at Mexico City had, however, been authorized on any favorable occasion which might present itself to second by his good offices any proper representations which British claimants might make to the Mexican government through their agents in Mexico.[30] Effective action under this authorization was made impossible by the Spanish invasion.

The revolution led by General Bustamante, immediately after the defeat of the Spanish invaders, resulted in the forced resignation of President Guerrero and the assumption of the executive power by Bustamante, as Vice-President.[31] The impression which British representations with respect to the foreign debt had made on the new government was reflected in the comments made on that subject by the Minister of Foreign Affairs in his report to the Congress on February 12, 1830. The non-fulfilment of the obligations solemnly entered into in the contracts for the loans of 1824 and 1825, said the Minister, had totally destroyed credit and confidence. The continual disturbances, the want of a regular system of government, and the violent measures which had followed as natural consequences had dissipated the phantom of stability created at the epoch of independence, and the ardor of the most decided friends of Mexican liberties had been made luke-

29 Priestley, *op. cit.*, pp. 267–268.
30 *B. and F. State Papers*, Vol. 18, pp. 1012–1014.
31 Bancroft, *op. cit.*, Vol. V, p. 94.

warm by the frustration of their hopes for the prosperity and aggrandizement of the nation. The glory won in the campaign against Spain must, he believed, greatly contribute to the re-establishment of Mexican credit abroad and to the revival of the kind feeling of the constant friends of Mexican liberty and independence. The time had arrived for giving fresh impulse to the foreign relations of the country. To accomplish this the most essential measure within the power of Congress was that of finding the means of fulfiling the obligations entered into for loans, since whatever facilitated the accomplishment of those solemn engagements would equally improve the credit and forward the diplomatic negotiations of the country.[32]

The report of the Minister of Finance in April, 1830, stated that the arrears accumulated on account of the foreign loans since October, 1827, would amount on June 30, 1830, to 4,178,529 pesos. The sums which the Act of May 23, 1828, had directed to be set aside for payment of interest and amortization had been applied to the most urgent necessities of the government. The greater part of the advance made by Baring Brothers for payment of interest in July, 1827, had been repaid. The government, desiring to restore the national credit at any sacrifice and to adhere strictly to the laws, despite the embarrassments which surrounded it, had ordered the punctual fulfilment of the act of May 23, 1828. The Mexican envoy in London had in consequence been directed to invite the bondholders to name agents in the ports of the republic to receive the eighth part of the future proceeds of the customs which had been destined by that law for the payment of interest.[33]

The arrangement indicated in the report of the Minister of Finance was brought to the notice of the British Foreign Office on June 3, 1830, by John Marshall, Chairman of a recently organized Committee of Mexican Bondholders. Marshall requested that his Committee be allowed to avail itself of the assistance of His Majesty's Minister in Mexico and of the British vice consuls at Veracruz and Tampico in connection with the

[32] *B. and F. State Papers*, Vol. 18, pp. 1415–1419.
[33] *Memoria de Hacienda*, April, 1830, pp. 13–14.

receipt of moneys in Mexico to be applied to the payment of interest due on Mexican bonds. The Foreign Office replied on June 8, 1830, that in consideration of the great respectability of the parties whom Marshall represented and of the magnitude of the interests at stake on this occasion, Lord Aberdeen was glad to have it in his power to comply with the request. His Lordship had accordingly instructed His Majesty's Chargé d'Affaires to give his friendly support to such representations as the bondholders might have occasion to make to the Mexican government. He had at the same time authorized the British vice consuls at Veracruz and Tampico to undertake the duty of receiving from the Mexican authorities, and transmitting to England, such sums of money as might be set apart at the ports mentioned for the payment of the dividends due to the holders of the bonds.[34]

Marshall's letter of the following day, communicating to the Mexican legation in London the substance of the reply from the Foreign Office, was published in the newspapers. The Foreign Office thereupon took exception to certain passages in Marshall's letter, which appeared to the Earl of Aberdeen to be likely to convey to the public an erroneous impression of the extent and character of the interference of the British government in behalf of the holders of Mexican bonds. These passages, if they were supposed to be sanctioned by the Foreign Office, might suggest even to the vice consuls at Veracruz and Tampico some doubt as to the real intention of the instructions with which they had recently been furnished on this subject. Lord Aberdeen considered it important that there should be no mistake as to the real character of the interposition of the vice consuls. These officials, in compliance with the request of the Committee of Mexican Bondholders, had been granted permission to receive and remit the money set apart for the payment of interest. It was for this object and for this alone, and not as agents of the bondholders in the more general and extended signification of that term, that Lord Aberdeen had granted the permission in question. His Lordship had been careful at the same time to ap-

[34] *B. and F. State Papers*, Vol. 28, p. 971.

prise the vice consuls that they were at perfect liberty to accept or decline the proposal of the Committee of Bondholders. They would undertake the business entirely on their own responsibility. They would not be placed in the situation of persons receiving remuneration from the Mexican government. Such a situation would be quite incompatible with the character of British vice consul.[35]

Before the receipt of the second communication from the Foreign Office Marshall had written to Pakenham, the British Chargé d'Affaires, explaining the views of his Committee with reference to the arrangements which it desired to have carried into effect. Replying on August 30, the Chargé d'Affaires assured the Chairman of the Committee of Bondholders that he had had great satisfaction in seconding the exertion of Manning, the Committee's representative in Mexico, and that he would continue to take every step consistent with his instructions which might appear to him to be likely to contribute to the advancement of so interesting an object.[36]

Capitalization of Interest

The efforts of Manning, seconded by the Chargé d'Affaires, had two days before the latter's communication to Marshall resulted in the submission to the Mexican Congress, by the Minister of Finance, of a proposal which took the form of a law on October 2, 1830. By this law the government was authorized to enter into an arrangement with the foreign bondholders for the issue of new bonds in satisfaction of all interest due or to become due on the loans of 1824 and 1825 up to April 1, 1831, and in satisfaction of half the interest to become due on the same loans during the five years following April 1, 1831. The holders of the Goldschmidt bonds were to receive new 5 per cent bonds at the rate of 1,000 pesos for 625 pesos of the interest funded, and the holders of the Barclay bonds were to receive new 6 per cent bonds at the rate of 1,000 pesos for 750 pesos of the interest funded. The new bonds were to be issued on April 1, 1836, and were to bear interest from that date. For the pay-

[35] *B. and F. State Papers,* Vol. 28, p. 971. [36] *Ibid.*

ment of the unfunded half of the interest due on the Goldschmidt and Barclay loans from April, 1831, to April, 1836, one-sixth of the proceeds of the maritime customs duties at Veracruz and Tampico was to be delivered immediately after collection to two persons, one named by the government and the other by the Committee of Bondholders at London.[37]

The law of October 2, 1830, was accepted by the Committee of Bondholders, subject to a change which was made by a supplementary decree of May 20, 1831, authorizing the issue of the new bonds before April 1, 1836, at such times and in such manner as might be agreed upon with the parties interested. Subsequently, in September, 1831, it was agreed that the new bonds, bearing interest from April 1, 1836, should be issued immediately for interest due and unpaid up to April 1, 1831, and that the new bonds for half the interest accruing from the latter date to April 1, 1836, should be issued from time to time during this period.[38] The effect of the operation actually made at this time is conveniently shown in the following table: [39]

The London debt before capitalization of interest

Bonds outstanding	
5 per cent loan of 1824	P10,652,500
6 per cent loan of 1825	15,754,500
Interest accrued to April 1, 1831	
5 per cent loan of 1824	1,997,340
6 per cent loan of 1825	3,544,760
Total	P31,949,100

The London debt after capitalization of interest

Old bonds	P26,407,000
New 5 per cent bonds for interest capitalized at 62.5 per cent	3,195,750
New 6 per cent bonds for interest capitalized at 75 per cent	4,726,350
Total	P34,329,100

[37] *Legislación Mexicana*, Vol. II, p. 289. [38] *Ibid.*, p. 329.

[39] Based on figures given by Casasús, *op. cit.*, pp. 135–137.

The bonded indebtedness of Mexico was thus increased by nearly 8,000,000 pesos. The new bonds for this amount were, however, to bear no interest until after April 1, 1836. Their "present value" was therefore hardly in excess of the sum of 5,500,000 pesos which had become due and payable as interest up to April 1, 1831. It was, moreover, obviously to the advantage of Mexico to obtain, through an arrangement regarding arrears of interest, a postponement for five years of one-half the interest which would have been due on the bonds of 1824 and 1825.

Suspension

The capitalization of arrears of interest in 1831 and the punctual observance, for approximately a year, of the provision of the law of October 2, 1830, with respect to the delivery of one-sixth of the customs duties of Veracruz and Tampico for the service of one-half of the London debt had a most favorable effect upon the political as well as the financial credit of Mexico.[40] At the beginning of the year 1832, however, it became evident that Bustamante was taking effective measures to secure his election to the post which he held by virtue of a revolution against a predecessor who in turn had expelled the regularly elected President. To forestall Bustamante's election, General Santa Anna headed a new revolution. By the end of September, 1832, Bustamante had been compelled to resign his office and General Melchor Muzquiz had been entrusted with the executive power as President *ad interim*. At the end of December, under an agreement between Santa Anna and Bustamante, who had taken the field, Gómez Pedraza was permitted to assume the office for the three remaining months of the term to which he had been elected in 1828.[41]

During the revolutionary disturbances of 1832 there was no serious thought of compliance with the arrangement of the previous year for payment of one-half the interest on the London debt. Hard pressed for funds, the administration of Bustamante,

[40] Statement of British chargé d'affaires to Mexican Foreign Office, February 7, 1833. *B. and F. State Papers*, Vol. 28, pp. 973–974.

[41] Bancroft, *op. cit.*, Vol. V, pp. 106–127.

characterized by its enemies as "a usurping and capricious government," borrowed money locally at rates as high as 5 per cent a month. According to an investigator appointed by Gómez Pedraza, it was willing

to sacrifice the nation in order to maintain itself in power against the will of the people and, calmly watching while thousands of victims poured out their blood, did not hesitate to burden the treasury to the extent of millions of pesos for the accomplishment of its private ends.[42]

On February 7, 1833, Pakenham, the British Chargé d'Affaires, wrote to González, the Mexican Minister of Foreign Affairs, as follows:

As peace and good order are now happily re-established throughout the country, the bondholders will naturally expect to be again placed in the enjoyment of that portion of the public revenue specially appropriated to the satisfaction of their claims.

The enlightened views of his Excellency the President, and his known regard for the credit and good name of his country, are, indeed, to me an earnest that in this expectation they will not be disappointed; but having it in instruction from my Government to use my good offices with the Government of Mexico, to obtain the strict fulfilment of an arrangement in which so many of His Majesty's subjects are interested, I have felt it my duty to request you, sir, to bring the subject under his Excellency's notice, with the fullest confidence that it will receive from him the attention which it deserves.[43]

On the ninth of February González stated in reply that he had been directed by President Gómez Pedraza to assure the Chargé d'Affaires that his government would regard it as one of its first duties to comply with the national engagement as soon as the public treasury came under the system and regulations which were actually in progress and which would procure for it the means of meeting the demands upon it.[44]

Supplementing his note of February 9, González transmitted to Pakenham on March 2, 1833, a communication dated February 22 which he had received from the Minister of Finance with further reference to Pakenham's note of February 7. In this communication the Minister of Finance stated that the President

[42] Romero, *Memoria, sup. cit.*, pp. 23, 115.

[43] *B. and F. State Papers*, Vol. 28, pp. 973–975.

[44] *Ibid.*

of the Republic had given the strongest proofs of his desire to uphold the national credit and to fulfil the engagements of the country with the strict good faith which ought to characterize every just government founded upon the laws. If he had not been able to perform all that he could have wished, it had been because of difficulties which it was not yet possible to overcome or because the resources of the public treasury were "inadequate to the expenses indispensably requisite to the existence of the nation and to pay its debt." The President, on taking charge of the executive power, after the paralysis and confusion incident to the revolution just ended, had been confronted with arrears of many months in salaries and pensions due from the public treasury, by an enormous debt contracted in Mexico during the last year, and by current expenses which could not be postponed. Nevertheless, he had within two months decreed a plan for the redemption of the greater part of the debt of 1832 and had relieved the distress of the employees, pensioners, and others. He had not lost sight of the provisions of the law regarding the assignment of duties for the redemption of the foreign debts. He would like to be able to fulfil these provisions; but as it was impossible to pay at once all the creditors of the nation or to meet all the exigencies of the state, it was also impossible to satisfy the claims of the foreign bondholders. The President had, however, ordered to be devoted to the payment of interest on the foreign debts 6 per cent of the proceeds of the maritime customs-houses at Veracruz and Tampico. This was all that could be done for the moment; but it was to be understood that if circumstances rendered necessary the temporary diminution of the assignment, everything promised that the circumstances would soon change and that the assignment for the debt would be restored to its former condition.[45]

Pakenham replied, on March 8, that His Majesty's Government would not fail to deplore the necessity which had obliged the government of Mexico to depart from the strict fulfilment of so solemn an engagement. It would, however, receive with satisfaction the assurance that the suspension of the existing arrangements would be but momentary and that the Mexican

[45] *B. and F. State Papers*, Vol. 28, pp. 973–975.

government only waited to be relieved from the pressure of the extraordinary demands on the treasury created by the late political occurrences to resume the faithful execution of its engagements toward its foreign creditors.[46]

In accordance with the order made at this time by President Gómez Pedraza, 6 per cent of the revenues of Veracruz and Tampico was set aside for the service of the foreign debt during the remainder of 1833. The amount actually remitted to London was 212,330,000 pesos — approximately 4.5 per cent of the revenues of those ports for the fiscal year 1832–1833. In 1834 only 20,678 pesos, or less than one-half of one per cent of the revenues of Veracruz and Tampico for the fiscal year 1833–1834, was remitted. The amount due in each of those years, under the arrangement of 1831 with the bondholders, was 738,940 pesos. The amounts left unpaid in those years therefore totalled 1,244,-872 pesos. In 1835 the factional strife which had begun again in the latter part of 1834 reduced the government to such straits that only 1,309 pesos was remitted. Nothing more was paid for the service of the foreign debt until after a new agreement with the bondholders in 1837. None of the bonds for capitalization of interest from 1831 to 1836 was issued in the meantime, as had been agreed in 1831.[47]

Possibility of an American Loan

The financial embarrassments described in the communication of February 22, 1833, from the Minister of Finance led the Mexican government to consider the possibility of obtaining a loan in the United States, either from the American government or from private capitalists. This possibility was suggested by a friend of the administration who informed the American Chargé d'Affaires, Colonel Anthony Butler, that it was likely to be brought to his official attention within a short time. Butler's opinion of the matter, as expressed in a private letter to President Jackson on February 10, 1833,[48] was that, whenever he was directly approached by the Mexican government, the situation should be turned to the best account in the adjustment of the

[46] *Ibid.*

[47] Payno, *op. cit.*, p. 45.

[48] MS. Desp. Mex., Vol. 6.

boundary question on which he had been negotiating. If Mexico refused to sell the territory desired by the United States (embracing the present States of Texas, New Mexico, Arizona, and California),[49] he would need further instructions. He believed that if the territory desired could be pledged as security for the repayment of money advanced to Mexico, the transaction would be understood from the beginning as a means of giving final title to the United States. In view of the condition of the Mexican treasury, not a single effort would, he thought, be made for the repayment of the money advanced by the United States. The territory pledged would be "suffered quietly to fall in to us."

The Colonel said that he would endeavor to simplify the transaction by negotiating an absolute sale if possible. His hopes of success in this direction were greater by reason of the fact that large grants of territory had been recently made to friends of the Mexican President, "evidently with a view to the New York market." It was to be expected that the adversaries of the party in power would raise violent objection to an absolute and unconditional transfer of Mexican territory to the United States, but against a contract in which the territory was merely pledged for repayment of a loan no solid objection could be maintained.

Butler's letter was referred by Jackson to Secretary of State Livingston, with an endorsement to the effect that the negotiations regarding the boundary question should be brought to a close. After the expected promulgation of a constitution by the Texans in the convention then fixed for April, 1833, Mexico, the President believed, would be unable to exercise control over the territory or the legislation of Texas. The Secretary of State was authorized to add anything that his judgment might suggest. Accordingly, on March 20, he instructed Butler to reject any proposal that might be made for a loan by the government of the United States to the government of Mexico. With respect to the possibility of a loan from American capitalists he said:

Individuals are, as you know, free to make such disposition of their funds as they may think advisable; but, in this case, the only agency which

[49] Manning, *op. cit.*, pp. 48, 289–290.

it would be proper for you to take would be to transmit their proposals, and advise them as to the proper persons to whom they might be addressed.

You cannot, it is believed, with propriety, give any confident hopes of success for such a negotiation with our moneyed men, without some certain pledge of repayment, and a ruinous rate of interest. The late events in Mexico have entirely destroyed all confidence in their stability, their resources, and their punctuality; and it is much doubted whether a loan could be effected for them on any terms.[50]

Local Loans and Arrangements (1835–1837)

It does not appear that the Mexican government made any effort to obtain a loan at this time from "our moneyed men." Instead, it had recourse to short-time loans which it obtained from capitalists in Mexico at extremely high rates. From these loans and other "extraordinary" sources the several administrations which succeeded one another during the next five years[51] derived more than one-third of the revenues for the maintenance of the army and navy and the civilian services. The nominal amounts thus obtained totalled some 35,000,000 pesos. The actual cash obtained was, however, in many transactions, less than half the amount of the obligation assumed; the remainder of the amount being represented by "credits" of various kinds which had been purchased at a fraction of their face value for delivery to the government as the equivalent of cash.[52] Failing to obtain sufficient funds through voluntary loans, even on terms apparently so advantageous to the lenders, the government had recourse to forced loans. These by April, 1837, according to a

[50] House Executive Document No. 351 (annex), 25th Congress, 2d Session, p. 95.

[51] Santa Anna, who had been elected President to replace Gómez Pedraza on April 1, 1833, served in person only intermittently. The "acting presidents," more or less subject to his direction, were Gómez Farías up to January, 1835; Miguel Barragán from that time to February, 1836; and José Justo Corro from the latter date to April, 1837. Anastasio Bustamante, having been elected President for a term of eight years, assumed the office on April 19, 1837, and occupied it until March 18, 1839, when Santa Anna became provisional president. Bustamante was allowed to resume the office four months later. He held it until he was again displaced by Santa Anna, as provisional president and virtual dictator, in October, 1841. Bancroft, *op. cit.*, Vol. V., pp. 129–236.

[52] Romero, *Memoria, sup. cit.*, pp. 131–132.

protest made by the French legation on behalf of local capitalists of French nationality, had become "the favorite combination" of Mexican Ministers of Finance and a constant source of ruin to the involuntary supporters of the treasury.[53]

The extent to which the government relied on extraordinary sources of revenue during this epoch may be seen from the following table of revenues and expenditures for the fiscal year 1836–1837:

Revenues

		(*In pesos*)
From ordinary sources		7,268,625
Import and export duties	4,663,299	
Half of the revenues from the States	1,152,511	
Direct taxes	512,884	
Revenues from the post, lottery, stamped paper and salt mines	311,064	
Other revenues	628,867	
From extraordinary sources		10,051,092
Loans	4,702,373	
Donations, etc.	828,073	
Deposits (judicial, cautionary, etc.)	1,799,963	
Contributions from the States	2,720,683	
Total revenues		17,319,717

Expenditures

Ministry of Relations	724,224
Ministry of Justice and Ecclesiastical Affairs	468,599
Ministry of War	6,605,332
Ministry of Navy	238,148
Ministry of Finance	9,574,426
Total expenditures	17,610,729

[53] *Diplomatic Correspondence of the United States*, 1867, Vol. 2, pp. 380–381.

With the aid of 1,358,000 pesos which had been in the treasury on June 30, 1836, the government was able to begin the next fiscal year with 800,000 pesos in hand. It would be able to avoid a deficit in that year, however, only by again resorting to forced loans and other unsound practices.

One reason for the reluctance of the local capitalists to lend money to the government was the disposition of the latter to insist upon new arrangements for the purpose of "reconciling the just demands of the creditors with the urgent needs of the treasury."[54] A striking example of this disposition was afforded in the early months of 1833. In February of that year the administration of Gómez Pedraza entered into an arrangement with local capitalists, including British and French subjects who were supported by their legations, for the acceptance of certain debentures of the Bustamante administration, of the preceding year, at 40 per cent of their face value in payment of customs duties. Within two months, however, the administration of Gómez Farías, acting in place of Santa Anna, announced that this arrangement must be revised because "it entailed too great a reduction of the revenues available for the expenses of the government." Friendly but urgent remonstrances were made by the British and French legations without avail, and a formal protest was filed by the British chargé d'affaires under instructions from his government.[55]

Another of the arrangements which the Mexican government deemed to be necessary was made two years later under a law providing that all the obligations resulting from loans and contracts concluded by the executive between January, 1832, and November, 1834, should be converted into "amortization certificates" receivable at the customs-houses in payment of duties, in proportions varying from six to thirty per cent according to the nature of the transactions in which the obligations originated. Arrangements more satisfactory to the creditors were made under the laws of January 20, 1836, and May 6, 1837. By these arrangements 15 per cent of the maritime customs duties were

[54] Romero, *Memoria, sup. cit.*, pp. 121, 130.
[55] *B. and F. State Papers,* Vol. 28, p. 976.

assigned for the repayment of advances made by one group of creditors, and 17 per cent of the same duties were assigned for the benefit of another group.[56]

The urgent need of funds during the period of five years here considered was due most largely to the determination of Mexico to reëstablish her mastery over the Texans, whose attempt to throw off their Mexican allegiance had been foreseen by President Jackson in March, 1833. The recognition of the independence of Texas by the United States in March, 1837, did not lead to any relaxation of Mexican efforts to recover dominion over the revolted province. On the contrary, it led the Mexicans to consider new measures for reattaching Texas to their own country. Among the measures proposed was the introduction of large numbers of British subjects as colonists. It was with a view to attracting such colonists, no less than to reëstablishing Mexican credit abroad, that the government proposed the next important measure with respect to the foreign debt.[57]

The Conversion of 1837

On April 4, 1837, the Mexican Congress directed the executive to "proceed to make effective the colonization of the lands that are or ought to be the property of the Republic, by means of sales, long leases or mortgages." The money obtained through these sales, leases or mortgages of public lands was to be applied to "the redemption of the national debt contracted or to be contracted." [58]

In pursuance of the act of April 4, the President *ad interim*, José Justo Corro,[59] on April 12, 1837, ordered the issue of warrants (*inscripciones*) giving title to vacant lands in the departments of Texas, Chihuahua, New Mexico, Sonora, and the

[56] Romero, *Memoria, sup. cit.*, pp. 141, 154, 171.

[57] Romero, *Memoria, sup. cit.*, pp. 153–155; Bancroft, *op. cit.*, Vol. V, p. 182.

[58] *Legislación Mexicana*, Vol. III, p. 352.

[59] Chosen by the Chamber of Deputies February 27, 1836, to act during the illness of Vice-President Barragán, to whom President Santa Anna had left the conduct of the government. Barragán dying March 1, 1836, Corro acted as President until April 19, 1837, when he yielded to Bustamante, who had been elected for a term of eight years. Bancroft, *op. cit.*, Vol. V, pp. 178–180.

Californias.[60] The quantity of land to which a warrant would give title was to vary from four hundred to ten thousand acres, valued at five shillings an acre. The warrants were thus to range from one hundred to twenty-five hundred pounds sterling (500 to 12,500 pesos) in nominal value. They were to bear 5 per cent interest from the date of issue to the date of the taking possession of the vacant lands; the interest not being paid meanwhile but being added to the value of the warrant as an instrument for the purchase of lands.

Concurrently with the land warrants new bonds bearing 5 per cent interest per annum from October 1, 1837, were to be issued in London. These bonds and the land warrants were to be delivered to holders of the bonds issued in 1824, 1825 and 1831 [61] in connection with the debt incurred in London, provided that the holders of the bonds of 1824, 1825 and 1831 would consent to accept the new bonds and the land warrants in equal nominal amounts in exchange for the bonds which they held and in satisfaction of arrears of interest on those bonds up to October 1, 1837. In consideration of the difference in the rate of interest the 6 per cent bonds of 1825 and 1831 would be exchanged at a premium of 12.5 per cent. As an inducement to the holders of the existing bonds to make the exchange, it was provided that if the interest on the new bonds were not paid when due, the holders of the coupons should have the right to demand of the Mexican financial agents in London certificates for the amount of the coupons plus six per cent, receivable as ready money in payment of customs dues at Veracruz and Tampico. "For the greater security of the payment of capital and interest" of the new bonds, which were to constitute the "consolidated debt," the government was to hypothecate especially 100,000,000 acres of the vacant lands for which warrants were given.[62]

The order of April 12, 1837, as indicated in a report made by the Council of State to the Congress, was designed primarily to

[60] Under the *Siete Leyes* of December 30, 1836 (the seven constitutional laws known by the partisans of federalism as the seven plagues), the government was centralized and the states became departments. Bancroft, *op. cit.*, Vol. V, p. 145.

[61] *Cf.* p. 61, *supra.*

[62] *Legislación Mexicana,* Vol. III, p. 359.

reduce the foreign debt by one-half and to secure the colonization of unoccupied lands. The choice for this purpose of lands situated in Texas and other departments bordering on the United States was, however, as Casasús suggests, undoubtedly motivated by the desire to preserve the national territory through giving to Great Britain, whose subjects were thus invited to settle in these departments, an interest in lending her "protection and assistance against the ambitious designs" of Mexico's "neighbors of the North."[63]

The proposed operation, in some of its details, was strongly opposed by the bondholders in London. As a concession to the bondholders, the Mexican Minister in London agreed on September 15, 1837, subject to ratification by his government, that one-sixth of the maritime customs duties of Veracruz and Tampico should again be irrevocably set apart for payment of interest and delivered to Mexican commissioners of whom one should be nominated by the agents of the bondholders. The certificates which the bondholders were entitled to demand in case of a delay in the payment of interest were, under this agreement, to be for the amount of the unpaid coupons plus 10 per cent instead of 6 per cent, as provided in the order of April 12. The Minister agreed also, subject to ratification, that in lieu of the proposed land warrants the bondholders submitting bonds and coupons for conversion should receive "deferred" bonds bearing 5 per cent interest from October 1, 1847. The deferred bonds could at the option of the holder be used in the purchase of vacant lands, at the rate authorized in the decree of April 12, 1837. If they were so used, interest at 5 per cent from October 1, 1837, would be credited toward the purchase.[64]

The conversion of the existing bonds into new bonds, either "active" or "deferred," was opposed on essential grounds by English periodicals and persons friendly to the cause of Texas, who pointed out the incompatibility between the terms of the order of April 12 and the declaration of the Texans that Mexico had neither right nor power to dispose of their territory. Free currency was given to the rumor that the law for the conversion

[63] Casasús, *op. cit.*, p. 142.
[64] Payno, *op. cit.*, App., pp. 11–13.

of the existing foreign debt was only a prelude to the negotiation of another loan by which Mexico would again impose upon "the credulous John Bull." [65]

In anticipation of the government's approval of the agreement of September 15, 1837, Messrs. F. de Lizardi and Company, who had become the financial agents of Mexico in London upon the resignation of Baring Brothers in 1836, proceeded to effect the conversion of the existing foreign debt in accordance with that agreement. While the conversion was in progress, with the agreement still awaiting approval, a new element of confusion was introduced into the situation by the submission of an ultimatum to the government on March 21, 1838, by the French Minister at Mexico City. The Minister demanded the cessation of forced levies on French nationals and the payment of an indemnity for various injuries inflicted upon such nationals during the war for independence and in subsequent years. His demands not being met, a French fleet established a blockade of Mexican ports.[66]

Although the agreement of September 15, 1837, was still unratified, the bondholders at London were so far interested in the maintenance of the trade of the two ports mentioned in the agreement that they addressed a petition to Lord Palmerston, on June 30, 1838, declaring that the French blockade was prejudicial to their interests and that Great Britain, always concerned for the protection of her subjects, ought to intervene in the Franco-Mexican conflict with a view to reopening the ports to the free commerce of all nations. This petition, the ensuing discussion in the House of Lords in August, 1838, and the urgent representations made by the British chargé d'affaires induced the Mexican executive to recommend to the Congress on December 18, 1838, the immediate approval of the agreement of September 15, 1837. By that time, however, the French had already captured the stronghold of San Juan de Ulúa, and the end of "the pastry war" [67] was in sight. The arrival, at the close of December, of a

[65] Casasús, *op. cit.*, p. 144.

[66] Bancroft, *op. cit.*, Vol. V, pp. 186–205.

[67] Casasús, *op. cit.*, pp. 157–159; Bancroft, *op. cit.*, Vol. V, pp. 186–205; Payno, *op. cit.*, App., p. 133. The undignified title given to the war by the Mexicans

British squadron of thirteen warships, exceeding the French in strength, may have prevented the immediate seizure of funds for the indemnification of the French claimants, but it did not relieve Mexico of the necessity of signing a convention, in March, 1839, by which she undertook to pay 600,000 pesos on account of indemnity within six months after the ratification of the convention. After the signature of the convention and of the treaty of peace concluded at the same time the ports of Veracruz and Tampico were, however, open to the trade of the world as the bondholders had desired.

The Congress was so deliberate in acting upon the executive's recommendation of December, 1838, that the bondholders in London considered calling a public meeting for the purpose of censuring "the versatile and incomprehensible conduct followed by the government for more than a year and a half." Finally, however, the agreement of September 15, 1837, was approved by an act of June 1, 1839.[68] By a supplementary order of July 29, 1839, it was provided that the issue of new bonds should be strictly limited to the amount necessary for the conversion of the existing bonds of 1824, 1825 and 1831 and the coupons due and unpaid up to October 1, 1837. As the bonds and coupons to be converted at par totalled 23,198,935 pesos and the bonds to be converted at 112.5 totalled 20,480,850 pesos, it was expected that the maximum amount of the new bonds, half of them "active" and half of them "deferred," would be 46,236,890 pesos.[69]

The conversion of the bonds and unpaid coupons of the London loans had, as already stated, been commenced by Lizardi and Company, the Mexican financial agents, immediately after the signature of the agreement of September 15, 1837. New bonds to the amount of more than 15,000,000 pesos had been exchanged for old bonds and coupons before the approval of the agreement in June, 1839. After that date the conversion

---

was due to the fact that one of the principal claims supported by the French was that of "a baker whose pastry had tempted the mob" in one of the revolutionary disturbances.

[68] *Legislación Mexicana*, Vol. III, p. 624.

[69] Casasús, *op. cit.*, pp. 159, 168–170; Payno, *op. cit.*, App. pp. 15–19.

proceeded more rapidly, so that before the end of the year 1840 practically all the old bonds and coupons of interest up to October 1, 1837, had been exchanged for new bonds. The completion of the operation was, however, delayed for three years longer by circumstances which will be described below.

The Debentures and Lizardi's Commissions

During the period of more than a year and a half which elapsed between the conclusion of the agreement of September 15, 1837, and the promulgation of the approving act of June 1, 1839, the arrears of interest on the London debt had continued to accumulate. Such of these arrears as had existed on October 1, 1837, were converted into new bonds under the agreement. For a part of the remainder of the arrears, plus 10 per cent, certificates receivable in payment of duties at Veracruz and Tampico were issued, as contemplated in the agreement. In consequence of the long delay in the approval of the agreement, the quantity of these certificates was much greater than had been anticipated and the duties assigned proved to be scarcely more than half enough for the payment of the certificates issued. After considerable correspondence it was agreed between the Committee of Spanish-American Bondholders and the Mexican financial agents at London on February 11, 1842, that eight semiannual coupons of interest due subsequent to October 1, 1837, amounting to 4,990,960 pesos, should be converted into debentures of the nominal value of 2,495,480 pesos. These debentures were not to bear interest but were to be redeemed by payments from time to time out of any funds remaining in the hands of the financial agents after satisfaction of current interest. In consideration of the sacrifice made by the bondholders the assignment of customs duties at Veracruz and Tampico, for payment of interest on the London debt, was to be raised from one-sixth to one-fifth.[70]

In deciding what action to take with reference to the agree-

[70] Casasús, *op. cit.*, pp. 174–187. The increase of the assignment had been authorized by a law of August 28, 1841 (*Legislación Mexicana*, Vol. IV, p. 29), but the execution of the law had been suspended until an agreement should be reached with the bondholders.

ment of February 11, 1842, the government was influenced by representations made by the British Minister at Mexico City in behalf of the bondholders. The Minister, on August 20, 1842, called attention to the losses which British subjects were suffering and to the advantages which the government would gain through the agreement. He urged that the doubt and uncertainty regarding a matter of such transcendent importance be removed by a definite decision of the government.[71]

The agreement was approved by the government on October 10, 1842. At the same time Lizardi and Company were authorized to pay themselves a commission of 5 per cent on the conversion of the coupons due subsequent to October 1, 1837, and a commission of 2.5 per cent on the conversion of the old bonds and the coupons unpaid up to October 1, 1837. The 5 per cent commission, amounting to approximately 250,000 pesos, was to be obtained at the option of the agents either by deduction from the proceeds of the customs assignment or by the issue of new bonds. The 2.5 per cent commission, amounting to 1,156,000 pesos and specified as payable in cash, was to be obtained by the issue of " active " and " deferred " bonds, in equal quantities, to such amount as might be necessary.[72]

The authorization of a commission on the operation approved by the government in 1839 had been acted on in advance by the financial agents. Instead of limiting themselves to the maximum figure of 46,236,890 pesos contemplated in the order of July 29, 1839, Lizardi and Company had issued " active " and " deferred " bonds, in equal quantities, to the amount of nearly 55,000,000 pesos. They now proceeded to sell for their own account " active " bonds to the amount of 4,380,160 pesos, at the market price of approximately 25 per cent of the face value, for the payment of their commission of 2.5 per cent. Of the " deferred " bonds, which under their authorization they should have sold in equal quantities with the " active " bonds for payment of this commis-

[71] Casasús, *op. cit.*, p. 187. The increase of the assignment had been authorized by a law of August 28, 1841 (*Legislación Mexicana*, Vol. IV, p. 29), but the execution of the law had been suspended until an agreement should be reached with the bondholders.

[72] Payno, *op. cit.*, App., p. 20.

sion, they made no use at this time. These "deferred" bonds, amounting to 3,921,750 pesos in excess of the quantity required for the conversion of 1837, were retained by the financial agents in their vaults. Some of these bonds appear to have been placed in circulation, but as late as the beginning of 1857 approximately one-half of them were still in the agents' hands.[73]

The 5 per cent commission of 250,000 pesos was paid with the proceeds of the sale of an additional issue of "active" bonds, to the amount of 1,000,000 pesos, authorized by the government in July, 1843.[74] The details of the conversion, as thus completed, are shown in the table on the following page.

Amount of the Foreign Debt Officially Declared

The placing on the market of more than 5,000,000 pesos in "active" bonds in excess of the amount which had been contemplated either in the agreement of September, 1837, or in that of February, 1842, had naturally a prejudicial effect upon the interests of the holders of the original bonds. The existence, in the Lizardi vaults, of nearly 4,000,000 pesos in "deferred" bonds which might be placed on the market at any time was also a disquieting factor in the situation. Mexican credit suffered such a severe blow and there was such confusion that the government deemed it necessary to declare authoritatively the amount of the legitimate foreign debt of the republic.[75] By a decree of December 13, 1843, the government denied responsibility for the un-

[73] Romero, *Memoria, sup. cit.*, pp. 228, 263, 274, 428, 466; Casasús, *op. cit.*, p. 255; Ortiz de Montellano, *op. cit.*, pp. 155–170. It was agreed between the government and Lizardi, in 1856, that only 3,250,000 pesos of the excess issue of "deferred" bonds need be delivered to the government, upon condition that Lizardi and Company should pay the value of any bonds of this excess issue which might appear on the market. In 1857 Lizardi and Company delivered to the Mexican legation in London 1,750,000 pesos of the "deferred" bonds. In 1866 they delivered 340,000 pesos in "active" bonds, which were accepted as the equivalent of 566,665 pesos in "deferred" bonds. In 1867 the obligation of Lizardi and Company on account of the "deferred" bonds was cancelled and a balance established in their favor against the government. See document No. 20, following page 221, Ortiz de Montellano, *op. cit.*

[74] Casasús, *op. cit.*, p. 263.

[75] *Ibid*, pp. 187–190.

DETAILS OF CONVERSION OF 1837*

Securities Converted			Securities Issued		
At Par		P 23,195,936	Active bonds		P 28,498,606
5 per cent bonds	P 10,652,500				
5 per cent capitalization bonds of 1831	3,195,750		Authorized in law of 1837	P 23,118,446	
Unpaid interest coupons to April 1, 1836, on loans of 1824 and 1825	6,465,791		Authorized (for commissions) in orders of October 10, 1842	5,380,160	
Interest coupons on bonds of 1824, 1825, and 1831 from July 1, 1836, to October 1, 1837	2,881,895				
			Deferred bonds		23,118,446
At 112.5 per cent		20,480,850	Debentures		2,495,480
6 per cent bonds of 1825	15,754,500				
6 per cent capitalization bonds of 1831	4,726,350		Total		54,112,532
At 50 per cent		4,990,960			
Interest on "active" bonds from October 1, 1838, to October 1, 1842	4,990,960				
Total		48,667,746			
Loss By Operation		5,444,786			
12.5 per cent on 6 per cent bonds of 1825 and 1831	2,560,106				
Bonds issued for commissions	5,380,160				
	7,940,266				
Less gain by conversion of interest 1838 to 1842 at 50 per cent	−2,495,480				
Total		54,112,532			

* The deferred bonds for P 3,921,750 issued by Lizardi without authorization are not included.

authorized issue of deferred bonds except as to P458,250 of these bonds which had been rendered "active" and used in the payment of interest due in April, 1843. The London debt, as recognized in the decree, was as follows: [76]

Active bonds		P28,958,250
For conversion of 1837	P23,119,840	
For commission on the same	4,380,160	
For commission on debenture issue of 1842	1,000,000	
For payment of interest April, 1843 ("deferred" bonds rendered "active")[a]	458,250	
Deferred bonds		23,120,000
Debentures representing eight coupons of interest after October 1, 1837		2,495,480
Total		54,573,730

[a] Two-thirds of the interest due April 1, 1843, had been paid in "deferred" bonds which were at that time transformed, by government order, into "active" bonds. Casasús, *op. cit.*, p. 262.

The Burden of the Debt in 1843

The total income of the Mexican government for the year 1843, after deduction of expenses of collection, was 28,819,083 pesos. More than one-third of this amount was derived from forced loans and other extraordinary sources. The total expenditures for the year were 29,220,119 pesos, only about 400,000 pesos in excess of the revenues. The showing thus made compared favorably, on the whole, with the accounts for the five years preceding, in which calculated deficits totalling 64,000,000 pesos, or nearly 13,000,000 pesos a year, had been made up only through forced loans and other extraordinary devices.[77] It could not, however, be said to be reassuring as to the ability of the government to meet its funded obligations.

[76] *Legislación Mexicana*, Vol. IV, p. 679.
[77] Romero, *Memoria, sup. cit.*, pp. 232–233.

In the official report for the year 1837–1838, Lebrija, then Minister of Finance, had said: [78]

> The nation can count upon only 9,870,728 pesos for its needs. Yet the demands upon it amount to 27,555,944 pesos, which exceeds its certain and normal resources by 17,285,216 pesos; an enormous difference which, in view of the solemn obligations of the Republic, requires a corresponding increase in the revenues. Since it is impossible to meet these obligations without establishing new taxes or altering the taxes which exist, the Congress and the government are placed in the truly frightful position of choosing the less of two extreme evils. There must be established a conflict of interest between the national authorities and the holders of private wealth, or else the administration, inadequately provided for, must allow public order to be shattered and society to be dissolved. For, indeed, unless the officials and employees are punctually paid, there can be no efficiency or discipline among them, nor can the government assert its authority beyond the walls of its council chamber. . . . Unless provision is made for the army, the soldier may become the enemy of the State instead of its servant. Unless the obligations assumed by the government in reciprocal contracts with individuals are met, its credit, already lost, cannot be restored.
>
> Although the people are always opposed to any increase in their burdens, yet it is certain that patriotism has not been extinguished, and that the repugnance to new burdens would diminish, or even disappear entirely, if a system of revenues were established with due regard for the liberty of industry and commerce and in proportion to the service rendered to the tax-payer. . . . It must be held to be a principle of fiscal science that *if every citizen bears his just proportion of the common expenses, none can be prejudiced by the burden.*

Lebrija had not been hopeful of the immediate adoption of a just and equitable system of taxation which would produce revenues enough for the needs of the government. The chances of a consummation admittedly so far removed from the realities of the day were greatly reduced by the "pastry war" with France, at the end of 1838; by the various expeditions for the reconquest of Texas; and by the frequent changes of government.[79] Santa Anna, who had seized the reins of power for a few months in 1839 and for a longer period in 1841, attempted, in 1842, to obtain additional revenues through levying monthly contributions upon manufacturers and shopkeepers; through tax-

[78] Romero, *Memoria, sup. cit.*, p. 174.

[79] *Cf.* note 51, p. 67, *supra.*

ing salaries and pensions, coaches and carriages, carriage horses, family servants, theater boxes, and all males between the ages of sixteen and sixty; through extending the stamp tax to new objects; and through establishing government monopolies of playing cards, sulphur, and saltpeter. All efforts made to improve the financial situation fell far short of their aim, and six years after the filing of Lebrija's wise recommendations extraordinary sources of revenue were still regularly tapped to an extent which could not be reconciled with the principles of sound financing.

The amount of the internal obligations of the Mexican government at this time cannot be ascertained. It was almost certainly beyond the power of the Ministry of Finance to reckon this amount, in view of the reckless and casual manner in which the obligations had been assumed. The total of these obligations was probably not less than 50,000,000 pesos. The rate of interest, as has already been indicated, was in some cases as high as five per cent a month. Whatever the amount of the obligations may have been, it is believed to be safe to say that no provision was made for its payment except as such provision became necessary in connection with new loans. It could hardly be otherwise when the government was going on each year from deficit to deficit.

In regard to one group of internal obligations existing at this time information is fairly full and precise. These were the obligations specifically charged upon the customs revenues. Among these may be mentioned a loan obtained by the government under a contract of November, 1840, with the English house of Montgomery, Nicod and Company, of Mexico City. Under this contract the government assumed an obligation of 2,000,000 pesos, bearing 6 per cent interest, in return for an advance of 920,000 pesos in cash and 1,080,000 pesos in "paper and credits" which had been bought at 15 per cent of their face value.[80] Another contract for the same purpose, concluded in June, 1841, with Ducoing, Magua and Atocha, an American brokerage house of Mexico City, brought into the treasury 1,000,000 pesos in cash

[80] Romero, *Memoria, sup. cit.*, p. 242; Payno, *op. cit.*, p. 70; *Pedido de los acreedores del erario nacional* (Mexico, 1842), pp. 4–12.

and 1,173,015 pesos in "credits"; the government assuming the obligation to repay 2,000,000 pesos in cash.[81] A loan in the nominal amount of 6,000,000 pesos, negotiated with local capitalists during the French blockade, and another of 8,000,000 pesos, authorized in July, 1841, for the purpose of withdrawing certain copper money in circulation, had no more satisfactory results. The loans obtained locally from the beginning of 1838 to the end of 1845 reached a total of over 43,000,000 pesos, of which considerably less than half was in cash.[82]

By October, 1841, 62 per cent of the maritime customs revenues had been assigned to local capitalists for the repayment of loans made by them. The charges upon these revenues were known as the 15, 17, 8, 10 and 12 per cent "funds." Since one-sixth of the same revenues was at that time pledged for the service of the foreign debt, the part left at the disposal of the government was less than 22 per cent. Finding this part inadequate to its needs, the government, on October 11, 1841, suspended payment on all the "funds" assigned to local capitalists. Three days later, however, it decided to continue setting aside 31 per cent of the maritime customs revenues, or one-half of the "funds" assigned, for the repayment of the internal loans. Payment on the "funds" was again totally suspended in February, 1842, but in consequence of protests made by several of the legations, including that of the United States,[83] it was ordered that from August 1, 1842, 15 per cent of the maritime customs duties should be paid to the holders of the bonds of the various assigned "funds." After several minor changes in this arrangement, the assignments of 15, 17, 8, 10 and 12 per cent of all the maritime customs revenues were replaced in May, 1843, by a new "fund" of 25 per cent of the import duties.[84]

81 *Pedido,* etc., *loc. cit.;* Despatch of Minister Thompson to Secretary of State, May 18, 1843, MS. Desp. Mex., Vol. II. Information as to the antecedents of Ducoing, Magua and Atocha is not available.

82 Romero, *Memoria, sup. cit.*, pp. 175, 182, 202, 214, 220, 233, 252, 258.

83 See p. 84, *infra*.

84 Romero, *Memoria, sup. cit.*, pp. 230–232, 241.

Diplomatic Conventions with the British Minister

In addition to the charges placed upon the maritime customs duties under arrangements between the Mexican government and the bondholders of the London debt and those of the "funds" mentioned above, charges of 2 per cent of the import duties at Veracruz and 1 per cent of those at Tampico were imposed under a convention made between the British Minister at Mexico City and the Mexican Ministers of Finance and Foreign Affairs on October 15, 1842. This convention was concluded for the benefit of British subjects to whom the Mexican government acknowledged a liability of 306,931.44 pesos on account of various claims based on advances of money, sales of goods or damage to property.[85]

A further charge of 5 per cent was laid upon the maritime customs revenues by an arrangement made between the government and the English house of Montgomery, Nicod and Company with the intervention of the British Minister. The transaction which was finally settled by this arrangement was the advance of the nominal sum of 2,000,000 pesos to which reference has already been made.[86] At the time of this advance, in November, 1840, the government had given its bonds in the amount of 2,000,000 pesos and had assigned to the lenders, subject to the exhaustion of a prior charge, 17 per cent of the maritime customs duties. In April, 1844, the bonds given in 1840 remained unpaid to the amount of 941,500 pesos. With the interest due on this amount and with additional "subsidies" which the lenders had given to the government, the obligation of the government, as agreed upon between the British Minister and the Mexican Ministers of Finance and Foreign Affairs, was 1,148,630 pesos. The agreement was apparently not embodied in a formal convention, but the debt on account of which the British Minister intervened at this time was thereafter considered a part of the "English convention debt."[87]

85 Payno, *op. cit.*, App., pp. 62–69. 86 *Supra*, p. 81.

87 Payno, *op. cit.*, pp. 67–68, and App., pp. 69–77. *Cf.* p. 101, *infra.*

American Interest in Mexican Finance

The suspension of payment in February, 1842, on the 15, 17, 8, 10 and 12 per cent " funds " established in favor of local capitalists was made the occasion of a formal protest by the American Minister at Mexico City, Powhatan Ellis. The only American citizens interested in these " funds " appear to have been the brokers, Ducoing, Magua, and Atocha, who had advanced a part of the sum of 2,000,000 pesos in cash and " credits," in consideration of which the 12 per cent " fund " had been established. The advance of 600,000 pesos made by these brokers was made almost entirely for the account of local clients.[88] Ellis notified the Mexican government that to deprive the holders of Mexican obligations of the means stipulated for the payment of interest was an unquestionable violation of their rights. So far as American citizens were concerned it was, he added, directly contrary to Article 14 of the treaty between the United States and Mexico, under which "the contracting parties promise and engage to give their special protection to the persons and property of the citizens of each other, of all occupations, who may be in their territories." [89]

The receipt of the despatch in which Ellis reported his protest against the suspension of payment on the assigned " funds " was acknowledged by Secretary of State Webster in April, 1842. The President, said Webster in the acknowledgment, desired Ellis to be informed that his course " in relation to the arduous and highly important business " which had devolved upon him, " especially of late," was " entirely approved." [90]

A year later, however, when the various assigned " funds " were replaced by a new " fund " considerably less than half as great, Waddy Thompson, who had succeeded Ellis at Mexico

[88] Despatch of Minister Ellis, No. 56, Feb. 18, 1842, MS. Desp. Mex., Vol. 10; Minister Thompson's despatch, above cited.

[89] Treaty of Amity, Commerce and Navigation, concluded April 5, 1831 — *Treaties, Conventions, International Acts, Protocols and Agreements between the United States and Other Powers*, 1776–1909 (Washington, 1910), Vol. I, p. 1089.

[90] Department of State, Washington, Manuscript Instructions, Mexico (hereinafter cited as MS. Inst. Mex.) Vol. 15, p. 155.

City, declined to protest in behalf of the American citizens concerned. Thompson expressed to the Department of State the opinion that the provision made for the local creditors of Mexico was the most liberal that could then be made by the government with due regard for its own necessities. The American brokers interested in the 12 per cent " fund " were, he said, satisfied with the new arrangement, but they had urged him to demand that this arrangement be given the additional guarantee of a treaty stipulation between the United States and Mexico. Thompson was unwilling to comply with the request of the brokers without specific instructions from the Department of State. With his views of the subject, indeed, he would not have taken the action which his predecessor had taken with reference to the suspension of the assignments in February, 1842. For he believed that it was only in cases of tort that a government had a right to interfere for the protection of its citizens. When such citizens made contracts with other governments, they trusted " alone to the good faith of such governments " and had " no right to evoke the aid of their own government."

" The evil consequences of an opposite rule," continued the Minister, " are too obvious to require that they should be stated." If he had the right to demand a treaty stipulation in favor of the American brokers interested in the 12 per cent " fund," he would have also the right " to demand payment in full or to interpose in any other way." To demand a treaty stipulation, moreover,

> would be practically of no benefit. For no one supposes that if it were made a matter of treaty stipulation and afterwards violated that we would make war on Mexico because she could not pay one or at most two hundred thousand dollars to our citizens.[91]

Although Thompson requested instructions with reference to any action which the Department might desire him to take in behalf of Ducoing, Magua, and Atocha, no instructions appear from the records to have been sent to him concerning the matter.

A matter of much deeper interest to the Department of State at this time was the settlement of the claims of American citizens for damages caused by the Mexican authorities prior to 1839.

[91] Despatch of Minister Thompson, May 18, 1843, MS. Desp. Mex., Vol. 11.

Awards totalling approximately $2,500,000 had been made in 1841 by an arbitral commission appointed under a convention signed two years earlier by representatives of Mexico and the United States. The means by which Mexico might be able to pay these awards were discussed in a memorandum presented to the Department by Brantz Mayer, secretary of the legation in Mexico City, in December, 1842.[92]

After referring to the "lamentable deficit" with which the Mexican government was confronted, Mayer observed that, considering the great internal resources possessed by Mexico in its church property and elsewhere and considering the anxiety felt by the government to avoid a warlike rupture with the United States, the progress of which would be marked by the dismemberment or destruction of the republic, he was inclined to hope that the government would make every effort to pay the claims awards. Mexico, he said, had been reduced to her existing miserably embarrassed condition by civil war and by the pressure of creditors. She was apparently disposed to comply with her engagements if possible; but, paralyzed by war and the bad management of corrupt rulers whose peculations on her revenues had become proverbial, she would require both time and forbearance before she could assume among the nations the place to which she was of right entitled. The government of the United States, in pressing the claims of American citizens upon Mexico, would be likely to be aided not only by the justice of its cause and the known strength of its people, but also by the interest of all the European commercial Powers, especially England and Spain, in the preservation of peace betwixt Mexico and the United States. The diplomatic representatives of England and Spain in Mexico would, in Mayer's opinion, ardently urge the government to satisfactory measures. England, indeed, if necessary, might be willing to yield to the United States temporarily a portion of the security held by the English creditors.

Subsequent events did not confirm Mayer's opinion as to the accommodating attitude of the British government and British creditors. Great Britain would doubtless have been glad to assist in bringing about better relations between the United States and

[92] MS. Desp. Mex., Vol. 11.

Mexico. On the one hand, she had delayed the official recognition of the independence of Texas for more than five years after the recognition of Texan independence by the United States. On the other hand, she had endeavored to convince the Mexican government of the futility of continuing the struggle for the reconquest of Texas. The British Minister at Mexico City had, moreover, been the willing intermediary between the Mexican and Texan governments in discussions of a plan for the payment of 5,000,000 pesos by Texas to the bondholders of the Mexican foreign debt in consideration of the recognition of Texan independence by Mexico. But neither the British government nor the British creditors of Mexico showed any disposition to relinquish in favor of the United States guarantees which had been won by arduous negotiations and at the expense of notable sacrifices.[93]

The most urgent demand made by the United States upon Mexico at this time was satisfied, temporarily, by the undertaking of Mexico on January 30, 1843, to pay the arrears of interest on the claims awards in April of that year and to remit the principal with later interest in quarterly instalments during the next five years. The arrears of interest, amounting to 270,000 pesos, were paid with funds procured by the levy of a compulsory loan upon capitalists in Mexico City. For the payment of the additional amounts due under the agreement a compulsory loan of 2,500,000 pesos, payable in quarterly instalments, was levied by quotas upon the provincial or departmental governments. The regular collection of these instalments was impeded by difficulties of communication and by political disturbances. The government was able, however, to pay the amounts due the United States up to and including July 30, 1844. On January 30, 1846, eight of the instalments were still due. The feeling which existed in Mexico in 1843 and 1844 because of the practical certainty that Texas would soon be annexed by the United States was naturally aggravated by the recurring demands of the United States for payment of the instalments overdue.[94]

After the passage of the Texan resolution of July 4, 1845,

[93] E. D. Adams, *British Interests and Activities in Texas* 1838–1846 (Baltimore, 1910), pp. 18, 26–29, 69–71, 88; Bancroft, *op. cit.*, Vol. V. pp. 249, 327.

[94] Bancroft, *op. cit.*, Vol. V, pp. 320, 338; Romero, *Memoria, sup. cit.*, p. 240.

accepting the American offer of annexation, the government of the United States made a last effort to settle by peaceable means the pending questions with Mexico in regard to the Texas boundary and the payment of the overdue instalments of the claims awards. It sent to Mexico City James M. Slidell, as Envoy Extraordinary and Minister Plenipotentiary for the discussion of these questions. At the moment of Slidell's arrival, in December, 1845, popular feeling against the United States was at its height. The administration of President Herrera, established just a year before upon the overthrow of Santa Anna, was on the point of being overthrown in its turn by General Paredes, who was to become President *ad interim* on January 4, 1846. In the circumstances Slidell was not officially received.[95]

During his stay of two months at the Mexican capital, Slidell reached the conclusion that nothing but financial embarrassment could induce the Mexican government to enter into negotiations with the United States. The entire national revenue, he wrote Secretary of State Buchanan, was not more than 10,000,000 to 12,000,000 pesos a year. As against this sum, the annual expense of the army, which must be paid to prevent revolt, was in excess of 21,000,000 pesos. The public debt, foreign and internal, could not be much less than 150,000,000 pesos. On a small portion of this debt payments of interest were occasionally made. For the balance no provision whatever was thought of. Every branch of the revenue was pledged in advance, and there was no possibility of the government's obtaining a loan from private capitalists, even on the most onerous terms, so long as there was a prospect of war with the United States.[96]

Before leaving the capital Slidell took care to convey to a person having confidential relations with President Paredes a hint that the financial difficulties of the government might be relieved if satisfactory arrangements could be made regarding the boundary with the United States. In so doing he anticipated the suggestion which he later received from Secretary Buchanan that he make it known to the government, in some discreet manner,

[95] Bancroft, *op. cit.*, Vol. V, pp. 292–293, 340–342.
[96] Slidell's No. 7, MS. Desp. Mex., Vol. 12.

that the United States was both able and willing to relieve Mexico of pecuniary embarrassment if she "would do us justice and settle the question of boundary." [97]

"Justice," however, was not to be done by Mexico for a pecuniary consideration. The trial by arms began on April 25, 1846.[98]

The Foreign Debt on the Eve of the War with the United States

The Mexican hope of saving Texas and the other northern departments of the republic through the introduction of British bondholders as colonists had been demonstrated to be ill-founded soon after the passage of the law of June 1, 1839, approving the issue of "deferred" bonds receivable in payment for land in those departments. Although Lord Palmerston, in December, 1840, had instructed the British Minister at Mexico City to give the colonization project his friendly countenance and support,[99] the bondholders had shown but little disposition to avail themselves of the privilege of immigration to Mexico. The well meant efforts of the British government to forward the project had, indeed, led "some educated men" in Mexico to apprehend "that the British government aspires to the acquisition of a certain part of the territory of this republic."

The persistence of the apprehension of British designs caused distress to Robert Crichton Wyllie, a member of the London Committee of Spanish-American Bondholders, who in July, 1840, had publicly commended the action of Mexico in providing for grants of land to the bondholders when the cash resources at her disposal were not adequate to satisfy her obligations.[100] In discussing the reason for the Mexican distrust of Great Britain in regard to the colonization scheme, Wyllie disclaimed exact knowledge of the

97 Slidell's No. 13, April 2, 1846, MS. Desp. Mex., Vol. 12.

98 Bancroft, *op. cit.*, Vol. V, pp. 346–352; Rippy, *op. cit.*, p. 11. War was formally declared by the American Congress on May 13 (Bancroft, *op. cit.*, Vol. V, p. 369).

99 Adams, *op. cit.*, p. 50.

100 Robert C. Wyllie, *The Present State and Prospects of the Spanish American Loans* (London, 1840), pp. 4–11.

"secrets or intentions" of Her Majesty's Government but emphatically expressed the opinion, based on the general policies and the known interests of his country, that Great Britain desired nothing but the peace, happiness, and prosperity of Mexico and that, far from aspiring to any part of the territory of that country, Great Britain would not accept sovereignty over it even if it were offered by the Mexican government. Nothing could be clearer, he thought, than the distinction between the financial relations of Mexico with British subjects and the political relations of Mexico with Great Britain. From the failure to grasp this distinction it had resulted that the British government, whenever it made representations in behalf of the British creditors of Mexico, was considered by Mexicans to be acting in its own behalf and for the advancement of political ends.[101]

Perceiving the failure of the colonization project and desiring to forestall the difficulties which were expected to arise when the "deferred" bonds began to draw interest in 1847, the Mexican Congress in April, 1845, passed a law for the "definitive settlement of the foreign debt" on the following bases:

1. Interest is not to be capitalized.

2. No higher rate of interest than five per cent per annum can be agreed to.

3. The present amount of the legitimate foreign debt cannot be increased.

4. For the payment of the same no national property can be alienated nor can the whole or any part of the territory of the republic be hypothecated.[102]

Negotiations with a view to the conversion of the foreign debt in conformity with these bases were in progress at the moment of the opening of hostilities between Mexico and the United States.

[101] Robert C. Wyllie, *México: Noticia sobre su hacienda pública bajo el gobierno español y despues de la independencia* (Mexico, 1843), pp. 52–53.

[102] Casasús, *op. cit.*, p. 193; *Legislación Mexicana*, Vol. V, p. 16.

CHAPTER IV

"CONFUSION WORSE CONFOUNDED"
(1846–1860)

THE CONVERSION OF 1846

AFTER more than a year of negotiations in London and Mexico City a contract for the conversion authorized in April, 1845, was concluded between the Mexican Minister at London and the Committee of Spanish-American Bondholders on June 4, 1846. This contract provided for the issue of a new 5 per cent loan in the amount of £10,241,650 (51,208,250 pesos) upon a general pledge of all the revenues of the republic and a special assignment of the tobacco revenue, the duty on the exportation of silver through the Pacific ports, and one-fifth of the import and export duties at Veracruz and Tampico. The new issue was to be applied in the first instance to the conversion of the existing bonds and debentures, which had been recognized in 1843 to the amount of nearly 55,000,000 pesos. The "active" bonds of the existing issue were to be converted at 90 per cent of their face value; the "deferred" bonds and the debentures at 60 per cent. Interest accrued on the active bonds, to the amount of nearly 4,000,000 pesos would be paid in cash at the rate of thirty-six and four-elevenths per cent; that is, with about 1,400,000 pesos. Only a little more than 40,000,000 pesos of the new issue would be required for the conversion. The remainder of the new bonds, amounting to nearly 11,000,000 pesos, were to be sold to provide cash for the current needs of the government and for the retirement of domestic obligations.[1]

The contract of June 4, 1846, arriving in Mexico in August, immediately after a revolutionary change of government,[2] and

[1] Casasús, *op. cit.*, pp. 195–210; Payno, *op. cit.*, App., pp. 31–33.

[2] Paredes resigned on July 28, 1846, leaving the executive office in the hands of the Vice-President, Nicolás Bravo. On August 3, a revolution began as the

during the war with the United States, was disapproved by the Minister of Finance. Two months later a new Minister of Finance approved it. The next month the approval was revoked. The contract was finally ratified by President Santa Anna in an order dated July 19, 1847. Meanwhile, however, there had been great excitement among the bondholders at London; the law officers of the British Crown had given their opinion to the effect that the contract was binding under the law of nations as having been signed by the Mexican Minister at London under previous authorization by his government; and the British Minister at Mexico City had, under instructions from his government, made representations to the Mexican government. The order of President Santa Anna, which was formally communicated to the British Minister, read in part as follows:

> . . . in view of the arguments presented to the Supreme Government by the interested parties in support of the rights which they have obtained by the said agreement; in view of the representations of Her Britannic Majesty's Government, which is bound to protect the said rights; in view of the respect due to this friendly Power; and in view of the considerations of public expediency which, if they be at all times worthy of attention, are more particularly so under the extraordinary circumstances in which the nation is placed at present by the war with the United States of the North; I have, with the concurrence of the Ministers of the State, . . . consented to ratify, as by the present I do ratify, the approval already given to the aforesaid arrangement for the conversion of the foreign debt of the republic.[3]

The details of the operation which was thus approved are shown on the following page.[4]

This operation, by which the Mexican government reduced the London debt by nearly 5,000,000 pesos and at the same time obtained over 10,500,000 pesos to be disposed of for its own account, has been characterized by an eminent authority[5] as

---

result of which General Salas was granted the supreme executive authority, by a decree of August 22. A liberal Congress was installed on December 6, and on the twenty-third Santa Anna was chosen President *ad interim*. Bancroft, *op. cit.*, Vol. V, pp. 299–304.

[3] Payno, *op. cit.*, App., pp. 36–37.

[4] Based on Ortiz de Montellano's table entitled "Quinta Operación," in the work already cited, and on Payno, *op. cit.*, pp. 15–16.

[5] Payno, *op. cit.*, p. 16.

Obligations of the London debt June 30, 1846		
Active bonds (excluding P1,000-000 for Lizardi's commission, authorized October 10, 1842) .	P27,950,250	
Deferred bonds (which were to bear interest after October 1, 1847)	23,120,000	
Debentures	2,495,480	
Interest on active bonds (after payment of one year's interest in cash)	2,448,145	
Total obligations		P56,013,875
New bonds used for conversion		
Active bonds at ninety per cent .	P25,162,475	
Deferred bonds at sixty per cent	13,872,000	
Debentures at sixty per cent	1,497,000	
New bonds at the disposal of the government	10,676,775	
Total new bonds		P51,208,250
Reduction of the London debt		P4,805,625

" one of the most advantageous and brilliant financial operations " ever made by that government. According to the same authority, it was also " one of the most equitable and best conceived [operations], since the interests of Mexico were reconciled with those of the bondholders, the debt was liquidated and the fund for payment of interest was increased." With it " should have ended all differences and difficulties." Unfortunately, such was not the case, for new difficulties arose " from the usual cause, that is, the lack of punctuality in the payment of interest." The new bonds placed at the disposal of the government were taken by a British firm in Mexico City in exchange for internal obligations of various kinds, accompanied by only 200,000 pesos in cash.[6] The government resorted to new sources of revenue, including the lands held by the clergy, which were levied upon to the extent of 25,000,000

[6] *Ibid.*

pesos. The demands of the army for the prosecution of the war against the United States were naturally very great. It was not surprising therefore that the deficit for the year 1847–1848, with no allowance made for payment of interest on the London debt, amounted to nearly 10,000,000 pesos.[7]

Palmerston's Circular of 1848

The representations of the British government which were acknowledged by Santa Anna to have been the principal inducement to his approval of the contract of June 4, 1846, were presumably not considered by the Foreign Office at London to have been "authoritative." The position of Her Majesty's Government with respect to the support which might properly be given to the interests of investors in foreign securities was at this time doubtless the same position which was announced by Lord Palmerston six months later in his famous circular of January, 1848.[8]

Her Majesty's Government, said Lord Palmerston in this circular, had frequently had occasion to instruct the representatives of Great Britain in various foreign states to make "earnest and friendly but not authoritative representations" in support of the unsatisfied claims of British holders of foreign government securities. It was, he declared, "entirely a question of discretion, and by no means a question of international right," whether the British government should or should not make such claims the subject of diplomatic negotiation. If the question was to be considered simply in its bearing on international right, there could be no doubt whatever of the perfect right of the government of every country to take up as a matter of diplomatic negotiation any well-founded complaint which any of its nationals might prefer against the government of another country. If the government of one country was entitled to demand redress for any one individual among its nationals, the right so to require redress could

[7] Romero, *Memoria, sup. cit.*, pp. 282–283.

[8] Quoted by Sir John Fischer Williams, in *International Law and International Financial Obligations Arising from Contract*, Bibliotheca Visseriana, Vol. 2 (Leyden, 1923), pp. 10–11.

not be diminished merely because the extent of the wrong was increased and because instead of one individual claiming a comparatively small sum there was a great number of individuals to whom a large amount was due.

Hitherto, continued Lord Palmerston, the successive governments of Great Britain had thought it undesirable that British subjects should invest their capital in loans to foreign governments instead of employing it in profitable undertakings at home. With a view to discouraging hazardous loans to foreign governments which might be unable or unwilling to pay the stipulated interest, the British government had hitherto thought it the best policy to abstain from taking up as international questions the claims made by British subjects against foreign governments which had failed to make good their engagements in regard to such pecuniary transactions. It had been considered that the losses of imprudent men who had placed mistaken confidence in the good faith of foreign governments would prove a salutary warning to others and would prevent any other foreign loans from being raised in Great Britain, except by governments of known good faith and ascertained solvency. The loss occasioned to British subjects through the non-payment of interest upon loans made by them to foreign governments might nevertheless, at some time in the future, become so great that it would be too high a price for the nation to pay for such a warning. In that case it might become the duty of the British government to make these matters the subject of diplomatic negotiations.

The Settlement of 1850

The war with the United States, which was one of the factors in the yielding of the Mexican government to the authoritative or unauthoritative representations of Great Britain in July, 1847, came to an end with the signature of the treaty of Guadalupe Hidalgo on February 2, 1848. Under this treaty, as compensation for the territory acquired by the United States, Mexico was to receive $15,000,000, subject to a deduction of approximately $3,000,000 for acknowledged claims of American citizens against the Mexican government.[9] During the war the bondholders at London had refrained from pressing for the immediate execution of the agreement approved by President Santa Anna in July, 1847; but as soon as the war was over, the Chairman of the Committee of Spanish-American Bondholders at London instructed the agents of the Committee in Mexico to request that the stipulated charges upon the revenues be made effective. He also instructed the agents to request that the three instalments of interest due on the bonds be paid out of the "indemnity" from the United States.[10]

The Minister of Finance replied, on July 8, 1848, that orders had already been given for making effective the assignment of duties for the benefit of the bondholders but that no disposition could be made of the American "indemnity" without the special authorization of Congress.[11] The bondholders thereupon consulted the law officers of the British Crown and obtained from them, on September 5, 1848, an opinion to the effect that since all the revenues of the country had been made collateral security under the debt agreement of 1846, approved in 1847, and since any act of the Mexican Republic diminishing its territory weakened by so much the security agreed upon, the Mexican government was under obligation to apply a fair part of the sum received for the surrendered territory to the payment of the principal and interest of the foreign debt.[12] Fortified by this opinion, the bondholders, in a public meeting on September 6, 1848, decided to send a special representative to Mexico to present their claim to a share of the sum in question.[13]

William P. Robertson, the representative of the Committee of Spanish-American Bondholders, arrived in Mexico in March, 1849, and entered into negotiations with the Minister of Finance. In these negotiations he had the unofficial support of Percy Doyle, the British Minister. On July 6, 1849, a contract was signed

[9] *Treaties, Conventions,* etc., *sup. cit.*, Vol. I, pp. 1115–1116.

[10] Casasús, *op. cit.*, p. 221.

[11] *Ibid.*

[12] William P. Robertson, *La deuda externa de México* (Mexico, 1849), pp. 21–25.

[13] Casasús, *op. cit.*, p. 222.

providing for the payment to the bondholders of $4,000,000 of the sum received from the United States. The contract was immediately submitted to the Mexican Congress for ratification. It was rumored in September that the British Minister had received "strong instructions" from his government and that he would shortly be authorized to demand favorable action under threat of coercive measures. The contract nevertheless still slumbered in the hands of a committee of the Congress, which was then preoccupied with the internal debt, and no action had been taken with reference to the foreign debt when Robertson returned to London in October.[14]

Finding the contract of July 6, 1849, opposed by a number of the members of the Committee of Spanish-American Bondholders, Robertson brought about the establishment of a new committee, known as the Committee of Mexican Bondholders, which was more favorably disposed towards Mexico.[15]

The decision finally reached by the Mexican Congress with reference to the settlement of the foreign debt was embodied in a law of October 14, 1850. By this law provision was made for the payment to the bondholders of $2,500,000 of the American "indemnity" in addition to the sums received at Mexican ports for the account of the bondholders up to the date of their acceptance of the law. The payment of the sums mentioned was subject to the condition of the bondholders' relinquishing all further claims to arrears of interest, which then amounted to 10,241,650 pesos, and agreeing to the reduction of the rate of interest for the future from 5 to 3 per cent. As special security for the payment of interest to accrue in future, the law authorized the assignment of one-fourth of all the import duties, three-fourths of the export duties on the Pacific coast, and one-twentieth of the export duties on the Gulf coast, with the right of ultimate recourse against all the revenues of the country. It provided also for the designation by the bondholders of agents for the purpose of receiving the amounts due for interest at the Mexican ports.[16]

[14] Am. Legation's Nos. 44, July 14, 1849; 47, Sept. 8; and 49, October 13, MS. Desp. Mex., Vol. 13.

[15] Casasús, *op. cit.*, p. 229.

[16] *Legislación Mexicana*, Vol. V, pp. 743–744.

The law of October 14, 1850, was accepted by the bondholders at London on December 29 of the same year, and new bonds to the amount of 51,208,250 pesos, bearing 3 per cent interest, were issued. These bonds were subsequently known as the London bonds of 1851. Certificates representing the arrears of interest from 1846 to 1851 were issued upon the surrender of the coupons which had become payable during that period. Within the next four years the holders of these certificates received 37 pesos for each 100 pesos of arrears of interest. The payments were made chiefly from the $2,500,000 received by Mexico from the United States. A sharp controversy developed between the Mexican government and the holders of the certificates. It was alleged that only a part of the sums received at Mexican ports for the account of the bondholders was applied to the payment of arrears of interest, as provided in the law. The controversy remained unsettled until the time of the Dublán conversion of 1886.[17]

Conversion of the Internal Debt

In reporting the passage of the law of October 14, 1850, the American chargé d'affaires, on October 22, raised the question whether the government of the United States would be disposed to advance the "indemnity" for the special purpose of paying British creditors to the exclusion of American citizens, who were said to hold large claims against Mexico not covered by the terms of the treaty of Guadalupe Hidalgo. The next move of the Mexican government, it was apprehended by the chargé d'affaires, would be the total suspension of all debts due to domestic as well as to foreign creditors.[18]

The next move of the government was in fact the passage of a law, on November 30, 1850, appropriating $2,360,000 of the

[17] A considerable number of the certificates in question were held by Dutch subjects, who applied to the Maximilian Government in 1865 without success, through the informal agency of the Dutch Consul General at Mexico City. Their efforts were renewed at various times up to 1886. Ortiz de Montellano, *op. cit.*, pp. 227–263; *infra*, pp. 203–211.

[18] Letcher's No. 33, MS. Desp. Mex., Vol. 14.

American "indemnity" for the partial payment of certain local creditors and reducing the amount of the acknowledged internal debt from 61,200,000 to 32,500,000 pesos. For this reduced sum the local creditors, whether of Mexican or foreign nationality, were to receive bonds bearing 3 per cent interest and secured by an assignment of 20 per cent of the maritime customs duties.[19]

The plan of conversion embodied in the law of November 30, 1850, was not carried out. The total amount of the internal debt was found to be much larger than it had been estimated to be. The sum appropriated from the American "indemnity" was therefore far from adequate to satisfy the claims of the creditors to the extent contemplated in the law. The government's need of funds for current expenses was, moreover, so urgent that even this inadequate sum was not actually applied to the purpose for which it was appropriated. The principle of establishing a single

[19] *Dictamen de la Mayoria de Crédito Público . . . y documentos relativos al arreglo de la deuda interior de la República* (Mexico, 1850); *Documentos relativos de la Deuda Interior* (Mexico, 1851). The principal items of the internal debt, as recognized in the law of November 30, 1850, are shown in the following table, which indicates also the provisions of the law with reference to the reduction of these items and the payment of funds from the American "indemnity" to holders of certain classes of the debt.

Items of Internal Debt	Debt as Recognized (In pesos)			Debt as Reduced (In pesos)	Amounts Appropriated from Indemnity (In dollars equivalent to pesos)
	Capital	Interest	Total Debt		
Pre-independence debt	14,000,000	16,000,000	30,000,000	10,200,000	....
Debt for amortization of copper money	2,000,000	900 000	2,900,000	2,600,000	....
Debt to employees	10,000,000	....	10,000 000	6,700,000	....
Debt secured on customs duties.......	12,424,000	2,635,000	15,059,000	11,270,000	1,334,000
Debt for expropriation of property........	638,000	126,000	764,000	334,000	351,000
Miscellaneous debts..	2,200,000	290,000	2,490,000	1,410,000	675,000
Totals...........	41,262,000	19,951,000	61,213,000	32,514,000	2,360,000

fund of the internal debt, with a uniform rate of interest, was abandoned, and separate agreements, on varying bases, were concluded with various creditors and groups of creditors.[20] The creditors of Mexican nationality succeeded in bringing about a modification of the law in May, 1852, but even after this modification the conversion of the obligations held by these creditors proceeded so slowly that as late as January, 1858, eleven million pesos of the bonds issued under the law of November 30, 1850, were still in the vaults of the Treasury.[21] The British, French, and Spanish holders of obligations of the internal debt, to the extent of some fourteen million pesos,[22] were able to induce their respective governments to obtain from the Mexican government undertakings in the form of diplomatic conventions in their favor.[23] American citizens being also interested in the internal debt, to an extent which does not appear, the American Minister, R. T. Letcher, protested against the law as "founded on injustice," "violative of legal vested rights," and "arbitrary and coercive in its character and tendency towards creditors."[24] No convention was, however, concluded between Mexico and the United States with respect to the rights of American creditors.

Diplomatic Conventions with Spain, Great Britain and France

The first of the diplomatic conventions with respect to foreign interests in the internal debt, as of November 30, 1850, was concluded on November 14, 1851, between José F. Ramirez, the Mexican Minister of Foreign Affairs, and Juan Antoine y Zayas, the envoy of Spain. It provided for the examination and adjustment of the claims of Spanish subjects,[25] "whether arising from debts contracted by the treasury of New Spain before its in-

[20] *Cf.* Pablo Macedo, *Tres Monografías que dan Idea de Una Parte de la Evolución Económica de México* (Mexico, 1905), pp. 418–419.

[21] For the completion of the conversion in 1859, see pp. 115–117, *infra*.

[22] Romero, *Memoria, sup. cit.*, pp. 343–344, 368.

[23] See pp. 100–104, *infra*.

[24] Letcher's No. 41, January 2, 1851, MS. Desp. Mex., Vol. 14.

[25] Not including that Padre Morán, for which see p. 102, *infra*.

dependence . . . or from later circumstances." All claims for forced loans or seizure of property were to bear interest at 5 per cent from the date of their origin or from September 27, 1821, if they arose before that date. The total amount of the claims which might be deemed valid was to be delivered to the Spanish Minister in bonds of the Mexican treasury bearing 3 per cent interest.[26]

On the fourth of December, 1851, Ramirez signed with Percy Doyle, the British Minister, an agreement, known subsequently as the Doyle Convention,[27] for the adjustment of the claims which had previously been comprised in the agreements made with Pakenham, the predecessor of Doyle, in October, 1842, and April, 1844, as well as for the redemption of certain bonds of the internal debt held by Martinez del Rio Brothers.[28] The total amount which Mexico thus undertook to pay was approximately 5,000,000 pesos.[29] It was agreed that Mexico should pay 5 per cent of this amount each year. Interest on the amount remaining unpaid was to be paid at the rate of 3 per cent a year. The Mexican government bound itself to assign enough of its import duties to meet the stipulated payments. It agreed, moreover, to increase the assignment, five years after the date of the arrangement, to an amount sufficient for the payment of 4 per cent interest and the redemption of 6 per cent of the principal each year.[30]

26 Payno, *op. cit.*, App., pp. 110–114. This convention replaced an earlier convention of a similar nature which had been the subject of controversy since its signature on July 17, 1847. See Payno, *op. cit.*, App., pp. 108–110.

27 Printed *infra*, as Appendix IV.

28 The Supreme Court of Mexico had decided, in October, 1846, that the government was bound to pay 35,000 pesos a month for redemption of these bonds, known as tobacco bonds, but that "a prudent arrangement ought to be made" in view of the war with the United States then in progress. Pursuant to the Court's decision, the Minister of Finance had arranged with the principal bondholders for resumption of payments three months after the end of the war. The claim of Martinez del Rio Brothers grew out of the non-fulfilment of the arrangement. (Payno, *op. cit.*, App., pp. 82–84.)

29 Payno, *op. cit.*, p. 93.

30 Payno, *op. cit.*, App., pp. 85–87. The assignment was fixed in February, 1852, at twelve per cent of all the import duties. At the same time, however, the same percentage of the same duties was charged with the payment of sums

On December 6, 1851, two days after the signature of the Doyle Convention, an agreement containing somewhat similar conditions was concluded between Ramirez and the Minister of Spain. The subject of this agreement was a debt of 825,000 pesos which had been acknowledged in conventions signed on November 7, 1844, and December 24, 1845, by the Mexican Minister of Foreign Affairs, the Minister Plenipotentiary of Spain, and Padre Morán, the representative of a Spanish order of missionaries to the Philippine Islands. Of this debt approximately one-half was due as compensation for property taken by the Mexican government between 1822 and 1829. The remainder was arrears of interest on the principal sum. Before the signature of the agreement of December 6, 1851, the rights accorded in the conventions signed by Padre Morán and the official representatives of Mexico and Spain in 1844 and 1845 had been acquired by one Cayetano Rubio for his own account. The new agreement was nevertheless known as the Padre Morán Convention. By this Convention the Mexican government bound itself to pay annually 5 per cent of the principal amount due and 3 per cent interest on the amount remaining unpaid. The government further undertook to assign duties for satisfaction of the obligation and to increase the assignment after five years, in order that the annual payments might be raised to 6 per cent of the principal amount and 4 per cent interest on the remainder.[31]

Two conventions regarding French pecuniary claims were made with the Minister of France at this time, one on December 10 and the other on December 17, 1851. In the first of these conventions the Mexican government recognized as due to Jecker, Torre and Company of Mexico City the sum of 109,143 pesos, representing advances made by them to the Mexican exchequer. For the payment of this sum it undertook to assign "the free part remaining to the government of the duties upon goods imported by these gentlemen at San Blás, Mazatlán and

due under the Padre Morán Convention mentioned in the next paragraph. *B. and F. State Papers*, Vol. 52, pp. 356–359.

[31] Payno, *op. cit.*, pp. 190–197. *Cf.* note immediately preceding.

Guaymas."[32] In the other convention the Mexican government recognized its obligation in the amount of 274,784 pesos to Serment P. Fort and Company, for advances made to the exchequer, and it undertook to assign for the payment of the claim one-half of the proceeds of the circulation and export duties on silver at Veracruz and Tampico.[33]

The assignment of one-half the duty on the exportation of silver, in the French convention of December 17, 1851, assumed unexpected prominence six months later, when the beneficiaries of this assignment strongly protested the grant of a free license for the export of the silver coin representing the portion of the American "indemnity" allocated to the bondholders at London. The coin was, nevertheless, shipped free of the export tax.[34]

Additional assignments of customs duties were made in favor of British and French subjects under agreements with the British Minister in December, 1852, and May, 1853, and with the French Minister in June, 1853. The British claims which benefited through these additional assignments, amounting to 4 per cent of the customs duties, were those which had been included in the Doyle Convention of December, 1851. The French claims were a new group of twenty-eight individual claims, arising from advances of money, from contracts for supplies or services, or from the depreciation of copper money through an order for its demonetization.[35]

The conclusion of the additional agreements with the British and French Ministers was followed on November 12, 1853, by the signature of a further agreement with the Spanish Minister. This agreement provided for the assignment of eight per cent of the import duties for the satisfaction of Spanish claims. It also contained a provision that the bonds representing these claims might be redeemed by the government at any time before maturity and that the redemption should be made "by auction,

[32] At the request of Jecker, Torre and Company orders for the sum due were later drawn upon the customs-houses at Veracruz, Manzanillo, Altata, San Blás and Guaymas. Payno, *op. cit.*, p. 224 and App., pp. 139–140.

[33] Payno, *op. cit.*, pp. 220–222.

[34] Casasús, *op. cit.*, p. 318.

[35] Payno, *op. cit.*, pp. 82, 225–244, and App., pp. 87, 140.

to be held solely among the holders of bonds of the Spanish Convention, . . . the minimum proposal acceptable being an exchange of 130 pesos in bonds for 100 pesos in cash." [36]

A Forsyth "Saga"

On the thirtieth of December, 1853, General Santa Anna, who had again become President of Mexico in April of that year and had maintained himself as virtual dictator against a rising tide of opposition and at increasing expense, signed a treaty by which he sold to the United States for $10,000,000 a portion of Mexican territory bordering on Arizona. The sale of this territory, known in Mexico as the Mesilla and in the United States as "the Gadsden purchase," was denounced by many Mexicans as treason. As the proceeds of the sale were applied to the current expenses of the government, and not to the service of the funded debt, the transaction was viewed in a scarcely more favorable light by the bondholders at London.[37]

In March, 1854, began the revolution of Ayutla. Santa Anna was driven from power in August, 1855. General Álvarez, one of the leaders of the successful revolutionists, became temporary president in October and was succeeded by General Comonfort, in the same capacity, in December. The position of the new government was far from secure during the year which followed the flight of the dictator. Payments of interest on the foreign debt remained in abeyance.[38]

In November, 1856, the party which had placed Comonfort in power was reported by the American Minister, John Forsyth, to be considering a novel means of firmly establishing its control of the country. This means was the conclusion of a treaty of offensive and defensive alliance with the United States. As incidents of the virtual protectorate to be established under such

[36] Payno, *op. cit.*, pp. 82, 225–244, and App., 117–121.

[37] Bancroft, *op. cit.*, Vol. V, pp. 623–629; Priestley, op. cit., p. 320; *Treaties, Conventions*, etc., *sup. cit.*, Vol. 1, pp. 1121–1125; Casasús, *op. cit.*, pp. 331–332.

[38] Eugène Lefêvre, *Intervention Française au Mexique* (Brussels, 1869), Vol. I, p. 23; Casasús, *op. cit.*, p. 332; Bancroft, *op. cit.*, Vol. V, pp. 664, 672; Priestley, *op. cit.*, pp. 322–323.

a treaty, the new government contemplated the encouragement of American immigration, the development of the great natural resources of Mexico, and the building of railroads. It was thought, moreover, that in consideration of a liberal commercial treaty and of an undertaking to do immediate justice to American claimants, the United States might be disposed to lend the new government several millions of dollars. It was even rumored in Mexico City that Forsyth had been instructed to make overtures to the Mexican government regarding a treaty of alliance or protectorate and to offer a loan of an unspecified number of millions of dollars.

All this perhaps [said Forsyth] is the creation of a dreamland and visionary speculation, but they are dreams that are occupying the minds of a large portion of this people. If they could be transmuted into realities should we not enjoy the fruits of annexation without its responsibilities and evils? Could we not secure for our countrymen the enjoyment of the rich resources of the Mexican country without the danger of introducing into our social and political systems, the ignorant masses of the Mexican people? [39]

In December, 1856, Miguel Lerdo de Tejada, the Mexican Minister of Foreign Affairs, informed Forsyth that the existing government could not sustain itself against the disorganized elements unhappily rife throughout the country without the pecuniary aid of some friendly power. For such aid it could look only to the United States as the natural ally of Mexico. Lerdo declared that he did not share the opinion, prevalent in Mexico and in other Spanish-American Republics, "that the ruling principle in the foreign policy of the United States was territorial encroachment and self-aggrandizement." On the contrary, he professed to regard the United States

as the exemplar of human rights, as aiming rather at the conquest of ideals than of arms, and as eager not for the victory of physical force but for the dissemination of the high principles of self-government.

Unfortunately, however, the cordiality which should subsist between the two nations was

[39] Forsyth's No. 5, Nov. 8, 1856, MS. Desp. Mex., Vol. 20.

weakened by the hereditary Spanish dislike of anything foreign and especially of the American or Anglo-Saxon race, a feeling which had been aggravated by the last war.

The assistance required by Mexico, continued Lerdo, was "simply pecuniary." He believed that "without doing violence to the national sensibilities of either nation," an arrangement could be made for the loan of an amount "of slight importance to the United States though of great avail" to Mexico.

In the absence of pertinent instructions from Washington, Forsyth indicated to Lerdo that he was disposed to consider the matter

upon the basis of adjusting all the matters in dispute between the two governments, the settlement of American reclamations, and the negotiation of those treaties which Mexico was aware the United States was solicitous to make.[40]

To the State Department he expressed the opinion that the moment was propitious "to take advantage of the financial straits in which Mexico finds herself to close up all of the business" of the American legation with the Mexican government and "to accomplish some objects of great interest to the United States." The plan which he had prepared, and which he would offer at his next interview with Lerdo, would, he admitted, "cost the United States some money," but in his judgment it was "not easy to perceive how a few millions can be disbursed from our plethoric treasury with superior results of profit and advantage." [41]

On February 2, 1857, still without instructions from Washington, Forsyth informed his government that he had signed with the government of Mexico a treaty of reciprocity, a postal treaty, a claims convention, and a treaty of commerce and loans. The most important of these instruments was the last named. This instrument, the title of which was later changed to "treaty of loan and anticipation of duties," provided for an advance of $15,000,000 from the government of the United States to the government of Mexico. Of this sum, $8,000,000 was to be regarded as "an advance made to the Mexican republic in anticipa-

[40] Memorandum accompanying Forsyth's No. 14, Dec. 19, 1856, MS. Desp. Mex., Vol. 20.

[41] Forsyth's No. 14, December 19, 1856, above cited.

tion of its customs revenues, denominated duties on imports and exports, derived from its direct trade with the United States." This $8,000,000 was to be used by the Mexican government for its own purposes. It was not to be repaid to the government of the United States but was to be the basis for a reduction of 20 per cent in the import and export duties payable by American merchants and shippers in Mexican customs-houses.

The remaining $7,000,000 of the advance provided for in the "treaty of loan and anticipation of duties" was to be applied to the payment of the pecuniary claims of American citizens against Mexico, estimated at $3,000,000, and to the liquidation of the "English convention debt," which then amounted to approximately $4,000,000.[42] This $7,000,000 was to be repaid to the government of the United States, with interest at 4 per cent per annum, with the proceeds of an assignment of 13 per cent of all the customs revenues of Mexico.

The Secretary of State, said Forsyth, would at once perceive that money was at the bottom of the whole negotiation and that without this element it would have been impossible to obtain the Mexican signature to any of the treaties. Pecuniary aid Mexico was obliged to have, and the question immediately presented itself to the government of the United States whether sound policy did not dictate the assumption of the commanding and influential position of creditor and benefactor to Mexico, in preference to leaving it open to one or more of the leading European powers, whose commercial and political influence in Mexico had always been in undue and injurious proportion to that of the United States. Viewed solely as a money proposition, it had appeared to Forsyth that policy demanded of the United States the extension of the aid of which Mexico stood in such pressing need.

It was of course possible that the Mexican republic might fall to pieces, as it had frequently been in danger of doing. On the other hand, gathering strength and courage from the timely aid of the United States, it might be able to deal successfully with the momentous questions before it, to reform its administration, and to develop the rich natural resources of its territory.

[42] Romero, *Memoria, sup. cit.*, p. 693.

In either event the United States had a great stake in the future of the neighboring republic and a profound interest in the maintenance of a controlling and friendly influence over its policy.[43]

On February 17, 1857, Forsyth reported to Washington that the treaties which he had signed had had a very happy effect in strengthening the Mexican government. They had also "produced a great sensation." He believed that the treaty of loan and anticipation of duties would "revolutionize the commerce of Mexico in favor of the United States." The British and French legations were "much disturbed and very indignant," and were expected to "enter their unavailing and written protest against some of the features" of the arrangement.[44]

The Forsyth treaties were received by Secretary of State Marcy on February 25, 1857. On the next day they were laid before President Pierce. The President instantly perceived that the treaty of loan and anticipation of duties, and the other instruments submitted for his approval, were calculated to make "important changes" in the relations of the contracting parties. To such changes he believed there were "weighty objections." The time available for action by his administration was, moreover, exceedingly limited, since the life of the Congress was to expire and a new President was to be inaugurated within a few days. He therefore determined not to submit the results of Forsyth's labors to the Senate. He avoided, however, taking any course which would interfere in any way with the action of his successor.[45]

Forsyth was informed of this state of affairs on March 3. A week later he was advised by Lewis Cass, the new Secretary of State, that President Buchanan concurred in the views of his predecessor and was not disposed to submit the three treaties and the convention to the Senate.[46]

In a despatch of April 24, Forsyth was concerned to justify his course in the negotiations with the Mexican government. His leading idea, he declared, had been that the true interest of the United States was to see Mexico wisely and firmly governed; in-

[43] Forsyth's No. 23, February 2, 1857, MS. Desp. Mex., Vol. 20.

[44] Forsyth's No. 25, MS. Desp. Mex., Vol. 20.

[45] Instruction No. 11, March 3, 1857, MS. Inst. Mex., Vol. 17.

[46] Inst. No. 12, March 11, 1857, MS. Inst. Mex., Vol. 17.

dependent of undue European influence; her relations, political and commercial, with the United States extended and strengthened; and herself elevated into the position of a good, useful, and friendly neighbor. He knew well the general sentiment of his countrymen in favor of further acquisition of Mexican territory, but he was sure it was not the desire of his government to satisfy this public appetite at the expense of the honor, dignity, and justice of the United States. It was, then, an object of interest to accomplish this by other means than filibustering.

At the outset of his negotiations the subject of territory had been fully in his thoughts. This, however, was a subject which could not have been broached directly to Mexico with any show of prudence. He had therefore proposed a loan by which "a species of floating mortgage" would have been imposed upon "the territory of a poor neighbor, useless to her, of great value to us, which in the end, would be paid, could be paid with honor, and could only be paid, by a peaceable foreclosure with her consent." In short, finding it impossible to acquire territory immediately, he had done the next best thing, which was "to pave the way for the acquisition hereafter." He had used his efforts to lead the government of Mexico to the point of alienation without encountering "the obstacles of the national pride and prejudice." He was persuaded that in no other way could the United States have "acquired the desired land so soon, so easily, and so cheaply."

The commercial aspect of the negotiations, Forsyth supposed, hardly required explanation. The 20 per cent discrimination in favor of American trade would certainly have given us the markets of Mexico, which had been almost monopolized by the commercial nations of Europe. The British government was reported to have declared that the treaties, if ratified, would cost British commerce with Mexico $15,000,000 annually. The universal sentiment among intelligent men was that the result would have been to revolutionize the trade of Mexico in favor of the United States. Beyond question, the discrimination of 20 per cent in our favor in the export duties on silver and coin, especially since the duty had been raised from 3.5 per cent to 6 per cent, would have afforded a margin of profit and would have diverted to the United States $25,000,000 a year which had formerly gone almost *en masse* to England.

It seemed to Forsyth quite susceptible of demonstration that this result could have been effected without loss to the treasury of the United States. The $8,000,000 which at first would certainly have been a bonus to American trade, manufacture, and navigation, would have come back to the treasury in port, warehouse, and other charges upon the augmented trade which it would have purchased. This view of the case refuted the objection urged by some of the press of the North that it was only the South which would be benefited by the treaty. Whoever manufactured the commodities that would have constituted, and owned the shipping that would have transported, the increased commerce must be the beneficiaries of the arrangement; and surely this was the North.

Equally erroneous and wide of the mark were those newspapers which regarded the liquidation of the English convention debt as a sum thrown by way of a "douceur" to the British Cerberus. This was far from the intention of the Mexican Cabinet or of Forsyth himself, and was very different from the light in which the British legation regarded it. To the British this was the most distasteful part of the whole arrangement, and the object of the Mexican Cabinet and Forsyth had been to take from the hands of Great Britain "a rod of influence and constraint" which she had "unsparingly used" over the Mexican government. It might be asked, why put it into the negotiations? If Mexico wished to discharge the convention debt, why could she not have done so out of the loan? The answer was that Forsyth wished to insure the extinguishment of the debt and of the British influence depending upon it. If the money had gone into the Mexican treasury, it was almost certain that it would not have been devoted to this object. It was most important that this debt be paid, and there was no way of making it certain apart from the convention.

While the negotiations, in the Minister's opinion, contained much for the promotion of the commercial interests of the United

States and were valuable in providing for the adjustment of the claims of American citizens against Mexico, it was in its political aspect and in the light of the international relations of the United States that the result of his negotiations seemed to him to be entitled to the greatest consideration. It was not safe for the statesmen of the United States to disregard the fact that other nations besides our own had their eager gaze fixed upon this rich and superb country. If she could not stand without the aid of some friendly power, what power was there that should occupy the commanding position of her benefactor and friend? If the United States refused, some other power must accept that position. What if foreign aid came in the form of a French occupation supported by 10,000 French bayonets? Or a British loan effecting that floating mortgage which the United States declined?

The United States could not play the dog in the manger with the Monroe Doctrine. Mexico could not afford to perish for want of " a medical interventor " because the United States chose not to assume that rôle. Mexico must lean upon some power. That power, " by every consideration of humanity, good neighborhood, and sound policy," must be the United States; for if it were a European power, Mexico, in a multitude of contingencies, might become the battleground for the maintenance of American supremacy in America and the theater of a practical illustration of the value and virtue of the Monroe Doctrine.[47]

Forsyth's eloquent defense of his treaty of loan and anticipation of duties did not induce his government to alter its position.[48] In an instruction dated November 17, 1857, Secretary Cass noted that that treaty had provided for a generous loan of money to Mexico without any other equivalent than that which was to be found in certain commercial arrangements of which the United States would have become practically the purchaser. If these arrangements had been far more valuable than they really were, said the Secretary, it would still have been a dangerous departure from the established policy of the United States to give a pecuni-

[47] Forsyth's No. 29, April 24, 1857, MS. Desp. Mex., Vol. 20.

[48] See Forsyth's No. 36, May 5, 1857, MS. Desp. Mex., Vol. 20; Dept's. Inst. No. 25, June 18, 1857, MS. Inst. Mex., Vol. 17.

ary equivalent for them. A treaty of commerce, in every just view of the subject, should rest upon the basis of reciprocity; and commercial privileges in one country should be paid for by commercial privileges in another country. Should the contrary rule prevail and should the nations of the earth go about bidding against one another for the monopoly of commerce, the laws of trade would be virtually abrogated and the longest purse would buy the richest market. Such a doctrine belonged to a past age of the world, and wherever else it might be sanctioned it could meet no favor in a republic such as the United States, whose interests demanded the most liberal competition and the freest trade. So far, therefore, as Forsyth's projects contemplated the purchase of commercial privileges by the payment of money, the President was unable to give them his approval.[49]

In November, 1857, Forsyth made a final effort to assist the Mexican government in its financial difficulties. He informed the Department of State that he was trying to induce bankers to lend to President Comonfort the sum of 2,500,000 pesos which was urgently needed for the suppression of threatening revolutionary movements. He added that he would be obliged to look to the Department for support if he took "decisive steps" to meet the exigencies of the situation.[50] Secretary Cass replied on January 6, 1858, that President Buchanan was unable to determine what "decisive steps" were referred to by Forsyth. It was not the policy of the government of the United States to interfere in the struggles of contending parties in other nations in order to give either of them an advantage over the other, either through pecuniary aid or otherwise. The rule of conduct which American representatives abroad were expected to pursue was that of non-intervention in the domestic politics of the countries to which they were respectively accredited, and no proceedings in violation of this rule could meet the approval of the Department.[51]

[49] Inst. No. 33, MS. Inst. Mex., Vol. 17.
[50] Forsyth's No. 56, Nov. 18, 1857, MS. Desp. Mex., Vol. 21.
[51] Inst. No. 36, MS. Inst. Mex., Vol. 17.

OPERATIONS OF THE *DE FACTO* GOVERNMENT AT MEXICO CITY

Before the receipt by Forsyth of Secretary Cass' warning against interference in the struggles of the contending factions, President Comonfort had been driven from power and Mexico had been divided between two factions opposing each other in "the first contest for principles" in the history of the republic. The "conservative" or "reactionary" faction, established at Mexico City and recognized as the *de facto* government by the diplomatic corps, was headed by General Zuloaga, who was installed as President on January 22, 1858. The "liberal" or "constitutional" régime, established first at Guanajuato and later at Veracruz, was presided over by Benito Pablo Juárez, who, as Chief Justice under Comonfort, had been declared on January 10, 1858, to have succeeded to the presidency, in pursuance of the constitution of 1857,[52] upon the forced resignation of his chief.[53]

Since Veracruz was in the hands of the Juárez government, the Zuloaga government was deprived of the revenues of that important port. Hard pressed for funds, the Zuloaga government decided to dispose of bonds to the nominal amount of 11,000,000 pesos which had been issued, under authority of the law of November 30, 1850, for the conversion of the internal debt, but which had remained in the treasury because of the delay of certain of the interested parties in complying with the terms of the law. The sale of these bonds at the extremely low prices offered in the market brought but little relief.[54] In March, 1858, advances to the amount of 320,000 pesos were obtained from Barron, Forbes and Company, an English house at Mexico City, upon the security of Church property obtained by the Zuloaga government from the clergy. In May an extraordinary contribution of one per cent was levied upon all industrial property. In September the local agent of Rothschild and Company, of London, agreed to advance 475,000 pesos in cash and 225,000 in bonds of

[52] This constitution, adopted February 5, 1857, was conspicuously liberal and anticlerical. Bancroft, *op. cit.*, Vol. V, pp. 695–697.

[53] Lefêvre, *op. cit.*, *loc. cit.*

[54] *Supra*, pp. 98–100; Payno, *op. cit.*, pp. 247–248.

the internal debt in exchange for an undertaking, secured upon specified Church property, to repay 700,000 pesos in cash.[55]

Notwithstanding the extremely straightened circumstances of the Zuloaga treasury, the "rod of constraint" which Forsyth had sought to take from the hands of the British government was wielded by the British Minister, L. C. Otway, in August, 1858, with such authority that the Mexican Minister of Foreign Affairs agreed that the bonds which had been issued in 1851 under the Doyle Convention and which were still outstanding to the amount of 4,175,000 pesos should thenceforth bear 6, instead of 3, per cent interest per annum. Although the maritime customs-houses at Veracruz and several other ports were in the possession of the Juárez authorities, Zuloaga's government agreed that the maritime customs revenues assigned for payment of interest on the bonds of the Doyle Convention and for the redemption of the principal should continue to be set aside, as formerly. If, in the immediate future, this assignment were found insufficient, the deficit was to be made up later. The new agreement was known as the Otway Convention. It was promptly approved by the British government. It was declared by Otway, in a communication addressed to the Mexican Minister of Foreign Affairs on November 5, to have been due to the benevolence and assiduity of that Minister and to the gracious acquiescence of His Excellency the President *ad interim* of the Republic, General Zuloaga.[56]

Toward the end of December, 1858, Zuloaga took refuge in the British legation from a revolution within his party. This revolution was terminated upon the assumption of the presidency of the government at Mexico City by General Miguel Miramón on February 1, 1859. To meet his immediate needs, Miramón levied a contribution of 1 per cent on all industrial property valued at 1,000 pesos or more and on the income of all persons deriving as much as five pesos a month from professions, trades, or employments. In May a contribution of 10 per cent was levied on property, and in July a new assessment of taxes was made with the provision that they must be paid for one year in advance.[57]

[55] Payno, *op. cit.*, pp. 117–138; Lefêvre, *op. cit.*, Vol. I, p. 26.

[56] Payno, *op. cit.*, App., pp. 90–91.

[57] Lefêvre, *op. cit.*, *loc. cit.*

An agent of Rothschild's, of London, was reported to be negotiating with the Miramón government at this time with a view to a loan of 4,000,000 pesos, to be secured by a pledge of the Church property and to be guaranteed by the Ministers of England and France.[58]

The guarantee which it was thought the English and French Ministers might give was not in fact given. Their governments, however, evidenced their desire to assist the Miramón government at this time by offering to mediate between Mexico and Spain in the difficulties which had arisen with reference to the execution of the Spanish claims convention of November, 1853,[59] and the indemnification of Spanish victims of recent criminal attacks in Mexico. These difficulties, which had been so grave as to cause the severance of diplomatic relations, were adjusted in a treaty, signed at Paris on September 26, 1859, by Alejandro Mon for the Spanish sovereign and Juan N. Almonte for Miramón. This treaty provided for the reëstablishment of the convention of 1853 "in all its force and vigor, as though it had never been interrupted." It provided also that the amount of the indemnities payable on account of the recent injuries referred to should be decided by the French and English governments.[60]

Two months before the signature of the Mon-Almonte treaty the Miramón government had decided to bring out a new issue of bonds to the total amount of 80,000,000 pesos. Of this issue approximately 50,000,000 pesos were to bear 6 per cent interest and were to be used chiefly in the conversion of the outstanding three per cent bonds of the internal debt. Persons presenting the latter bonds for conversion within fifteen days from the date of the new issue were to receive the new bonds to the same amount as the old bonds, provided that they gave the government a premium of 5 per cent in cash. During the second period of fifteen days after the date of the new issue the old bonds submitted for

[58] J. M. Callahan, *Evolution of Seward's Mexican Policy* (Morgantown, W. Va., 1909), p. 9; *cf.* Payno, *op. cit.*, pp. 117–130.

[59] *Supra*, p. 103. Execution of the Convention had been suspended in 1855 under orders of October 14 and 26 of that year. (*Legislación Mexicana*, Vol. VII, pp. 574, 586).

[60] Payno, *op. cit.*, App., pp. 122–128.

conversion would have to be accompanied by a premium of 7 per cent in cash. In the next period of fifteen days the premium must be 9 per cent. In the fourth and last it must be 11 per cent. In the second, third, and fourth periods approved "credits" against the government could be presented at 35, 30, and 25 per cent of their face value, respectively, in exchange for the new bonds.

On another portion of the new issue, amounting to 16,666,954 pesos and intended for use in the funding of pensions, interest was to be paid at the rate of 12 per cent.

The remainder of the issue, 13,333,340 pesos, was to bear no interest and was to be exchanged for coupons of interest due on the old bonds of the internal debt.

Of the authorized amount of 80,000,000 pesos only about 57,000,000 pesos of the new bonds were actually issued. In return for these bonds the government obtained a little less than 57,000,000 pesos in bonds of the internal debt, besides approximately 2,000,000 pesos in "credits" and 443,000 pesos in cash.[61]

The entire operation with respect to the Peza bonds, so-called from the name of the Minister of Finance under whom they were issued, was characterized by Payno as "preposterous and scandalous."[62] In judging the operating it should, however, be borne in mind that the 3 per cent bonds, to the redemption of which nearly all of the Peza issue was devoted, were genuine bonds of the Mexican government. The 443,000 pesos obtained in cash were also doubtless sorely needed by the Miramón administration. That administration would have been most exceptional in political history if it had not identified its own continuance with the welfare of the nation.

An operation even more "preposterous and scandalous" than that of the Peza bonds was authorized by General Miramón at the end of October, 1859. This operation was effected in pursuance of a contract concluded on October 29, 1859, between the Ministry of Finance and J. B. Jecker and Company of Mexico City, a banking institution headed by a Swiss national and

[61] Payno, *op. cit.*, pp. 287–299. Full details of the operation have been diligently sought without success.

[62] *Ibid.*, p. 248.

largely patronized by French subjects. Under this contract, bonds to the amount of 15,000,000 pesos bearing 6 per cent interest and receivable in payment of duties and taxes, up to 20 per cent of any sum due, were delivered to the house of Jecker. In return for these bonds the government received from Jecker 723,000 pesos in cash; 468,000 pesos in orders for military equipment and orders upon customs-houses; [63] and 14,378,700 pesos in bonds of the internal debt, chiefly the Peza bonds, which could be bought in the market at from one-half of one per cent to 5 per cent of their face value. Jecker's total expenditure in connection with the transaction was not much in excess of 1,000,000 pesos. As the annual interest due on the bonds which he received was 900,000 pesos, the practical effect of the transaction was that the Miramón government borrowed at about 90 per cent per annum.[64]

In the circumstances the terms on which the bonds were issued are scarcely surprising. The bankers assumed an exceedingly heavy risk. Presumably, they calculated that a 90 per cent annual return upon their investment would be adequate compensation for this risk!

In November, 1860, the Miramón government, desperate in the face of the growing strength of its rivals at Veracruz, committed a fatal error, so far as its relations with Great Britain were concerned, by seizing the sum of 660,000 pesos which had been collected for the account of the London bondholders by the Juárez authorities and which had been placed in a room of the British legation under official seal. The fact that the chargé d'affaires had shortly before the seizure withdrawn from Mexico City, in order to emphasize his government's disapproval of the general course of action which was being followed by Miramón, was not deemed a notable palliation of the offense. A more lawless outrage, declared Lord John Russell, in a communication to

[63] Such orders were frequently given by the government in exchange for cash. The holders had the hope, often long deferred, of obtaining at the specified customs-houses amounts much larger than those advanced.

[64] Lefêvre, *op. cit., loc. cit.*; Payno, *op. cit.*, pp. 247–252; Romero, *Memoria, sup. cit.*, p. 506; Émile de Kératry, *La Créance Jecker, les Indemnités Françaises et les Emprunts Mexicains* (Paris, 1868), pp. 10–15.

the chargé d'affaires, had never been committed by persons assuming to be a regular government.[65]

The bondholders at London were loud in their demands for redress of the wrong done them by the seizure of their funds. They deeply deplored the fact that their funds had been exposed to the "rapacity" of the Miramón government by the withdrawal of the chargé d'affaires from the capital. They indicated that if Her Majesty's Government was not prepared to protect the bondholders by the employment of force, it would be expected at least to compensate them for their loss.[66]

Replying to the bondholders, the British Foreign Office observed that redress for various wrongs complained of by British subjects, including the bondholders, could be obtained only after the establishment of a government which would respect British persons and property. Her Majesty's Government would use its influence toward the establishment of such a government in Mexico, but it was not itself prepared to effect the change desired. For the particular act complained of by the bondholders it would use its best efforts to obtain reparation.[67]

In writing to the chargé d'affaires, George B. Mathew, on January 12, 1861, Russell was more explicit with respect to the means of obtaining redress for the seizure of the funds on the legation premises. It was evident, he said, that if Her Majesty's Government enforced reprisals on the property of Mexicans at Veracruz it would, by so doing, aid and abet General Miramón in his further depredations. Nothing less than marching a British army to the capital of Mexico would reach General Miramón. Her Majesty's Government did not contemplate such a measure. What it could do was to open negotiations with President Juárez. He might be told that the robbery of the bondholders had been an act of state plunder so shameless that Her Majesty's Government could hold no relations with the government responsible for that act. If Juárez concurred in this opinion and

[65] Casasús, *op. cit.*, pp. 338–342; *B. and F. State Papers*, Vol. 51, pp. 577–578; Payno, *op. cit.*, p. 31.

[66] *B. and F. State Papers*, Vol. 51, pp. 585–586.

[67] *Ibid., loc. cit.*

was disposed, in case he succeeded in establishing his authority in Mexico City, to acknowledge the debt incurred by the Miramón authorities through the act of "plunder" referred to, and if he would also acquiesce in the principle of satisfying other established claims of British subjects for spoliation and violence inflicted on them at various times, Her Majesty's Government would be ready to recognize him as the head of a legal government and to give him the moral support of Great Britain.[68]

The *de Jure* Government at Veracruz

The government of Juárez, which the British chargé d'affaires was thus provisionally directed to recognize at the beginning of 1861, had been given a measure of recognition two years earlier in an arrangement between the Governor of Veracruz and a captain in the British Navy. This arrangement had been effected by an exchange of notes in which the Juárez government was referred to as "the party in possession of Veracruz."[69]

In the first of these notes, dated January 24, 1859, Captain Dunlop, commanding a detachment of the British Navy then stationed in the Gulf of Mexico, demanded the payment of the interest due on the bonds of the London debt and of the English convention debt. He demanded also that an agent appointed by the British Minister at Mexico City, on behalf of the holders of these bonds, be stationed at each of the customs-houses controlled by the Juárez authorities for the purpose of assuring the punctual and full payment of the assignments of revenues in favor of the bondholders.[70]

The demands of Captain Dunlop were acceded to by Governor Zamora on February 2, 1859, except as regards the appointment of an agent of the British creditors at each port. Such an appointment, said the Governor, would be in the greatest degree

68 *Ibid.*, pp. 577–578.

69 *B. and F. State Papers*, Vol. 49, pp. 1253–1261.

70 The bondholders of the London debt, it will be recalled, were entitled to 25 per cent of the import duties at all the customs-houses. Sixteen per cent of the same duties were pledged to the bondholders of the English convention debt. *Cf.* pp. 98–103, *supra*.

humiliating to the dignity of the authorities, as implying that they were suspected of being capable of falsifying the monthly statement of the liquidation of the British assignments, which was in future to be rendered from all the customs-houses under the control of the party in possession of Veracruz. The Governor, however, gave his word of honor that the administrators of the customs-houses would be instructed to afford every possible facility at all times to Her Majesty's consuls in the different ports to compare and verify the monthly statements, when this should be considered necessary to rectify or clear up any part of those statements which might not be clearly understood.

The Captain having accepted the Governor's assurances in lieu of the appointment of special agents for the English creditors, the obligation to set aside 25 per cent of the customs revenue for the London bondholders and 16 per cent for the bondholders of the English convention debt was assumed by Zamora, in the name of the Juárez government, on February 7. The concluding paragraph of the note of February 7, which had been approved by Melchor Ocampo, Juárez' Minister of Foreign Affairs, was as follows:

> Should his Excellency the Constitutional President *ad interim* of the Republic come into possession of the capital, as his right to do so and the wish of a majority of the nation lead us to hope, he will maintain, as appears to him just, the stipulations to which he has now agreed; but he declares that, with regard to those stipulations ever serving as the base of a future diplomatic Convention, he thinks it proper to reserve to himself, and does in fact reserve, the natural right, should such negotiations be regularly and duly instituted, of discussing the nature of any such Convention.[71]

A correspondence of the same tenor as that summarized above was carried on at the same time between the Juárez authorities and Vice-Admiral Penaud of the French navy. An arrangement concluded on January 26, 1859, provided that 8 per cent of the duties on goods imported in vessels other than French should be devoted to the payment of arrears on the French convention debt and of treasury orders belonging to French subjects.[72]

[71] *B. and F. State Papers*, Vol. 49, pp. 1253–1261.

[72] Romero, *Memoria, sup. cit.*, pp. 487–489.

While the Dunlop and Penaud arrangements were being made, a special agent of the United States, William M. Churchwell, appointed in December, 1858, was investigating conditions in Mexico and preparing a report favoring recognition of the Juárez government by the United States. American relations with the government at Mexico City had, in fact, been broken off six months before by Forsyth, and the message of President Buchanan to the Congress at Washington, shortly preceding the appointment of Churchwell, had indicated strong sympathy for "the liberal party in Mexico." The sympathy was given more emphatic expression in March, 1859, after Churchwell had sent to Washington a memorandum signed by Juárez indicating that he was willing, under certain conditions, to sell Lower California to the United States and to grant to the same country perpetual rights of way across the Isthmus of Tehuantepec and from the Rio Grande to Guaymas and Mazatlán. In instructing the newly appointed Minister to Mexico, Robert M. McLane, Secretary of State Cass said, on March 7, 1859:

Undoubtedly, . . . the sympathies of the United States have been strongly enlisted in favor of the party of Juárez which is now established at Veracruz, and this government would be glad to see it successful. This arises not only from the fact that it is believed to be a constitutional party, but because, also, its general views are understood to be more liberal than those of the party opposed to it, and because, moreover, it is believed to entertain friendly sentiments toward the United States. Notwithstanding this preference, our government cannot properly intervene in its behalf without violating a cardinal feature of our foreign policy. Yet, it would be an agreeable duty to give it the full weight of our recognition, at the earliest period when its condition and prospects would justify us in doing so. The single fact that it is not in possession of the City of Mexico, ought not to be a conclusive consideration against it. . . .

You are authorized, whenever under your instructions you shall have recognized a Government in Mexico, and shall find it willing to negotiate a satisfactory treaty of commerce and limits with the United States, to enter upon such negotiation without delay.[73]

The Juárez government was recognized by McLane in April, 1859, and the negotiations envisaged by Cass were immediately commenced. The proposed sale of Lower California, to which

[73] Instruction No. 2, March 7, 1859, MS. Inst. Mex., Vol. 17.

Juárez had been willing to assent, encountered strong objections in the liberal Cabinet. The Minister of Finance, Miguel Lerdo de Tejada, who was considered the ablest member of the Cabinet, would consent to the sale at not less than 30,000,000 pesos — a figure so high as to be taken as indicating effective opposition to the sale. Before the end of June McLane reached the conclusion that the proposed sale could not be effected at that time and that the most practicable measure for securing American ascendancy in Mexico and establishing a government of constitutional freedom in that country was a treaty for the purchase by the United States of a perpetual right of way across the Isthmus of Tehuantepec, with the privilege of using military forces for the protection of the right of way and incidentally for the support of stable government.[74] McLane's negotiations to that end were suspended in July, 1859, when Lerdo proceeded to the United States for the purpose of obtaining a loan upon the security of the Church property which had just been expropriated by the government.[75]

Upon the eve of Lerdo's departure McLane informed Secretary of State Cass that should the Minister of Finance succeed in obtaining the desired loan it was not likely that he or his colleagues would be disposed to cede Lower California to the United States. If the Minister's attempt failed, he would, on the other hand, almost certainly cease to oppose the sale of the desired territory.[76]

In November, 1859, Lerdo returned from the United States empty handed. It does not appear that his efforts to obtain a loan were in any way impeded by the government of this country. The failure of his efforts did not result in the sale of Lower California to the United States. It was doubtless, however, one of the factors in the decision of the Juárez government to sign with McLane, in December, 1859, a treaty ceding to the United States for the sum of $2,000,000 the perpetual right of way and incidental right of military action which McLane had envisaged six

[74] McLane's despatches of June 22 and June 25, 1859, MS. Desp. Mex., Vol. 23.

[75] McLane's No. 26, July 12, 1859, MS. Desp. Mex., Vol. 23.

[76] *Ibid.*

months earlier. In submitting this treaty to the Department of State, McLane predicted that if the United States declined responsibility for assuring public order in Mexico there would be intervention from some other quarter.[77]

The McLane treaty was disapproved by the United States Senate in May, 1860. The decision apparently turned upon the sectional issue between the northern and southern States of the American union, the treaty being denounced as a plot of the slave interests to extend their territory and augment their population.[78] The unfavorable action of the Senate left the Juárez government $2,000,000 poorer than it had hoped to be.

The urgent financial needs of the Juárez government for its military activities against the Miramón government were met to some extent in September, 1860, by the seizure at Laguna Seca of some 1,100,000 pesos in transit from the interior to the port of Tampico. As the funds seized belonged chiefly to nationals of Great Britain, France, Spain, and Germany, there were immediate protests from the consulates of those Powers. Some 400,000 pesos, belonging chiefly to British subjects, were immediately returned. For the remainder, in which the British still shared, acknowledgments bearing one per cent interest a month were given. The complaints of the injured nations were nevertheless not much assuaged.[79]

On the 15th of December, 1860, ten days before Juárez, "the Constitutional President *ad interim* of the Republic," came "into possession of the capital,"[80] an arrangement was concluded at Veracruz between his Minister of Foreign Affairs and Captain Aldham, of the British Navy, for the adjustment of difficulties which had resulted from the infraction of the arrangement concluded two years before with Captain Dunlop. By the new arrangement the Juárez government bound itself to make an

[77] Callahan, *op. cit.*, p. 10; Rippy, *op. cit.*, pp. 223–226.

[78] Rippy, *op. cit.*, p. 221.

[79] Payno, *op. cit.*, pp. 103–106; Casasús, *op. cit.*, pp. 342, 354; Bancroft, *op. cit.*, Vol. V, pp. 787–788. For the privileged character given to this debt, see pp. 130, 145, *infra*.

[80] The expressions quoted are from Governor Zamora's note of February 7, 1859, to Captain Dunlop, *supra*, p. 120.

additional temporary assignment of ten per cent of the import duties at Veracruz and Tampico for the benefit of the holders of the English convention debt and the London debt. It engaged solemnly not to tolerate in future the violation of either the Dunlop or the Aldham arrangement.[81]

The Empty Treasury at Mexico City

On Christmas day, 1860, President Juárez occupied the capital city. The republic of which he was now generally recognized to be the President was exhausted by the recent struggles. Its revenues were so heavily charged in favor of foreign creditors as to be far from sufficient for its legitimate needs. The assignments of import duties in favor of foreign creditors were at this time as follows: [82]

Creditors	Amount	Veracruz and Tampico	Other Customs-Houses
London Debt [a]	P 62,000,000	30 per cent	25 per cent
English Convention Debt	4,000,000	16 per cent (both)	16 per cent (both)
Padre Morán Debt	800,000		
Spanish Convention Debt	6,000,000	8 per cent	8 per cent
French Convention Debt	190,000	25 per cent of duties paid by French vessels	25 per cent of duties paid by French vessels
Arrears of interest on English Convention Debt	1,800,000	5 per cent of duties paid by all vessels; 8 per cent of duties paid by all but French vessels	8 per cent of duties paid by all but French vessels

[a] For this debt were also assigned 75 per cent of the export duties on the Pacific coast and 5 per cent of those on the Gulf coast.

81 *Legislación Mexicana,* Vol. VIII, p. 778.

82 *Legislación Mexicana,* Vol. V, p. 743, Vol. VII, p. 315, Vol. VIII, p. 363, 664; Payno, *op. cit.*, p. 321 and App., pp. 89–90, 119, 141; Romero, *Memoria, sup. cit.*, pp. 487–489; Inclosures with Sir Charles Wyke's despatch of August 26, 1861, *B. and F. State Papers,* Vol. 52, pp. 356–359.

The government was supposed, especially by the bondholders at London, to have at its disposal ample resources for meeting all its obligations. These resources were believed to be represented by the Church property which had been the subject of a decree of nationalization in July, 1859. It was known that a considerable part of this property, being outside the control of the Juárez authorities during the revolutionary struggle, had been sold by the clergy to private parties — in some instances, in order to raise money for the support of the faction opposing Juárez. It was known also that a substantial portion of the Church property had already been sold by the Juárez authorities at prices ranging as low as 15 per cent of its normal value. Yet it was thought that enough of the Church property must remain in the hands of the Juárez authorities to afford a large annual income.[83]

The truth in regard to the Church property appears to have been that the estimates of its normal value had been greatly exaggerated, that its market price was enormously reduced by the unsettled conditions and lack of confidence, and that almost all of the property had been disposed of before the beginning of 1861. It may not have been true, as later asserted, that this property was "frittered away" and "squandered," but the fact remained that it was no longer a source of revenue for the government.[84]

The government which had triumphed in the "first contest for principles" in the history of the republic was under the urgent necessity of finding new sources of revenue. It was believed by the British chargé d'affaires that nothing short of foreign interposition could save the republic from dismemberment and bankruptcy.[85]

[83] Payno, *op. cit.*, pp. 37–39, 117–119; Romero, *Memoria, sup. cit.*, p. 500; *B. and F. State Papers*, Vol. 52, pp. 250–255.

[84] *Ibid. Cf.* Macedo, *op. cit.*, p. 420.

[85] *B. and F. State Papers, loc. cit.*

CHAPTER V

A EUROPEAN INTERLUDE
(1861–1867)

Foreign Relations of the Juárez Government

The Juárez government, as already noted, had been recognized by the United States nearly two years before its triumph over Miramón. In July, 1860, when the issue of the contest between the two governments still seemed doubtful, Secretary of State Cass had rejected the invitation of the British Minister at Washington to join Great Britain and France in asking the leaders to arrange some method of settling their difficulties. In December, 1860, only a few days before the entry of Juárez into Mexico City, when there were rumors that Great Britain, France and Spain intended to use forcible means to obtain redress for injuries to their subjects, McLane, the American Minister, sent a member of his legation from Veracruz to the neighborhood of Mexico City to declare to the diplomatic representatives there that his government denied to the European governments "the right to interfere *directly* or *indirectly* with the political independence of the republic of Mexico." "The government of the United States," it was asserted, "will to the extent of its power, defend the nationality and independence of said republic."[1]

This declaration was not intended as a defiance of the three European powers most largely interested in Mexican affairs. Those powers had, in fact, already assured the United States that they would undertake no interference with the nationality or independence of Mexico. The declaration was, however, undoubtedly designed to give the Juárez government the impression that it could rely upon the United States in case of menaces from Europe. The preoccupation of the United States with its

[1] Rippy, *op. cit.*, pp. 227–228.

own internal affairs, especially after the secession of South Carolina in December, 1860, altered the methods but not the aims of American policy with reference to the apprehended schemes of Great Britain, France, and Spain in Mexico. The desire of the United States for close and friendly relations with Mexico was indicated by the choice of the successor to McLane. The new Minister, appointed in March, 1861, was Thomas Corwin, who fifteen years before had expressed in Congress the hope that Mexico would welcome American soldiers with bloody hands to hospitable graves.[2]

The resentment which the Juárez government felt against all the European diplomatic representatives, on account of their recognition of the rival government at Mexico City, was particularly bitter in the case of the Spanish Ambassador, Juan B. Pacheco, who was believed to have given active support to Miramón against Juárez. The liberal government had been installed in Mexico City less than three weeks when it informed Pacheco that he could be regarded only as an enemy because of the efforts he had made in favor of the usurping rebels who had occupied the capital for the last three years. The Ambassador was therefore ordered to leave the country. The President, however, desired it to be understood that his respect and esteem for Spain were undiminished and that his objections to Pacheco were based on individual grounds. The Ambassador replied immediately that he was leaving the country with his entire suite.[3]

In connection with the incident of the dismissal of Pacheco the President made it clear that he would not be bound by the treaty, regarding Spanish claims, which had been signed on September 26, 1859, by Almonte, the representative of Miramón at Paris, and Mon, the Ambassador of Spain at that capital.[4] The reasons for the rejection of this treaty included the belief that it was "immoral" and that approval of it would have involved a recognition "that the reactionary administration had the right to make agreements in the name of the Republic."[5]

[2] *Ibid., loc. cit.*, and p. 257.

[3] *B. and F. State Papers*, Vol. 51, pp. 609–611.

[4] *Supra*, p. 115.

[5] Lefêvre, *op. cit.*, Vol. I, p. 28.

For similar reasons Juárez refused to recognize without modification the contract under which the Swiss house of Jecker and Company had obtained bonds to the amount of 15,000,000 pesos in return for an expenditure of approximately 1,000,000 pesos in cash.[6] Jecker and Company, presumably because of the interest of French subjects in their operations,[7] had been taken under the protection of the government of Napoleon III. The new French Minister, de Saligny, who had presented his credentials in March, 1861,[8] declared that the claim of these protégés of France was the only claim which could give rise to serious difficulty between his country and Mexico.

It seemed to de Saligny to be superfluous to discuss the principle of the "solidarity" of the several governments which might succeed one another in any country. This principle his own country, in the midst of many changes of government during the last fifty years, had always respected, sometimes at the cost of grievous sacrifices. However kindly his government might feel toward Mexico, it could not admit the right of Mexico to violate this principle in the matter of the liability of 15,000,000 pesos incurred toward the house of Jecker. The basis for the settlement of this liability proposed by de Saligny was the recognition of a debt of 10,000,000 pesos and the imposition of a charge of fifteen per cent on the customs revenues for its repayment. This basis of settlement was unacceptable to the Juárez government.[9]

Somewhat more satisfactory relations existed between the Juárez government and Great Britain. The conditions of recognition proposed by Lord Russell were accepted by Juárez in February, and recognition was immediately accorded.[10] It was realized, however, that Sir Charles Wyke, the new Minister of

[6] Kératry, *op. cit.*, p. 12; *cf.* pp. 116, 117, *supra.*

[7] The most important French interest in the Jecker bonds was apparently that of the Duc de Morny, illegitimate half-brother of Napoleon III and President of the French Chamber of Deputies, who was reported to have acquired some thirty per cent of the bonds. Priestley, *op. cit.*, p. 341; Pérez Verdía, *op. cit.*, p. 355; *La Grande Encyclopédie,* Paris, 1899, Vol. 24, p. 359; Thomas R. Lill, *National Debt of Mexico* (New York, 1919), p. 45.

[8] Lefêvre, *op. cit.*, Vol. I, p. 46.

[9] Kératry, *op. cit.*, p. 14.

[10] *B. and F. State Papers,* Vol. 51, pp. 631–632.

Great Britain, would be likely to have occasion to make strong representations with a view to securing the fulfilment of the promises which the Juárez government had made for the benefit of British subjects.

In instructing the new Minister with reference to his duties, Lord Russell emphasized the importance of the outstanding pecuniary claims of British subjects. Referring particularly to the debts contracted in London in 1824 and 1825, he said that it had not been the custom of Her Majesty's Government to interfere authoritatively, although it held itself free to do so, on behalf of those who had chosen to lend their money to foreign governments. The holders of the bonds issued on account of the London debts had not been an exception to the rule. The claims of these bondholders had, however, acquired the character of an international obligation in consequence of the arrangements concluded by the constitutional government at Veracruz with Captain Dunlop and Captain Aldham. Sir Charles Wyke was accordingly to insist upon the punctual fulfilment of the obligation thus contracted.

The holders of the bonds of the London debt had, moreover, sustained a grievous loss through the robbery on the legation premises, in November, 1860. Her Majesty's Government did not expect any determined refusal on the part of the constitutional government to afford the redress which it had promised in this case. In the event of such refusal, however, the Minister was to apprise the Mexican government that he was authorized and enjoined at once to call upon Her Majesty's naval forces to support, and if necessary to enforce, his demand for reparation. The fact that the scene of the outrage was the residence of the British legation, added Lord Russell, gave Her Majesty's Government a special right to enforce reparation in this particular case.[11]

On April 30, 1861, M. A. de la Fuente, former Minister of Finance and of Foreign Affairs, was sent to represent Mexico at Paris and London. In the instructions given to him before his departure he was reminded that his government, in order to com-

[11] *B. and F. State Papers*, Vol. 52, pp. 237–239.

ply with its financial engagements, had sacrificed the greater part of its revenues and burdened the maritime customs in such a way that their proceeds scarcely sufficed for the payment of the employees of the administration. He was urged to devote all his thought and efforts to establishing the truth that so long as foreign claims were large the possibility of payment would necessarily be small. The government was in need of money for the pacification of the republic, an object in which foreigners were no less interested than Mexicans, since it was only in the shadow of peace that the administration could be organized and industry and commerce could be energized. De la Fuente was to adopt all possible measures with a view to obtaining for his country a moment of respite.[12]

The Act of May 29, 1861

On the twenty-ninth of May the Mexican Congress passed an act designed to afford the country the " moment of respite " which was believed to be necessary. This act provided that all payments on account of the national debt, with the exception of two classes of the debt, should be suspended for one year. The debts excepted were those due to the owners of the funds seized at Laguna Seca[13] and those recognized in the diplomatic conventions with Great Britain, France, and Spain. The executive was directed to " institute measures regarding the suspension of the diplomatic conventions."[14]

The news of the promulgation of this act was received with indignation by the bondholders in London. At a meeting on July 4, they passed resolutions respectfully but firmly requesting Her Majesty's Government to continue its demand for the repayment of the 660,000 pesos seized at the British legation, to require the fulfilment of the engagements previously made by Mexico with respect to assignment of revenues, and to insist upon the appointment of special agents at the ports. They also expressed the hope that their government would intervene for the enforcement of their demands for adequate security. To that end they

[12] Lefêvre, *op. cit.*, Vol. I, p. 57.

[13] *Supra*, p. 123.

[14] Payno, *op. cit.*, App., p. 91.

urged that the Mexican government be required to cede to them immediately the remaining Church property and all the public lands of the country and to sign a diplomatic convention respecting the London debt, as had been contemplated in the Dunlop arrangement of 1859, in such a manner as to make it in future impossible for the Mexican government to escape from its engagements.[15]

In an interview with Lord Russell the bondholders were given to understand that Her Majesty's Government would insist on the repayment of funds seized by the Mexican government and on the fulfilment of the agreements with the British bondholders, with Captain Dunlop, and with Captain Aldham. Lord Russell also promised to take into consideration the question of the appointment of special agents at the ports. With reference to the other requests of the bondholders he observed that Her Majesty's Government could not espouse all the claims which the bondholders might consider themselves justified in making.[16]

The Wyke-Aldham Plan of Action

The passage of the act of May 29 was one of the incidents which led the British Minister to state in a report to his government on June 25, 1861, that no further reliance could be placed on the promises or even on the formal engagements of the Mexican government. The situation would be even worse if the old Church party succeeded in driving the ultra-liberal administration from power. Under such circumstances it appeared to him that only two courses were open to Great Britain; namely, either to withdraw the diplomatic mission altogether from a country where its dignity was compromised and where consequently it had become useless, or else to support its influence by such means as would compel obedience to its just demands and obtain for the wrongs and grievances of British subjects that redress which they were lawfully entitled to claim. The only way of obtaining such redress was by the employment of Her Majesty's naval

[15] Report of the Committee of the Mexican Bondholders (London, 1862), App., pp. 172–173.

[16] *Ibid.*, p. 68.

forces simultaneously at the ports of both coasts of the Republic. The moral effect thus produced " would equal the material pressure " and would assure prompt compliance with any conditions which Great Britain might choose to impose.[17]

Captain Aldham, who during the last three years had gained a very clear insight into the Mexican situation, was reported by Sir Charles Wyke to be of the opinion that the time for leniency was past, and that if Great Britain meant to protect the lives and properties of her subjects coercive measures must be employed. A blockade was considered by the Captain to be inadvisable on account of the large forces that would be required for that purpose on so extensive a line of coast, to say nothing of the commercial difficulties to which it would give rise and of the fact that by establishing a blockade the British would actually be robbing themselves of their percentage of the duties levied at Veracruz and Tampico. The next best thing to be done was, in the Captain's opinion, to take possession of the customs-houses at Veracruz, Tampico, and Matamoros on the Atlantic and at Acapulco, Mazatlán, or San Blás on the Pacific; to lower the duties on all goods landed at those places; and to deduct the percentage to which the British were entitled, but which they never obtained, " owing to the rascality of the Mexican authorities," who either suspended payment altogether or delivered only one-fifth of what was due. Reducing the tariff would largely increase the importations and thus make possible the rapid payment of long arrears.

Against Captain Aldham's plan it might be urged that the Mexican government would place a line of interior customs-houses for levying other duties and thus partly defeat the object in view. Such an objection was easily set aside by anyone who really knew the country. The " badly paid and venal officers " serving on this second line would not be able to resist the temptations which the importers who had paid only a low entrance duty at the ports would " know how to throw in their way." The Mexican traders themselves would not allow such an impost to be levied and would for their own interests force the goods into the interior, where by their sale they would realize large profits.

17 *B. and F. State Papers,* Vol. 52, pp. 269–271.

Should Her Majesty's Government adopt the course recommended, the Minister said in conclusion, the sooner measures were taken for carrying the plan into execution the better.[18]

Corwin's Plan

A different course from that proposed by Sir Charles Wyke and Captain Aldham was suggested by the American Minister. Mexico, said Corwin, in a despatch to Secretary of State Seward on June 29, 1861, was exhausted by forty years of almost uninterrupted civil war. She was looking, and had for some time been looking in vain, for help from other nations. England pressed her and claimed from her the scanty resources at her command, for payment of interest on a debt of about 62,000,000 pesos due to British subjects. France was urging with equal persistence the claims of French subjects into whose hands had fallen bonds to the amount of 50,000,000 pesos issued by the Zuloaga and Miramón governments during the struggle which had terminated in the victory of Juárez. These bonds, which had been sold to French subjects at prices varying between one-half of one per cent and five per cent of their face value, were now claimed as a debt of the republic to be paid in full. Meantime there was not one peso from day to day in the treasury, and a heavy forced loan had been levied in order to raise money for the payment of troops.[19]

These facts Corwin stated in the hope of being authorized to negotiate a treaty which " for ample equivalents " might stipulate for the payment to Mexico by the United States of a sum varying from five to ten million dollars in cash or United States bonds. Such a sum, delivered in instalments, might perhaps enable the government to keep on foot a sufficient force to save it from ultimate subjugation to one of three European monarchies, or from a partition of its territory amongst the three.

The sale of territory, Corwin continued, was the last expedient to which the government would resort. A course perhaps more likely to be favored by both the Mexican and the American

[18] *Ibid.*

[19] Corwin's No. 21, June 29, 1861, MS. Desp. Mex., Vol. 28.

governments was a fifty per cent reduction of duties on American products, in return for an advance of money to Mexico.

It had been supposed, said the Minister, that the Church property which had been secularized and made available to the government would furnish an ample fund to enable the government to preserve itself and to pay the interest and principal of the debt. This fund, had, however, been almost entirely exhausted during the struggle of the last three years, and it was no longer a resource to be calculated upon.

England desired to possess (as, owing to the American neglect in this quarter, she very nearly did possess) the commerce of the Gulf states as well as that of the Western coast. Spain, in her rising fortune, could not but desire to repossess herself of her lost American colonies. The towering ambition of Napoleon, when it should have been gratified in Europe, would seek to dazzle the world by impressing upon the American continent the idea of French glory and French supremacy. Indeed, it had been rumored that France and England were already considering the project of intervention in Mexican affairs. How, asked Corwin, would any or all of these ideas, if realized, affect the great idea of free government on this continent? Surely American statesmen should be awake to even a suspicion that such portentous events were possible.

The Act of July 17

The act of May 29 proving an inadequate measure for the relief of the financial situation, the Congress of Mexico, on July 17, 1861, passed an act suspending for two years payments on all Mexican obligations, including the diplomatic convention debts.[20] The British and French Ministers immediately protested against this act and severed official relations with the Mexican government. Similar action was impossible on the part of Spain for, as already observed,[21] the relations with that country had been broken in the preceding January.

In the course of an informal correspondence with the British

[20] *Legislación Mexicana*, Vol. 9, pp. 243–245.
[21] *Supra*, p. 127.

Minister in regard to the act of July 17, the Minister of Foreign Affairs, Manuel María Zamacona, on July 25, stated that payments on the debts had been stopped only because the government could not continue making such payments out of the funds at its disposal. The government had given its creditors a twofold guarantee — first in a plan for fiscal reorganization set forth in the act of July 17 and second in the assignment of a special fund (Church property, promissory notes, etc.) which would constitute better security than the customs assignments had been. Mexico was not haggling about money. On the contrary, she was defending principles of order and seeking to establish a system and a method which would enable her in future to avoid being accused of slovenliness and mismanagement by those who regarded as a national vice what was only an inseparable incident of a state of revolution.

Mexico recognized her engagements, and she would abide by them without taking exception to the manner in which they had been contracted. The Minister of Foreign Affairs was convinced, however, that all who were familiar with the history of the foreign debt of Mexico, all who were acquainted with the primary elements of the British convention debt and knew how the parties interested in that debt were allowed the advantages of increased interest in the midst of a ruinous civil war, would see something strange in the allusion which the Minister of Great Britain had made to the prodigal indulgence of the foreign creditors and the systematic abuse of that indulgence by Mexico. Had the demands of the creditors been somewhat fewer, the fulfilment of international engagements might perhaps have come within the range of possibility. Mexico had been like those fields in which, the harvests having been out of proportion to the fertility of the soil, the day came when the land was impoverished, yielded nothing, and was obliged to lie fallow for one or two years.[22]

The Corwin Plan Approved by Seward and Lincoln

The attitude of the Mexican government continuing to be unsatisfactory to the British and French Ministers, Corwin, on

[22] *B. and F. State Papers*, Vol. 52, pp. 285–286.

July 29, communicated to his government his apprehension that the ports of Mexico and eventually the whole country would be occupied by the military forces of Great Britain and France, with the possible coöperation of Spain. The prevention of such action, he suggested to Secretary of State Seward, was the duty as well as the interest of the United States. The amount due annually on the Mexican debt was, he said, less than 2,000,000 pesos. This sum the United States might guarantee for a period of five years, in return for a pledge of all the public lands and mineral rights in Lower California, Chihuahua, Sonora, and Sinaloa. Such a pledge would probably end in the cession of sovereignty to the United States, " the only safe guardians of the independence and true civilization of this continent." [23]

Corwin's dispatch of July 29 was followed by another on the same subject on August 28. Many plans for pecuniary relief had, he said, been suggested by friends of the Mexican government and one or two by the Mexican Ministry of Foreign Affairs. Since none of these plans had seemed practicable, he had not yet presented a proposition for a treaty providing for the payment of money to Mexico by the United States. He had no doubt that a treaty giving the Mexican government five to ten million dollars in monthly instalments of say $250,000 would enable it to crush opposition, restore security, and adjust the foreign debt.[24]

The suggestion of an official loan to Mexico was favorably received by Secretary Seward and President Lincoln. On September 2, Corwin was informed that the President had determined to authorize him to negotiate a treaty with Mexico for the assumption of the payment of interest at 3 per cent on the funded debt due to the bondholders for a term of five years, on a pledge of reimbursement, with 6 per cent interest, secured by a specific lien on all public lands and mineral rights in the states named in the Minister's dispatch. The property so pledged was to become " absolute in the United States " at the expiration of six years from the time when the treaty should go into effect, unless the reimbursement had been made before that time. The Presi-

[23] *House Executive Document, No. 100,* 37th Congr., 2d Sess., 1862, p. 15.
[24] *Ibid.*, p. 20.

dent, said Seward, would submit his action to the consideration of the Senate for the constitutional sanction.

The instructions to Corwin were, Seward declared, subject to modification as regards the amount of the loan, its terms, the security, etc. They were, moreover, conditional upon the consent of the British and French governments to forbear from resorting to action against Mexico for non-payment of interest until after the treaty was submitted to the Senate and, in case the treaty was ratified, so long thereafter as the interest should be punctually paid by the United States. The American Ministers at London and Paris were to be instructed to apply to the British and French governments for their assent. Corwin was to urge the Mexican government to support the representations of the American Ministers in London and Paris.[25]

Soundings in England, France, and Spain

A week before this indication of the President's approval of the plan for a loan to Mexico, Secretary Seward had directed Charles Francis Adams, the American Minister at London, to discuss the plan with Earl Russell and to ascertain whether the British government would forbear hostilities against Mexico upon the conditions suggested by Corwin. A few days after the instructions to Corwin the Secretary of State took occasion to discuss the plan with Lord Lyons, the Minister of Great Britain at Washington. The American interest in the financing of Mexico, Lyons reported to his government on September 10, was due to the importance which the United States attached to Mexican independence.[26]

William L. Dayton, the American Minister to France, discussing the proposed loan with the French Minister of Foreign Affairs, pursuant to his instructions, found the subject not new to the Quai d'Orsay. It had in fact been discussed already between Thouvenel and Cowley, the British Ambassador at Paris. Thouvenel had declared to Cowley that the United States could not be prevented from offering money to Mexico but that in his

[25] *Ibid.*, p. 22. [26] *Ibid.*, p. 304.

opinion France and Great Britain should not recognize the transaction. Dayton was accordingly given no reason to suppose that France would be satisfied by the payment of interest on the French convention debt out of funds advanced by the United States. The French claims against Mexico, said Thouvenel, were not primarily for interest on the funded debt, but for a capital sum of twenty-five to thirty million francs. The danger to the territorial integrity of Mexico, he added, was not so great from European countries as it was from the United States.[27]

The result of Adams' interview with Russell was somewhat similar. Adams declared that his government was considerably alarmed by the statements in newspapers with respect to an intervention which Great Britain, France, and Spain were supposed to be contemplating in Mexico with a view to organizing a new government in that country. Such an intervention, and especially the active participation of Spain in it, would excite strong feelings in the United States and would be regarded as the kind of interference in the internal affairs of America to which the government of the United States had always been opposed. There was a sort of understanding that so long as European Powers did not interfere in America the United States might abstain from European alliances. If, however, a combination of powers were to organize a government in Mexico, the United States would feel obliged to choose its allies in Europe and to take its part in the wars and treaties of Europe. Such a necessity, it was believed, would be avoided if Great Britain and France would accept the payment of interest by the United States until Mexico should be able to defray her own obligations.[28]

Russell replied by relating what had taken place in Mexico. He then referred to a proposal made by Thouvenel that the government of the United States be invited to act in Mexico in coöperation with France, England, and Spain. To this proposal the British government had replied that it had in view only the security of British persons and property and the fulfilment

[27] *House Executive Document, No. 100,* 37th Congr., 2d Sess., 1862, pp. 211, 307.

[28] *Ibid.,* p. 308; *B. and F. State Papers,* Vol. 52, pp. 329–331.

of all the obligations of Mexico to Great Britain. Adams, he continued, would see that these obligations could hardly be transferred to the United States without raising an infinite number of questions of detail, upon which Great Britain and Mexico would have to appeal to the equity of the United States. He considered it desirable that Great Britain and the United States have as few entangling questions and clashing interests as possible. He would be afraid that the friendly relations of the two countries might be endangered with the increase of the number of points upon which they might come into collision. The American proposition he believed to be open to very grave objections.

Russell had a counter proposition, which he thought deserved the serious consideration of the American government. He was no less apprehensive than Adams was of an attempt to build upon the foundation of debts and injuries a claim to organize a new government in Mexico. He was convinced that of all countries Mexico was the one in which intervention would bring the most severe disappointment to its authors. The factions in that country were too hostile to each other and too sanguinary in their tempers to be reconciled by a small force of Europeans in the name of order and moderation. But might not the evils feared by both the United States and Great Britain be guarded against by defining terms of coöperation with Spain which would exclude interference in the internal affairs of Mexico? Would not this be a better course than leaving Spain to seek her own vindication and afterwards opposing the results of her operations?

The appropriateness of seeking the Spanish approval of the plan for rehabilitating the Mexican finances was apparently not fully realized by Secretary Seward until October 14, when he informed Carl Schurz, the American Minister at Madrid, of the plan and of the indispensability of the assent of Spain. When Schurz conferred with the Spanish Minister of Foreign Affairs on November 3, he was informed that so far as the financial question was concerned the Corwin plan could not be considered by the Spanish government in view of the agreement which Spain had signed with Great Britain and France on October 31 for a joint intervention in Mexico. The plan would, in any case, have left untouched the more serious and delicate questions growing out of the dismissal of the Spanish Ambassador in January, 1861, and the absence of guarantees of the rights and security of Spanish subjects.[29]

The Pact of Intervention

The agreement of October 31 referred to by the Spanish Minister of Foreign Affairs had been signed after several weeks of discussion between the signatory powers. In this discussion the British government indicated that it was in principle opposed to forcible interference in the internal affairs of an independent nation. Mexico, it was acknowledged, might form an exception to the rule. Few cases of internal anarchy, bloodshed, and murder could exceed the atrocities perpetrated in that country. On the other hand, there was no case in which a remedy by foreign interference appeared so hopeless. The contending factions were spread over a vast extent of territory. Spanish troops would be peculiarly obnoxious to the liberal party and British troops would be equally odious to the Church party. There would, moreover, be universal alarm both in the United States and in the Confederate States of America at the contemplation of European interference in the domestic quarrels of an American republic. "Without at all yielding to the extravagant pretensions implied by what is called the Monroe Doctrine," Russell thought that as a matter of expediency it would be unwise to provoke the ill feeling of North America unless some paramount object were in prospect and tolerably sure of attainment.[30]

The French government in this discussion took the position that the employment of force for the legitimate purposes in view would be very likely to encourage the well-disposed part of the Mexican people, who might feel the gall of the yoke to which they were subjected, to profit by the moment to throw it off and to substitute something better in its place. Should such turn out to be the case, the French government did not see why a movement of that kind, if it proved to be decidedly popular, should not re-

[29] *House Exec. Doc. No. 100, sup. cit.*, p. 225.
[30] *B. and F. State Papers,* Vol. 52, p. 367.

ceive the support of the powers who had come to Mexico to seek from an acknowledged bad government redress for injuries done to their subjects and for the violation of engagements toward themselves. While admitting the inexpediency of forcible interference in the internal affairs of an independent nation, France drew a distinction between forcible interference and the indirect encouragement which the presence of foreign forces might give the Mexican people to emerge from an odious tyranny.[31]

The Spanish government took substantially the same position as the French.[32]

The convention which was signed on October 31 recited that in consequence of the arbitrary and vexatious conduct of the authorities of the Mexican republic, the sovereigns of the signatory states found it necessary to require of those authorities a more efficacious protection for the persons and property of their subjects, as well as the execution of obligations contracted towards those sovereigns by the republic. The high contracting parties accordingly agreed to send to Mexico land and sea forces sufficient to seize and occupy the fortresses and military positions on the coast. Each of them undertook, in the use of coercive measures under the convention, to seek no acquisition of territory and no special advantage for itself and to exercise in the internal affairs of Mexico no influence of such a nature as to prejudice the right of the Mexican nation to choose and to establish freely the form of its government. Desiring, moreover, that the measures which they intended to adopt should not have an exclusive character, they agreed to invite the government of the United States to accede to the convention.[33]

The invitation to accede to the convention of October 31 was duly presented to Secretary of State Seward by the Ministers of the signatory powers at Washington. It was declined on December 4 in a communication in which Seward declared that the United States was not disposed to resort to forcible remedies while Mexico was disturbed by factions within her borders and

[31] *Ibid.*, p. 368.

[32] *Ibid.*, p. 367.

[33] *House Exec. Doc. 100, sup. cit.*, pp. 134–137.

by the prospect of war with foreign nations. The Minister of the United States at Mexico City, he pointed out, had been empowered to conclude a treaty which might enable Mexico to satisfy the just claims of Spain, France, and Great Britain and to avert the impending war. The proposal of a loan had been made not in hostility to the three powers, but in the hope of being able, with the approval of the President and the Senate, to submit a satisfactory proposition to those powers in behalf of Mexico.[34]

Progress of the Corwin Plan

The negotiations alluded to by Seward in his note of December 4 had been steadily prosecuted throughout the autumn. On September 7, before the receipt of the presidential authorization, Corwin wrote the Secretary of State that as a consideration for the desired advance of money Mexico would gladly reduce the tariff on American goods by fifty per cent for a period of five or ten years. Such an arrangement would, however, thought Corwin, be likely to be rejected on the same grounds as the McLane Treaty of 1859.[35] It might also meet serious foreign opposition. He requested instructions as to whether the United States would agree to pay in money immediately from five to ten million dollars, upon the receipt of stipulations of any kind from Mexico. He apprehended an attack upon Mexico by Confederate forces in case a foreign intervention occurred.[36]

Replying to this despatch on October 2, Seward advised Corwin that it would be impracticable as well as likely to encounter popular and senatorial opposition for the United States to advance in one sum so much money as suggested by the Minister. He doubted the wisdom of negotiating for a reduction of the tariff, which would require senatorial advice before the commencement of negotiations. He preferred a pledge of lands and mineral rights.[37]

[34] *House Exec. Doc. 100, sup. cit.*, p. 189.

[35] He probably meant the Forsyth treaty of loan and anticipation of duties. *Cf.* pp. 104–112, *supra*.

[36] *House Exec. Doc. 100, sup. cit.*, p. 23.

[37] *Ibid.*, p. 30.

On October twenty-first Corwin reported that he had proposed and Mexico had assented to two loans: one of $5,000,000 for five years at six per cent in monthly payments of $500,000; the other of $6,000,000 at the same rate of interest, to be made available over a period of three years. Mexico was to file bonds before the receipt of the money. The loans were to be secured by the pledge of the public faith, by all the public lands of the republic, and by the undisposed-of national property formerly belonging to the Church. Corwin had no doubt that interest would be punctually paid and that the principal would be returned within five years. If Mexican lands were mortgaged to the United States, he pointed out, the troops of both the United States and Mexico could oppose the Confederate forces on these lands.

On the assumption that the contemplated loans would be granted, the British Minister at Mexico City, said Corwin, had concluded an arrangement with the Mexican government which that Minister believed would be entirely satisfactory from the point of view of British interests. The French government would also be satisfied. The amount proposed in the draft treaty was, in Corwin's opinion, absolutely necessary to keep the Mexican government on its feet for the next three years.[38]

The Wyke-Zamacona Convention

The arrangement concluded between the Mexican government and the British Minister on the assumption of the realization of the loans proposed by Corwin was the subject of a report by Sir Charles Wyke to Earl Russell on the twenty-eighth of October. According to this report, Zamacona, the Mexican Minister of Foreign Affairs, on learning that Corwin was authorized to sign a treaty providing for a loan to Mexico, had felt sure that Corwin would guarantee the payment of the interest on the English debt and thereby settle at once the disagreeable questions existing between Great Britain and Mexico. Zamacona had seemed so pleased with this new solution of his difficulties that Wyke had found it quite painful to wake him out of his happy daydream by the declaration that such a "combination" could not be enter-

[38] *Ibid.*, p. 33.

tained and that his government alone must be held responsible for what it owed to British subjects. After he had recovered from the perception of this unpleasant truth, the Minister of Foreign Affairs had reflected that the money would still be forthcoming and that he had only first of all to receive it from the United States in order to pay it to Great Britain.

In long interviews Wyke had day by day gained ground, until at length he believed he had carried his point and brought the Mexican Minister of Foreign Affairs to agree to a settlement of the difficulty on terms which would prove satisfactory to Her Majesty's Government. As it would have been impossible for the Mexican government to fulfil such engagements without the pecuniary aid to be received from the American government, and as that aid would not be forthcoming until January, 1862, the stipulations of the convention, which he hoped to sign within a fortnight, would not come into force until the first day of the month indicated.

Since it was under the pressure of fear that the Mexican government had yielded, it was absolutely necessary, the British Minister believed, that a respectable naval force should soon make its appearance in the waters of Veracruz. He should, moreover, be authorized, in case the Mexican government at any time failed to comply with its engagements, to employ such naval forces as he could procure from Jamaica or elsewhere, without awaiting instructions from home to that effect.

Wyke could not speak in terms of sufficient praise of his American colleague, who had refused to negotiate his own convention with the Mexican government until he learned that Wyke had settled all pending difficulties with that government. Corwin had been determined that the money to be advanced by the United States should be applied for the purpose for which it was intended, and not uselessly squandered.

Inasmuch as the interest due on the French convention was a mere trifle in comparison with the interest due to British creditors, Wyke had strongly urged the Mexican government to satisfy the full claims of the French legation growing out of the suspension of payment. He had been assured that the Mexican government would use its best efforts to come to a satisfactory arrangement with de Saligny.[39]

The negotiations recounted in the British Minister's dispatch of October 28 continued until November 21, when a convention was signed. Meanwhile, through arguments presented both to the Minister of Foreign Affairs and to the newly appointed Minister of Finance, who accepted the office only after long urging by the British Minister, the government was induced to submit to the Congress a bill for a reduction of 50 per cent in the import duties and a smaller reduction in the additional or extra duties. The British merchants at Mexico City, summoned by Wyke to a conference, were unanimous in the opinion that the reduction was very much in favor of trade generally, but the agent of the London bondholders considered that his principals would be the losers by the reduction. Wyke explained to the agent that so long as Mexico really benefited trade by reducing her tariff, the bondholders had no right to insist upon her effectually crippling herself for the sake of being able to square the balance sheet of the London debt. They had no right, either, to fix the exact ticket to be placed on each separate piece of shirting that came into the country.

The government's proposals with respect to tariff reductions were rejected by the Congress. The government was, however, authorized to reform the tariff upon the basis of a 40 per cent reduction on the import duties and about 42 per cent on additional duties. This plan, said Wyke, was not quite so beneficial for trade generally as that proposed by the executive, but it affected pretty equally both the bondholder and the merchant and had the immense advantage of taking the tariff reform out of the hands of the Congress and placing it under the exclusive control of the executive.

The convention signed by Wyke and Zamacona on November 21 provided that the 660,000 pesos forcibly taken from the British legation and the sum due to British subjects out of the moneys seized at Laguna Seca should be repaid to the lawful owners by an assignment of 10 per cent of certain additional

[39] *B. and F. State Papers*, Vol. 52, pp. 382–389.

duties known as *mejoras materiales*.[40] All treaties, conventions, and arrangements previously concluded between Great Britain and Mexico were to remain binding on both parties. The supreme decrees of October 14, 1850, and January 23, 1857,[41] were likewise to remain in full force so far as they concerned the London bondholders. The British consular agents and the agents of the bondholders at the different ports of the republic were to be entitled to require the production of all customs-house books and papers having reference to their nations' or clients' interests and to call for ships' manifests, bills of lading, and all other documents which they might consider it necessary to examine.

Accompanying the convention on its submission to the Congress was an exchange of notes between Wyke and Zamacona which were intended to make it appear to the Congress that the government had been acting from a spirit of justice, instead of under pressure of menaces from the legation. The convention was nevertheless rejected by a large majority, on the ground that it was humiliating to the nation and constituted an almost complete surrender of the customs administration to the English agents. Wyke thereupon presented to the Mexican government an ultimatum demanding the repeal of the act of July 17 and the establishment of British commissioners at the Mexican ports with power to collect the assignments of revenue due under previous agreements and with discretion to reduce the existing tariff by one-half or more.[42] The act of July 17 was repealed on November 23, but the consent of the Mexican government to the establishment of British commissioners at the ports, with the power and discretion desired, was not immediately granted. Wyke therefore, on November 25, informed his government that the

[40] Imposed in order to raise revenue for public works.

[41] Under the first of these decrees, 25 per cent of all the import duties, 75 per cent of the export duties at Pacific ports, and 5 per cent of the export duties at Gulf ports were assigned for payment of interest on the London debts. Under the second decree, bills of exchange, representing customs duties payable, were to be delivered by the customs administrators to the local agents of the London bondholders. Romero, *Memoria, sup. cit.*, pp. 339, 463.

[42] *Report of the Committee of Mexican Bondholders* (London, 1862), App., pp. 111–112.

settlement of British claims would depend upon the employment of brute force.[43]

A conclusion substantially the same as that announced by Wyke in his despatch of November 25 was communicated by Russell a few days later to the British representatives at the French and Spanish Courts. The latest advice which the Foreign Office had received from Mexico at that time was to the effect that the arrangement actually signed on November 21 was approaching completion. The terms obtained by Wyke, said Russell, fulfiled, generally speaking, the separate requirements of Great Britain, but there was no security that these terms would be observed any better than former stipulations and engagements. Such security, if to be found at all, was to be found in the convention of October 31.[44]

The Beginning of the Intervention

The first move taken in pursuance of the convention of October 31 was the seizure of Veracruz by Spanish naval forces just at the end of the year 1861. British and French troops were landed at the same port on January 7, 1862. Three days later Commissioners of the intervening powers proclaimed to the Mexican people that the three powers, whose primary interest might seem to be "satisfaction for the outrages inflicted upon them," had "a higher interest and one that has more general and beneficent consequences." The proclamation was promptly disavowed by the British government, which declared that its object was "limited to the protection of British persons and British property." Such protection, with satisfaction for past injuries, was in fact all that was demanded in the name of Great Britain in the ultimatum presented to the Mexican government on January 14 by General Prim, the Spanish Commissioner, acting for himself and his colleagues. Prim and the British Commissioner, Wyke, refused to support the demand of de Saligny,

[43] *B. and F. State Papers,* Vol. 52, pp. 398–403.

[44] *Ibid.,* pp. 389–391; *supra,* p. 140. See also, on the general subject of the intervention, Chapter V in John H. Latané, *The United States and Latin America* (New York, 1920).

the Commissioner of France, for the recognition of the Jecker contract of October, 1859, and the payment of claims loosely estimated at 12,000,000 pesos.[45]

The government of Napoleon III, it soon became apparent, was convinced that the government of Juárez was an "oppressive and violent minority" and that the name of the Archduke Maximilian of Austria, put forward by General Almonte of the Mexican Church party, would elicit a general burst of enthusiasm and form an immediate basis for the establishment of a new government of a monarchical type in Mexico. The British and Spanish governments were less sanguine as to the effect of a move toward the constitution of a new government under foreign auspices. Wyke, indeed, at the end of January, 1862, was of the opinion that General Doblado, the Mexican Minister of Foreign Affairs, who had been invested with large powers by Juárez, was

> using those powers in a manner calculated to centralize the forces of the government, and to give a death blow to that federal system [which had been] the bane of the country, and prevented the establishment of a strong and respectable government.[46]

In response to the ultimatum of the Commissioners, General Doblado stated, on January 23, that his government was disposed to acknowledge all just claims against it. The way was thus opened for negotiations. Pending the outcome of these negotiations, a convention was signed at La Soledad, on February 19, providing for the removal of the foreign troops from the fever-ridden swamps of Veracruz to the higher and more healthful region of Orizaba. In this convention the Commissioners declared that the intervening powers had no designs against the independence, sovereignty, and integrity of the republic.[47]

In March additional troops arrived from France. At the beginning of April the French Commissioner, in a conference with his colleagues at Orizaba, insisted on an immediate march to Mexico City. The Commissioners of Spain and Great Britain were uncompromising in their opposition to the proposal. It was

[45] Lefêvre, *op. cit.*, Vol. I., pp. 119–120, 155–160; *B. and F. State Papers*, Vol. 53, pp. 393–437.

[46] *B. and F. State Papers*, Vol. 53, pp. 418, 518–520.

[47] Lefêvre, *op. cit.*, Vol. I, p. 188.

therefore without the concurrence of his colleagues that de Saligny two weeks later, on April 16, formally declared that a state of war existed between France and the government of Juárez.[48]

The Corwin Treaty

While the conferences and negotiations which preceded the French declaration of war were in progress, the American Minister continued his efforts to assist Mexico by means of a loan from the United States. The proposal for such a loan had been withdrawn immediately after the action of the Mexican Congress, which Corwin regarded as "foolish in the extreme," in rejecting the Wyke-Zamacona convention of November 21, 1861. The landing of the British, French, and Spanish troops produced such a change in Mexican sentiment that by January 26, 1862, Corwin was able to express to Secretary Seward the opinion that treaties would be made with the intervening powers on the basis of the convention previously rejected. The Mexican Cabinet was content with his draft of a treaty for the loan of an amount equivalent to that to be paid to European claimants, but he had not deemed it proper to make the treaty in the absence of assurances that Great Britain and France would be satisfied.[49]

On February 18, 1862, Corwin reported that the only security acceptable to any of the intervening powers was a mortgage on the revenues arising from imposts. To make this security such as would no doubt be insisted upon, Mexico would be required to surrender, for a limited period, a very large proportion of these revenues. This she could not do without imminent danger to her internal peace, unless the United States would step in and make her the loan proposed in the draft treaty. If the intervening powers did not agree as to the securities to be received by each of them and if Mexico for want of the proposed loan were unable to give what was demanded of her, then war might ensue and the subjugation of the country to European domination would probably be the result. Corwin was sure that the time was approaching when the United States would be obliged either to pay

[48] *B. and F. State Papers,* Vol. 53, pp. 558–559.

[49] Corwin's No. 14, *House Exec. Doc. No. 100,* 37th Cong., 2d Sess., 1862, p. 48.

the interest on the Mexican debt or to abandon Mexico to such fate as the intervening powers might choose to award her.[50]

The solicitude of the American Minister with reference to the effect of the financial embarrassments of Mexico upon her political independence was shared by Secretary Seward and President Lincoln. The proposed treaty for a loan to Mexico was considered by the President to be of such importance that the draft prepared by Corwin and discussed with the Mexican authorities had been submitted to the United States Senate for its advice at the beginning of the session in December, 1861. It was understood that the project was favored by the members of the Committee on Foreign Relations, but no authoritative information regarding the attitude of the Senate reached the Department of State until the end of February, 1862. This information was in the form of a resolution to the effect that it was not advisable to negotiate a treaty which would require the United States to assume any portion of the principal or interest of the debt of Mexico or which would require the concurrence of European powers. It was later learned that the Senators who opposed the loan belonged to three groups: first, those who apprehended that it would lead to annexation of Mexican territory; second, those who considered it derogatory to the honor of the United States to discuss Mexico with foreign nations; and third, those who feared that the grant of a " subsidy " to Mexico might prejudice the credit of the United States.[51]

Whatever the cause of the senatorial disapproval of the project, its immediate effect was to modify in essential particulars the instructions under which the American Minister was negotiating with the Mexican government. After thinking the matter over for a month, the Secretary of State informed the Minister, on April 3, that in view of the adverse advice of the Senate, the President was unable to suggest any mode of relief for Mexico. Since, however, the House of Representatives had called for the papers regarding the Mexican situation, it was possible that some

[50] Corwin's No. 16, *House Exec. Doc. No. 100, sup. cit.*, p. 50.

[51] Seward's Nos. 36 and 40, Jan. 24 and Feb. 28, 1862, *House Exec. Doc. No. 100, sup. cit.*, pp. 46 and 49; Seward's instruction of June 24, 1862, *Dip. Cor. U. S.*, 1862, pp. 748–749.

plan might be found.[52] Before this instruction reached Mexico City, Corwin had signed with the Mexican Minister of Foreign Affairs a treaty providing for a loan of $9,000,000. This treaty was approved by President Juárez on April 6, 1862.[53]

The declaration of war between Mexico and France made it improper for the United States, as a neutral, to advance money to Mexico. On May 28, accordingly, Secretary Seward informed Corwin that the treaty negotiated by the latter would be held up. Ten days later, however, Corwin was advised that the President had deemed it his duty to refer the treaty to the Senate in a confidential manner for the uninfluenced consideration of that body. The President had not considered it inconsistent with the purpose of the reference to declare his own sincere convictions as to the importance of the matter and his sympathies with the people of Mexico.[54]

On July 14 Corwin was informed that his treaty had been laid upon the table in the Senate.[55] It appeared later that the Juárez government had considered the treaty so far effective as to make it the basis for negotiating drafts on the United States. These drafts were of course protested when they reached the Department of State.[56]

The Wyke-Doblado Agreements

The French declaration of war, on the sixteenth of April, was apparently not regarded in Mexico as an insuperable obstacle to the ratification of the Corwin treaty and the grant of the proposed loan by the United States. The Corwin loan was, in fact, under a convention signed by Sir Charles Wyke and General Doblado on April 28, to be used in part for the payment of British pecuniary claims for damages amounting to some 2,000,000 pesos. It was provided in this convention, however, that in case the loan from the United States were not realized the payment of the

[52] Seward's No. 43, *House Exec. Doc. No. 100, sup. cit.*, p. 51.

[53] Corwin's dispatch of April 28, *Dip. Cor. U. S.*, 1862, p. 739.

[54] *Dip. Cor. U. S.*, 1862, pp. 747–748.

[55] *Ibid.*, p. 753.

[56] Seward's No. 201, August 23, 1862, to Dayton (*House Exec. Doc. No. 54*, 37th Cong., 3d Sess., 1863, p. 546).

British claims should be made out of the property that was to have formed the security for the Corwin loan.[57]

The convention of April 28 was supplemented on May 12 by an agreement that, during the continuance of the existing civil war and disturbances in Mexico, British naval forces should have the right to occupy Mexican ports whenever the percentage of duties assigned to British subjects under various conventions and decrees was not paid in due course.[58]

The convention and the supplementary agreement, having been approved by President Juárez, were forwarded to the British Foreign Office for further action. There they encountered the disapproval of Earl Russell, who regarded them as recognizing the Corwin treaty " in a most inconvenient manner." Her Majesty's Government, said Russell, was not fully informed of all the articles of the Corwin treaty. That treaty might contain provisions injurious to the independence of Mexico. Previous recognition of it might, moreover, be held to bar objections which Her Majesty's Government would later feel bound to make. The title to the waste lands which were to be granted to Great Britain under the convention of April 28, in case the treaty with the United States was not ratified, might be disputed; and while the assertion of such a title might involve Great Britain in a conflict with other powers and with Mexico herself, the abandonment of the title might render the British government liable in an inconvenient degree to the claims of British bondholders. The supplementary article was, in Russell's opinion, open in a much greater degree to objections of the same nature.[59]

Progress of the Intervention

Although the French troops had the support of General Almonte and of a considerable faction which proclaimed him chief of the nation on April 19, 1862, it was more than a year before they were able to reach the capital. At the end of May, 1863, Juárez and his government removed from Mexico City to San Luis Potosí. During the next month General Forey, the French commander-in-chief, occupied Mexico City and ordered the for-

[57] *B. and F. State Papers,* Vol. 53, pp. 573–578.
[58] *Ibid.,* pp. 588–590.
[59] *Ibid.,* pp. 593–602.

mation of a "Superior Council of Government" composed of thirty-five persons named by the French Minister. The Council appointed an executive, consisting of General Almonte and two other Mexicans, Archbishop Labastida and General Salas. On July 10, 1863, an assembly of 215 "notables," convoked by the Council, declared unanimously in favor of a hereditary empire under Maximilian, Archduke of Austria. Formal overtures were immediately made to Maximilian.[60]

In March, 1864, the Archduke was in London, with his father-in-law, King Leopold of Belgium, endeavoring to obtain the British recognition of his new position. The British government, reported the American Minister, Charles Francis Adams, on March 24, had declined to act immediately on the subject, but had given hope that it would recognize Maximilian as soon as the situation in Mexico appeared to justify such action. It was understood that Spain and Belgium would accede more readily to the French program.[61]

The Bond Issues of 1864

In his communication of March 24, Adams stated further that a loan to Maximilian had been negotiated in London for £8,000,000. The holders of the bonds issued in 1851 in exchange for earlier bonds of the London debt had been the principal supporters of the plan for the new loan, and they were greatly distressed to find that no provision had yet been made for the payment of arrears of interest due to them.[62]

The contract for the new loan was signed on March 20, 1864, by Count Zichy, acting for Maximilian, and by a representative of the house of Glyn, Mills and Company of London. On the tenth of April, the day of his formal acceptance of the throne of Mexico, Maximilian established a Mexican Finance Committee, to consist of one representative of Mexico, one representative of the French bondholders, and one representative of the English bondholders. The French representative, Count de Germiny, Senator and former Minister of Finance, was appointed Chairman of the Committee. On the following day the new Emperor

60 Lefêvre, *op. cit.*, Vol. I, pp. 293–296.

61 *Dip. Cor. U. S.*, 1864, Vol. 3, p. 740.

62 *Ibid.*

approved the contract with Glyn, Mills and Company. His decree provided that the rate of interest should be 6 per cent and that the issue price should be 63. Two years' interest was to be reserved out of the proceeds of the loan.[63]

A separate decree of the same date provided for the conversion of the twenty unpaid coupons of interest from January 1, 1854, to July 1, 1863, inclusive, on the old bonds of the London debt, into new 3 per cent bonds, at the rate of £60 in coupons for £100 in bonds. As the unpaid interest amounted to £3,072,495, the holders of the coupons were entitled to £5,120,817 of the new bonds.[64] Only nineteen of the coupons were actually converted. The new bonds issued for the conversion totaled £4,864,800.[65]

The £8,000,000 loan was immediately offered for sale in London and Paris. The sales in London were much below expectations. In Paris, however, the bonds were eagerly bought from the Crédit Mobilier, which had been induced by the French Minister of Finance to associate itself with the English bankers; and in the French provinces there were many subscribers, partly because the receivers-general of taxes, by direction of the French government, gave every possible assistance to the operation. More than £1,000,000 of the bonds offered for sale remained undisposed of. These were delivered to the Mexican Finance Committee at Paris. The cash proceeds of the loan, after deduction of commissions, were £3,719,290. From this amount £615,000 was deducted for interest on the old London debt for the two years beginning January 1, 1864.[66] An additional sum of £1,260,000 was deducted as interest in advance for two years on the new 6 per cent loan and on the 3 per cent bonds issued for conversion of arrears of interest; £300,000 was applied to the payment of interest on the additional issue of bonds referred to in the next paragraph; £317,462 was delivered to Maximilian for the

[63] Mexico, *Diario Oficial,* May 4, 1868; Kératry, *op. cit.,* pp. 85–87.

[64] *Ibid.*

[65] *Memoria de Hacienda,* 1888–1889, p. XXXV; Manuel Payno y Flores, *Cuentas, Gastos, Acreedores y Otros Asuntos del Tiempo de la Intervención Francesa y del Imperio* (Mexico, 1868), pp. 767, 785.

[66] The interest for the last six months of 1863 was to be paid out of the assigned customs duties.

settlement of his personal obligations before his departure from Miramar. The sum actually received from the loan by the government in Mexico, in return for the assumption of an obligation of £8,000,000, was only £1,217,532.[67] It is not surprising that this sum was stated by a contemporary writer in a Mexican periodical to be but "a pie in the dog's mouth."[68]

In addition to the 6 per cent bonds for £8,000,000 offered for sale in London and Paris and the 3 per cent bonds for approximately £5,000,000 made available for the conversion of arrears of interest on the bonds of the old London debt, bonds to the amount of 110,000,000 francs, bearing 6 per cent interest, were delivered to the French government in accordance with the terms of a convention concluded between that government and Maximilian on April 10, 1864. Bonds of this issue to the amount of 20,000,000 francs, accepted as the equivalent of 12,000,000 francs in cash, were to be used for the payment of claims of individual French subjects. The remaining 90,000,000 francs of the issue were to be applied at a valuation of 54,000,000 francs, toward the payment of the sum of 270,000,000 francs which Maximilian acknowledged to be due to France for the expenses of the French expedition up to July 1, 1864.[69] All the bonds of the issue of 110,000,000 francs were deposited in the French treasury, where they remained until they were exchanged for bonds of another issue a year later.[70]

The three issues of bonds made at this time by Maximilian were the occasion for a protest made on June 10, 1864, by Jesús Escobar y Armendáriz, agent of the Juárez government in

[67] Romero, *Memoria, sup. cit.*, pp. 602–608; Payno, *Cuentas, Gastos*, etc., *sup. cit.*, p. 767.

[68] *La Acción*, Saltillo, June 18, 1864, quoted in *Dip. Cor. U. S.*, 1865, Vol. 3, p. 580.

[69] Romero, *Memoria, sup. cit.*, p. 599. The balance of 216,000,000 francs acknowledged to be due up to July 1, 1864, was to be reduced gradually by payments out of the 25,000,000 francs which Maximilian agreed to remit annually to France. The annual remittance of 25,000,000 francs was, however, to be used in part also for the maintenance of a steamship service between France and Mexico; the payment of a French army corps of 25,000 men until such time as their presence in Mexico should no longer be required; and the further indemnification of individual French claimants against Mexico.

[70] *Infra*, p. 157.

Europe. The Mexican nation and its constitutional government, declared Escobar, would never at any time recognize or admit the obligations which might be contracted by any other functionaries than those who held their authority from the constitution — whether such obligations had the object of creating a debt to the French government, augmenting the amount of the debt already in existence, or modifying the English or any other debt legally recognized.[71]

The Maximilian Bonds of 1865

Maximilian arrived at the capital of his empire in August, 1864. He immediately perceived the poverty of his financial situation and the necessity of obtaining further assistance from abroad. Accordingly, on the twenty-sixth of November, 1864, he authorized Corta, a member of the French Parliament who had been sent to Mexico by the French government; Barron, a capitalist in Mexico; Bourdillon, a lawyer, also residing in Mexico; and de Germiny, Chairman of the Mexican Finance Committee in Paris, to contract a new loan in Europe. The bonds of this loan, in the nominal amount of 250,000,000 francs, bearing 6 per cent interest, were brought out in Paris in April, 1865, at 68 per cent of their face value. They were sold also in London, Antwerp, and Frankfort. An attractive feature of the offering was the provision for semiannual redemption bonuses amounting to 1,500,000 francs, to be awarded to the holders of numbers determined by lot. A still more attractive feature was the provision for immediately setting aside against each bond a sum which would be delivered to the holder as a premium at the end of fifty years, and which would then amount to the price paid for the bond. These features and the enthusiastic report of Mexican resources given to the French Chamber of Deputies on April 10 by Corta enabled the loan to command a ready sale. The amount realized by the Maximilian government on this issue, after deduction of commissions and interest in advance, was 96,724,768 francs.[72]

[71] *Dip. Cor. U. S.*, 1865, Vol. 3, p. 582.

[72] Kératry, *op. cit.*, pp. 91–92, 99–101; Romero, *Memoria, sup. cit.*, p. 644; *Dip. Cor. U. S.*, 1866, Vol. 3, p. 287.

The success of April, 1865, was followed in September of the same year by the conversion of the 6 per cent bonds issued in 1864. The new bonds, offered in the proportion of 80 to 100, bore the same rate of interest as those which they replaced, but they were made more attractive by the repetition of the lottery and premium features of the loan of April, 1865. Approximately two-thirds of the public holdings of the £8,000,000 issue made under the contract with Glyn, Mills and Company in 1864 were presented for conversion into the new bonds. The bonds of the issue of 110,000,000 francs deposited in the French treasury were also converted.[73]

Upon the completion of the two operations of 1865 the outstanding new bonds issued by Maximilian amounted to approximately 690,000,000 francs or 138,000,000 pesos. The increase of the bonded indebtedness of Mexico through the operations of 1864 and 1865 is indicated in the following table: [74]

The Foreign debt (exclusive of the Convention debts) on January 1, 1864		
3 per cent bonds of 1851	P51,208,250	
Arrears of interest since July 1, 1854	15,362,475	
		P66,570,725
New bonds issued in London and Paris		
6 per cent bonds of 1864 .... (remaining unconverted in 1865)	12,325,990	
3 per cent (capitalization) bonds of 1864	24,324,000	
6 per cent bonds of 1865	100,000,000	
	136,649,990	
Deduction for arrears of interest capitalized	15,362,475	
Increase of bonded debt		121,287,525
The foreign debt (exclusive of the convention debts) at the end of 1865		P187,858,250

[73] Kératry, *op. cit.*, pp. 106–112. The new bonds obtained by the French treasury, in exchange for the issue of 110,000,000 francs, were immediately sold to French bankers.

[74] Based on Kératry, *op. cit., loc. cit.*

In return for the new bonds which he issued, Maximilian received only about 25,000,000 pesos in cash. This sum was applied toward the reduction of the apparently inevitable current deficit.[75] Among the uses to which the proceeds of the loans were put, it is important to mention the payment of the sum of 2,865,000 pesos to the house of Jecker and Company on account of the bonds delivered to that house by Miramón in 1859.[76] This payment, it may be noted, was approximately twice the amount of Jecker's expenditure, plus compound interest at 6 per cent.[77]

The Juárez Loans in the United States

While through the operations above described the government of Maximilian was obtaining small amounts of money in return for the assumption of large obligations, the government of Juárez, clinging to the edge of Mexico, was endeavoring to obtain money from its neighbor of the north.

On the twelfth of November, 1864, two weeks before Maximilian authorized the loan of April, 1865, Juárez authorized General José M. Carbajal, the governor of the State of Tamaulipas, to accept the military services of one to ten thousand foreigners, to purchase a limited quantity of arms and munitions, and to contract a foreign loan sufficient to equip the foreigners enlisted. As security the governor was empowered to pledge the federal as well as the state revenues collected in Tamaulipas.

The extent to which his authorization might be employed was apparently not realized by General Carbajal immediately. It was only after he had made the acquaintance of General Lewis Wallace, of the United States Army, then on duty near the Mexican border, that he decided to attempt to enlist foreigners outside his own country and to undertake active negotiations in the United States with a view to obtaining a loan. General Wallace, according to Matías Romero, who was at this time the Minister

[75] Romero, *Memoria, sup. cit.*, pp. 684–688.

[76] This is the figure given by Kératry, *op. cit.*, pp. 59–61. Payno (*Cuentas, Gastos*, etc., *sup. cit.*, pp. 800–811) gives a different figure: 2,532,000 pesos. Jecker had been promised 2,000,000 pesos in addition to the sum which he actually received.

[77] *Cf.* pp. 116, 117, *supra*.

of the Juárez government to the United States, persuaded the Mexican General that his authorizations were " sufficient to allow him to come to the United States, raise means, arms, munitions, and everything else that he might desire." The two officers left the Rio Grande together about the end of March, 1865, and arrived in Washington a month later, just as the Civil War was closing.[78]

At Washington Carbajal learned that Romero, who had also been authorized to negotiate a loan in the United States, regarded the negotiation as an arduous undertaking, which would require mature meditation and the coöperation of American business men, as well as a concurrence of contingent circumstances of which the Minister was not altogether hopeful. The General's plans and his haste to carry them out were in open contradiction to the Minister's own views, but in order to give the General an opportunity to satisfy himself of the impracticability of these plans, the Minister consented to his going to New York and attempting to raise the funds, which he thought he could obtain merely by asking for them.[79]

On the thirteenth of July Carbajal surprised Romero by reporting that a strong company in New York had offered to lend him $2,000,000 in cash, to provide all the war material he might need, and to accord ample facilities for raising money on the largest scale.[80]

Romero immediately determined to go to New York himself in order to obtain better information concerning the nature of Carbajal's arrangements and at the same time to try to comply with his own instructions in regard to the negotiation of a loan. Accordingly, on July 23, he addressed to Secretary Seward a communication in which, after referring to the general plans of his government, he said that his immediate wishes were to negotiate a loan in the United States and to purchase arms and munitions in this country for export. It was indubitable, he declared, that the duties of neutrality did not require the United States

[78] Romero to Seward, April 20, 1867, *Dip. Cor. U. S.*, 1867, Vol. 2, p. 547.

[79] *Ibid.*

[80] *Ibid.*

to prevent the sale of Mexican bonds in this country. If the French also desired to negotiate a loan here upon the same bases as the Juárez government — "that is, as a private speculation, with which the government [of the United States] has nothing to do" — the right to do so could not be denied them.[81]

Replying to Romero's communication on August 7, Secretary Seward said that he was "not aware of any law or executive order" prohibiting "the exportation of arms, or of money, from the United States to Mexico, by either of the parties at war in that country, or by the individual citizens or subjects of the respective parties." "Any proceedings for that purpose must, however, not be connected with proceedings which tend to infringe the impartial neutrality which this government has hitherto in every instance maintained." The Secretary added:

> You are well aware that the government of the United States has official relations with the republican government in Mexico only, and heartily desires that that form of government may, by the unity, virtue, valor and perseverance of the people in Mexico, be maintained in that country, as the United States earnestly desire that, in the same manner, it may be perpetuated in every other country in the American hemisphere where it has heretofore been established.[82]

The Woodhouse Contract

Before the receipt of Seward's reply, Romero had gone to New York. There, on August 3, he learned that General Carbajal had signed a contract for a loan of $50,000,000 with Daniel Woodhouse, secretary and financial agent of the United States, European and West Virginia Land and Mining Company. The contract, though negotiated and signed in New York in July, was dated May 15 and purported to have been concluded in San Carlos in the State of Tamaulipas. The reason for this fiction was presumably a lingering doubt in the General's mind as to his authority to contract a loan outside Mexico. The mere contracting of the loan was less startling to Romero than the inclusion in the contract of "grants of railroads, etc., for which

[81] *House Exec. Doc. No. 73*, 39th Cong., 1st Sess., pp. 177–178.
[82] *Ibid.*, pp. 178–179.

he [Carbajal] had not the slightest pretext of authority." The company had issued drafts which it proposed to pay with the proceeds of the bonds, after their sale.[83]

Upon inquiring among established business men in New York, Romero ascertained that the company with which Carbajal had contracted was quite unknown; that it had apparently been formed entirely with a view to handling the proposed loan; that it had no funds, credit, or security; that Woodhouse, the principal partner, was a lawyer of the lowest class, without pecuniary responsibility; and that of the persons whose names appeared in the loan prospectus as members of the company, some were insolvent, others could not be found, and the only ones who had means and credit disclaimed all knowledge of Woodhouse or stated that he had used their names without their knowledge or consent. It was only with the greatest difficulty, however, that the Minister was able to disabuse General Carbajal of the hallucination of which he had been a victim, and to induce him to cancel the contract.[84]

On the last day of August, General Wallace, who had been Carbajal's adviser in his negotiations in New York, and had accompanied him to Washington to obtain the assurance of Secretary Seward that there was no legal obstacle to the flotation of the loan, invited Romero to attend a meeting of several highly respectable persons, including E. D. Morgan, Moses H. Grinnell, L. E. Chittenden, and Cornelius Vanderbilt, who Woodhouse said had agreed to participate in the reorganization of his company. The Minister declined to attend the meeting. So did most of the highly respectable persons whom Woodhouse had mentioned. By the seventeenth of January, 1866, Woodhouse's company had changed its name to the National American and Mexican Company. Ten days later Romero was informed that the members of the company had become disgusted with Woodhouse and had determined to reorganize under the name of the International American and Mexican Company. Both Romero and Carbajal refused to have anything further to do with Woodhouse or his associates, by whatever name they were called.[85]

[83] Romero's note of April 20, 1867, above cited. [84] *Ibid.* [85] *Ibid.*

Meanwhile, on September 15, 1865, President Juárez had declared that Carbajal had exceeded his powers in making the contract with Woodhouse and that the contract was void. Woodhouse, however, had persisted in the claim that the contract was valid, and sometime before the end of 1865 he had caused to be engraved a quantity of bonds purporting to have been issued in pursuance of the contract. The existence of these bonds was an element prejudicial to the success of the legitimate issue of Mexican bonds under the contract which Carbajal concluded with a reputable New York banking house on September 11, 1865.[86]

The Carbajal-Corlies Loan

The collapse of the hopes which had been built upon the Woodhouse contract left Carbajal in a painful situation. Upon the basis of the loan promised by Woodhouse he had contracted numerous obligations and had engaged his personal prestige as well as his financial credit by inviting a number of Mexican officers to come to New York in order to return with him to the frontier. He was accordingly eager to make another contract as soon as possible. This contract, which was signed with John W. Corlies and Company, of New York, provided for the sale of Mexican bonds of the nominal value of 30,000,000 pesos, bearing 7 per cent interest. The security for the bonds was to be three-fifths of all the state and federal revenues in the states of Tamaulipas and San Luis Potosí, besides certain "waste lands and vacant mines" in those states. The bonds were to be sold at not less than "sixty cents in lawful money of the United States for each peso." The bankers' commission was fixed at 25 per cent of the bonds sold, provided that the commission should be in any case not less than 1,000,000 pesos in bonds.[87]

The nature of the services performed by the bankers in consideration of their commission was indicated in their communication of August 25, 1865, in which they explained to General

[86] Romero's note of April 20, 1867, above cited.

[87] *Contratos hechos en los Estados Unidos por los comisionados del gobierno de México durante los años de 1865 y 1866* (Mexico, 1868), pp. 436–512.

Carbajal "the difficulties notoriously surrounding the loan in question."

Your government [said the bankers] is in a certain sense a government in disorganization. There is within its territory an empire which claims to be established in the exercise of full governing power, imposed *vi et armis* by powerful nations, maintaining diplomatic relations with many other empires and monarchies, and holding an organized court which is attended by diplomats of various nations.—It is true, as you say, that your government has been iniquitously imposed upon and that it nevertheless retains a regular organization; but it sees itself constantly attacked by the usurper and obliged to move from place to place. . . . There is, however, one circumstance favorable for the offering of the loan to the public, and that is the sympathy of our people toward you; yet when it is recalled that we have just passed through the terrible crisis of civil war and have incurred an enormous debt the greater part of which is due to our own people, it must be admitted that the difficulties are so great that they cannot be overcome without almost superhuman efforts. How can this be done?

1. A very powerful public sentiment must be created in favor of your government. For this it is necessary to procure the influence of our government and of the press; whatever interest the matter may gain in the abstract, it is well known that the most powerful stimulus will consist in private interest. To accomplish this, it will be necessary to offer and give very liberal recompense to the newspapers and even to influential persons in high circles.

2. A series of well considered articles on several points of interest will have to be written by intelligent writers, who must be compensated.

3. Advertisements must be published in great profusion and in all the popular forms—which is very costly.

4. It will be necessary to interest the principal bankers, to secure their active and energetic coöperation.—To do this as it ought to be done, it will be necessary to spend a great part of what is assigned as remuneration or commission in our contract.

5. To avoid the necessity of a detailed explanation to each of those who consider purchasing bonds, and to strengthen the confidence of those who are totally or partially convinced by such explanation, it will be quite indispensable that various of the most celebrated lawyers of the United States, after examining the matter carefully, pass on the regularity of all the proceedings relative to the issue of the bonds, the obligation of your government for the loan, and the validity of the mortgage of the properties, etc., which constitute the security for payment. . . . To obtain this opinion, after the necessary examination, will require liberal expenditures.[88]

[88] *Ibid.*, p. 87.

The "almost superhuman efforts" of the bankers had begun, and the bonds of the Carbajal-Corlies loan were about to be offered for public sale, when a further obstacle appeared in the person of General Gaspar Sánchez Ochoa. This officer, having tried in vain to sell in San Francisco an issue of 10,000,000 pesos of bonds authorized by President Juárez in December, 1864, came to New York at the end of October, 1865, hoping to sell some of his bonds there. Corlies, Carbajal, and Romero, greatly agitated, immediately set about dissuading Sánchez Ochoa from offering his bonds in New York. Sánchez Ochoa readily perceived the prejudice to Mexican credit which would be certain to follow any attempt to sell the two issues at the same time, especially in view of the fact that Carbajal's contract with Corlies contained a clause binding the Mexican government not to offer other bonds for sale until after the disposal of the Corlies issue. He agreed to withhold his bonds, which had already been printed. At the time of his visit to New York they were in the possession of a San Francisco capitalist, Samuel Brannan, who had undertaken to act as agent for the sale of the bonds and had advanced $30,000 in cash.[89]

Disposal and Utilization of the Carbajal-Corlies Loan

Of the authorized issue of 30,000,000 pesos only 2,925,450 pesos in bonds of the Carbajal-Corlies loan had been disposed of up to August 8, 1867. Nine thousand pesos in bonds were sold for cash, at sixty per cent of their face value. The bankers retained 1,000,000 pesos of the bonds for commission and expenses.[90] Twelve thousand five hundred pesos of the bonds were delivered to Dr. George M. Ramsay in payment for a torpedo boat valued at $7,500 in paper money of the United States.[91] One million,

[89] Romero's note of June 4, 1867, to Secretary Seward (*Dip. Cor. U. S.*, 1867, Vol. 2, p. 556).

[90] An agreement for final settlement between the bankers and the Mexican government was concluded at Mexico City on February 25, 1868. From the terms of this agreement, it appears that the bankers had disposed of the bonds allocated for commission and expenses; at what price is not shown. *Cf.* Romero, *Memoria, sup. cit.*, p. 751.

[91] The paper dollar of the United States at the time of the Carbajal-Corlies

nine hundred and three thousand, nine hundred and fifty pesos of the bonds were delivered to General Herman Sturm, a retired officer of the United States Army, who used them in the purchase and shipment to Mexico of war material, including twenty thousand rifles and carbines.[92]

The war material purchased by General Sturm was obtained from twenty-one different dealers, who accepted the Corlies bonds in payment at the rate of sixty dollars in American paper money for one hundred pesos in bonds. The prices paid by General Sturm were compared by him with those which the United States had paid for similar material during the Civil War and with the prices at which such material was offered for sale by the United States in July, 1867. According to the list furnished General Sturm by General Horace Porter, Chief of Arsenal, Enfield and Springfield rifles of the kind which Sturm purchased for Mexico at 16.50 pesos in bonds had been purchased by the United States during the War at $26 and were offered for sale by the United States in July, 1867, at $16.27. For carbines, which Sturm bought at the rate of 35 pesos in bonds, the United States had paid during the War $35; no carbines were for sale by the United States in 1867. For rifle cartridges, for which the United States had paid $1.50 a thousand during the War and which it was selling at $1.26 in 1867, Sturm paid private firms 1.10 pesos a thousand in bonds. "Although the arms for the government of Mexico were paid for in bonds which had no value in the market of the United States, they [the prices] were," wrote Sturm to Romero, "equitable and in some cases lower than those" paid by the United States during the War.[93]

Romero's own opinion of the transaction, in which he himself figured prominently as authorizing various advances to Sturm, was indicated in November, 1867, as follows:

Considering that all this [war material] was purchased at a time when every rifle had an inestimable price for us, and when our credit was not and

---

contract was worth 49½ cents in American gold. (Davis R. Dewey, *Financial History of the United States* [New York, 1902], p. 367.)

[92] *Contratos hechos*, etc., *sup. cit.*, pp. 486–493.

[93] *Ibid.*, pp. 494–509.

could not be very high; bearing in mind the extreme need for arms, . . . the good service that these arms gave, and the moral effect which the news of the issue of the bonds and the purchase of armament produced in the republic, discouraging our enemies — Napoleon included — and heartening our friends . . . , and recalling that the entire affair was accomplished with less than two million pesos, in bonds which at the current market quotation could be redeemed at much less [than their issue price], no one, I think, will believe that there has been wastefulness or that the republic has been unduly burdened.[94]

Efforts to Obtain Assistance from the United States Congress

On January 5, 1866, General Sturm, who had a very comprehensive contract of service with General Carbajal, was requested by the latter to proceed to Washington with a representative of Corlies and Company and to endeavor to obtain from the government of the United States either a direct loan or a guarantee of a loan of forty to fifty million dollars. He remained in Washington from January to July, 1866, in frequent conference with members of Congress.

That Sturm made some headway is evidenced by the fact that so influential a Congressman as Thaddeus Stevens proposed to the House Committee on Foreign Affairs in June, 1866, an inquiry into the propriety of lending $20,000,000, to the Mexican republic. This sum, it was thought by Stevens, would enable the republic to "prevent the overthrow of its government and the establishment of a monarchical government on the continent of North America." The French troops having been withdrawn from Mexico, in consequence of pressure from Secretary Seward and of the general political situation in Europe,[95] France could no longer be considered to be at war with Mexico. Hence the proposed loan could not constitute a breach of neutrality as between Mexico and France. The possibility that Maximilian might regard the loan as a cause of war would alarm no one. It might, indeed, have the advantage of giving the United States an

[94] *Contratos hechos*, etc., *sup. cit.*, pp. 12–13.
[95] *Infra*, p. 168.

opportunity to vindicate its honor, which had become dim under "the Micawber policy" of Secretary Seward.[96]

A factor which worked against the success of the General's efforts in Washington was the lack of confidence in the stability and reliability of the Juárez government. Besides the doubt which still existed as to the issue of the contest with Maximilian — a doubt which was fed by active agents of Maximilian opposing the desired loan — there was the recollection of the fiasco with Woodhouse, who was endeavoring to obtain Congressional support for his often amended loan project. Two projects for loans to professed liberal rivals of Juárez were, moreover, being urged in the United States at this time. One of these rivals of Juárez was General Santa Anna, who sought to float a loan of some 750,000 pesos in the United States on the security of large estates which he claimed in Veracruz, New Granada, and the Island of St. Thomas. The other rival was Jesús González Ortega, Chief Justice and Vice-President in the Juárez administration, who claimed recognition as constitutional president, in place of Juárez, and attempted to obtain a loan of 50,000,000 pesos in this country. With so many factors against it, the project for an American official loan, or guarantee of a loan, to the Juárez government proved fruitless.[97]

Collapse of the Imperial Government

The "Micawber policy" of which Representative Stevens complained had not prevented Secretary Seward, as soon as the military power of the United States was available for use outside the country, from entering into correspondence with France with a view to expediting the departure of French forces from Mexican soil. This correspondence had by February 12, 1866, reached a point at which Seward denied the right of France to intervene in Mexico for the purpose of restoring order.

The United States, said Seward, would not deny that Mexico had been for a long time the theater of faction and internal war.

[96] Callahan, *op. cit.*, p. 82.

[97] Herman Sturm, *The Republic of Mexico and Its American Creditors* (Indianapolis, 1869), p. 21; Callahan, *op. cit.*, p. 82.

From the American point of view, however, all the anarchy in Mexico of which the French complained had been necessarily and wisely endured in the attempt to lay sure foundations of broad republican liberty. The injuries and wrongs which Mexico had committed against any other state had found a severe punishment in consequences which legitimately followed their commission. Nations were not authorized to correct one another's errors except in so far as was necessary to prevent or redress injuries affecting themselves. If one state had a right to intervene in any other state to establish discipline, constituting itself a judge of the occasion, then every state had the same right to intervene in the affairs of every other state, being itself alone the arbiter both in regard to the time and the occasion. The principle of intervention, thus practically carried out, would seem to render all sovereignty and independence and even all international peace and amity uncertain and fallacious.[98]

The representations of Secretary Seward against the continued presence of French troops in Mexico were of course greatly strengthened by "the dogged persistence of the troops of Juárez, supported and encouraged by the clandestine introduction of American arms and munitions." [99] There was also very powerful opposition in France to the Mexican enterprise of the Emperor Napoleon. The Duc de Morny, Napoleon's illegitimate half-brother and leading supporter of the Mexican venture, in the success of which he was believed to be financially interested, had died in 1865, but not in time to avoid listening to heated attacks and veiled accusations of improper motives on the floor of the Corps Legislatif over which he presided.[100] The most important factor in the decision of Napoleon to withdraw his troops was probably, however, the beginning of a shift in the European balance of power in comparison with which the Mexican enterprise was "but a holiday diversion." [101]

98 *Dip. Cor. U. S.*, 1866, Vol. 3, p. 817.

99 Rippy, *op. cit.*, p. 274.

100 *Grand Encyclopédie*, *loc. cit.*; *Sen. Ex. Doc. No. 11*, 38th Cong., 1st Sess., pp. 125–169, 212, 223, 424–440.

101 *The Daily News* (London), August 10, 1866, quoted in *Dip. Cor. U. S.*, 1866, Vol. 3, p. 288.

Napoleon's announcement of his intention to withdraw his troops from Mexico immediately was made in May, 1866. Within the next few months events moved so rapidly that at the beginning of August, when Maximilian's consort, the Empress Carlotta, arrived in Paris for the purpose of imploring further aid for Maximilian, a London periodical made the following comment:

> The empress will perceive that this is a crisis in which the imperial banker at Paris must in justice to himself draw together all his resources, close outstanding transactions, taking from his debtors whatever they are able to pay, but on no account parting with more. If the Mexican empire can stand when the French troops have been recalled, and supplies of French money have ceased to flow, well; if not, the empress will hardly find it worth while to make another voyage across the Atlantic.[102]

Deprived of French military and financial support, the government of Maximilian quickly declined. Its financial weakness had been indicated in its budget for the year ending June 30, 1866. The total expenditures had been calculated at 48,263,870 pesos — including 1,700,000 for the Emperor; 4,807,692 for the French troops; and 12,048,292 for interest and amortization on the foreign debt. Against these expenditures had been set the sum of 43,073,611 pesos as estimated revenues — including 22,-200,000 from the French loans of 1865.[103] Immediately before the withdrawal of the French forces a convention had been concluded for the assignment of one-half of the maritime customs duties for the payment of interest on the new loans of 1864 and 1865 and on the acknowledged debt of approximately 50,000,000 pesos for the costs of the intervention.[104] One-fourth of the same duties, it will be recalled, had been pledged in 1851 to the bondholders of the London debt. The assignments of 24 per cent of the same duties for the service of the English and Spanish convention debts were also regarded as still in force.[105] There remained, therefore, for the use of the government, subject to

102 *Ibid.*

103 Romero, *Memoria, sup. cit.*, pp. 685–686.

104 *Dip. Cor. U. S.*, 1866, Vol. 3, pp. 278–279. The assignment of export duties on the Pacific coast was temporarily limited to 25 per cent.

105 Romero, *Memoria, sup. cit.*, pp. 695, 699.

charges on account of the internal debt, only one per cent of these duties.

In January, 1867, the imperial government endeavored to obtain funds by means of a forced loan. The effort failed. The government thereupon issued a decree imposing an extraordinary tax of one per cent, which was denounced by the diplomatic corps at Mexico City as a forced loan in disguise. Before the end of March it levied upon the city of Mexico a forced loan of 850,000 pesos which added to the commercial distress resulting from previous taxation and morally weakened the imperial cause.[106] At the end of April the members of the diplomatic corps, including the Minister of France, ceased all relations with the imperial government.[107] On the fifteenth of May Maximilian surrendered to Juárez, and on June 19 the young emperor's adventure ended with his execution.[108]

[106] *Dip. Cor. U. S.*, 1867, Vol. 2, p. 391.

[107] *Ibid.*, p. 401.

[108] Lefêvre, *op. cit.*, Vol. II, pp. 389–395; 449–450.

CHAPTER VI

THE REËSTABLISHMENT OF MEXICAN CREDIT (1867–1887)

Repudiation of the Imperial Debt

The most urgent problem of the Juárez authorities who took possession of Mexico City on June 20, 1867, was that of obtaining funds for the necessities of the army. This problem was met for the moment by means of a voluntary loan of 200,000 pesos, without interest, which was obtained from local capitalists through the efforts of Marcus Otterbourg, American Consul in charge of the interests of the United States. Before undertaking to raise this loan, Otterbourg had made to Porfirio Díaz, the young general commanding the Juárez troops

> a strong representation . . . of the danger to the constitutional government, if by a repetition of forced loans and contributions it should attract to itself any of the odium belonging to the military power [of Maximilian], which had exasperated and impoverished the citizens by extortionate demands upon their property.

In informing Díaz of the success of his efforts the Consul referred to "the desire of the United States government to see established in Mexico a permanent government," and assured "the citizen general" of his readiness to "aid in the settlement of peace and order in Mexico."[1]

The loan of 200,000 pesos was but a temporary expedient. Confronted by the problem of providing permanent sources of revenue, the government of Juárez was forced to decide whether it should continue in effect the assignments of customs duties existing at the time of the collapse of the empire. These assign-

[1] Otterbourg to Secretary of State, June 27, 1867 (*Senate Executive Document No. 20*, 40th Cong., 1st Sess., pp. 267–268).

ments, it will be recalled, had been increased by Maximilian up to ninety-nine per cent of all the maritime customs duties.[2]

As might have been expected in view of the circumstances of the establishment of the empire, the government of Juárez not only repudiated all the assignments of customs duties made by Maximilian but also declared:

> The republic neither can, nor ought, in any shape, [to] recognize the obligations which the Emperor of the French attempted to force upon her through his intervention in our domestic affairs. The government cannot find language sufficiently strong to express the force of its determination in this respect.[3]

A legal case for the recognition of at least a substantial part of the financial obligations assumed by Maximilian could doubtless have been made out by the persons interested. The government of Maximilian, however objectionable it may have been to the majority of the Mexican people, had clearly been for some years in effective control of the greater part of the territory of Mexico. It had, moreover, been recognized as the government of Mexico by every important power except the United States. Even upon the theory of the temporary usurpation of the powers of the legitimate "sovereign" by Maximilian, the republican government, resuming its powers, was bound by well established rules of the *jus postliminii* to recognize as valid some of the acts of the usurper. Under these rules, according to Heffter,[4] private rights created during the usurpation must be respected "in so far as they can be reconciled with the reëstablished order of things." Alienations of the capital or revenues belonging to the State are also, in the opinion of the same author, to be considered valid, as having been obviously within the power of the usurping sovereign.[5]

[2] *Supra*, pp. 169, 170.

[3] Report of Romero, Minister of Finance, to the Mexican Congress (*For. Rel. U. S.*, 1868, Vol. 2, p. 410).

[4] *Europäische Völkerrecht* (8th ed., Berlin, 1888), §§ 187–189.

[5] Heffter admits that the question of the recognition of such alienations is highly controversial. On the general question of the legal effect of the acts of *de facto* governments, *cf.* Taft, William H., *Opinion and Award in the matter of an Arbitration between H. M. the King of the United Kingdom of Great Britain and Ireland and His Excellency the President of the Republic of Costa Rica* (New York, 1923).

No serious effort appears to have been made by any government at this time to oppose, on legal grounds, the action which the government of Juárez had determined to take with reference to the obligations assumed and the assignments effected by Maximilian. It was evidently realized by both France and Great Britain, the two powers whose subjects were concerned, that the only argument which could alter the determination of Juárez and his Cabinet was the argument of force. That argument, for obvious reasons, France was indisposed to invoke. She chose, instead, to grant an indemnity of 87,000,000 francs to the French investors in the bonds of Maximilian. This indemnity amounted to nearly fifty per cent of the amounts actually paid for the bonds.[6] The disinclination of Great Britain to support by force the claims of British purchasers of these bonds may be attributed to the considerations which had been set forth by Palmerston in his circular of 1848. It was only because of peculiar circumstances that the British government had departed in 1861 from its established policy of non-intervention in behalf of bondholders.[7] The situation in 1867 was radically different.

Repudiation of Pre-Intervention Assignments

Upon motives somewhat similar to those which caused the rejection of responsibility for the financial commitments of Maximilian, the government of Juárez determined to repudiate also the assignments of customs duties which had been made in favor of foreign creditors before the intervention. In the first place, the government needed all the funds it could lay hands on. In the second place, Great Britain and Spain, whose nationals were the principal foreign creditors, were the objects of deep resentment because of their participation in the first stages of the intervention and because of their recognition of Maximilian as emperor. It was this resentment that led Juárez to refuse to enter into relations with the British and Spanish diplomatic and consular representatives who had been in intercourse with the

[6] *The Economist*, September 28, 1889.

[7] *Supra*, pp. 119, 123, 129, 141.

imperial authorities. It was this also that led him to say to the Congress at Mexico City on December 8, 1867:

> The intervention broke up our relations with the European powers. By a convention in London, three of them declared war against the republic. Two of them soon withdrew, and France was left alone, as actively hostile to us. The others, however, soon recognized the monarchy established by the French, and thus became our moral enemies because they did not declare neutrality. In that manner many of the European governments violated their treaties with the republic, and broke off their friendly relations with us.[8]

In regard to the diplomatic convention of 1853 with Spain, under which eight per cent of the maritime customs duties were assigned for the benefit of creditors originally Spanish (but later largely Mexican), the Department of Finance made the following statement:[9]

> The citizen President has well-founded motives for considering insubsistent the treaties which united Mexico with the powers who disowned the republican government of this country, and recognized the so-called imperial government which the French intervention pretended to establish, it being those powers who by such conduct broke said treaties.
>
> As among those treaties figures the Spanish convention, it is in the same case as any of the others, and must, in consequence, be considered as insubsistent. The government, however, does not for this deny the obligation of the national treasury to pay the legitimate and recognized titles of this extinguished convention. All that it denies is that such obligation retains an international character, and that the terms of payment stipulated in a no longer existing arrangement should subsist.

A similar statement was made by the same department with reference to the arrangements under which sixteen per cent of the customs duties had been assigned, jointly, to the Padre Morán and English convention debts.[10]

The assignment of one-fourth of the customs duties in favor of the bondholders of the London debt of 1851 was repudiated on the ground that these bondholders had released the republic from all undertakings in their favor by concluding with Maximilian a new arrangement in regard to the debt. In vain was it urged,

[8] *Dip. Cor. U. S.*, 1868, Vol. 2, p. 378.

[9] *Ibid.*, p. 419.

[10] *B. and F. State Papers*, Vol. 58, pp. 682–683.

in behalf of the bondholders, that this new arrangement related exclusively to arrears of interest on the London debt and "rather diminished the physical force of that [the imperial] order of things, than contributed to increase its moral power." In vain did their agent offer to abandon "the rights created in their favor by the operation effected with the Empire" upon condition of the government's acknowledging that this operation could not "vitiate previous acts in every sense valid and executed with Mexican governments whose legitimacy the present one cannot disavow." The government of Juárez remained unmoved, acknowledged its obligations for principal and interest of the London debt, and indicated that it was prepared to consider new arrangements regarding the manner of meeting its engagements.[11]

The Financial Program of Romero

Pending the conclusion of new agreements with the foreign creditors or with their governments, the government of Juárez announced its intention of proceeding to the redemption of the bonds of the London debt and the convention debts. The redemption was to be effected in accordance with a program outlined by Minister of Finance Romero in a report to the Mexican Congress dated January 31, 1868.[12]

The public debt, said Romero in this report, had undoubtedly been the principal difficulty with which former administrations had had to struggle. It might be said without exaggeration that it had served as a pretext for the intervention just ended. European nations had imposed upon Mexico, as an international obligation, a debt which by its origin and in accordance with every principle of equity and justice, recognized by all nations, could have no other character than that of a national debt, in which no foreign power ought to interfere in any way. The government

[11] For the position of the Mexican government, see *Dip. Cor. U. S.*, 1868, Vol. 2, pp. 500–501. The arguments of the bondholders are summarized in a memorial to the Congress of Mexico, a translation of which accompanied Minister Rosecrans' No. 54½, April 27, 1869, to the Department of State. MS. Desp. Mex., Vol. 35.

[12] Romero, *Memoria, sup. cit.* pp. 722–724; *Dip. Cor. U. S.*, 1868, Vol. 2, pp. 379, 410.

had thus found itself deprived of the resources indispensable for the preservation of public order and had not even been able to pay the interest on the debt. The demands of the powers had reached a really intolerable point and had at last produced a misunderstanding which was fatal to the powers but which had for the Mexican people the beneficial result of freeing them from the tutelage to which they had been subject.

The government, continued the Minister, would endeavor, first of all, to restore public tranquillity, which was still far from assured. It would insist upon a punctual observance of the revenue laws by all the inhabitants of the republic, including the authorities of the states, by whom a large part of the federal income had been collected during the intervention. It would adopt or propose to Congress such reforms in the financial laws as experience might show to be needful, taking care not to destroy any of the existing sources of revenue without substituting others. It would refuse to enter into ruinous contracts for advances of money in anticipation of the receipt of duties. It would introduce economy in administrative expenditure. Finally, it would constantly bear in mind the fact, which had not usually been realized in the past, that Mexico possessed within herself all the necessary elements for her existence and that through the development of her immense material resources she would attain the high degree of welfare and prosperity to which she was apparently destined by a benign and prodigal nature.

Availing itself of the rights given by the new situation and animated with a sincere desire to comply with all the legitimate obligations of the republic, the government had decided upon a method of paying off the national debt gradually by the use of not less than 50,000 pesos a month in the purchase, at public "auction," of the largest possible quantity of the outstanding bonds.[13] If, as might be expected, the auctions produced good results, a large part of the debt would have been redeemed within a few years and the constant motives which had existed for diffi-

[13] The amortization of the English and Spanish convention debts by means of auctions had been authorized by the Minister of Finance in a circular of October 22, 1867 (*Legislación Mexicana,* Vol. X, p. 107).

culties with European powers would have been removed. If those powers desired to renew relations with Mexico on new bases, there would no longer be any cause for differences.

Auctions of Bonds

Ten days after the announcement of the government's program for liquidation of the public debt, the first of the proposed auctions was held. The sum of 90,000 pesos in cash was offered to those who were willing to surrender the largest quantity of bonds of the English and Spanish convention debts. The reason for specifying the convention debts was that the funds with which the auction was held had been taken from the local agents of the bondholders of these debts. The result of the auction was that bonds of the English convention debt of the nominal value of 168,073 pesos were surrendered in exchange for 49,000 pesos in cash, and bonds of the Spanish convention debt of the nominal value of 316,781 pesos were exchanged for 41,000 pesos in cash. In further auctions up to the end of May, 1868, the government acquired for 204,995 pesos in cash, bonds of the English and Spanish convention debts of the nominal value of 1,093,414 pesos.[14]

The purchase of bonds at auction was strongly condemned by Edward L. Plumb, the American chargé d'affaires, in a dispatch of March 12, 1868, to the Department of State.[15] These bonds, said Plumb, were depreciated because the interest had not been paid for years. If there were funds at the disposal of the government, it would seem that they should first be applied to the payment of interest. They could not rightfully be used for the purchase of the depreciated principal until the interest was paid.

Aside from the question of morality and public good faith, a question of sound policy was involved. All the money the government could raise, and more, was required and would for some time be required in the work of reëstablishing and maintaining public order. Until very great changes were introduced into the

[14] *B. and F. State Papers*, Vol. 58, pp. 682–683, 693–695; *Dip. Cor. U. S.*, 1868, Vol. 2, pp. 399–419; *Diario Oficial*, February 11, 1868.

[15] No. 87, MS. Desp. Mex., Vol. 32.

revenue system, commerce relieved of the existing restrictions, and public order more firmly established, the means of the government would be "greatly inadequate to the mere expenses of its existence" and to "those more pressing demands which every government must liquidate in full." If the government still had funds available "after meeting these primal necessities," such funds should be applied "in the first instance under the peculiar circumstances of the case, to the payment of the claims of citizens of the United States," which had been "waived for a time as a means of special relief to Mexico."

"As a general system," it appeared to the chargé d'affaires to be necessary that all the obligations of the government, both foreign and domestic, be called in, revised, and consolidated into one or two debts. In this way alone, and by the regular and prompt payment of interest on the consolidated debts, could the credit of the government be raised.

The views of the chargé d'affaires with respect to the special interest of the United States in the sale of the bonds of the convention debts were not shared by the Department of State. However objectionable might be the Mexican policy in this matter, said Secretary Seward in an instruction of April 13, the United States did not appear to be specially called upon to protest against that policy, inasmuch as no portion of the debts in question had been contracted to the government or citizens of the United States. It would seem ungracious for the United States to take the position that the sale of the bonds of these debts at auction gave to foreign creditors an undue preference over American claimants. This position could hardly be assumed without bringing into question the friendly feelings of the United States toward the republic of Mexico. Seward was looking forward to a time, not far distant, when he could propose a convention for the mutual adjustment and settlement of claims between citizens of the United States and citizens of Mexico.[16] It had not yet been thought expedient to press the subject, inasmuch as the United

[16] Seward's No. 53, *Dip. Cor. U. S.*, 1868, Vol. 2, p. 530. Such a convention was in fact signed on July 4, 1868 (*Treaties, Conventions*, etc., *sup. cit.*, Vol. I, p. 1128).

States itself, in view of the derangement of political and financial affairs produced by the late War, had up to that time declined to enter into negotiations with foreign states for the adjustment of the claims of their subjects growing out of the transactions of the War.

The point of view expressed by Plumb, though not supported by his own government, was of sufficient strength among certain members of the Mexican Congress to occasion an attack upon the policy of auctions. That policy Romero was accordingly obliged to defend in a session of the Congress on March 17, 1868. The government, said Romero, would consider it a great evil if the Congress directed the suspension of the auctions. In the two months in which the auctions had been held they had produced the most satisfactory results. With great gain to the creditors and evident benefit to the treasury, there had been canceled more than half a million pesos a month of the public debt. If this could continue, the debt would at the end of a few years be very considerably reduced or entirely extinguished.[17]

The auctions of the British and Spanish convention bonds were continued. An appropriation of 1,080,000 pesos was made, moreover, for the purchase of bonds of the London debt in the same manner. The extension of the system of auctions to the bonds of the London debt was defended by the Minister of Finance in a speech in Congress on May 20, 1868, in which he quoted a letter from the secretary of the Committee of Mexican Bondholders at London, urging the commencement of negotiations for the resumption of interest payments. In view of this indication of the disposition of the Committee to enter into arrangements it would, said the Minister of Finance, be a mistake for the Congress to declare that it was about to appropriate money for the payment of interest. Such a declaration would prejudice the negotiations and nullify the advantages which the government had a right to expect.[18]

[17] *Dip. Cor. U. S.*, 1868, Vol. 2, pp. 436–437.

[18] *Ibid.*, pp. 475–479.

Welcome Relief from Diplomatic Pressure

Neither the repudiation of the pre-intervention customs assignments nor the initiation of the policy of auctions appears to have occasioned any official representations by the governments of Great Britain and Spain. The absence of such representations was doubtless due in part to the fact that direct relations did not exist between those two governments and Juárez. Representations made through the Minister of the United States, in charge of British and Spanish interests, might have lost somewhat of their force in the process. It was taken for granted by European observers that Juárez would be glad to renew relations with the principal powers of Europe. Accordingly, the agent of the London bondholders, sent to Mexico upon the invitation of the Minister of Finance, sought to advance his negotiations by offering a possible exercise of the influence of the Committee of Bondholders to bring about a resumption of relations between Mexico and Great Britain. He was surprised to find that Juárez and his advisers were almost wholly indifferent toward all the European powers.[19]

An editorial written in August, 1868, by Francisco Zarco, a member of the Mexican Congress and a former Minister of Foreign Affairs, voiced the almost universal public sentiment in Mexico with reference to diplomatic relations with Europe.[20]

The republic, said Zarco, had ever since its triumph over the foreign usurpation been entirely without diplomatic relations with European powers. From this situation there had not resulted any evil to the country nor to the foreigners residing in it. The government had been free from the pressure which the legations of Europe had always exercised, and foreigners had been favored and protected by the Mexican laws and authorities. The absence of diplomatic relations had not interrupted the relations between people and people, which consisted in navigation and commerce. It had been demonstrated that diplomatic relations were not indispensable for the development of commerce, for the exchange

[19] Plumb's No. 179, August 22, 1868, *Dip. Cor. U. S.*, 1868, Vol. 2, p. 570.
[20] *Ibid.*

of ideas between peoples, nor for the interests of foreigners resident in Mexico.

The legations had been a constant embarrassment; had violated the rules of neutrality and of public law; had allied themselves almost always with the retrograde faction in Mexico; and had afforded no protection to their nationals. Absolutely nothing should be done by Mexico to hasten the reëstablishment of diplomatic relations with Europe. The attitude of Mexico should be that of mere expectation. In making new treaties the government should be exceedingly cautious, rejecting the old clause of reciprocity, falsely so-called, and establishing the rule that foreigners in Mexico must have the same rights and the same obligations as Mexicans.

Such an attitude would not prevent Mexico from cultivating and drawing closer its good relations with the United States, in which there was not the least peril for Mexican nationality nor for the integrity of Mexican territory. At the same time Mexico could and should promote the alliance of all the American republics against all projects of reconquest, invasion, or intervention on the part of Europe. The strength of Mexico as an independent nation was to be derived not from foreign alliances but from its own political institutions and material progress.[21]

Possibility of an American Guarantee

Perceiving the bent of the government toward the cultivation of closer relations with the United States, as recommended in Zarco's editorial, the agent of the bondholders of the London debt urged upon the Mexican Minister of Foreign Affairs, in February, 1869, the conclusion of an arrangement with the United States for the guarantee of the payment of future interest on that debt. On the strength of such a guarantee, the agent would undertake to secure a reduction of the principal of the debt from approximately 80,000,000 pesos to 50,000,000 pesos. To this proposal, according to a confidential report of the American Minister, General Rosecrans, on March 3, 1869, the Mexican official replied:

[21] *Siglo XIX* (Mexico City), August 13, 1868, translation quoted in *Dip. Cor. U. S.*, 1868, Vol. 2, pp. 570–572.

"Oh no! that would never do, — never do, it would place us under the tutelage of Americans." He likewise rejected the agent's alternative suggestion of a sale or pledge of one of the Mexican states, say Yucatán, on the basis of which the agent thought he might induce the British government to assume the payment of the debt.[22]

From these negotiations, said General Rosecrans, it was obvious that the foreign debt was a weapon which might be used either by or against the United States. It was also evident that though Sebastián Lerdo de Tejada, the Minister of Foreign Affairs, appeared officially to reciprocate the good will frankly expressed by the American Minister, he would seize any opportunity to work against the United States. It therefore seemed wise for the United States to "take care to control all the elements of opposition" to Lerdo, who was practically the government of Mexico. From these elements of opposition, General Rosecrans was sure, could be obtained all that would be necessary for the development of the country as required by its own best interest and that of the United States.

With adequate guarantees, the General continued, the United States could "people" Mexico and render it "enormously productive" in a short period of time. It was by no means the poor mining country which he had expected to find it. Its laboring population, numbering five millions, were "simple, docile and patient of labor, easily governed" and needing only "intelligent, industrial chiefs for guidance, an example to make them a valuable element of the country." Its mining and agricultural resources were enormous. If the Department considered it desirable, he would be pleased to enter into details in order to show how a country which had been declared to be composed of "seven and a half millions of unhappy people and one hundred thousand rascals" could become "a powerful, wealthy and very friendly neighbor, whose entrance into our family might become unobjectionable, provided prompt and speedy action be taken."[23]

Without awaiting a request from the State Department, Rose-

[22] Rosecrans' No. 36, March 3, 1869, MS. Desp. Mex., Vol. 35.

[23] *Ibid.*

crans proceeded on April 10, 1869, to give some of the details of his plan for the development of Mexico. Extensive railway construction, along routes which he indicated, should be undertaken and executed by American capital and enterprise, with the backing of the American government, in such a way as to give to the United States "the prestige of a success only seen among Americans." The effect of such construction would be at once to open the country and to facilitate the guarantees of stability and justice so necessary to inspire the Mexican people with confidence. A more direct means to the same end would be for American capitalists, with the consent of their government, to buy and control the Mexican public debt and advance the needful means to the Mexican government to "get organized under our auspices." These capitalists should, in the General's opinion, be guaranteed by the United States government the payment of a certain percentage of the nominal value of the debt. A part of "the discount" would presumably be given to Mexico. Liberal margins of profit would, however, be allowed to the purchasers of the bonds. The United States would have to assume the responsibility for the payment of some $8,000,000 a year as interest for perhaps five years, at the end of which time Mexico, under proper development, would probably be able to pay the interest and a part of the principal annually.

Europe, declared Rosecrans, had its "sick man." America had, in Mexico, a "sicker man," whom it became "our genius to cure by prompt and energetic action in the spirit of humanity for the material improvement, elevation and freedom of the Mexican people." [24]

Toward the end of April, Rosecrans was encouraged in his plans by the arrival of an English steamer bringing authorization to the agent of the British bondholders to negotiate with him for the sale of the London debt.[25] No negotiations to that end appear

[24] Rosecrans' No. 48 (confidential), April 10, 1869, MS. Desp. Mex., Vol. 35.

[25] The Bondholders' Committee had, according to Rosecrans, made a direct communication on the subject to Reverdy Johnson, American Minister at London, on April 10, 1869. An overture made through Minister Adams two years earlier had drawn from Secretary Seward the statement that the President did not think it necessary to charge the Minister with any duty with reference to the sug-

to have been held. Rosecrans' successor had, in fact, already been appointed before the arrival of the bondholders' authorization for such negotiations.

" Intrigues " of the Bondholders

A year later Thomas H. Nelson, the successor of Rosecrans at Mexico City, had reason to suspect that the bondholders of the London debt were " intriguing " with the Minister of Foreign Affairs with a view to obtaining a concession for the construction of a ship canal across the Isthmus of Tehuantepec in consideration of the extinguishment of a large part of the London debt. His suspicions were confirmed in an interview which he had with the Minister of Finance at the end of July, 1870. The Minister of Foreign Affairs, without consulting Romero, in whose province the matter primarily lay, had offered to grant the Tehuantepec concession in consideration of the cancellation of half the London debt. The offer had been rejected by the bondholders in a meeting at London. Nelson was of the opinion that the agent of the bondholders had not contemplated the investment of further capital in the construction of the Tehuantepec canal. He believed that the agent had hoped to dispose of the concession to the highest bidder or to the Tehuantepec Railroad Company of New York, which had for some time been seeking it.[26]

Customs Assignments for Railway Construction

The Tehuantepec Company of New York, to which the agent of the London bondholders had hoped to sell the proposed concession for the construction of a canal, was among the first of the foreign concerns to undertake extensive public works in Mexico. The actual construction of a railway, carriage road, and telegraph line projected by this Company was initiated with formal public ceremonies on January 9, 1871.[27] This was, however, nearly a score of years later than the inception of a more

gested purchase of the bonds of the London debt by the United States. (*Dip. Cor. U. S.*, 1867, Vol. 1, pp. 93–101).

[26] Nelson's No. 255, July 29, 1870, *For. Rel. U. S.*, 1870, pp. 486–490.

[27] Nelson's No. 276, Jan. 23, 1871, *For. Rel. U. S.*, 1871, pp. 612–613.

ambitious project, backed by British capital, for a railway from Veracruz to Mexico City. The British project had, moreover, in November, 1868, been given the advantage of two large assignments of customs duties.

The first assignment of customs duties in favor of the British-owned railway, known as the Mexican Railway, was in the form of bonds issued to the amount of 560,000 pesos a year for twenty-five years and receivable in payment of import duties up to 12 per cent of any sum due. The second assignment was in the form of a legal requirement that, up to the end of the year 1872, 15 per cent of all the maritime import duties should be paid in the stock of the railroad company, purchased at par. The total assignment was calculated to produce in excess of 900,000 pesos by way of annual subsidy to the company.[28]

The Mexican Railway having been completed in 1873, the Tehuantepec Railroad Company was at the end of the following year given a subsidy of 12,500 pesos for each mile of construction on its proposed line across the Isthmus of Tehuantepec. For the payment of this subsidy 50 per cent of the customs duties at Minatitlán and Salina Cruz were pledged. At the same time subsidies of $15,288 were awarded to the Central Railroad of Mexico, owned by British and Mexican capitalists, and to the American-owned International Railroad Company of Texas for each mile of construction on their lines from Mexico City to León and from León to a point on the Rio Grande. The subsidy in favor of the Central Railroad was charged upon 8 per cent of the customs duties at Veracruz, Tampico, Manzanillo, Mazatlán and Guaymas. That in favor of the International Company was to be paid out of 25 per cent of the customs duties at Matamoros and the other frontier customs-houses on the Rio Grande.[29]

Prospects for Adjustment of the Foreign Debt

The construction of railways and other public works was considerably hampered by frequent political disturbances throughout the country. The Juárez government had not proved

[28] Plumb's No. 222, Nov. 14, 1868, *Dip. Cor. U. S.*, 1868, Vol. 2, pp. 614–616.

[29] Minister Foster's No. 409, December 23, 1874, *U. S. For. Rel.*, 1875, Vol. 2, pp. 853–855.

equal to the task of maintaining the public tranquillity which Romero had said it would be its first endeavor to restore. The disturbances had become particularly serious toward the end of the year 1871, when Lerdo, Díaz and others forcibly but fruitlessly opposed the desire of Juárez to be reëlected to the presidency. The long-continued strife impoverished the treasury. Although Romero still served efficiently as Minister of Finance, the best prospect he could hold out to the Congress in his budget for the year 1872–1873 was an income of 15,860,561 pesos from ordinary sources, as against expenditures of 23,079,443 pesos. The estimate of expenditures, it should be noted, included no provision for payments on the foreign debt.[30]

When Lerdo became provisional President in July, 1872, upon the death of Juárez, he found it necessary to raise a loan of 400,000 pesos, for urgent expenses, from capitalists in Mexico City. This loan was, however, raised with comparative ease, and according to the American Minister, commerce, agriculture, and mining immediately took an impulse from the hopes of peace.[31]

During the year 1873 general conditions in Mexico improved appreciably. Before the end of this year, as a result of the friendly offices of the United States, diplomatic relations had been restored between Mexico and Spain, Prussia, and Italy. France and Great Britain, however, were still adamant in their refusal to renew relations.[32] The absence from Mexico of a British diplomatic representative was believed by the bondholders at London to be seriously prejudicial to their interests. "The interest of bondholders," it was declared in the report of the London Corporation of Foreign Bondholders for 1873,

> are generally antagonistic to any measures which can place H. M. Government in simple antagonism to that of another country, and still less to seek hostile interposition which must come home in disturbance of our own commerce, besides the creation of dangerous complications.

[30] *Projecto de Presupuestos de Ingresos y Egresos del Erario Federal para 1872–73* (Mexico, 1871), p. 62.

[31] Bancroft, *op. cit.*, Vol. VI, pp. 384–396; Nelson's No. 340, August 15, 1872, *For. Rel. U. S.*, 1872, Vol. 1, pp. 453–454.

[32] Bancroft, *op. cit.*, Vol. VI, pp. 358–359.

The efforts of the bondholders in Mexico were declared to be directed to the restoration of diplomatic relations rather than to any new interference with them.[33]

At the end of 1873 the Mexican Minister of Finance reported to the Congress that the foreign debt of Mexico was 76,451,163.19 pesos, including 63,498,130 pesos for the London debt, 4,351,348 pesos for the English convention debt, 8,200,000 pesos for the two Spanish convention debts, and 401,685.19 pesos for the American claims adjusted by a Mixed Commission which had been established in 1869.[34] Besides the debt thus acknowledged there were later declared by the Minister to be outstanding bonds of the Carbajal-Corlies issue to the amount of $1,438,050. Bonds to the amount of $500,000 of the issue of General Sánchez Ochoa were stated to be in the custody of Eugene Kelly and Company of New York, under an order of the Supreme Court of that State.[35] For the collection of the principal and interest on the Carbajal-Corlies bonds, the American Minister, John W. Foster, was instructed by Secretary of State Fish on January 31, 1874, to employ only his good offices.[36]

On January 12, 1874, Foster, in the absence of official relations between Great Britain and Mexico, introduced to President Lerdo in an unofficial manner John Geiger, representative of the London Corporation of Foreign Bondholders. In presenting Geiger to the President, Foster took occasion to remark that the government of the United States would regard with interest and pleasure all steps taken in the direction of more friendly relations between the government and people of Mexico and Great Britain. The President expressed to Geiger the earnest desire of his government for an adjustment of the London debt and the willingness of his government to resume the payment of interest as soon as the condition of the treasury and its resources would permit. He declined to make any proposition for such adjustment and re-

[33] Page 33 of the report cited.

[34] Under the convention of July 4, 1868, mentioned *supra*, p. 178.

[35] *For Rel. U. S.*, 1874, pp. 720–735. The Clerk of the Court states in a letter to the Committee that his records contain no reference to the order mentioned. For information regarding the Sánchez Ochoa bonds, see p. 164, *supra*.

[36] MS. Inst. Mex., Vol. 19, pp. 66–67.

sumption, but stated that he would be pleased to receive and consider a proposition from the bondholders.

The subject of the resumption of diplomatic relations between Great Britain and Mexico was favorably alluded to in the conference between the President and Geiger. Foster understood that the Mexican government was entirely ready to resume diplomatic relations and to receive an official representative from Great Britain but that, in view of the circumstances attending the war of intervention and the withdrawal of the former British Minister, Mexico was not disposed to take the initiative.[37]

Upon the return of Geiger to London the Council of the Corporation of Foreign Bondholders resolved to take "more decided action" with a view to inducing Mexico to conclude arrangements with her foreign creditors. A factor in the Council's decision was "the advantage the country derived from the construction of the Mexican Railway, effected by means of funds procured by the hypothecation of a part of the securities which had been already assigned to the bondholders."[38] After consultation with the bourses on the Continent, the Council notified the Mexican government that it would no longer be allowed to avail itself, directly or indirectly, of European markets for the purpose of raising capital. The effect of this notification, says the Corporation in its report for 1874, became immediately apparent. After unsuccessful attempts to raise money in the United States, as well as in Europe, President Lerdo at length authorized overtures to be made to the Committee of Mexican Bondholders at London.[39]

The Beginning of the Díaz Régime

Negotiations between the bondholders and the government were under way during the summer of 1876, while President Lerdo was attempting to put down a revolution headed by General Díaz. The latter accordingly deemed it necessary, in a proclamation issued on September 26, to declare that any obliga-

[37] Foster's No. 94, January 15, 1874, MS. Desp. Mex., Vol. 50.

[38] Corporation of Foreign Bondholders, London (hereinafter cited as C. F. B.), *Second Annual Report*, 1874, pp. 44–45.

[39] Page 44 of the report cited.

tions which President Lerdo's government might contract with the bondholders of the English debt in regard to the recognition of that debt would be null and void.[40] It was charged by Díaz that Lerdo had agreed to recognize the London debt in consideration of the payment of 2,000,000 pesos to himself. Díaz also charged that Lerdo contemplated an arrangement for the assumption of the London debt by the United States, "which was equivalent to selling the country to the neighboring republic."[41]

At the time of Díaz' proclamation Foster, the American Minister, was absent on leave in the United States. So far from certain was the triumph soon afterwards gained by Díaz that the Minister, then at New Orleans, *en route* to his post, wrote to Secretary of State Fish, on October 21, that Lerdo would be able to maintain himself if he had the funds which he needed.[42] Lerdo's Cabinet, according to information given Foster by a member of the Mexican Congress, had considered the possibility of inducing the government of the United States, upon satisfactory security, to guarantee the payment of interest on a loan of six to eight millions of dollars. Without expressing any opinion on the questions of policy which might be raised in connection with the possibility suggested, Foster observed that the grant of the loan desired might enable the United States to make a commercial treaty which would secure Mexico as a market for American manufacturers and producers. It would also present some questions of deep interest to the United States, including the question how long and to what extent the American government could allow the internecine struggle to continue in the neighboring republic without some kind of interposition, friendly or otherwise.[43]

Before the end of November, 1876, the forces of General Díaz had occupied Mexico City. On November twenty-eighth the merchants and capitalists were called to the national palace and asked for a loan of 500,000 pesos. Only a part of the amount requested was obtained. Díaz, however, abstained from irregular

[40] Foster's No. 472, Dec. 8, 1876, *For. Rel. U. S.*, 1877, p. 386.

[41] Bancroft, *op. cit.*, Vol. VI, p. 421.

[42] MS. Desp. Mex., Vol. 57.

[43] *Ibid.*

exactions and forced loans, having recourse instead to a general tax of 6 to 10 per cent of the profits derived from all classes of property. The decree establishing this tax stated that the proceeds should be applied in part to the payment of an instalment of 300,000 pesos due to the United States under awards of the Mixed Claims Commission. The Department of State accordingly, on January 19, 1877, realizing that the instalment could not well be received before the recognition of the Díaz government, authorized the American Minister to recognize that government, provided that such a step was not made inexpedient by events which were not then foreseen.[44]

Díaz assumed the office of President on April 2, 1877, pursuant to his election in the manner provided for in the Constitution of 1857. At the end of May he was officially recognized by the German government. Recognition by Spain followed in June. France, Great Britain, and other European powers held back. Disturbances having occurred on the Mexican-American border, recognition by the United States was also deferred until March, 1878. Meanwhile, in September, 1877, President Díaz had prophesied to the Mexican Congress an epoch of regeneration and prosperity.[45]

Financial Embarrassments

On May 4, 1878, Foster reported that the Mexican government had resumed the practice, which it had followed in 1868 and 1869, of purchasing its own bonds at auction. In the recent auctions only the Spanish convention bonds had been purchased, but these had been bought at less than one-fourth the price which they had commanded in 1868 and 1869. From data recently published it appeared that the bonds purchased in the years mentioned had, contrary to the information then available, included certain of the Carbajal-Corlies bonds sold and held in the United States. The existence or knowledge of this fact, the Minister suggested, might have modified the tenor of Seward's

[44] *For. Rel. U. S.*, 1877, pp. 385–395.

[45] *For. Rel. U. S.*, 1878, pp. 526–543; Foster's No. 545, June 16, 1877, MS. Desp. Mex., Vol. 59.

instruction of April 13, 1868, to the effect that the United States was not specially called upon to protest against the system of auctions.[46] The receipt of the new information furnished by Foster does not appear to have been followed by any protest on the part of the United States.

Before the end of the summer of 1878 considerable dissatisfaction with the state of affairs in Mexico had begun to manifest itself. One of the chief sources of dissatisfaction, said Foster, in a despatch of September 7, was "the great scarcity" of the federal treasury. All departments of the government except the legislative were in arrears of pay for the month of August and all public improvements, which the government was striving to push forward, would have to be held up. The lack of funds was stated by the Minister of Finance to be due to the disorganized and bad condition of the commerce of the country, in consequence of the decrease of orders for importations and the increase of smuggling. The endeavors of the Minister of Finance to find additional methods of taxation had, according to Foster, alarmed all the property and business interests of the country, and these interests, according to the past experience of Mexico, might be expected to encourage a revolutionary change of government in the hope of avoiding an impending tax or forced loan.[47]

The government was still financially embarrassed on October 8, when Foster made two detailed reports concerning the foreign debt.[48] There was "very little hope," he said, "of an early resumption or rather commencement of payment of interest" on the Carbajal-Corlies bonds issued in the United States in 1865. The pledge of the federal and state revenues of the States of Tamaulipas and San Luis Potosí for the payment of interest and amortization on these bonds would have been amply sufficient for the purpose if the revenues mentioned had not been encumbered by other pledges. None of the pledges had actually been honored, but this fact had been due not so much to the unwillingness of the government as to its constant financial em-

[46] Foster's No. 701, *For. Rel. U. S.*, 1878, p. 548.

[47] Foster's No. 777, *For. Rel. U. S.*, 1878, pp. 587–589.

[48] Foster's Nos. 802 and 803, October 8, 1878, MS. Desp. Mex., Vol. 64.

barrassments. No unfavorable discrimination had, however, been shown against Americans.

The straitened condition of the federal treasury was referred to again by Foster in a dispatch of October 25, 1878, in which he said that the worst feature of the situation was that it seemed to presage increased taxation, extraordinary contributions, or forced loans, which were the sure forerunners of revolution. Aside from financial embarrassments, there was no outward indication of civil war, and if the army could be paid with reasonable punctuality peace was likely to be preserved, at least for the immediate future.[49]

Abortive Agreements with Bondholders at London

In December, 1878, the negotiations which had been in progress for more than a year between the Minister of Finance and the agent of the bondholders in London resulted in the signature of a contract *ad referendum* providing for the consolidation of the public debt, embracing nineteen different classes of obligations, in connection with an arrangement for the construction of a railway from Mexico City to the Pacific Coast. The ability of the Mexican government to carry out the contract and the advisability of the acceptance of its terms by holders of the Carbajal-Corlies bonds were questioned by the American Minister in a despatch written before the contract was actually signed. The contract was rejected by the bondholders in London.[50]

A modified agreement drawn up in London in July, 1879, subject to the approval of the Mexican Congress, was rejected by the Congress. This agreement, according to the report of the Council of the Corporation of Foreign Bondholders for 1880,[51] was blocked by American capitalists (headed by General William J. Palmer)[52] who obtained a concession for the construction of the railway line contemplated in the agreement. These

49 Foster's No. 817, *For. Rel. U. S.*, 1878, pp. 660–661.

50 *Memoria de Hacienda*, 1878–79, pp. 459–460; Foster's No. 855, Dec. 16, 1878, MS. Desp. Mex., Vol. 65; C. F. B., *Sixth Annual Report*, 1878, pp. 35–38.

51 Pages 40–42.

52 *Cf.* p. 197, *infra*.

capitalists were declared by the Council to have had the official support of the government of the United States.[53]

THE "DAWN" OF AMERICAN INTERVENTION

The London bondholders were not alone in the belief that American official influence was being used in favor of American capitalists. According to a report made to the Department of State by Foster in September, 1879,[54] the conviction was widespread in Mexico that the United States earnestly coveted more Mexican territory and would take advantage of any plausible pretext to bring about a conflict or an intervention or to establish a protectorate. To this end, it was thought, the government of the United States would not only support the economic projects of American citizens in Mexico, especially the projects for railways connecting the two countries, but it would also take advantage of any failure of Mexico to pay instalments of the awards of the Mixed Claims Commission established in 1869 or to pay interest on the Carbajal-Corlies bonds of 1865.

In the opinion of one Mexican observer, Tomás Mendoza, there was beginning to "dawn upon Mexico the American intervention, against which there ought to be sought a European alliance by means of credit and commerce." This opinion was developed by Mendoza in a pamphlet, entitled "The Future of Mexico in the Light of her Financial Questions," in which he said:[55]

> . . . as if nothing should be wanting in the frightful conjuncture of horrors which are unchained against the Mexican Republic, a real complication is discovered in the relations with the United States of the North, which might very well commence with an armed intervention, in order to conclude with the spoliation of a part of the national territory. Revolution and anarchy will bring the first; the failure in payment of any instalment of the debt adjusted in Washington (the claims awards), or a reclamation on the account of the Carbajal bonds would decide the second. To confine in time those evils, is a patriotic duty which ought not to be postponed for a moment.

[53] *Ibid.* The declaration as to official support is not confirmed by the records of the Department of State.

[54] No. 1023, MS. Desp. Mex., Vol. 68.

[55] *Ibid.*

After quoting the text of the Carbajal-Corlies bonds, he continued:

> The necessary consequence of a failure of payment (when due), needs no explanation. The reading of the text of the bond copied will be sufficient to be thoroughly satisfied of the imminent danger which the Mexican nationality incurs by such an imprudent hypothecation of its territory. The States of Tamaulipas and San Luis Potosí would scarcely be sufficient to satisfy the cupidity of the North American speculators. . . . The intervention of the United States is indudable [sic] if the foresight of the Government does not with anticipation provide the resources for that national payment.

For the repayment of the American loan, the rescue of the treasury from bankruptcy, and the development of the resources of the country, the author recommended the borrowing of 10,000,000 pesos in France upon a pledge or a lease of the government mints.

The official journal of the government, said Foster, had published an editorial in which it sought to show that, in view of the past policy of the United States with reference to contracts of its citizens with foreign governments, there could be no danger of American diplomatic intervention in behalf of the holders of the Carbajal-Corlies bonds. In this connection the editorial stated that the British government, though jealous of the rights of its nationals, had not made a national question of the English debt. This assertion, declared Foster, showed a lamentable forgetfulness of Mexican diplomatic history. The British government had on no fewer than seven different occasions intervened in behalf of British subjects who had voluntarily entered into contracts with or made loans to the Mexican government. The Mexican executive had, moreover, recognized the right of intervention in these instances by concluding treaties or conventions with respect to them.

The seven interventions referred to by Foster were those which resulted in the conclusion of the Doyle Convention (December 4, 1851); the supplement to the Doyle Convention (December 9, 1852); the Otway Convention (August 10, 1858); the Dunlop Arrangement (February 7, 1859); the Aldham Arrangement (December 15, 1860); the Wyke-Zamacona Convention (November 21, 1861); and the Wyke-Doblado Convention (April 28, 1862). The first three of these instruments, it should be recalled, related exclusively to claims for damages or to short-time advances by English capitalists in Mexico, and not to the loans contracted in London. The last, likewise, related to pecuniary claims independent of the London loans, and was, moreover, not ratified by the British government. The Dunlop and Aldham Arrangements did, indeed, contain stipulations in favor of the London bondholders and were considered by the British government to have imposed obligations of an international character on the Mexican government. The Wyke-Zamacona Convention followed the precedent set in the Dunlop and Aldham Arrangements, and its rejection by the Foreign Office in London was apparently due not to any objection in principle but rather to the conviction that it was not adequate to the situation.[56]

The fear of American intervention was not sufficient to deter the government from purchasing at depreciated rates in August, 1881, bonds of the Carbajal-Corlies issue as well as bonds of the English and Spanish conventions.[57] Provision for the redemption of the Carbajal-Corlies bonds at their face value was not made until the end of 1883, when the Mexican Consul at New York was instructed to inform holders of those bonds that from January 1, 1884, the bonds and coupons attached would be received in payment of import duties up to 5 per cent of such duties at Veracruz and up to 10 per cent at Tampico, Matamoros, Monterey, Laredo, and Mier y Camargo.[58]

[56] *Supra*, pp. 101, 103, 114, 119, 123, 145, 151.

[57] Minister Morgan's No. 263, Aug. 25, 1881, MS. Desp. Mex., Vol. 73.

[58] Morgan's No. 728, Dec. 26, 1883, MS. Desp. Mex., Vol. 81. The amount of the Carbajal debt on June 30, 1880, was 2,844,510 pesos, of which 1,326,100 pesos was capital and the remainder was interest. During the next six years the amount was reduced to less than 75,000 pesos. (*Memoria de Hacienda*, 1880–1881, pp. 155–160; 1884–1885, p. 237; 1886–1887, p. xlvi.) The redemption of the debt appears to have been completed by 1890.

Further Efforts of the London Bondholders

Notwithstanding the unfavorable action of the Mexican Congress on the agreement of September, 1879, the bondholders at London were, at the end of the following year, distinctly hopeful of an early settlement with Mexico. The mind of the country, they believed, had been awakened to the necessity for the reëstablishment of the national credit in order that the requisite capital for public works might be procurable. For such capital, it was thought, Mexico must rely chiefly upon the European market, which could be opened to Mexican securities only after a settlement with the European creditors and the resumption of the regular service of the debt.[59]

Among the encouraging developments during the year 1880 was President Díaz' appointment of a committee for the formulation of a project for the settlement of the debt. Another favorable augury was the reëstablishment, in October, of diplomatic relations between Mexico and France — subject, however, to the understanding that no claims would be made against Mexico on account of past financial transactions.[60] The restoration of relations with France, incidentally, prepared the way for the establishment of the Banco Nacional Mexicano,[61] under a contract of August 23, 1881, between the Mexican government and Edward Noetzlin, on behalf of the Franco-Egyptian Bank of Paris. The new bank was authorized to commence operations with a minimum capital of 3,000,000 pesos and to issue notes up to that amount for every 1,000,000 pesos in stock or on deposit. It was bound by the contract to open for the Mexican treasury, upon request of the government, an account current for advances of specie up to 4,000,000 pesos.[62]

Despite the inability of the Mexican government to borrow money in Europe, the *Diario Oficial* was able to state at the be-

[59] C. F. B., *Eighth Annual Report* (London, 1880), pp. 40–42.

[60] *The Economist* (London), Sept. 18, 1880, p. 1090; *B. and F. State Papers*, Vol. 71, p. 752.

[61] The name of the bank was changed in 1884 to Banco Nacional de México (Morgan's No. 847, MS. Desp. Mex., Vol. 83).

[62] *The Economist* (London), Oct. 1, 1881, pp. 1221–1222.

ginning of the year 1882 that day after day new applications were being made for railway concessions. In July, 1882, an issue of 10,000,000 pesos of bonds of the Mexican National Railway Company, owned by the American capitalists who had two years before obtained a concession for the construction of railways from Mexico City to Laredo, Texas, and Manzanillo, on the Pacific Coast, was offered on the London market.[63] These bonds were secured by a government subsidy of approximately $11,000 for each mile of construction, charged upon a percentage of the customs duties claimed by the London bondholders. A warning was accordingly issued to the public by the Bondholders' Committee. The immediate result was that the bonds were virtually withdrawn from the European market.[64]

A further consequence of the warning issued by the Bondholders' Committee was the arrival in London, in the spring of 1883, of a representative of Mexico with authority to treat for a settlement of the London debt, *ad referendum*. An agreement signed by this representative and the Bondholders' Committee on May 12, 1883, provided for the issue of new three per cent bonds to the amount of £20,000,000. Three-fourths of these bonds were to be used in the conversion of the bonds and coupons of the existing London debt, which then totalled £15,106,450. The remainder of the bonds were to be used in the payment of interest in advance, the conversion of certain local debts, and the meeting of incidental expenses.[65]

The terms of the agreement were generally approved by observers in London. It was believed that there was a better chance than ever before that the interest to become due would actually be paid. The government of Mexico, it was noted, was more stable than it had been since the intervention, and the revenues were increasing rapidly.[66] The most effective influence toward a

[63] U. S. Dept. of Commerce, *Railways of Mexico* (Washington, 1925), pp. 7–8. *Cf.* p. 192, *supra*.

[64] C. F. B., *Tenth Annual Report*, 1882, pp. 48–52; *The Economist*, July 8, 1882, p. 848.

[65] Casasús, *op. cit.*, pp. 447–449.

[66] In 1882–1883 the revenues, which had amounted to only about 20,000,000 pesos three years before, rose to 30,320,222 pesos. The next year they were 32,-

compromise on the part of the government was declared to be that of American capitalists who had "seen their way to profit in Mexico if only credit can be restored." Apart from the reported American projects of annexation, it was clear that "the Americans can make things very disagreeable for any Mexican government without annexation." [67]

THE LAW OF JUNE 14, 1883

Before the agreement *ad referendum* of May 12, 1883, reached Mexico, the Mexican Congress had on June 14, 1883, passed a law providing for the consolidation of the entire public debt of Mexico, the internal as well as the external. The new consolidated debt, it was declared, should have a purely national character and should not be charged upon any specific revenues. The law provided also for the negotiation of a new loan of 20,000,000 pesos. In view of the provisions of the law substantial changes in the agreement were suggested to the Committee of Bondholders.[68]

In October, 1883, the American Minister at Mexico City, Philip H. Morgan, reported that a contract for a loan of $10,000,000 had been signed by the government with representatives of an unnamed New York syndicate. Interest was to be paid in New York at nine per cent per annum. As security for the loan, the government was to deliver to the syndicate orders on specified customs-houses which would be obliged to accept the orders as the equivalent of cash in payment of a percentage of the duties to be determined later. In case the government desired to increase the loan to $20,000,000, as it was authorized to do, the New York syndicate would have the privilege of handling the transaction.[69] This contract does not appear to have been carried out.

The government was in urgent need of the loan of 20,000,000

808,265 pesos. In 1884–1885 they reached the high point of 37,442,625 pesos. *Anuario Estadistico* (Mexico, 1895), Año II, No. 2, p. 16.

[67] *The Economist*, May 26, 1883.

[68] Casasús, *op. cit.*, pp. 449–451.

[69] Morgan's No. 705, Oct. 16, 1883, MS. Desp. Mex., Vol. 80.

pesos authorized in the law of June 14. The increase of revenues, which in the fiscal year just ended had reached a total of over 30,000,000 pesos, was not sufficient to obviate a deficit. The expenditures for the fiscal year 1883–1884 amounted to more than 37,500,000 pesos as against revenues of less than 33,000,000 pesos.[70] Although in the autumn of 1883 a deficit of nearly 5,000,000 pesos was clearly foreseen, the government refused to combine the proposed loan with the conversion operation provided for in the agreement of May 12. In justification of its stand it declared that the issue of additional bonds in order to obtain a loan simultaneously with the conversion would depress the market price of the entire issue; that inasmuch as the bonds to be issued under the agreement of May 12 were to bear only three per cent interest and to be redeemable at half their face value, the government could not hope to obtain more than 5,000,000 pesos in exchange for additional bonds issued on the same terms to the nominal amount of 20,000,000 pesos; that there was no peculiar appropriateness in the combination of the two operations; and that the combination of these operations might lay the government open to the reproach of having sought to promote a settlement of the debt question in order to raise money — "an idea that never entered into its head."[71]

The efforts of the government to obtain the loan of 20,000,000 pesos were renewed in Paris in the spring of 1884. Although it appeared likely in April that these efforts would result in an advance of half the sum desired to President González[72] and an advance of the remaining half to his successor, the negotiations finally came to nothing.[73]

A Spanish Protest

The provision of the law of June 14 that the entire debt of the republic should have an exclusively Mexican character, and should not be charged upon any of the national revenues, was

[70] *Anuario Estadistico, sup. cit., loc. cit.*

[71] *The Economist,* Jan. 5, 1884, p. 9; Casasús, *op. cit.,* pp. 457–458.

[72] Elected Sept. 25, 1880, for a term of four years beginning Dec. 1, 1880.

[73] *The Economist,* April 18, 1884, pp. 482–483; Casasús, *op. cit.,* p. 456.

the occasion of an emphatic protest by the Minister of Spain at Mexico City. This provision, the Minister declared, was at variance with a stipulation in the Spanish-Mexican convention of November 12, 1853,[74] according to which the assignment of duties made for the benefit of bondholders of that convention could not be altered without the express and formal consent of Spain.

In replying to the Spanish Minister, the Minister of Foreign Affairs declared that the convention of November 12, 1853, had been terminated by the state of war which President Juárez and his successors had regarded as resulting from the support given by Spain to the French intervention and to the government of Maximilian. President González had instructed him to say, without intending the least bravado, but simply for the purpose of exactly defining his position, in the interest of the two nations, that the Mexican government maintained and would maintain that that convention no longer existed. The President was determined to accept any situation, no matter what, rather than consent to put the republic back twenty years to the position which it had occupied in 1861.[75]

The correspondence was believed by the Minister of the United States to be more theoretical than practical, since nearly all the bonds in question were held by Mexican citizens and not by Spaniards.[76]

Resumption of Diplomatic Relations with Great Britain

The bondholders of the English convention debt were more fortunate than those of the Spanish convention debt and of the debt contracted in London. The payment of the amounts due to the first-mentioned group was provided for in an agreement concluded between Special Commissioners of Mexico and Great Britain on August 6, 1884, as the result of official negotiations initiated by Earl Granville in April, 1883. Unofficial communications exchanged at the beginning of the year 1883, with a view to establishing a basis for the resumption of diplomatic relations

[74] *Cf.* p. 103, *supra.*

[75] Morgan's No. 665, July 10, 1883, *For. Rel. U. S.*, 1883, p. 663.

[76] *Ibid.*

between the two countries, had been fruitless because of "the difficulty anticipated in the settlement of certain financial questions long pending." The Mexican government adhering to its refusal to take the initiative in official negotiations for the resumption of relations, the British government had at last decided "to take a first step" and proposed "that the two Governments should simultaneously accredit Special Envoys to London and Mexico, respectively, who should be charged with the duty of conducting the negotiations on behalf of their Governments."

In response to this overture Ignacio Mariscal, the Mexican Minister of Foreign Affairs, had stated on May 18, 1883:

> The President of the Republic, desirous of removing every obstacle to the cultivation of cordial relations with Great Britain, has requested from Congress, through the medium of the Financial Department, an authorization for the general adjustment of the public debt. As soon as he obtains it, he proposes to make with the English creditors fair and equitable arrangements, which, resting not only on good faith but on the capacity of the public Treasury to fulfil them, will have a yet more solid basis than the Conventions formerly in force.[77]

The agreement of August 6, 1884, was signed by Mariscal and Sir Spenser St. John, as Special Commissioners in behalf of their respective governments. It provided for the reëstablishment of normal diplomatic relations between the two governments, as well as for the payment of the amounts due to the bondholders of the English convention debt and to various holders of pecuniary claims. It was definitely understood, however, that the agreement did not embrace the question of the London debt. This question the Mexican government was "desirous of settling by direct negotiations with the bondholders." In a note addressed to Mariscal on the date of the signature of the "preliminaries," St. John stated that his government would not in the future invoke in support of the claims of British subjects any treaty, convention, pact, or agreement between the two countries for the time anterior to the date of the exchange of the ratifications of the agreement.

The agreement of August 6, 1884, having been approved by

[77] *Parliamentary Session Papers* (Great Britain), LXXXVII, 1884, "Papers respecting the renewal of diplomatic relations with Mexico."

the two governments before it was signed by the Commissioners, normal diplomatic relations between Mexico and Great Britain were resumed at once.[78]

The Noetzlin Agreement

In September, 1884, the Committee of Bondholders at London concluded with Edward Noetzlin, head of the Banco Nacional de México, acting for the Mexican government, an agreement which it was thought could not fail to be ratified by the Congress. Before signing this agreement the Committee took care not only to verify the authenticity and examine the scope of Noetzlin's powers but also to ascertain that the President-Elect, General Díaz, acquiesced in the grant of such powers and in the nature of the accompanying instructions. The agreement was nevertheless rejected by the Congress, on the ground that it was contrary to the provisions of the law of June 14, 1883.[79]

The agreement was indeed obviously in conflict with the law of June 14, 1883, in that it authorized a pledge of ten per cent of all the import duties for the service of the London debt. It was charged, moreover, in Mexican periodicals and in the Mexican Congress, that the rate of conversion of the old bonds was unduly high and that the agreement as a whole was humiliating to the dignity of the nation. The rejection of the agreement was attributed in part to the opposition of indignant citizens, including many students, who took possession of the lobbies of Congress and overwhelmed the complacent majority with an avalanche of groans and hisses.[80]

The rejection of the agreement was not greatly regretted by certain of the bondholders, especially a group of Dutch investors who had acquired a small quantity of the bonds of the London debt and who had protested against the agreement at the time when it was signed. The agreement was also criticized by *The*

[78] *Parliamentary Session Papers* (Great Britain), LXXXVII, 1884, "Papers respecting the renewal of diplomatic relations with Mexico."

[79] Casasús, *op. cit.*, pp. 458–468.

[80] *Ibid.;* Minister Jackson's confidential despatch of August 31, 1885, MS. Desp. Mex., Vol. 86; *B. and F. State Papers,* Vol. 76, pp. 856–859.

Economist of London, which believed that it entailed sacrifices for the bondholders but secured no real guarantee in their favor. But for the want of cohesion among the vast body of bondholders, said *The Economist*, some distinct expression would have been given to the growing feeling against the ready acceptance of arrangements of this kind. The principle on which the Committee of Mexican Bondholders worked was declared to be unethical, since the provision for compensating the Committee with a percentage of the amount obtained from Mexico made it to the interest of the Committee to effect some kind of settlement in any case, irrespective of the sacrifices that might be required of the bondholders.[81]

The Dublán Conversion

The rejection of the Noetzlin agreement of September, 1884, had naturally a damaging effect upon Mexican credit in London. This effect was the more pronounced because that agreement was the result of the direct negotiations which Mariscal had declared it to be the intention of his government to hold with the bondholders. The government, understanding the position in which it had been placed by the rejection of the agreement, "did not think of sending new agents nor of initiating new negotiations, which it supposed would be fruitless, but determined to act as it had done in 1850, with the general applause of the creditors, laying down the bases on which it believed it could fulfil the obligations of the republic provided that such bases were accepted freely and spontaneously by those interested."[82]

Manuel Dublán, who became Minister of Finance at the beginning of Díaz's second term as President, found the financial plight of the government "in every respect unbearable."[83] According to his *Memoria* of October, 1885,[84] 94.87 per cent of the revenues of the customs-houses of Tampico and Matamoros were pledged for various internal obligations (the pledges in favor of

[81] *The Economist*, September 27, 1884, p. 1164.

[82] Casasús, *op. cit.*, p. 469.

[83] Macedo, *op. cit.*, p. 439.

[84] As quoted by Macedo, *op. cit.*, *loc. cit.*

foreign bondholders being still ignored); 87.87 per cent of the customs revenues at Veracruz, Laredo, and Mier y Camargo, and 87.37 per cent of all the other customs revenues were similarly pledged. The entire taxes of the Federal District of Mexico and the entire net proceeds of the National Lottery were payable to the Banco Nacional de México on account of loans. Approximately 100,000 pesos a year was due on account of advances made by another bank. The government mints, which were leased to private companies, were subject to debts aggregating nearly 2,500,000 pesos, on which interest had to be paid, for the most part at 6 per cent per annum. With a deficit of 23,000,000 pesos at the outset of his service as Minister, and with the revenues 6,000,000 pesos less than in the preceding year, Dublán was of the opinion that the difficulties of the situation could not be exaggerated.

One of his first official acts, continued the Minister in his *Memoria,* was the conclusion of an arrangement with the Banco Nacional under which the greater part of the indebtedness to that institution was paid and the pledges of customs revenues in favor of the bank, in its own behalf or as agent for other creditors of the government, including railways entitled to subsidies and certain contractors for port works, were reduced from 45 to 15 per cent of those revenues. Numerous administrative changes were made by Dublán with a view to increasing the revenues and effecting economies, but a more radical solution of the difficulties was evidently imperative.

Although the administration, through the arrangement with the Banco Nacional and through various economies, was able to meet ordinary payments and claims, its situation was declared by President Díaz to be far from easy or satisfactory. So long as no provision was made for the payment of the floating and consolidated debts it would clearly be quite impossible to obtain the foreign capital so much needed for the development of different enterprises in the country. The President therefore appointed a Commission to draw up a plan for the settlement of the debt, according to the bases determined by the law of June 14, 1883. The plan drawn up by this Commission was embodied in two decrees issued by the President, under special powers from the Congress, on June 22, 1885.[85]

By one of these decrees provision was made for the issue of treasury bonds, bearing 6 per cent interest per annum, to be exchanged "for unpaid orders and for credits of the floating debt" contracted from July 1, 1882, to June 30, 1885. By the other and much more important decree, the salaries of all public officials were greatly reduced, all pledges of the public revenues were suspended, and provision was made for the issue of a new "Consolidated Debt of the United Mexican States" to replace all obligations arising against the government, under bonds or otherwise, prior to July 1, 1882. The new consolidated debt was to embrace, among others, the following obligations:[86]

1. The bonds of the debt contracted in London and converted under the law of October 14, 1850.[87]

2. The 3 per cent bonds authorized by the law of November 30, 1850, and issued up to December 17, 1857; and those subsequently issued, provided they bear the annotation prescribed in the order of January 17, 1861.[88]

3. The bonds of the abrogated English Convention of December 4, 1851.[89]

4. The bonds of the abrogated Spanish Conventions of December 6, 1851, and November 12, 1853.[90]

[85] *The Consolidation and Conversion of the Mexican National Debt* (Mexico, 1885), pp. 11–27; Ortiz de Montellano, *op. cit.*, pp. 553–574.

[86] Enumerated in Article 16 of the law. Details regarding most of the other obligations enumerated in this article may be found in Romero, *Memoria, sup. cit.*, pp. 357, 366, 392, 532–534, 575, 579, 731, 732; *Memoria de Hacienda*, 1868–1869, pp. 506–508; *Legislación Mexicana*, Vol. IX, p. 17; Report of Comisión para formar un proyecto de ley para el arreglo de la deuda pública (Mexico, 1881), pp. 62–84.

[87] *Supra*, p. 98. Interest due and unpaid on the London debt from July 1, 1854, to date was to be "the subject of special arrangement with the creditors." (*Cf.* p. 207, *infra.*)

[88] *Supra*, pp. 99–100; Romero, *Memoria, sup. cit.*, p. 533. The order of January 17, 1861, authorized the treasurer general to validate such bonds as he found to have been issued by the "reactionary" government in satisfaction of legitimate claims.

[89] *Supra*, pp. 101, 174.

[90] *Supra*, pp. 102, 103, 174.

5. The bonds issued at San Luis Potosí in November, 1863.[91]

6. The bonds issued at San Carlos de Tamaulipas on July 4, 1865, with the intervention of the Mexican Legation at Washington.[92]

7. The bonds and securities of different classes, issued prior to the law of November 30, 1850, and which, in virtue of that law, remained deferred; the securities of the same class which were not presented, accepted, and adjusted; and the securities which were issued before the law of November 30, 1850, and which were not included therein.[93]

8. The balances of salaries, pensions, and other unsettled balances of the budget of expenses up to June 30, 1882, provided that the persons entitled to such balances be not comprehended in article 7 of the law of October 13, 1870.[94]

9. Claims against the Treasury arising from nationalized property.

10. Claims allowed and those pending before the judicial courts or in any way pending decision by the Executive, as soon as they may be settled and allowed, according to law.

11. Claims originating from the furnishing of supplies to the army, from seizures of property, from forced loans, or from any other act imposing a debt upon the Nation's Exchequer, and, in general, all other claims once settled according to law.

It was specifically provided that the consolidated debt would not include obligations alleged to have been incurred by the *de facto* governments which had existed in Mexico City from December 17, 1857, to December 24, 1860, and from June 1, 1863, to June 21, 1867.

Of the obligations to be included in the consolidated debt all were to be admitted at par with the exception of obligations for

[91] Bonds of the internal debt to the amount of 1,500,000 pesos were issued while the government of Juárez was situated at San Luis Potosí. All but 72,000 pesos of these bonds had been amortized before the end of 1868. Romero, *Memoria, sup. cit.*, pp. 589, 737.

[92] *Supra*, pp. 162, 195.

[93] *Supra*, p. 98. *Cf.* Romero, *Memoria, sup. cit.*, p. 340.

[94] By the law mentioned, deserters from the military service and persons guilty of treasonable or seditious acts were granted amnesty but were denied the right to present claims against the treasury. *Diario Oficial*, Vol. IV, No. 287.

interest, which were to be the subject of special arrangements between the government and its creditors, and with the further exception of the "unconsolidated liabilities pertaining to the debt contracted in London," which were to be converted into bonds of the new issue at 20 per cent of their face value.[95]

All bonds of the consolidated debt were to bear one per cent interest in 1886; 1.5 per cent in 1887; 2 per cent in 1888; 2.5 per cent in 1889; and 3 per cent in subsequent years. Payments of interest were to be made by the Banco Nacional de México out of customs duties received by the bank directly from the customs-house at Veracruz. Bonds and coupons were to be expressed in American and English as well as in Mexican money, and interest was to be payable in New York and London as well as in Mexico. The mention of foreign money in the bonds and the designation of places outside the republic for payment of interest were, however, declared to have "no other object than to respect the agreements on which certain credits are based." The consolidated debt was thus to be regarded as of "essentially Mexican character," that is, as an internal debt.

The law of June 22, 1885, although declared by President Díaz to have been a necessary measure in overcoming the financial difficulties of the government, was denounced by many persons in Mexico, including some of those interested in the railways, as the result of pecuniary corruption in high quarters, dexterously played upon by English diplomacy. It was rumored that former President González and his brother-in-law, Ramón Fernández, Minister to France, were the owners of some 30 to 50 per cent of the entire English debt, by which was meant presumably the convention debt, and it was noted that there had been of late a striking intimacy between the British chargé d'affaires on the one side and the Mexican Ministers of the Interior and of Foreign Affairs on the other.[96]

The law was regarded by the bondholders at London as open to several objections. At a meeting on September 9, 1885, the

[95] Ortiz de Montellano, *op. cit.*, table following p. 125; *Memoria de Hacienda*, 1886–1887, pp. 72–74. *Cf.* p. 209, *infra*.

[96] Jackson's confidential despatch of August 31, 1885, MS. Desp. Mex., Vol. 86.

bondholders decided to send a special representative to Mexico to discuss modifications of the law.[97] The decision was revoked upon the receipt of an intimation from the Mexican Minister at London that his government preferred that the negotiations be conducted in that city. The negotiations which followed between the Bondholders' Committee and General Mena, Mexican Minister to Germany, acting as financial agent of Mexico in London, led to the signature of an agreement on June 23, 1886.

By this agreement it was provided that the bonds issued by Maximilian in 1864 to the amount of £4,864,800, in satisfaction of arrears of interest from July 1, 1854, to July 1, 1863, should be exchanged for new 3 per cent bonds at 50 per cent of their face value. Interest due since July 1, 1866, amounting to £6,144,990, was to be converted into new bonds at 15 per cent. The bonds of 1851 were to be submitted for stamping, after which interest would be paid on them as provided in the law of June 22, 1885, but the date for their exchange for bonds of the new issue was left to be determined by the Mexican government. The government reserved also, up to December 31, 1890, the right to purchase at the market price or to redeem by drawings at 40 per cent of their face value bonds of the issue of 1851 or of the new issue.[98]

The agreement of June 23 was accepted by the bondholders on June 30 and approved by President Díaz on July 15.[99] Both houses of the Mexican Congress subsequently passed resolutions recording their satisfaction at the completion of an arrangement of such vital importance to the credit of the republic, and President Díaz informed the Congress that by this agreement, made in pursuance of the law of June 22, 1885, the good name of the republic had been upheld and its credit established abroad.[100]

By the end of August, 1888, when the right of conversion finally expired, approximately 99 per cent of the existing securities of the London debt and of the English convention debt had been exchanged for new bonds of the internal consolidated debt

[97] C. F. B., *Thirteenth Annual Report*, 1885, pp. 99–105.

[98] *Memoria de Hacienda*, 1886–1887, pp. 72–74.

[99] *Ibid.*, p. 70.

[100] C. F. B., *Fourteenth Annual Report*, 1886, pp. 84–92.

or, in the case of the bonds of 1851, had been impressed with a stamp that made the exchange dependent on the discretion of the Mexican government. The holders of securities not presented for exchange or stamping were not considered to have forfeited their rights to the principal amounts of their securities, but, under the law of June 22, 1885, they were to receive no interest "until upon the termination of the general conversion, the manner of treating their respective claims may be declared." Provision for the redemption of the securities withheld at this time was ultimately made by a decree of September 6, 1894.[101]

The results of the conversion of securities of the London debt and of the English convention debt, as of September 10, 1888, are shown in the following table: [102]

Items of Debt Converted	Percentage Rate of Conversion	Old Securities Existing	New Bonds Issued	Economies Obtained (Subject to slight reduction after eventual re demption of securities withheld)
5 per cent deferred bonds of 1837	20	£ 434,350	£ 73,320	£ 361,030
5 per cent active bonds of 1843	29	200,000	57,913	142,087
5 per cent active bonds of 1846	54½	21,492	11,713	9,779
Certificates of 1851	40	180,000	54,100	125,899
4 per cent bonds of 1864	50	4,864,800	2,395,972	2,468,828
Certificates of 1866	20	75,532	7,535	67,997
Interest on 1851 bonds, 1866–1886	15	6,144,900	912,632	5,232,268
Bonds and coupons of English convention debt [a]	[a]	1,180,456	871,887	308,569
Totals		£13,101,530	£4,385,073	£8,716,457

[a] Under agreements with the bondholders on October 15 and December 30, 1886, the English convention bonds of 1843 (amounting to 870,000 pesos) were to be converted at 20 per cent of their face value, and the remaining bonds of the English convention debt (approximately 2,600,000 pesos), with arrears of interest amounting to more than 2,000,000 pesos, were to be converted at 150 per cent of the face value of the bonds. *Memoria de Hacienda*, 1886–1887, p. XLIII.

The bonds of the Spanish convention debts, which were among the securities scheduled for conversion in the law of June 22, 1885,[103] were, like the bonds of the English debt of the same character, the subject of a special agreement with representatives

[101] See p. 223, *infra.*

[102] The table is based on a combination of figures given, respectively, in C. F. B., *Sixteenth Annual Report*, 1888, p. 114, and in Dublán, *Informe . . . sobre el emprestito contratado en Europa de £10,500,000* (Mexico, 1888), p. 42.

[103] *Cf.* p. 205, *supra.*

of the bondholders. By this agreement, which was concluded on May 1, 1890, it was provided that the bonds and overdue coupons of the two Spanish convention debts, amounting to more than 8,500,000 pesos,[104] should be exchanged for bonds of the 3 per cent consolidated debt at 145 per cent of the face value of the Spanish bonds. As the Spanish bonds outstanding were estimated at 3,860,285 pesos,[105] the new bonds required for the conversion would amount to approximately 5,600,000 pesos, and the "economy" anticipated, in addition to the reduction of the rate of interest from 6 to 3 per cent, would be approximately 3,000,000 pesos. The bonds and coupons of the Spanish convention debts converted up to June 30, 1890, totalled 4,791,401 pesos.[106]

Kind of Obligation Converted	Capital	Interest	Total
Tobacco bonds	P 16,816	P 32	P 16,848
Copper bonds	229,965	....	229,965
Cotton bonds	221,354	....	221,354
5 per cent bonds	335,851	860,022	1,195,873
3 per cent bonds	3,689,226	3,570,078	7,259,304
3 per cent certificates	132,157	22,491	154,648
"Redemption certificates"	1,422,365	....	1,422,365
Nationalization certificates	207,764	....	207,764
Bonds and certificates of various kinds	3,659,637	1,573,133	5,232,770
"Ministraciones"	4,153,442	560,200	4,713,642
Unconverted credits	1,797,856	1,458,943	3,256,799
Balances of salaries	7,536,126	....	7,536,126
Totals	P23,402,559	P8,044,899	P31,447,458

While the conversion of various items of the foreign debt was pending or in progress, Minister Dublán was able to make considerable headway with the conversion of the numerous classes of internal obligations enumerated in the law of June 22, 1885. Up to June 30, 1890, more than 31,000,000 pesos of these obliga-

104 *Cf.* Ortiz de Montellano, *op. cit.*, table following p. 125.

105 *Ibid.*

106 C. F. B., *Eighteenth Annual Report*, 1890, p. 138, quoting statement of Mexican Treasury.

tions, including some 8,000,000 pesos for interest, had been converted at par into bonds of the new consolidated 3 per cent debt. The variety of the obligations thus converted is indicated in the table on page 210.[107]

The conversion (of the items of the internal debt included in the law of June 22, 1885,) had not been completed as late as September 6, 1894, when a new law, to be fully discussed in the next chapter, was found to be necessary.[108]

[107] Adapted from the statement of the Mexican Treasury quoted in C. F. B., *Eighteenth Annual Report*, 1890, pp. 138–139.

[108] *Cf*. pp. 221–226, *infra*.

CHAPTER VII

GROWTH OF THE FOREIGN DEBT (1888–1914)

The Loan of 1888

The Dublán conversion, as already noted, did not include the internal obligations, known as the floating debt, arising subsequent to June 30, 1882. These obligations it was considered essential to the credit of the government to meet in cash with the least possible delay. Funds to the extent of nearly £6,000,000 would also be required before the end of the year 1890 in order that the London bonds of 1851 and the new bonds issued under the agreements of 1886 might be redeemed, in accordance with the option reserved, at 40 per cent of their face value. In view of the favorable impression that had been made abroad by the definite moves toward the settlement of the foreign debt, and in view of the comparative scarcity of capital in Mexico available for loans to the government, it was deemed advantageous, even before the conversion of the existing foreign debt had been completed, to seek a new loan abroad. A law authorizing the negotiation of such a loan was passed by the Mexican Congress on December 13, 1887. The nominal amount of the loan, it was provided, should be not more than £10,500,000; the rate of interest should not exceed 6 per cent per annum; and not less than 70 per cent of the nominal amount should be obtained in cash.[1]

The contract for the new loan was signed at Berlin on March 24, 1888. The bankers who undertook to raise the loan were S. Bleichroeder of Berlin, Antony Gibbs and Sons of London, and the Banco Nacional de México. The interest rate agreed upon was 6 per cent. The sinking fund, payable in 1893 and each year thereafter until the redemption of the loan, was fixed

[1] *Memoria de Hacienda,* 1887–1888, p. 88.

at one-half of one per cent of the bonds issued. The guarantees stipulated were one-fifth of the customs revenues of the republic and the whole of the net proceeds of the revenues of the Federal District. The bankers' allowance for the expenses of the issue was 1.25 per cent of the amount involved. A commission of one-fourth of one per cent was to be allowed on the future payment of coupons and redemption of bonds. It was agreed that bonds to the amount of £3,700,000 should be issued immediately at 70 per cent of their face value and that up to July 1, 1889, the bankers should have the option to purchase the remainder of the bonds authorized at 86.5 per cent. It was further stipulated that the government should have the right to increase the sinking fund or to redeem all outstanding bonds of the loan at par at any time after the end of the year 1898.[2]

The bonds for £3,700,000 were offered to the public simultaneously at Berlin, London, and Amsterdam. They were more than twenty times oversubscribed. An important factor in their popularity was the high standing of the bankers who participated in the transaction. An equally important factor was declared to be the prosperous condition and excellent prospects of Mexico, where, it was generally believed, a new era had dawned.[3]

The amount received by the Mexican government for the bonds of this first issue was £2,506,949. Of this amount £315,000 was deposited with Bleichroeder for interest in advance. £195,-278 was used in the redemption of certain bonds of the Ferrocarril Interoceanico de Tehuantepec, which had been acquired by the government in 1881 after the forfeiture of the concessions of the Tehuantepec Railroad Company[4] in 1878 and after the lapse of a further concession granted in the same year for the construction of a railway across the Isthmus.[5] The remainder of the proceeds of the first issue of the Bleichroeder loan, approximately £2,000,000, was used toward the retirement of the floating debt.[6]

[2] *Ibid.*, pp. lx–lxvii.

[3] *The Bullionist*, London, March 31, 1888.

[4] *Cf.* p. 185, *supra*.

[5] *Cf.* U. S. Dept. of Commerce, *op. cit.*, p. 38.

[6] *Memoria de Hacienda*, 1889–1890, pp. xviii, xix.

The bonds for the remaining £6,800,000 of the loan were issued periodically to the contracting bankers, at 85 per cent of their face value,[7] in exchange for bonds of the London debt and bonds of the Dublán conversion of the nominal value of £14,450,000 for which the bankers had paid the holders £5,780,000 in cash. Of the acknowledged obligations of the foreign debt there remained outstanding only the Spanish convention debts, with a capital of 3,860,000 pesos and arrears of interest amounting, on June 30, 1889, to approximately 4,250,000 pesos.[8] The acknowledged foreign debt had thus been reduced in the space of three years from over £23,000,000 to approximately £12,000,000. Of this £12,000,000, moreover, nearly £2,000,000 represented new funds received from abroad under the loan of 1888. The details as to the improvement of the position of the government in relation to the foreign debt, through the Dublán conversion and the Bleichroeder loan up to June 30, 1889, are indicated in the following table:[9]

		(*In pounds sterling*)
The foreign debt at the end of 1885		
Bonds of 1851 (3 per cent)		10,241,650
Arrears of interest on bonds of 1851 from 1854 to 1863 and from 1866 to 1885 (ignoring capitalization bonds of 1864)		8,500,569
Various small issues of bonds and certificates in connection with the London debt (3 per cent)		1,910,607
English convention debt (6 per cent)		1,180,476
capital	549,189	
arrears of interest	631,287	
Spanish convention debts (6 per cent)		1,461,120
capital	772,057	
arrears of interest	689,063	
Total		23,294,422

[7] The purchase price of the bonds for £6,800,000 had been fixed in the contract at 86.5, but it was deemed equitable to modify the contract in favor of the bankers. *Cf. Memoria de Hacienda,* 1888–1889, p. xxxii.

[8] *Cf.* p. 210, *supra,* as to eventual settlement regarding these debts.

[9] For details regarding the reduction of the relatively insignificant Carbajal-Corlies debt, see p. 195, *supra.*

	(*In pounds sterling*)
The foreign debt on June 30, 1889	
Bleichroeder bonds of 1888 (6 per cent)	10,500,000
Spanish convention debts (6 per cent)	1,600,000
Total	12,100,000

The Tehuantepec Railway Loan of 1889

The prominent part taken by German capital in the transaction of 1888 encouraged some persons to proclaim the approach of an increase of commercial relations between Germany and Mexico. Others doubted whether the trade between the two countries would admit of any rapid or important growth. German firms in Mexico, it was said, already had a sort of monopoly of the foreign trade, and there was believed to be little room for development unless the circle of consumers were increased by immigration from the United States and elsewhere.[10]

The aid of German capital was again invoked by the Mexican government at the beginning of the year 1889. The loan which was then obtained was for the completion of the government-owned National Railway of the Isthmus of Tehuantepec, which had been authorized in May, 1882.[11] The contract for the loan was made in October, 1888, between the government and Colonel Edward MacMurdo, a resident of London. It was approved by Congress and declared in effect in December, 1888. It was amended in certain respects a year later.

Under the contract of 1888 and the amending contract of 1889, bonds were to be issued to the amount of £2,700,000 or 55,080,000 Imperial German marks, bearing 5 per cent interest from January 1, 1889. They were secured by a mortgage of the railway and its branches, an assignment of one-half the gross revenues of the railway, and a pledge of the government to supply any deficiency from other revenues. They were to be redeemed at par by semi-annual drawings in equal amounts over a period of fifty years beginning July 1, 1899. Interest was made payable

[10] *The Economist,* March 31, 1888, pp. 412–413.
[11] *Cf.* pp. 185, 213, *supra.*

in London by the house of Seligmann Brothers or in Berlin by the Dresdner Bank.[12]

The Tehuantepec bonds were offered publicly in Berlin and London. They were sold at approximately 77.5 per cent of their face value.[13]

" Dark Clouds "

During the year 1889, according to the report of the Corporation of Foreign Bondholders for that year,[14] the sound fiscal policy inaugurated by President Díaz [15] continued, with the active coöperation of Minister of Finance Dublán. The result was shown in the increase of the revenues, the enhancement of the public credit, and the introduction of foreign capital, principally British, for the development of the natural resources of the republic. The one " dark cloud " in the immediate future of Mexican finance, the Corporation believed, was the yearly increasing railway subsidies, which were thought to be absorbing a disproportionate part of the national revenues.[16]

Another dark cloud, which was soon dissipated, was raised by a rumor widely circulated in October, 1889, to the effect that the French government intended to press upon Mexico the claims of French nationals for payment of the loans obtained by Maximilian in 1864 and in 1865. Approximately one-half of the amount invested by French nationals had been repaid to the

[12] *Ferrocarril Nacional del Istmo de Tehuantepec, contrato celebrado entre el Ciudadano General Carlos Pacheco, Secretario de Estado y del Despacho de Fomento en representación del Ejecutivo de la Unión, y el Señor Coronel Edward Mac-Murdo,* etc. (Mexico, 1888).

[13] C. F. B. *Fifty-fifth Annual Report,* 1927, p. 295.

[14] Pages 104–106.

[15] Díaz had been reëlected for a term of four years beginning December 1, 1888.

[16] Twenty-three per cent of the customs revenues had been assigned for payment of subsidies, as follows: to the Central Railway 8 per cent, to the Mexican National and the Mexican Railways 6 per cent each, and to the Interoceanic 3 per cent. During the fiscal year 1889–1890 subsidies amounting to more than 1,000,000 pesos, not charged upon the customs revenues, were paid to the railways. Dublán, *Cuenta . . . del uso . . . de la autorización . . . para consolidar y convertir las deudas ferrocarriles* (Mexico, 1891); *Cuenta del Tesoro Federal,* 1889–1890, pp. 507–508.

investors by the French government, shortly after the fall of Maximilian. The investors had at that time renounced all further claims against their own government and had received from it, in exchange for their bonds, certificates which were called "petits bleus." Subsequently, in 1880, when diplomatic relations were reëstablished between France and Mexico, the French government had made a total renunciation of claims for payment of the Mexican debt. The holders of the "petits bleus" had, nevertheless, recently formed an association for pressing their claims upon the Mexican government. To quiet the rumor that the claims of this association would be supported by France, the French Minister, under telegraphic instructions from his government, presented to the Mexican government a formal document ratifying in every respect the previous renunciation of claims.[17]

The "dark cloud" which had been descried by the Corporation of Foreign Bondholders on the future of Mexican finance became a "sword of Damocles" in a report submitted to the British Foreign Office at the beginning of the year 1890 by Sir Francis Denys, Secretary of the British Legation at Mexico City. It was "imperative," said Sir Francis, for the Mexican government to find a way to meet the liabilities which it had assumed toward the railways. The danger had by this time been appreciated by the government itself, and consideration was being given to the possibility of obtaining a new loan in order to release the customs revenues assigned for the payment of the subsidies to the Mexican, the Mexican National, the Central, and the Interoceanic Railways.[18]

The Railway Subvention Loan of 1890

On July 15, 1890, two New York capitalists, Henry Seligman and Jesse W. Lillienthal, were reported by the American Minister, Thomas Ryan, to have been negotiating with the Mexican government with a view to a loan of 30,000,000 pesos for the redemption of the railway subsidies. Although the government had denied

[17] *The Economist*, Sept. 28, 1889; Chargé Whitehouse's No. 142, Oct. 12, 1889, MS. Desp. Mex., Vol. 100. *Cf.* pp. 173, 196, *supra*.

[18] *The Economist*, February 8 and May 10, 1890, pp. 172, 585, 586.

that any arrangements had been consummated, the Minister thought it probable that the American negotiators had reached a tacit understanding with the government. They appeared, he said, to have encountered sharp competition from " Breichloder " (sic) of Berlin and the Spanish house of Murrieta and Company of Paris. It was believed that a recent bear movement against the Bleichroeder bonds of 1888, which had fallen from 99 to 93.75, had been designed to drive the Americans out of the contest, but it did not seem to have had that effect.[19]

That Ryan was unduly sanguine regarding the outcome of the negotiations of Seligman and Lillienthal was indicated by the announcement, a month later, that the Mexican government had arranged with the firm of Bleichroeder for the issue of the desired new loan.[20]

The new loan, in the nominal amount of £6,000,000, was issued in September at Berlin, London, and Amsterdam. The rate of interest was 6 per cent, payable in Berlin at the house of Bleichroeder, in London at Antony Gibbs and Sons', in Amsterdam at Lippman, Rosenthal and Company's, and in Paris at the Comptoir National d'Escompte.[21] The price of sale was 88.75, from which one per cent was to be deducted for expenses. The customs revenues assigned as security were reduced to 12 per cent instead of the 23 per cent previously assigned for payment of the railway subsidies.[22] It was pointed out by *The Economist*, of London,[23] that the railways should welcome the redemption of subsidies with the cash proceeds of the loan, since they would receive capital needed for development and would no longer be obliged to maintain agencies for the sale of the customs certificates in which the subsidies had been paid. Only two of the railways, however, considered it to be to their interest to give up their assignments of customs duties. These were the Mexican and the Central, which held assignments of 14 per cent of the

[19] Personal letter to Secretary Blaine, March 5, 1890, MS. Desp. Mex., Vol. 104.

[20] *The Economist*, August 16, 1890, p. 1052.

[21] Dublán, *op. cit.*

[22] C. F. B., *Eighteenth Annual Report*, 1890, pp. 129–133.

[23] August 16, 1890.

customs revenues. The National and the Interoceanic, which held assignments of 9 per cent of the customs revenues, declined to relinquish them. The funds thus left at the disposal of the government were applied to the liquidation of its account with the Banco Nacional.[24]

Project for a Further Loan

The railway subvention loan had not been closed before the government began considering the flotation of another loan. This loan, according to information communicated to Secretary of State Blaine by Minister Ryan on September 23, 1890,[25] was to be for the nominal amount of £60,000,000 and was to be applied to the consolidation of the entire debt and to certain other objects. Ryan understood that a committee representing Paris and London banks was interested in making this loan and had proposed to make a deposit of £6,000,000 as evidence of good faith. The Bleichroeders, however, were also anxious to handle the loan, and as they were in favor with the Mexican Minister of Finance they had a well-founded hope of success. As the bankers had made a net profit of $1,500,000 on the loan recently brought out and $5,000,000 on the loan of 1888, the loan under consideration would be a bonanza for the syndicate which obtained it. A factor in the negotiations, added Ryan, was the conviction that the interests of the United States made the American government "surety for the public peace" of Mexico.

The Bank Credit of 1892

The project reported by Ryan in 1890 does not appear to have been developed further. Two years later, in August, 1892, Ryan received information which led him to believe that a new loan had been negotiated with the Mexican government. Upon inquiring at the Ministry of Foreign Affairs, he was told that there had been a financial operation which was "not properly a loan" but rather a credit of £600,000 at 7 per cent interest ob-

[24] *Memoria de Hacienda*, 1888–1890, p. 224; Dublán, *op. cit.*

[25] Personal letter, MS. Desp. Mex., Vol. 106.

tained through the Banco Nacional de México and certain European houses without an issue of bonds.[26] Recourse to this operation was attributed by the Mexican *Financial Review* [27] partly to the low price of silver, which had caused such a rise in exchange as to increase largely the sum in Mexican money payable as interest in gold on the foreign debt.[28]

The Public Debt in 1893

The external bonds of Mexico outstanding in 1893, exclusive of a new issue authorized and partly made in that year,[29] were as follows: [30]

	(*In pounds sterling*)
6 per cent loan of 1888	10,443,280
5 per cent Tehuantepec Railway loan of 1889	2,700,000
6 per cent Railway subvention loan of 1890	5,983,800
Total	19,127,080

[26] Ryan's No. 1057, August 30, 1892, MS. Desp. Mex., Vol. 113.

[27] Quoted in *The Economist*, Oct. 15, 1892, pp. 1300–1301. For a detailed summary of the financial situation at this time, see Macedo, *op. cit.*, pp. 449–453.

[28] Since the fiscal year 1874–1875, when the bullion price of the Mexican peso in London was 49.10 pence, the peso had declined as follows (files of *The Economist*, London, for the years mentioned):

1875–1876	47.12
1880–1881	44.58
1885–1886	40.81
1890–1891	40.75
1891–1892	36.84
1892–1893	32.90

The decline continued until 1905–1906 as follows (files of *The Economist*, *The South American Journal*, and *The Statist*, London):

1893–1894	27.80
1894–1895	25.14
1895–1896	26.21
1899–1900	23.27
1902–1903	19.68
1903–1904	22.18
1904–1905	23.68
1905–1906	24.47

[29] *Cf.* p. 222, *infra*.

[30] C. F. B., *Twenty-First Annual Report*, 1893, p. 203.

The recognized internal debt was at the same time 69,115,721 pesos, in detail as follows: [31]

	(In pesos)
3 per cent consolidated debt of 1885 ...	33,344,150
6 per cent railway subsidy bonds [a]	5,643,000
6 per cent subsidy bonds for port works [b]	1,783,675
5 per cent subsidy bonds for port works [c]	450,000
Railway subsidies due in cash [d]	8,375,877
Railway subsidies due in bonds [e]	877,000
Cash due to lessees of mints	1,836,296
Claims awaiting conversion into bonds of 1885	2,842,517
Bonds of 1885 bearing no interest until July, 1894	2,925,600
Bonds of the London debt not yet presented for conversion	234,250
Credit notes in circulation	2,952,167
Unpaid balances of former fiscal years ..	7,851,189
Total	69,115,721

a To the Monterrey and Gulf Railway P5,466,000; to the Chiapas Railway P177,000.

b At Veracruz P1,333,675; at Tonalá P450,000.

c At San Benito.

d To the Mexican National, under assignment of 6 per cent of customs revenues, P6,119,233; to the Interoceanic, under assignment of 3 per cent of customs revenues, P768,791; to other railways P1,487,853.

e To the Monterrey and Gulf P711,000; to the Michoacán P166,000.

On the basis of the current exchange rate of thirty pence to the peso, the recognized public debt of Mexico in 1893 was 222,132,361 pesos, or £27,766,520.

The Foreign Loan of 1893

In May, 1893, José Yves Limantour, the recently appointed Minister of Finance, addressed to Congress, with the approval of President Díaz,[32] a request for authority to take the necessary

[31] *Ibid.*

[32] Reëlected for a term of four years beginning December 1, 1892.

measures for the final settlement of the national debt. He pointed out that the operation contemplated in the laws of June 14, 1883, and June 22, 1885, had not been completed, inasmuch as various claims and credits against the government had not yet been presented for conversion. It was important for the credit of the country to know precisely the amount of the government's obligations and to declare forever barred the claims and credits not presented within a specified time. It would also be advantageous to unify the various securities issued by the government.[33]

The authority sought by the Minister of Finance was granted on May 29, 1893. The law of that date provided for the issue of bonds payable in Mexico to such an amount as the executive might deem necessary. It also authorized an issue of bonds up to £2,500,000, payable outside Mexico and specially secured upon 12 per cent of the customs duties, with a cumulative sinking fund of one-fourth of one per cent a year. The authorized amount of the foreign issue was raised to £3,000,000 in November of the same year. Bonds for this amount at 6 per cent interest were sold at an average price of approximately 64, which, after deduction of a commission of 1.25 per cent, netted the government only £1,890,073. The operation was nevertheless declared by Limantour, some years later, to have been one of the most interesting facts in the financial history of Mexico, by reason of the assistance which it gave the treasury in meeting the crisis brought on by the failure of crops, the prevalence of epidemics, and the necessity of paying the foreign debt in gold while the exchange value of the Mexican peso in the London market was dropping from 40.75 pence in 1891 to 25.14 pence in 1895.[34]

The Internal Loan of 1894

The immediate issue of the internal bonds authorized in May, 1893, was deemed inadvisable in view of the embarrassments

[33] José Yves Limantour, *Informe en cumplimiento del Articulo 20 del Decreto de 29 de Mayo de 1893, que autorizó el Ejecutivo para consumar el Arreglo de la Deuda Nacional* (Mexico, 1894).

[34] *Ibid. Cf.* table in note 28, p. 220, *supra,* and Limantour's report of 1900 (summarized in *Mexican Herald,* July 13, 1900). The exchange value of the peso, it will be observed, was usually somewhat higher than the bullion price.

attending the crisis mentioned above. It was not until September of the next year that Limantour was able to proceed with the operation. By that time, according to his report to the Mexican Congress,[35] foreign capital had ceased to be available for employment in industry and in the development of the natural resources of the country, and it was necessary to offer inducements to native capital. Since a large part of this capital consisted of inactive credits against the government, it was indispensable to devise some means of raising the market price of these credits and thus restoring to circulation the capital which they represented.

A decree of September 6, 1894,[36] issued by President Díaz under Limantour's advice, provided for the issue of bonds of the three per cent consolidated debt, without allowance for prior interest, in liquidation of duly established obligations presented before July 1, 1895, and belonging to the following categories:

1. Obligations antedating the decree of June 28, 1824,[37] and fulfiling the conditions of that decree, to be converted at 30.72 per cent of their face value.

2. Obligations arising between June 28, 1824, and November 30, 1850,[38] to be converted at 46.08 per cent of their face value.

3. Obligations arising between November 30, 1850, and July 1, 1882, and not previously barred by the decrees of June 22, 1885, and May 27, 1889,[39] to be converted at 61.44 per cent.[40]

4. Bonds and securities issued under previous conversions (with the exception of those recognized in the agreement of June 23, 1886, which were to remain subject to the terms of that agreement),[41] to be converted at 61.44 per cent.

[35] The *Informe* above cited.

[36] *Legislación Mexicana,* Vol. 24, pp. 264–275; quoted at length in C. F. B., *Twenty-Second Annual Report,* 1894, pp. 215–221.

[37] *Cf.* p. 18, *supra.*

[38] *Cf.* pp. 98–100, *supra.*

[39] *Cf.* pp. 204 *et seq., supra,* and *Legislación Mexicana,* Vol. 19, p. 417.

[40] By way of exception to the scales of conversion established with respect to this and the two preceding categories, obligations for salaries and pensions arising before July 1, 1882, and presented by persons other than the original claimants or their heirs were to be converted at only 11.52 per cent.

[41] *Cf.* p. 208, *supra.*

5. Obligations arising between June 30, 1882, and July 1, 1894, on account of salaries, pensions, and the like,[42] to be converted at par.

The conversion of the obligations above enumerated was declared to be voluntary for all creditors whose rights had originated later than June 30, 1882. The rights of such creditors were, however, subjected to the following restrictions:

1. Obligations for services rendered prior to July 1, 1890, would be forfeited unless presented for conversion by June 30, 1895.

2. Obligations for salaries, pensions, and the like,[43] originating subsequent to June 30, 1890, and prior to July 1, 1893, and not presented for conversion before July 1, 1895, would draw no interest after that date and would be paid not earlier than July 1, 1899, and at not more than thirty per cent of their face value.

3. Certificates issued for deferred interest under the law of June 22, 1885, and not presented for conversion before July 1, 1895, would draw no interest after that date and would be paid not earlier than July 1, 1899, at not more than eight per cent of their face value.

By another decree of the same date, September 6, 1894, provision was made for the issue of 5 per cent bonds of the "Redeemable Internal Debt of the United Mexican States" to be used (1) in the conversion of outstanding bonds previously issued for subsidies for railway enterprises and public works, and (2) in the consolidation of the part of the floating debt originating after June 30, 1882, from subsidies to railway enterprises and public

[42] In detail, the following obligations, which were placed in the "second category" in Article 5 of the decree (C. F. B., *Twenty-Second Annual Report*, 1894, p. 216):

"Credits for salaries, officials' travelling expenses, military and civil pensions; emoluments, fees, bonuses, participation in fines and remunerations; certificates for unpaid balances issued in accordance with the provisions of 28th of May, 1886, and 10th of November, 1888; those issued in conformity with the law of the 8th of November, 1892; and, in general, all credits not expressly included in the first category" (for which see note 44, *infra*).

[43] *Cf.* footnote 42, immediately preceding.

works, from loans in cash, and the like.[44] The bonds of this debt were to be issued in series as required and as authorized by special decrees. They were to be exchanged at par for obligations of the floating debt of the character indicated above. For certificates or bonds issued subsequent to June 30, 1882, as subsidies for railway enterprises and public works, the new bonds were to be exchanged in proportions to be fixed by the Ministry of Finance on the basis of the actual value of the securities to be converted. Creditors entitled to receive five per cent bonds of the "Redeemable Internal Debt" were given the privilege of demanding, instead, three per cent bonds of the consolidated internal debt in the proportion of 145 pesos of the latter bonds to 100 pesos of the former. The bonds of the "Redeemable Internal Debt" were to be redeemed in silver pesos of the current Mexican coinage by the application every six months of a fixed sum equivalent to 2.625 per cent of the face value of all the bonds issued. Redemption was always to be at par.[45] The provision for redemption only at par would, the Minister of Finance believed, assure the bonds a higher quotation on the market. From the moral point of view moreover, he observed, the government which contracted a debt ought to see to it that the security representing the debt should not suffer depreciation through acts of the government.[46]

The first issue of the bonds of the "Redeemable Internal Debt" was authorized in the decree of September 6, 1894, in the nominal amount of 20,000,000 pesos. This issue was followed by two others, each in the same amount, from 1895 to 1899. The

[44] In detail, the following obligations which were placed in the "first category" in Article 5 of the decree quoted in note 42, *supra:*

"Credits claimable in cash, and having their origin in subventions to railway undertakings and other public works, the sums due for freights and passages on account of the Government, and, in general, Credits arising from Loans, whether privileged or not, but made in cash, Mortgage Credits, and those arising from contracts of purchase or rentings, by virtue whereof the Government may have been expressly bound to make payments in cash, and the time for which may have expired, as well as the promissory notes not cleared off issued by the General Treasury on various offices."

[45] C. F. B., *Twenty-Second Annual Report,* 1894, pp. 218, 222.

[46] *Informe* above cited.

fourth and fifth series, amounting to 20,000,000 and 16,000,000 pesos, respectively, were issued between 1899 and 1909.[47] The operations with respect to the internal debts of 1885 and 1894 are conveniently shown, as of June 30, 1913, in the following table:

INTERNAL DEBT OF MEXICO 1886–1913

(In pesos)

Period (Years Ending June 30)	Amount Outstanding Beginning of Period	Interest Due Beginning of Period	Bonds Issued	Bonds Redeemed	Net Increase or Decrease
1886–1894	..........[a]	........[a]	58,573,300	24,357,550	.........[a]
1894–1895	34,215,750	541,074	27,649,950	173,450	27,476,500
1895–1897	61,692,250	986,063	20,555,200	739,150	19,816,050
1897–1899	81,508,300	834,347	23,888,800	1,307,725	22,581,075
1899–1901	104,089,375	900,117	20,174,900	1,101,000	19,073,900
1901–1903	123,163,275	978,661	22,374,500	1,585,600	20,788,900
1903–1913	143,952,175	1,309,477	16,222,600	26,424,450[b]	10,201,850
1913	133,750,325	1,530,677	....	....	....

[a] The amount of the internal debt was unknown at the beginning of this period.

[b] Included in the amount redeemed in this period were provisional certificates of the fifth series of the 1894 loan amounting to 16,842,500 pesos. These were redeemed by proceeds of the 4.5 per cent Treasury Obligations listed under external loans (p. 262, *infra*).

The Loan of 1899

Under the guidance of Limantour the exercise of strict economies was continued. Peace was assured throughout the country by the strong hand of President Díaz. Commerce expanded. The customs revenues increased. The steady decline in the price of silver was fortunately offset to some extent by a demand for large quantities of silver bullion in the Far East. Despite the fact that more than forty per cent of the annual revenues were required for the service of the debt, the government was at last able to attain a surplus of revenues over expenditures. Before

[47] Cf. *Memoria de Hacienda*, 1900–1901 (p. 95), 1901–1902 (p. 98), 1902–1903 (pp. 91–92), 1904–1905 (p. 629), 1905–1906 (p. xiv), 1906–1907 (p. xiii), 1907–1908 (p. xiv), and 1908–1909 (p. xii).

the end of the year 1897 Mexican credit had so far improved that the government received from financiers in the United States, England, and Germany proposals for loans at much more favorable rates than that of the existing foreign debt. Formal negotiations with a view to the floating of such loans were initiated shortly before the Spanish-American War.[48]

After the end of the War, the government was informed by the house of Bleichroeder that that house had been authorized to act as the representative of all the interested parties. Negotiations were thereupon resumed. They were suspended, however, when the bankers insisted on provisions, such as had been made in previous contracts, for the deposit of a half year's interest in advance and for a lien on the direct taxes of the Federal District.[49]

In April, 1899, a representative of several banks in the United States went to Mexico and informed the Minister of Finance that his principals were prepared to consummate the transaction on more advantageous terms than could be secured elsewhere. The Minister, being at this time obliged to take a trip to Europe for his health, made it convenient to stop in New York for a week *en route* and to discuss financial matters with firms in that city. The offers made by the New York banks were so favorable that Limantour considered it inadvisable to accept them before ascertaining whether still more favorable terms might not perhaps be obtainable in Europe. He had in mind also that it might not be advantageous to exchange the European creditors of Mexico for American creditors, inasmuch as (1) the American offers did not provide for the issue of new securities at a lower rate of interest; (2) European bankers and bondholders were already familiar with the Mexican financial situation; (3) Mexico ought not, in his opinion, to be dependent upon the banks and exchanges of a single country; (4) the American market was more likely than European markets to be affected by "circumstances foreign to the special status of Mexican loans"; and (5) a break with London and Berlin firms might alienate those firms. There was no reason, however, the Minister suggested to the New York

[48] Limantour's report of 1900, above cited.
[49] *Ibid.*

bankers, why American firms and the American investing public should not coöperate in a transaction effected in Europe.[50]

Upon his arrival in Paris, Limantour was sought out by the head of the firm of J. P. Morgan and Company of New York as well as by representatives of Bleichroeder and the Deutsche and Dresdner banks. A contract for a new loan of £22,700,000 at 5 per cent was signed in Berlin on July 1, by representatives of the three German institutions, who subscribed for 67 per cent of the issue; in Paris on July 2, by a representative of the Banco Nacional de México, who subscribed for 6 per cent; and at London on July 3, by a representative of J. S. Morgan and Company of London and J. P. Morgan and Company of New York, who together subscribed for 27 per cent. Under this contract the holders of the 6 per cent bonds of 1888, 1890, and 1893 and of the 5 per cent bonds of the Tehuantepec Railway Company, issued in 1889, were invited to deposit their bonds for conversion at par with cash bonuses of one per cent to the holders of the railway bonds, 1.5 per cent to the holders of the 1888 and 1890 issues and 2 per cent to the holders of the 1893 issue. The outstanding bonds eligible for conversion aggregated £21,457,220, but as it was expected that a substantial number of these bonds would not be presented for conversion, £4,700,000 of the new bonds were offered for subscription in cash in New York and Amsterdam.[51]

As a guarantee for the payment of interest and amortization on the new bonds, 62 per cent of the customs revenues of Mexico were pledged. The guarantee was made ample for the object in view, said Limantour in his report to Congress, because it was believed that half a guarantee would have been more hurtful than none at all, in that it would have led to surmises injurious to the confidence which it was desired to inspire. It was not reasonable, he suggested, to suppose that the new bonds could be issued without a special guarantee, inasmuch as the bonds for which they were to be exchanged had been abundantly protected by guarantees. The credit of the republic had not yet

[50] Limantour's report of 1900, above cited.
[51] *Ibid.*

attained such a degree of "solidity" as to make it possible for a large loan, at a low rate of interest, to attain a conspicuous success in the foremost markets of the world with no other guarantee than the word of the nation. It was important to score a moral success which would be a gratifying confirmation of the recognition of the progress achieved by the country in point of order and good government — a success so great as to induce most of the holders of former securities to submit them for conversion.[52]

The success of the loan of 1899 was all that could have been hoped for. By the end of the year approximately three-fourths of the bonds eligible for conversion had been presented for that purpose. The new bonds offered for sale were readily disposed of at 99 or better. The government was particularly congratulated upon the placing of its bonds in the American market, in which the only Mexican securities previously taken to any extent had been those of the railways.[53]

Amount of the Public Debt in 1900

Upon the completion of the loan of 1899 there remained outstanding less than £100,000 of bonds of previous issues payable exclusively in foreign money. The total public debt on June 30, 1900, was declared to be as follows: [54]

	(*In pounds sterling*)
Payable in foreign money	
6 per cent loan of 1888	36,040
6 per cent loan of 1890	7,320
6 per cent loan of 1893	600
5 per cent Tehuantepec Ry. loan of 1889	53,700
5 per cent loan of 1899	22,628,920
Interest accrued on these loans	309,142
Total	23,035,722

[52] *Ibid.*

[53] *Ibid.*

[54] C. F. B., *Twenty-Ninth Annual Report,* 1901, p. 251.

	(*In pesos*)
Payable in silver currency	
3 per cent loan of 1885	49,834,525
5 per cent loan of 1894	62,564,200
6 per cent railway subvention loans .	9,377,000
5 per cent railway subvention loan ..	42,000
6 per cent port works bonds	7,025
Interest accrued	1,294,232
Floating debt	1,015,836
Total	124,134,818

At the prevailing rate of exchange, the two divisions of the debt amounted approximately to 350,000,000 pesos or £35,000,000. To meet the service of this debt in the fiscal year 1899–1900 the government disbursed 21,612,126 pesos, or 37.065 per cent of its total expenditure of 58,309,933 pesos.[55]

Encouraging Aspects of the Financial Situation

The expenditure of the government in the fiscal year 1899–1900 was some 6,000,000 pesos below the revenues, which amounted to 64,261,076 pesos. A surplus almost equally gratifying had been obtained in each of the preceding five years, as shown in the following table:[56]

(Amounts in pesos)

Year	Ordinary Revenue	Ordinary Expenditure	Surplus
1894–95	43,945,699	41,372,264	2,573,434
1895–96	50,521,470	45,070,123	5,451,347
1896–97	51,500,628	48,330,505	3,170,123
1897–98	52,697,984	51,815,285	882,698
1898–99	60,134,212	54,499,542	6,639,670

[55] C. F. B., *Twenty-Ninth Annual Report,* 1901, p. 251.

[56] Limantour's reports to Congress, December, 1899, and December, 1900, as quoted in C. F. B., *Twenty-Eighth Annual Report,* 1900, p. 233, and *Twenty-Ninth Annual Report,* 1901, p. 241.

The cost of collecting the revenues had, moreover, been reduced during the same quinquennium as follows: [57]

(Percentage of revenue)

Year	Customs Duties	Stamp Duties	Taxes of Federal District
1894–95	9.163	7.93	.....
1895–96	7.780	7.29	.....
1896–97	8.017	6.60	4.992
1897–98	8.423	6.49	4.888
1898–99	6.880	6.33	4.645

The Minister of Finance, though pleased with the results shown in these tables, was conservative in estimating their significance. The Congress, he declared in his report of December 14, 1899, should not rely on the unbroken continuance of the favorable circumstances which had influenced the development of the national industries during recent years.

We have had [he said] several years of good crops and others of more than average ones; we have benefited by a relative stability of foreign rates of exchange, and, up to the present, we have not suffered from the inconveniences of an excessive production in any of our industries, and during this quinquennial period, the country has not been afflicted by any kind of general calamity. It seems, therefore, prudent to guard ourselves against the results arising from any of these accidents which might suddenly befall us, and to base our calculations for the future upon a situation neither so critical as that which the country had to contend against from 1892 to 1895, nor so exceptionally prosperous as that existing today.[58]

The prudence enjoined upon the Congress was not considered by the Minister to be incompatible with the reduction of certain taxes and the increase of the appropriations for public works and education. In accordance with the Minister's recommendations, several stamp duties were suppressed or reduced and the sum of 4,000,000 pesos was appropriated for the construction of schools and other public works and for the strengthening of the fleet.[59]

[57] Limantour's report, December, 1899, *sup. cit.*

[58] As quoted in C. F. B., *Twenty-Eighth Annual Report*, 1900, p. 233.

[59] *Memoria de Hacienda*, 1899–1900, pp. 52–56.

The most strikingly encouraging feature in the financial situation at the turn of the century was the reduction of war expenditures to less than one-fourth of the total. The application to military and naval purposes of only 22.984 per cent of the total sum expended by the government in 1900 was in most favorable contrast with the application in 1825 of 19 per cent more than the total budgeted revenues, including foreign loans. It was only a decade since 30 per cent of the revenues had been required for the maintenance of the military and naval establishment.[60]

Guaranteed State Bonds

The interest shown by the federal government in the prosecution of public works in 1900 was further manifested a year later by the grant of financial aid to the sanitary and harbor projects of three of the States of the Mexican Union. "Our system," declared Limantour in a communication to the Congress in May, 1901, "does not permit the Federation to undertake works of a local character which do not clearly and directly form part of the services of the ports or of the federal offices established in the maritime and frontier towns." The Minister nevertheless recommended, and the Congress, in June, 1901, authorized, the making of contracts by the federal executive, in association with the governors of the States, for the execution of certain kinds of public works. Under a contract signed later in the same year by Limantour in pursuance of the law of June, 1901, the federal government agreed to pay interest for twenty-five years on 5 per cent bonds to the amount of 5,000,000 pesos to be issued by the State of Veracruz. Similar undertakings were assumed by the federal government, in pursuance of the same law, with respect to later issues of bonds by the States of Veracruz, Tamaulipas, and Sinaloa. These bonds, all of which bore 5 per cent interest, reached a total of 9,629,000 pesos.[61]

[60] Report of Ministry of Finance to Congress, December, 1890, as quoted in C. F. B., *Nineteenth Annual Report*, 1890, p. 133.

[61] *Memoria de Hacienda*, 1900–1901, pp. 166–167, 321–322; 1901–1902, pp. 3–4; 1905–1906, pp. 237–238; 1906–1907, pp. 243–246, 257–260; Moody, *Analyses of Investments. Government and Municipal Securities* (New York, 1924), p. 524.

Bonds of the Municipalities of the Federal District

The national debt was still further increased in 1903 as a result of the reorganization of the administration of the municipalities of the Federal District, which embraces Mexico City and vicinity. The obligations of the several municipalities were assumed by the federal government. These obligations included 5 per cent bonds of the City of Mexico to the amount of £1,990,200 which had been sold, principally in London, in 1889. The revenues of the Federal District were adequate for the payment of the interest and amortization on these bonds and on the other obligations assumed by the federal government at this time.[62]

Stabilization of the Peso

Between 1900 and 1903 the Mexican silver peso, which had been quoted at 36.84 pence in 1892, the year of Limantour's appointment as Minister of Finance, declined from 24.59 pence to 19.68 pence.[63] In the fiscal year 1892–1893 the interest on the debt payable in foreign currency had been 5,000,000 pesos in excess of the amount of such interest at the "normal" rate of 48 to 50 pence. By 1903 the additional appropriation required for payment of interest, to offset the decline in the rate of exchange, had risen to approximately 13,000,000 pesos.

The seriousness of the problem presented by the decline and variation of the exchange value of the Mexican peso had been realized by Limantour since the beginning of his term in the Ministry of Finance. A commission had been appointed in February, 1893, to study the problem and to formulate plans for its solution. The commission had soon become convinced that the problem was of international scope and incapable of solution without international coöperation. It had therefore initiated a movement for an international conference on the subject. During the year 1903 five conferences, attended by representa-

[62] *Memoria de Hacienda*, 1902–1903 (pp. 113–121), 1903–1904 (p. xvi), and 1904–1905 (p. 307). The amount of the bonds was originally £2,400,000. They were issued at 85 per cent of their face value.

[63] *Cf.* table in note 28, p. 220, *supra*.

tives of the United States, Great Britain, France, Germany, Russia, Netherlands, and China, as well as Mexico, were held in different countries. The measures recommended as a result of these conferences were rendered "purely platonic" by the outbreak of war between Russia and Japan. Limantour's commission was therefore obliged to attempt a national solution of the problem. The law which the commission finally worked out was passed by the Congress and approved by the President in December, 1904. It came into force on May 1, 1905.[64]

The chief provisions of the law were the following: [65]

1. The theoretical unit of the monetary system is represented by seventy-five centigrams of gold and is called the peso.

2. The silver peso of 24.4388 grams of fine silver is retained as full and legal tender to any amount, and has attributed to it the value of 75 centigrams of pure gold.

3. The obligation on the part of the mints to coin all silver presented to them for that purpose is abrogated, and the right of issuing coin is confined to the Executive.

4. A special fund is created for the purpose of maintaining parity of foreign exchange value between the gold and the silver peso.

The effect of the law was to give to the Mexican peso a parity with the Japanese yen, which differs from a half dollar of the United States by only a small fraction.[66]

The Loan of 1904

During the period in which the silver reform was under consideration, the government issued 4.5 per cent treasury notes to the amount of $18,500,000 United States gold; special certificates to the amount of 6,000,000 pesos; and 6 per cent bonds to the amount of 15,122,000 pesos. The treasury notes were used in paying for debentures of the Interoceanic Railway and

[64] *Memoria de Hacienda*, 1904–1905, pp. 7–16; Carlos Díaz Dufoo, *Limantour* (Mexico, 1910), pp. 145–162, 167–170; Maurice de Perigny, *Les États Unis du Mexique* (Paris, 1911), pp. 84–94.

[65] *Legislación Mexicana*, Vol. 37, pp. 348–355.

[66] C. F. B., *Thirty-Second Annual Report*, 1904–1905, p. 277.

stock of the National Railway, in which the government had decided to acquire controlling interests,[67] and in meeting a part of the cost of public works at the ports of Coatzacoalcos, Salina Cruz, Veracruz, and Manzanillo. The special certificates were applied to payment for the same public works. The bonds were issued by way of subsidy to the Mexican Southern Railway and the Veracruz and Pacific Railway.[68]

With a view to redeeming these obligations and obtaining

[67] *Cf.* p. 237 *et seq., infra.*

[68] By the issue of these bonds the total of the subsidies given by Mexico for railway enterprises was brought to more than 150,000,000 pesos. As the greater part of these subsidies antedated the striking decline of the peso, the total was in excess of $100,000,000 United States gold. The following table, based on that of Macedo, *op. cit.*, p. 230, shows the subsidies up to June 30, 1902:

Railway Subsidies	Cash or Customs-House Certificates	5 or 6 per cent Bonds Redeemable at Par	Total
Mexican	P 13,685,195	....	P 13,685,195
Interoceanic	6,356,378	P 180,000	6,536,378
Tehuantepec	12,619,729	22,288,700	34,908,429
Mexican Central	21,526,007	2,320,000	23,846,007
Mexican National	11,929,870	380,000	12,309,870
Mexican Southern	880,805	10,368,000	11,248,805
Tonalá and Frontera	....	444,000	444,000
Monterrey to Gulf	....	5,534,572	5,534,572
Veracruz to Pacific	....	3,569,500	3,569,500
Mexico, Cuernavaca and Pacific	....	5,225,800	5,225,800
Thirty-four other railways	8,734,788	8,048,400	16,783,188
Totals	P 75,732,772	P 58,358,972	P 134,091,744

In return for these subsidies, it should be noted, the railways accorded to the government certain valuable privileges. Under the general railway law of 1899 (*Diario Oficial*, May 13, 1899) the government had the following rights, among others:

1. Transportation of troops, employees and agents on official business, ammunition and other articles destined for the public service, at 50 per cent below the maximum legal rates.

2. Special trains at 50 per cent of the average charge.

3. Telegraphic and other services at one-half the maximum legal rates.

4. Requisition, on condition of indemnification, of railway personnel and equipment upon such occasions and for such uses as the interests of the country require.

additional funds for the prosecution of the public works at the ports, Limantour on October 31, 1904, signed a contract with representatives of Speyer and Company of New York, Speyer Brothers of London, Lazard Speyer-Ellison of Frankfort, the Deutsche Bank of Berlin, Teixeira de Mattos Brothers of Amsterdam, and the Banco Nacional de México. This contract provided for a loan of $40,000,000, United States gold, at 4 per cent per annum, to be taken by the contracting bank at 89 per cent of its nominal value. No special security was assigned. The loan was to be redeemed within fifty years by means of an amortization fund of 0.325 per cent a year. After December 1, 1909, the government was to have the right to use this fund in the purchase of the bonds of the loan at their market price. The bankers were to have a commission of one-fourth of one per cent on payments of interest and amortization.[69]

Of the total issue of $40,000,000 the Banco Nacional de México took 6.25 per cent. The remainder of the issue was divided among the other contracting banks. About $25,000,000 of the bonds were placed privately. The rest were sold on the European and American markets at 94 per cent of their face value.[70]

Limantour's Theory of Progress

At the end of the year 1905 Limantour, in presenting the estimates for the fiscal year 1906–1907, reported at length on the currency reform. The minor inconveniences occasioned by the adoption of the gold standard,[71] said the Minister, were susceptible of being easily redressed by measures such as the revision of the duties on imports and the granting of franchises to the mining industry. The satisfactory situation of the country, he added, had been enhanced by a fortunate rise in the value of silver, which had enabled the government to export and dispose of some 13,500,000 pesos of silver currency at a substantial profit.[72]

[69] *Memoria de Hacienda,* 1904–1905, pp. 81–87.

[70] *Ibid.; cf.* C. F. B., *Thirty-Fifth Annual Report,* 1907, p. 275.

[71] *Cf.* p. 234, *supra.*

[72] *Mexico, Financial Documents, being the budget for the fiscal year 1906–*

Considering the financial situation of the country from a more general point of view, Limantour noted that the public debt required annual payments of as much as 24,000,000 pesos, of which not more than 1,000,000 remained in Mexico. The railways also, he observed, remitted abroad over 20,000,000 pesos a year, while several additional millions were annually remitted to Europe by the Banco Nacional de México, the Bank of London and Mexico, and the mining, industrial, agricultural, and commercial concerns. On the other hand, there was a constant influx of foreign capital for the development of the resources of the country. The situation did not appear to the Minister of Finance to be actually unfavorable to Mexico, inasmuch as

> the aggregate of advantages which every new industry and every expansion of existing industries confer on the country serve to enhance the prosperity of all its inhabitants without distinction of classes or nationalities. The day will come, as has been exemplified by the story of other modern nations, when the population, increased by the multiplication of the means of livelihood and trained in more laborious habits, will by degrees redeem itself from indebtedness, and when that happens, the bonds, shares and other securities of our most flourishing enterprises will be held at home and will not be allowed again to leave the country.[73]

The Railway Merger

It was not overlooked by Limantour that the foreign interests which he welcomed to Mexico might acquire a predominant influence prejudicial to the national welfare. The danger of the acquisition of such an influence was most imminent in connection with the railways, of which approximately 8,500 miles had been constructed, chiefly by competing foreign interests, before the end of the century.[74] It was evident that if these foreign interests ceased to be rivals, they would possess a formidable power over the economic life of the country.

1907, and the analysis of the state of the Mexican Treasury for the year 1904–1905. Presented to the Mexican Congress December 1905 by Señor Limantour. English translation by C. Simonds (Mexico, 1905), pp. 3–22.

[73] *Ibid.*, at page 9.

[74] Mexico, *Secretária de Comunicaciones y Obras Públicas, Reseña Condensada de los Ferrocarriles de los Estados Unidos Mexicanos* (Mexico, 1910), Diagram 1.

In 1903 there was good reason to believe that the two principal railway systems, the Mexican National[75] and the Mexican Central, "in the control of rival American interests led by the house of Speyer and H. Clay Pierce," were about to be merged. To prevent the merger, Limantour first expended 9,000,000 pesos in the purchase of debentures of the Interoceanic Railway, of which the Mexican National was attempting to gain control. Shortly after the purchase of these debentures he was able to conclude an arrangement with Speyer and Company of New York under which the debentures were accepted by the Mexican National, with $4,500,000 in cash, as full payment for a controlling interest in the latter company. As the Mexican National had previously acquired the control of the International Railway, the government through this arrangement gained a deciding voice with respect to three of the four great railway systems of Mexico. It could afford for the future to assume a passive attitude, and it did in fact announce that it had no intention of acquiring additional railway stock.[76]

Within the next three years, however, the railway situation changed in essential respects, and in December, 1906, Limantour asked the Congress to authorize the acquisition of the Mexican Central Railroad and its consolidation with the Mexican National. The "three main arguments for the incorporation of the two great systems, the National and the Central" he stated as follows:[77]

> First to avoid friction between different corporations when the two are competing lines or when one of them fears being antagonized by a combination in which the Government holds a controlling interest; secondly, to avoid the absorption of properties, not controlled by the Government, by one of the great railway systems of the United States; and thirdly, the prospect of realizing considerable economies through the consolidation of all the great railways under a single management.

[75] The Mexican National Railroad is to be carefully distinguished from the National Railways of Mexico, or Ferrocarilles Nacionales de México, the system which was formed by the consolidation of the Mexican National and the Mexican Central in 1909. *Cf.* p. 239, *infra.*

[76] *Mexican Yearbook,* 1908, p. 349.

[77] *Ibid.,* pp. 690–692.

The merger was completed early in 1909, when the National, with its subsidiaries, and the Central were incorporated as the National Railways of Mexico (Ferrocarriles Nacionales de México) with roads aggregating approximately 6,987 miles, or about 55 per cent of the mileage of railways in operation in Mexico at the time.[78] The capital of the new company consisted of 2,300,000 shares of stock of the nominal value of 200 pesos each, divided as follows: 300,000 first preferred 4 per cent; 1,250,000 second preferred 5 per cent; and 750,000 common. Of the common stock there were allotted to the Mexican government, "on account of guaranty and other considerations,"[79] 637,300 shares. The first and second preferred shares received by the government in exchange for its previous holdings in the National and the Mexican Central were sufficient to give the government 51 per cent of the total stock of the new company.

The new company was authorized to issue 4.5 per cent prior lien bonds to the amount of $225,000,000 United States gold, and 4 per cent general mortgage bonds to the amount of $160,000,000 United States gold. The general mortgage bonds were to be guaranteed unconditionally, as to both principal and interest, by the Mexican government. Of the prior lien bonds, approximately $100,000,000 were used in the retirement of outstanding bonds and notes, in the purchase of equipment, and "for other corporate purposes"; $6,000,000 were delivered to the Mexican government "on account of its guaranty and other considerations"; and $10,000,000 were sold for cash required in connection with the merger. The remaining $109,000,000 of these bonds were reserved for future issue. Of the guaranteed general mortgage bonds, approximately $63,500,000 were used in the retirement of outstanding bonds and notes, in the purchase of equipment, and "for other corporate purposes"; $2,450,000 were delivered to the Mexican government "on account of its

[78] The "Plan and Agreement of Readjustment and Union" was published by the readjustment managers in New York in 1908. Further information is available in the *Mexican Yearbook*, above cited; in Fred Wilbur Powell, *The Railroads of Mexico* (Boston, 1921) pp. 4–8; and in United States Department of Commerce, *Railways of Mexico*, *sup. cit.*, pp. 16–19.

[79] *Cf.* p. 235, *supra*.

guaranty and other considerations"; and $6,750,000 were sold for cash required in connection with the merger. The remaining $87,300,000 of these bonds were reserved for future issue.

The banking interests which assisted in the formation of the merger were Kuhn, Loeb and Company, Speyer and Company, Ladenburg, Thalmann and Company, and Hallgarten and Company of New York; Speyer Brothers of London; the Bank für Handel und Industrie of Berlin; and the Berliner Handelsgesellschaft of Berlin.

THE FINANCIAL CRISIS OF 1907–1909

During the fiscal year 1906–1907, in which Limantour was authorized by the Congress to acquire the Mexican Central Railroad and consolidate it with the Mexican National, the revenues of the federal government reached the high point of 114,286,122 pesos, as against expenditures of 85,076,640 pesos. The surplus of over 29,000,000 pesos thus realized brought the total of surpluses since 1895–1896 to 112,000,000 pesos. Of these surpluses, according to Limantour's report to the Congress, 38,500,000 pesos had already been expended in public works and 23,000,000 pesos more had been set aside for the same purpose.[80] A further surplus, amounting to more than 17,500,000 pesos, was obtained in the year 1907–1908, when the revenues totalled 111,771,867 pesos and the expenditures were only 93,967,339 pesos.[81]

The surplus of 1907–1908 was far above the most sanguine expectations of Limantour. The revenues for that year had been budgeted at 99,000,000 pesos, as against estimated expenditures of 93,000,000 pesos. Midway of the year, moreover, the effect of the "bankers' panic" in the United States, and to a less extent in Europe, had begun to be felt in Mexico. It was clear, as Limantour pointed out in his report to the Congress in December, 1907, that the large disbursements which Mexico was obliged to make each year for interest or profits on foreign capital in-

[80] *Memoria de Hacienda*, 1905–1906, p. 3.

[81] Díaz Dufoo, *Una Victoria Financiera*, *sup. cit.*, p. 121.

vested in the country could be kept up only upon condition of the natural and spontaneous entry of new foreign capital for investment as well as the maintenance of a distinctly favorable balance of trade. The dislocation of the European and American markets and the accompanying lack of confidence made it necessary for Mexico to depend almost entirely upon her own resources. Scarcity of money induced high rates of interest, existing enterprises were restricted, and new enterprises were postponed. At the same time the excess of exports over imports, which had amounted to over 50,000,000 pesos in 1905–1906, dropped to 21,000,000 pesos in 1907–1908.[82]

In the circumstances, Limantour felt obliged to be extremely cautious in the formulation of the budget for 1908–1909, which he submitted to the Congress in December, 1907. Income was budgeted at 103,385,000 pesos (11,000,000 pesos below the actual revenues for 1906–1907), and expenditures at 103,203,824 pesos. It was feared by President Díaz as well as by Limantour that a deficit could not be avoided. The revenues for the year did in fact prove to be nearly 5,000,000 pesos below Limantour's estimate, but through rigid economies in the federal departments expenditures were kept more than 10,000,000 pesos below the budgeted amount. There was therefore, instead of a deficit, a surplus of 5,808,117 pesos.[83]

The effects of the crisis finally disappeared in the fiscal year 1909–1910, when the balance of trade was more than 65,000,000 pesos in favor of Mexico and the federal revenues were 106,328,-485 pesos as against expenditures of 95,028,650 pesos.[84]

The Caja de Préstamos Bonds

At the height of the difficulties of the years 1907 to 1909 Limantour set on foot a plan, to which he had devoted much

[82] Limantour's report, as translated in C. F. B., *Thirty-Sixth Annual Report*, 1908, pp. 283 ff; *Mexican Yearbook* (1908), p. 223; *Memoria de Hacienda*, 1909, p. 25; C. F. B., *Thirty-Fifth Annual Report*, 1907, p. 273, and *Thirty-Eighth Annual Report*, 1910, p. 264.

[83] Díaz Dufoo, *Una Victoria Financiera*, *sup. cit.*, pp. 118–126.

[84] C. F. B., *Thirty-Eighth Annual Report*, 1910, p. 264.

thought, for the encouragement of agriculture and irrigation. The plan was initiated by the grant to four banks of a concession for the establishment of the Caja de Préstamos para Obras de Irrigación y Fomento de Agricultura (Loan Bank for Works of Irrigation and Promotion of Agriculture). The date of the concession was September 3, 1908. The concessionnaires were the Banco Nacional de México, the Banco de Londres y México, the Banco Central Mexicano, and the Banco Mexicano de Comercio é Industria. Of the capital of 10,000,000 pesos one share was held by the government and the remaining shares by the four banks. The Caja was authorized to obtain additional funds by the issue of bonds, for not more than 50,000,000 pesos, unconditionally guaranteed by the government. In pursuance of the authorization, a contract for the issue of bonds for the amount mentioned was signed on October 12, 1908, with Speyer and Company of New York, acting for themselves and as representatives of Speyer Brothers of London, Lazard Speyer-Ellison of Frankfort, the Deutsche Bank of Berlin, and Teixeira de Mattos Brothers of Amsterdam. The bonds bore 4.5 per cent interest and were to be redeemed within thirty-five years. One-half of the issue was immediately purchased outright by the contracting banks at 89 per cent of its face value. Before the middle of February, 1909, the same banks had purchased the remaining half of the issue: 15,000,000 pesos at 90.25 and 10,000,000 pesos at 90.5.[85]

Mexican Credit at Its Peak in the Loan of 1910

At the middle of the year 1910 general mortgage bonds guaranteed by the Mexican government in connection with the railway merger were outstanding to the total amount of 101,000,000 pesos. Of these bonds it is estimated that more than 90,000,000 pesos were held by foreigners. More than 100,000,000 pesos of the internal debts of 1885 and 1894 had by this time found their way into foreign hands. The bonds issued abroad by the Mexican government amounted to approximately 250,-

[85] *Memoria de Hacienda,* 1908–1909, pp. 198–202; 1909–1910, p. 283, *Informe de la Secretaría de Hacienda,* November 23, 1908.

000,000 pesos. The total direct or contingent obligations of the Mexican government to foreigners was thus in the neighborhood of 450,000,000 pesos — equivalent, since the currency reform of 1905, to $225,000,000. The railways were, however, in a prosperous condition, with no indication that the government would be called upon to fulfil its guarantee; commerce and industry were steadily growing; and the régime of peace and order established by Díaz was regarded as having become at last the normal régime of the country. The net annual revenues of the government were in excess of 100,000,000 pesos. In the circumstances the burden of the public debt, which was due almost exclusively to foreigners, was not considered to be out of proportion to the national wealth. The burden of the debt was, indeed, so easily borne that, when the centennial of the Mexican declaration of independence was celebrated in September, 1910, practically all of the outstanding bonds of foreign issues, bearing 5 per cent interest per annum, were apparently about to be converted, without increase of the principal, into new bonds bearing only 4 per cent interest.

The contract for the loan of 1910 was signed at Paris on July 2 of that year by Limantour and representatives of banking houses in Paris, Berlin, London, New York, and Mexico City.[86] It provided for a bond issue of £22,200,000 to be used toward the redemption of the outstanding 5 per cent bonds of 1899, amounting to £22,700,000,[87] or, at the option of the holders, in the conversion of those bonds into the new 4 per cent bonds at par. One-half of the issue was purchased outright by the bankers at 94.75, and an option was given to the bankers to purchase the other half at the same rate at any time before April 1, 1911. The French bankers took 42.5 per cent of the £11,100,000 of the

[86] A translation of the contract (from *Memoria de Hacienda*, 1910-1911, pp. 306–318) is given in Appendix VI. The French banks were the Banque de Paris et des Pays-Bas, the Crédit Lyonnais, the Société Générale pour Favoriser le Développement du Commerce et de l'Industrie en France, and the Comptoir National d'Escompte de Paris. The German group was composed of Bleichroeder, the Deutsche Bank, and the Dresdner Bank. The other participants were Morgan, Grenfell and Company of London, J. P. Morgan and Company of New York, and the Banco Nacional de México.

[87] *Cf. supra*, pp. 226 ff.

bonds issued in 1910; the German, English, and American groups together took the same amount; and the remaining 15 per cent of the issue were taken by the Banco Nacional de México.[88] The bonds were sold to the public at 97.625 per cent of their face value.[89]

The security stipulated in the contract of July 2, 1910, was the same assignment of 62 per cent of the customs revenues which had been granted for the loan of 1899. The new bonds were to be redeemed not later than January 1, 1945. For the purpose of redemption 1.37 per cent of the principal of the loan was to be set aside each year.

The Beginning of the Decline

Behind the pomp of the centennial celebration of September, 1910, and beneath the smooth surface exhibited to the foreign bankers who were helping to put Mexican credit on a 4 per cent basis, were elements of discontent which the aging hand of the dictator could not much longer suppress. These elements had been actively at work since the spring of 1908, when Díaz declared that Mexico was ready for democracy and that he would be willing to surrender to a successor chosen by the nation the power which he had held for almost a generation. Political ambitions long held in check had been given free rein by the President's declaration, and grievances of the landless classes and of all who stood to gain from disturbances of the social order had found eloquent, if not always sincere or well-balanced, champions among the jealous aspirants to the succession. The reëlection of Díaz in 1910, pursuant to his decision that the welfare of the country demanded his continuance in office, united many of his new rivals against him. The foreign delegates who thronged the castle of Chapultepec and marvelled at the wonders which the dictator had wrought could not fail to discern the fires of revolution answering the gorgeous illuminations of the centennial.[90]

[88] *Cf. supra*, pp. 226 ff.

[89] *L'Economiste Français* (Paris), July 9, 1910, pp. 70–71.

[90] Priestley, *op. cit.*, pp. 396–398.

From San Antonio, Texas, on October 5, 1910, Francisco Madero, visionary apostle of social reform, but lately released from the prison in which he had been confined in consequence of personal attacks on Díaz in the promotion of his own presidential candidacy, issued a call to revolution under the title of the Plan de San Luis Potosí. In November he returned to Mexico and began the systematic organization of a revolt to nullify the election. Within a few months he had made such progress that most of the country was in arms.[91]

In March, 1911, United States warships were dispatched to both the coasts of Mexico for the protection of the lives and property of American citizens. At the same time hasty preparations were made for United States Army manoeuvres on the Mexican frontier. It was suggested in some quarters that the United States intended to uphold the Monroe Doctrine by forestalling European intervention in the interests of foreign investors. There was even a rumor, for which no foundation seems to have existed, that the preparations for manoeuvres on the border were due to an intimation by the British Ambassador at Washington that if the United States held back Great Britain might be compelled to send military or naval forces for the protection of British interests.[92] Another rumor, equally ill-founded, was that the movement of troops toward the border was dictated by American business interests. It was pointed out that the railway and rubber interests, in particular, had direct access to the President's ear through his brothers Henry W. and Charles P. Taft. In well-informed circles, however, the immediately influential cause of the demonstration was believed to be the constant protests of the Díaz government against alleged operations of American citizens who were said to have furnished arms, ammunition, and supplies to the revolutionary forces and, in some cases, to have been personally active in organizing such forces. It was realized that the United States was bound by the comity of nations, if not by international law, to prevent such operations as were alleged to have been carried on by American citizens.[93]

[91] *Ibid.*, pp. 398–399.

[92] *The Economist*, March 11 and 18, 1911, pp. 487, 559.

[93] *Ibid.*, April 15, 1911, pp. 785–786.

The revolutionary forces triumphed over President Díaz in May, 1911, and on the twenty-fifth of the month Francisco León de la Barra was installed as provisional President, pending an election. Madero, who was expected to be chosen President in the forthcoming elections, took occasion, on June 10, to deny the "canards" which had associated Wall Street or high finance with his cause. Not one American dollar, he declared, had helped in the triumph of the cause led by him.[94] That a considerable amount of other currency had been used by the revolutionists was, however, indicated by the rapidity with which the treasury surplus of 62,483,119 pesos, left by President Díaz, was exhausted by payments for services rendered during the revolution.[95]

The Public Debt in 1911

The direct public debt of Mexico at the end of the month following the triumph of the Madero revolution was as follows:[96]

	(*In pesos*)
Outstanding bonds of 1888, 1889 (Tehuantepec), 1890, 1893	23,476
5 per cent bonds of 1889 (City of Mexico)	15,753,219
5 per cent bonds of 1899	103,856,261
4 per cent bonds of 1904	76,680,839
4 per cent bonds of 1910	106,663,830
3 per cent bonds of 1886	44,117,870
5 per cent bonds of 1894 to 1909	92,054,178
Bonds for railway subsidies and port works	457,952
Interest due on guaranteed bonds of States	96,469
Total	439,704,094

The obligations of the railways guaranteed by the government as to both principal and interest amounted at the same time to 138,475,000 pesos.[97] The total debt, direct and indirect, was thus 578,179,094 pesos.

[94] *Com. and Fin. Chron.*, March 11, 1911, p. 626.

[95] Díaz Dufoo, *Una Victoria Financiera, sup cit.*, p. 138.

[96] *Memoria de la Secretaría de Hacienda*, 1910–1911, p. XL.

[97] In addition to the guaranteed general mortgage bonds of the National

The Loan of 1912

In consequence of the revolutionary disturbances of 1911 the bankers who had taken half of the bond issue of £22,200,000 contemplated in the contract of July 2, 1910, did not exercise their option to purchase the other half of the issue. These bankers were naturally, therefore, not favored by Madero when he found, soon after his inauguration as President, that money was required to replenish his treasury. The loan desired by Madero was furnished by Speyer and Company of New York, who, at the end of May, 1912, accepted treasury notes at 99 per cent of their face value in return for an advance of $10,000,000 at 4.5 per cent interest. The advance was made for one year only, the reason for the short period being declared to be that before the expiration of that period the government would be able to place an issue for a longer time on more favorable terms. It was believed in American financial circles that the placing of this loan in the United States would exert a beneficial influence on Mexican public sentiment towards this country and would tend to moderate the bitterness which had been shown by those who had feared American intervention.[98]

A Desperate Situation

The need for another loan was felt in September, 1912, partly to finance the efforts to suppress the elements of disorder still at work in the country and partly to stabilize the exchange value of Mexican money, which was fluctuating to a marked degree. The government at this time appeared to many competent observers to be confronted with a dilemma, one horn of which was bankruptcy, followed by American intervention, and the other a foreign loan with foreign supervision of the revenues and expenditures.

At the beginning of February, 1913, while discussing in the

Railways of Mexico, this amount includes bonds issued in 1904 and 1909 by the Tehuantepec National Railway and the Veracruz and Pacific Railroad. *Cf.* Ferrocarriles Nacionales de México, *Third Annual Report* (Mexico City, 1911), p. 29.

[98] *Com. and Fin. Chron.*, June 1, 1912, p. 1472.

Mexican Senate the proposal of a loan, Manuel Calero, recently returned from his post as Ambassador to the United States, created a sensation by declaring that the situation of the country was desperate and that he had lied to the American government for ten months. The Minister of Finance retorted that Calero was an indiscreet ambassador and a bad financier. Naturally the incident was reflected in the price of Mexican securities in foreign markets.[99]

A tentative plan for financing the Mexican government on a large scale was being considered by an American group of bankers in concert with French, English, and German groups on February 18, 1913, the day of the arrest of President Madero by General Victoriano Huerta. Neither the coup d'état of Huerta on February 20 nor the insinuations as to his complicity in the shooting of Madero two days later interrupted the consideration of this plan. On March 3, 1913, officials of the Taft administration, which was to expire the following day, were reported to be giving their attention, not to the question of the recognition of General Huerta, but to that of the financing of his government. The American Ambassador at Mexico City, though not authorized to give formal recognition to Huerta, had established informal relations with the officials of Huerta's government, and it was not foreseen that formal recognition of Huerta would be long withheld by the incoming administration of President Wilson. Bankers in the United States, England, and France were reported to be pulling political wires and trying in other ways to obtain a large foreign loan which was contemplated by Huerta.[100]

The Loan of 1913

By the middle of April it had become apparent that the failure of the Wilson administration to recognize Huerta was deliberate, and Huerta was represented as considering the United States responsible for his inability to bring to a successful con-

[99] *Com. and Fin. Chron.*, February 8, 1913, pp. 385–386.

[100] *New York Times*, March 3, 1913; Manuel Calero, *The Mexican Policy of President Woodrow Wilson as it appears to a Mexican* (New York, 1916), p. 12.

clusion the negotiations which he was conducting with foreign bankers for a loan of £20,000,000. The bankers had at first made the recognition of Huerta by the United States a *sine qua non* of the loan. This condition had been withdrawn before May 20, when the Mexican Congress gave its sanction in principle to the proposed loan. The negotiations were further embarrassed, however, on May 24, when a Mexican constitutionalist committee at Paris, representing the Carranza party opposed to Huerta, gave formal notice to the French government that Carranza, if his revolution succeeded, would not acknowledge the financial obligation which Huerta was seeking to establish.[101] The issue of a loan in bonds of the treasury of a nominal value not to exceed £20,000,000 and for a period not less than ten years was finally authorized by the Mexican Congress in a law which was promulgated on May 30, 1913. The purposes of the loan, as set forth in the law, were to pay off various floating debts, to strengthen the treasury, and to provide for various general needs.[102]

In pursuance of this law, the Federal Executive of the United Mexican States (Huerta's government), represented by Luis L. de la Barra, its financial agent at London, signed a contract at Paris on June 8, 1913, with representatives of the Banco Nacional de México and of banking houses in Paris, Berlin, London, and New York.[103] The amount of the loan was fixed at £16,000,000; the rate of interest at 6 per cent; and the period at ten years. The security stipulated was the 38 per cent of the Mexican import and export duties not already pledged to the service of the loans of 1899 and 1910. These duties, it was declared in

[101] *New York Times*, May 22 and 25, 1913.

[102] *Diario Oficial*, Vol. 126, p. 362.

[103] The French banks were the Banque de Paris et des Pays-Bas; the Société Générale pour Favoriser le Développement du Commerce et de l'Industrie en France; the Comptoir National d'Escompte de Paris; the Banque de l'Union Parisienne; Morgan, Harjes and Company; A. Spitzer and Company. The German group was composed of S. Bleichroeder, the Deutsche Bank, and the Dresdner Bank. The English participant was Morgan, Grenfell and Company. The American banks were J. P. Morgan and Company and Kuhn, Loeb and Company. A translation of the contract is printed in the Memorial of the American Agent to the General Claims Commission, United States and Mexico, in behalf of John W. de Kay.

a prospectus issued by the bankers, had during the last four years averaged annually more than 46,000,000 pesos, 38 per cent of which was more than 17,000,000 pesos as against an interest charge of less than 10,000,000 pesos on the proposed issue.

Of the total issue of £16,000,000 only £6,000,000 were brought out at this time. These were purchased outright by the bankers at 90 per cent of their face value; the Banco Nacional de México taking 5 per cent of the bonds, the French group 40.125 per cent, the German and English groups 19 per cent each, and the American group 11.875 per cent. The bonds were offered to the public at 96 per cent of their face value. At this figure they were readily disposed of. The rate of the loan and the issuing price, however, it was noted by some observers, "contrasted strangely" with the level of three years earlier, when Mexican credit was practically on a 4 per cent basis.[104]

The amount payable to the Huerta government by the bankers (54,000,000 pesos, less the cost of printing, etc.) was "assigned before any other use" to the formation of a reserve fund equal to six months' interest on the bonds (1,800,000 pesos) and to the formation of funds "for the settlement of various short-term obligations of the Government." These short-term obligations included drafts and notes, falling due in September, 1913, for somewhat more than $20,000,000 gold (40,000,000 pesos). The drafts had been "accepted by various Banks and Bankers for payment of $10,000,000 gold, plus interest on Mexico Treasury Bonds maturing June 10, 1913, placed by Messrs. Speyer and Company of New York" in 1912. The notes, for $10,000,000 plus interest, had been issued by the Mexican Monetary Commission, endorsed by the Banco Nacional de México, and placed by Speyer and Company. The sum actually received by the Huerta government for its general requirements was thus only about 12,000,000 pesos.

With respect to the £10,000,000 of bonds provided for in the contract of June 8, 1913, but not issued at this time, options at 90 per cent, expiring within one year from July 1, 1913, were

[104] *The Economist*, July 2, 1913, p. 59.

given to the bankers. For a period of two years, expiring July 1, 1915, the Huerta government undertook

> not to conclude or issue any foreign public debt loan, and not to negotiate any treasury bond or certificate payable in gold, including the bonds of the present loan on which the options have not been redeemed, unless there be a previous agreement with the Banque de Paris et des Pays Bas, as to itself and the Contracting Groups.

By this operation, in which American bankers took a leading part, the reproach cast upon the United States and its people by many Mexicans and Americans interested in Mexican business was believed by observers in New York to have been largely removed. With the financial aid thus received, Huerta should, it was thought, be able to reduce the armed opposition, which he had reported to be neither general nor formidable. The objections to the refusal of the United States to grant immediate recognition to Huerta would thus lose nearly all their force.[105]

Europe Looks to the United States for Action

Before the end of June the Huerta government had been recognized by most of the European powers, including Great Britain, France, Germany, Spain, Russia, and Portugal, and it was confidently believed by European observers that the United States would not long delay recognition. On July 16 representatives of several European powers met at Paris and decided to endeavor to obtain from the government of the United States a declaration of its intentions with reference to intervention in Mexico or recognition of Huerta. Secretary of State Bryan found it necessary, on August 1, to characterize as entirely without foundation the statement which had appeared in some of the newspapers to the effect that European governments were bringing pressure to bear on the United States to compel aggressive action in Mexico. At the date of this denial Bryan and President Wilson were in conference with Ambassador Henry Lane Wilson, who had been summoned from Mexico City to make a personal report. The Ambassador strongly favored immediate

[105] *New York Times*, June 3, 1913.

recognition of Huerta, but the President and Bryan remained unconvinced.[106]

"MEXICO'S NEAREST FRIEND"

On August 4 the Department of State announced that the resignation of Ambassador Wilson had been accepted and that ex-Governor John Lind of Minnesota had been sent to Mexico as the personal representative of the President to act as adviser to the Embassy in the existing situation. Lind's instructions from President Wilson contained the following statement:

> The Government of the United States does not stand in the same case with the other great Governments of the world in respect to what is happening or what is likely to happen in Mexico. We offer our good offices, not only because of our genuine desire to play the part of a friend, but also because we are expected by the powers of the world to act as Mexico's nearest friend.[107]

On the twenty-second of August, after some preliminary correspondence, Lind handed to Federico Gamboa, Huerta's Minister of Foreign Affairs, a note in which he proposed that Huerta immediately resign the provisional presidency and bind himself not to be a candidate for President in the election which had been fixed for October 26. Lind stated that if General Huerta acted immediately and favorably upon this proposal and others contained in his note, President Wilson would assure American bankers and their associates that the government of the United States would look with favor upon the extension of an immediate loan sufficient in amount to meet the temporary requirements of the existing Mexican administration.[108]

Lind's proposals were indignantly rejected by Gamboa, as indicating a disproportionate interest in the internal affairs of Mexico. Gamboa pointed out, however, that under the constitution of Mexico General Huerta, who had been advanced to the office of Provisional President from that of Secretary of State,

106 *The Economist*, June 28 and Aug. 2, 1913, pp. 1555, 223; *Com. and Fin. Chron.*, July 19, Aug. 2, 1913, pp. 141, 262.

107 *For. Rel. U. S.*, 1913, pp. 817, 821–822.

108 *Ibid.*, p. 832.

was barred from appearing as a candidate for President in the forthcoming election. With reference to President Wilson's conditional offer to recommend a loan to the existing administration, Gamboa remarked that when the dignity of the nation was at stake he believed that there were not loans enough to induce those charged by the law to maintain that dignity to permit it to be lessened.[109] The mention of money in this connection was later characterized by Calero as "an unheard-of stupidity." The offer of a loan could not fail to be regarded by Mexicans, said Calero, as an attempt at bribery.[110]

Funds from Local Banks

The financial assistance which the government of Huerta was unwilling to accept from American bankers and their associates on the conditions indicated by Lind was promised a few days later, on August 29, by nine banks in Mexico City, subject to approval by the foreign capitalists who controlled some of the banks. The amount thus promised, at first 10,000,000 pesos, shortly afterwards increased to 18,000,000 pesos, was believed to be sufficient to meet the needs of Huerta's government up to the end of November.[111] Considerable delay in the advance of this amount was occasioned by the refusal of some of the French and English capitalists to approve it. It was reported that these capitalists were influenced by urgent suggestions from their governments to the effect that a refusal of money would force Huerta to yield to the demands of President Wilson and would promote peace without bloodshed. The exertion of pressure by the French and British governments was said to have been intended as a direct coöperation with President Wilson's effort to crush Huerta.[112]

The contract under which the loan was made to Huerta by the banks in Mexico City was signed on September 30, 1913. The rate of interest provided for was seven per cent. The loan,

[109] *Ibid.*, p. 834.

[110] Calero, *op. cit.*, p. 117.

[111] *Com. and Fin. Chron.*, Sept. 6 and 20, 1913, pp. 619, 764–765.

[112] *Mexico, A Weekly* (New York), Sept. 13, 1913, p. 7.

unless extended by subsequent agreement, was to be repaid in gold, with interest, not later than January 1, 1914. As a special guarantee for repayment of the 10,000,000 pesos first advanced, the government issued to the banks provisional certificates constituting a charge upon £1,206,640 of the bonds provided for in the contract of June 8, 1913, and subject to option in favor of the banks signatory to that contract. The amount of the bonds so pledged was to be proportionately increased in the event of further advances by the banks in Mexico City. It was stipulated that the bonds pledged should remain subject to the option established by the contract of June 8.[113]

President Wilson's Duty

On the eleventh of October, the Mexican Congress was dissolved by Huerta as an impediment to the establishment of peace. One hundred and ten of the deputies were arrested. On the thirteenth of October, Secretary of State Bryan instructed Nelson O'Shaughnessy, the American chargé d'affaires at Mexico City, to inform the Foreign Office that Huerta's course in dissolving the Congress and arresting the deputies was regarded by President Wilson as an act of bad faith toward the United States, as well as a violation of the constitutional guarantees and an obstacle to a free and fair election. The President, said Bryan, would not feel justified in accepting the result of an election held under the existing conditions. The instruction to O'Shaughnessy was immediately communicated to the Foreign Offices of Great Britain, France, Germany, Spain, and twenty other countries with a request for comments. The comments received were generally favorable, the Russian Minister of Foreign Affairs going so far as to say that his government would welcome the annexation of Mexico by the United States.[114]

The election scheduled for October 26 having been indefinitely postponed, Secretary Bryan, on November 7, instructed the diplomatic officers of the United States in various countries

[113] Memorial in behalf of John W. de Kay, *sup. cit.*, pp. 381–388.

[114] *For. Rel. U. S.*, 1913, pp. 838–841.

to inform the governments to which they were accredited that it was the clear judgment of President Wilson that it was his immediate duty to require General Huerta's retirement from the Mexican government and to employ such measures as might be necessary to secure this result. The government of the United States, added Bryan, would not regard as binding upon the people of Mexico anything done by Huerta since his assumption of dictatorial powers. President Wilson hoped that other governments would use their influence to impress upon General Huerta the wisdom of retiring in the interest of peace and constitutional government.[115]

" Financial Starvation "

Soon after this announcement of President Wilson's determination to eliminate Huerta, it became clear that the principal measure contemplated by the President to that end was what he called financial starvation. The possibility of financial assistance being given to Huerta by German capitalists under existing conditions was, according to news advices from Berlin, under date of November 12, entirely out of the question. In London the leading bankers were reported to be aware that the British government would look with extreme disfavor upon any action tending to justify suspicions of opposition to the American policy in Mexico. Downing Street, it was acknowledged, exercised no direct control over private initiative, but it was in the utmost degree unlikely that any British financial house would run counter to the known wishes of the government in such a hazardous proposition. In Paris, where the operations of the Bourse were more directly influenced by the government, a loan to the Huerta régime was removed from the realm of possibility by the declaration of the Minister of Finance that the government intended to reserve the financial resources of the nation for the national needs, and that it would not permit bonds issued by Huerta to be quoted on the Bourse.[116]

[115] *Ibid.*, pp. 856–857.

[116] *New York Times*, November 13, 1913; Calero, *op. cit.*, p. 18.

Suspension of Interest

On December 18, the efforts to obtain funds abroad having failed and the ordinary revenues supplemented by local loans having proved inadequate for the needs of the Huerta government, the new Congress convened by Huerta authorized an internal five per cent loan of 100,000,000 pesos to be used in the payment of railway subsidies, the construction of ports, the indemnification of Chinese victims of a recent riot, and for other specified purposes. The first issue of the bonds of this loan was to be in the amount of 20,000,000 pesos. Later issues were to be made under special decrees, which would fix the amount of each issue.[117]

On December 23, 1913, General Huerta declared a moratorium to last until January 2, 1914. By later decrees the moratorium was extended to January 15, to February 28, and finally to March 31, 1914. Efforts made by the Minister of Finance to obtain in London and Paris a loan sufficient to pay the interest due January 1, 1914, on the national debt were wholly unsuccessful.[118] On January 13, 1914, the dictator issued a decree suspending for six months the payment of interest on the foreign and internal indebtedness of the Republic. It was specifically stated in the decree that the coupons falling due while payment of interest was suspended would earn interest at the same rate as the bonds to which they were attached.[119]

Talk of European Intervention

This suspension of payment of interest, like the similar measure adopted by President Juárez in July, 1861, provoked a diplomatic crisis. Seizure of the customs-houses or more thoroughgoing intervention was urged by impatient bondholders in 1914, as similar action had been urged in 1861. The European

[117] *Diario Oficial*, Vol. 129, p. 453. Information as to the issues actually made is lacking.

[118] *Com. and Fin. Chron.*, Dec. 27, 1913, p. 1848, and Jan. 17, 1914, p. 186; *New York Times*, Dec. 31, 1913.

[119] *Com. and Fin. Chron.*, Jan. 17, 1914, p. 186.

and American bankers interested in the debt telegraphed strong protests to the Huerta government on January 20, taking care to reserve the right of themselves or their governments to adopt stronger protective measures.[120] A protest was made at the same time by the diplomatic representative accredited to Huerta by France. This protest was declared by the French government to be without prejudice to its "privilege of forced collection of the customs duties."[121]

The "forced collection of the customs duties" by France or any other power was not actually within the realm of immediate probability. The use of force in behalf of bondholders in advance of the presentation and rejection of proposals for arbitration was indeed prohibited by the terms of a convention which thirty-four powers, including France, Great Britain, Germany, the United States, and Mexico, had signed at the Hague in 1907.[122] The European powers, had, moreover, recently decided to give their tacit support to the policy of the United States with reference to Mexico. That policy, which came to be known as "watchful waiting," was manifested in the continued refusal of President Wilson to recognize Huerta, in his warning to American citizens to leave Mexico, and in the financial boycott resulting from his opposition to advances of money to Huerta by foreign governments or their nationals. It was said to be an open secret that

[120] *New York Times*, Jan. 21, 1914.

[121] *Com. and Fin. Chron.*, Jan. 24, 1914, p. 260.

[122] Convention respecting the Limitation of the Employment of Force for the Recovery of Contract Debts, signed October 18, 1907; ratifications deposited at the Hague, November 27, 1909, by the United States, Germany, Great Britain, the Netherlands, Mexico, and four other powers; ratification deposited by France October 7, 1910 (*Treaties, Conventions, International Acts*, etc., *sup. cit.*, Vol. II, pp. 2248–2259; James Brown Scott, *The Hague Conventions and Declarations of 1899 and 1907*, New York, 1915, p. 236). Article I of the Convention is as follows:

"The Contracting Powers agree not to have recourse to armed force for the recovery of contract debts claimed from the Government of one country by the Government of another country as being due to its nationals.

"This undertaking is, however, not applicable when the debtor State refuses or neglects to reply to an offer of arbitration, or, after accepting the offer, prevents any 'Compromis' from being agreed on, or, after the arbitration, fails to submit to the award."

foreign governments had been notified that any such advance would be regarded by the United States as an unfriendly act.[123]

Revocation of Suspension

The financial boycott established by President Wilson was not sufficiently effective to prevent the advance of funds by banks in Mexico more or less controlled by foreign capital. A number of these banks on March 24, 1914, in order to procure the abandonment of proposals for the establishment of a federal bank and the imposition of a capital tax of one per cent, concluded with the dictator an arrangement for an advance of 45,000,000 pesos. This advance, like the advances previously made by local banks under the contract of September 30, 1913, was secured upon a part of the unissued balance of the 6 per cent bonds of 1913.[124]

As a result of this arrangement with local banks, the government, on March 31, revoked the decree of January 13 for the suspension of payments on the debt and announced that payments would be resumed on April 15. The usual amount of the customs receipts was to be deposited for this purpose in the Banco Nacional de México, where it would remain until the exchange, then very unfavorable to Mexico, should return to normal rates. The retention of the money, it was pointed out, would give the bondholders a vital and direct interest in bringing to bear all possible influence for the improvement of the rate of exchange.[125]

The de Kay Bonds

On March 2, 1914, the financial agent of Huerta in London signed with John W. de Kay, an American citizen, an agreement providing for the delivery to de Kay of £3,025,000 in bonds of the unissued balance of the loan contracted in Paris in June, 1913. This agreement was a modification of two agreements which de Kay had concluded with the Huerta administration at Mexico

123 Am. Acad. Pol. and Soc. Science, *International Relations of the United States, 1914* (Philadelphia, 1914), p. 234.

124 *Com. and Fin. Chron.*, March 28, 1914, p. 1012.

125 *Com. and Fin. Chron.*, April 4, 1914, p. 1024; *The Economist*, April 4, 1914, pp. 822–823.

City early in January, 1914. Under the new agreement de Kay, who owned the majority of the common stock and of the voting trust certificates of the Mexican National Packing Company, Limited, was to transfer his stock and certificates to the Mexican government (the Huerta administration) and was to receive for his own account, from the financial agent, £1,025,000 in the bonds above mentioned. The remainder of the £3,025,000 in bonds delivered to him he was to use in paying for war materials supplied or to be supplied by European munitions dealers. All of the bonds so delivered were, according to the agreement of March 2, 1914, to be considered "in all respects *pari passu* with the bonds of the same loan issued according to the contract of the 8th of June, 1913, made with the Banque de Paris et des Pays-Bas and other banks." Interest was to be paid on these bonds as well as upon those issued through the banks party to the contract of June 8, 1913, but the bonds were to be subject to the prohibition, in that contract, against the sale before July 1, 1915, of any of the bonds of the unissued balance of the loan of 1913. Up to July 1, 1915, moreover, the Mexican government was to have the right to demand the return of the new bonds, upon payment of 85 per cent of their face value in the case of the bonds delivered to de Kay for his own account and upon payment of the cash value of war materials supplied in the case of the other bonds delivered to de Kay.[126]

Temporary bonds in the amount of £3,025,000 were issued and delivered by the financial agent of Huerta in March, 1914, and were replaced, for the most part, before the end of June, 1914, by definitive bonds of "Series C" of the loan of 1913. The financial agent had meanwhile accepted delivery from de Kay of 51 per cent of the common stock and voting trust certificates of the Mexican National Packing Company, Limited, and de Kay had concluded with French munitions dealers and a Swiss bank contracts under which £2,000,000 of the bonds had been deposited with the bank. A large shipment of war materials paid for by the bank, and charged against the bonds, was *en route* to Mexico in April, 1914, at the moment of the occupation of Vera Cruz

[126] Memorial in behalf of John W. de Kay, *sup. cit.*, pp. 252–256.

by the United States, in the circumstances to be described below.[127] Some £824,000 of the bonds delivered to de Kay were deposited with W. B. Peat and Company, of London, in May, 1914, as security for a public offering of six per cent trust certificates, in the amount of £700,000, exchangeable in July, 1915, for the bonds.[128]

The Elimination of Huerta

In February, 1914, the weapon of financial starvation which President Wilson had been using against Huerta was supplemented by the removal of restrictions upon the shipment of arms from the United States into Mexico across the border. With the arms thus made available, the forces opposing Huerta, under the leadership of Carranza, obtained an immediate advantage. American property in Mexico and the few American citizens who had remained in the country despite President Wilson's warning began to be subjected to increasingly violent treatment at the hands of the Huertistas. Demands for intervention for the protection of American lives and property were made throughout the United States and were loudly echoed in the halls of the Congress at Washington. The issue was sharpened by an incident which occurred at Tampico.

A detachment of American warships had been stationed for some months off the eastern coast of Mexico, partly for moral effect and partly for the purpose of intercepting shipments of war materials to Huerta. The presence of these vessels was naturally resented by Huerta, and the landing of forces from them had been strictly prohibited. On April 10, 1914, a party of American marines landed at Tampico to obtain gasoline. They were promptly arrested but were shortly afterwards released with an expression of regret. The Admiral in command of the American vessels insisted upon a formal apology and a salute to the American flag. Huerta refused the salute except on condition of a formal written agreement by the chargé d'affaires of the United States that the salute be returned gun for gun. This condition

127 Memorial in behalf of John W. de Kay, *sup. cit.*, pp. 252–256.

128 *New York Times*, May 20, 1914.

was rejected by President Wilson on the ground that since the salute would be returned as a matter of course, in accordance with international custom and courtesy, an agreement on the subject was unnecessary, and on the additional ground that the proposed agreement might be construed as a recognition of Huerta's government. On April 20 the President laid the matter before the Congress at Washington "with a view of taking such steps as may be necessary to enforce respect to the flag." It was immediately resolved by both houses of the Congress that the President was "justified in the employment of the armed forces of the United States to enforce his demands for unequivocal amends for affronts and indignities committed against the United States." On April 21 the port of Veracruz was occupied by American naval forces.[129]

During the American occupation the customs duties at Veracruz were collected by the occupying forces.[130] The government at Mexico City was therefore unable to comply with Huerta's promise of March 31, 1914, to deposit the usual portion of the duties in the Banco Nacional for eventual payment of interest on the foreign debt.

The prosecution of any plan which President Wilson may have had for a thoroughgoing solution of Mexican problems was forestalled by the mediation of Argentina, Brazil, and Chile. It was finally agreed that Huerta should yield the provisional presidency to Francisco Carbajal, and a new election should be held. Carbajal was forced to yield in August to Carranza, who styled himself "First Chief of the Constitutionalist Army, in charge of the Executive Power of the Republic." The American troops were withdrawn from Veracruz in November.[131]

The Public Debt in 1914

The external debt of Mexico at the end of 1914, including the bonds actually issued in 1913 and the interest in arrears since

[129] *For. Rel. U. S.*, 1914, pp. 447–483.

[130] The final determination as to the disposition of these duties has not yet been announced.

[131] *For. Rel. U. S.*, 1914, pp. 488–562.

the beginning of the year, but not including the bonds issued in 1914 nor the railway obligations guaranteed by the government, was in round numbers £40,000,000. The internal debt represented by bonds of the government, which were held almost exclusively by foreigners, was at the same time approximately 135,000,000 pesos. The changes in the amounts of the external debt during the period covered by this chapter are indicated in the following table: [132]

EXTERNAL LOANS OF MEXICO 1888–1914 [a]

(In pounds sterling)

Period (Years Ending June 30)	Amount Outstanding at Beginning of Period	Interest Due at Beginning of Period	Addition to Capital New Loans	Deductions from Capital: Converted or Redeemed by New Loans	By Agreement	Redeemed from Revenues	Net Increase or Decrease
1888–1890	14,822,300[b]	......	10,500,000	5,881,760	8,822,640	....	−4,204,400
1890–1893	10,617,900	171,997	8,700,000	28,340	43,385	45,575	8,582,700
1893–1899	19,200,600	268,357	3,000,000	....	10,910	676,370	2,312,720
1899–1903	21,513,320	299,177	22,700,000	21,483,400	1,250	444,890	770,460
1903–1904	22,283,780	291,796	5,668,200	1,000	225	157,005	5,509,970
1904–1910	25,872,261[c]	159,555	8,213,127	1,896,114	5,257	1,724,165	4,587,591
1910–1911	30,459,852	318,916	11,084,044	10,403,084	....	295,332	385,628
1911–1913	30,845,480	185,326	2,054,909	468,902	....	671,469	914,538
1913–1914	31,760,018	221,577	5,991,375	2,054,909	....	317,234	3,619,232

[a] Loans included in this table are: Mexican Consolidated External Six Per Cent Loan of 1888, Five Per Cent Tehuantepec Railway Loan of 1889, External Six Per Cent Loan of 1890, External Six Per Cent Loan of 1893, Five Per Cent External Consolidated Gold Loan of 1899, City of Mexico Five Per Cent Sterling Loan of 1889, Four and One-Half Per Cent Treasury Obligations of 1903 and 1904, Four Per Cent External Gold Loan of 1904, Four Per Cent External Gold Loan of 1910, Four and One-Half Per Cent Treasury Obligations of 1912, and Six Per Cent Ten-Year Treasury Bonds of 1913. Data are taken from *Memorias de Hacienda* and *Cuentas del Tesoro*, where they are given in pesos — converted from pounds at the rate of 5 to 1 up to 1904, and thereafter at par of exchange (24.58 pence = 1 peso).

[b] Amount of the London Debt outstanding at this time.

[c] This figure is less than the amount outstanding on June 30, 1903, plus the net increase during the next fiscal year, for the reason that in the *Memorias* and the *Cuentas* the smaller amounts of bonds outstanding continued to be reckoned after 1904 at the rate of exchange formerly used.

[132] For changes in the amount of the bonded internal debt, see the table on page 226.

CHAPTER VIII

"A VIA CRUCIS OF PENURY"[1]

(1915–1929)

FINANCIAL MEASURES OF RIVAL FACTIONS

THE Carranza troops which took possession of Mexico City in August, 1914, had experienced great difficulty in obtaining sufficient funds for their operations. They had, in general, refrained from forced levies upon individuals and had adopted instead "the system of issues of paper money, which [according to Carranza], regardless of the disadvantages which the future might bring, nevertheless presented, as a revolutionary procedure, the advantage of being the most equitable distribution of loans among the inhabitants of the regions occupied by the revolutionary armies."[2] Of this system they had made such free use that before the entry of Carranza into Mexico City more than 60,000,000 pesos in paper money had been issued by him or with his authorization. Some 43,000,000 pesos of paper were issued by Carranza at Mexico City before he was driven out by his late ally Francisco Villa in November, 1914. At Veracruz, where he remained for nearly a year after his loss of the capital city, Carranza issued 600,000,000 pesos of additional paper money. As this money was purely fiat currency, its value in terms of gold varied with the fortunes of the Carrancistas. In the summer of 1915 its gold value was only ten centavos to the peso.[3]

Of even less value in terms of gold was the paper money issued by Carranza's rivals, who had been associated with him

[1] The title is from a decree of President Obregón dated June 30, 1924.

[2] Carranza's address to the Mexican Congress April 15, 1917, quoted in *Mexican Review* (Washington), August, 1917.

[3] Law of Payments, December 24, 1917, Article 10 (*Diario Oficial*, Dec. 29, 1917).

in his fight against Huerta. Villa, "even prior to his disloyalty," had issued paper money far in excess of the amount which Carranza had authorized him to issue. After the Military Convention of Aguascalientes of October, 1914, at which the leadership of Carranza was repudiated by Villa and several other revolutionary generals, the "government" emanating from that Convention established itself at Mexico City and issued a considerable quantity of new paper money. This "government," known as the Conventionist government, at the same time declared the currency issued at Mexico City by the Carranza or Constitutionalist government to be worthless unless "revalidated" by the Conventionist authorities. The bills issued or "revalidated" by the latter authorities were, in turn, denounced by the Carranza government.[4]

At the end of January, 1915, the possession of Mexico City was temporarily recovered by General Alvaro Obregón, one of Carranza's supporters. During his occupation of the city he levied a capital tax of three-fourths of one per cent upon "all banks, business houses, stock companies, mortgage holders, and private individuals operating within the Federal District, including all foreign corporations and private business men." This tax was expected to yield 20,000,000 pesos. The United States and other powers protested to General Carranza against the threats accompanying the imposition of this tax and against the short time, only seventy-two hours, allowed for payment.[5]

The Recognition of Carranza

In August, 1915, a Conference of seven American republics initiated by the United States appealed to the chiefs of the contending factions to meet on neutral ground somewhere in Mexico and agree on the first steps necessary for the pacification of the country. The appeal was reported to have been preceded by

[4] Carranza's address, above cited.

[5] *Com. and Fin. Chron.*, Feb. 27, 1915, p. 670; *The Economist*, Feb. 6 and March 20, 1915, pp. 228 and 587. (Here, as elsewhere throughout the present chapter, periodicals are cited in connection with statements the accuracy of which has been checked so far as possible against other sources.)

intimations that the United States might assist a new government in Mexico by promoting a loan to it.[6]

The United States and the other participants in the Conference finally recognized Carranza as provisional President on October 19, 1915.[7] The recognition was not accompanied by a promise of financial assistance on the part of any of the powers nor by a promise on Carranza's part to recognize the financial obligations which Huerta had assumed.

"Well-Wishing Aloofness"

According to statements made by the Carranza agency at Washington on October 29, 1915, the Carranza government had decided not to attempt the negotiation of a foreign loan. This decision was believed by officials in Washington to have postponed a problem for the United States, which was apparently not prepared at that time to enter into an arrangement with Mexico for the exercise of such a measure of control over Mexican revenues as would be indispensable for the success of a Mexican loan in the American market.[8]

In February, 1916, well informed financiers who had gone into Mexico with capital professed to see no hope for the Carranza government so long as the United States maintained its attitude of "well-wishing aloofness." Bankers and their customers, it was said, had lost so much money on their Mexican ventures that no inducement unsupported by an official pledge of the United States government had any attraction for them. Even if the Carranza government were strongly entrenched, it could obtain no funds abroad because of its inability to collect sufficient revenues for its current expenses. A solution of the deplorable situation, it was believed, could be reached if the Mexican people were to invite the government of the United States to send a commission to take charge of the collection and disbursement of Mexican revenues until the defaulted obligations were redeemed.[9]

[6] *The Economist*, August 21, 1915, p. 290.

[7] *For. Rel. U. S.*, 1915, p. 772.

[8] *Com. and Fin. Chron.*, November 6, 1915, p. 517.

[9] *New York Times*, February 7, 1916.

The attitude of "aloofness" with which American financiers reproached their government was abandoned, temporarily, in March, 1916, when Villa, at the head of about a thousand men, attacked the garrison at Columbus, New Mexico, and killed several American soldiers. General Funston reported to Washington that the Carranza troops were "grossly apathetic and inefficient" and that, in his opinion, unless Villa were relentlessly pursued into Mexico he would continue his depredations upon the American border. By direction of President Wilson, an armed force was sent into Mexico, under General John J. Pershing, to capture Villa and to prevent further raids. The Carranza government at first evinced a "cordial and friendly spirit of coöperation in the efforts of the authorities of the United States to apprehend and punish the bands of outlaws." Within a few days, however, the Minister of Foreign Affairs at Mexico City declared that the consent of his government to the crossing of American troops into Mexico was being "erroneously understood." Agreement on the conditions of the continuance of the "punitive expedition" in Mexico proving impossible, the American troops were regarded by the Carranza government as hostile invaders. An armed engagement between forces of Carranza and a part of Pershing's column occurred at Carrizal, in Chihuahua, on June 21, 1916. Immediately thereafter several of the Latin-American countries offered to mediate between Mexico and the United States. A joint commission for the settlement of differences was proposed by the Carranza government on July 12, 1916. In November, the joint commission of six members, appointed in pursuance of the Mexican proposal, reached an agreement regarding the withdrawal of the punitive expedition. This agreement was rejected by the Carranza government, and it was not until February, 1917, that the American troops returned to the United States, without having captured Villa.[10]

In the meantime the financial distress of the Carranza government had continued. It had, in fact, been aggravated by the necessity of obtaining funds for the equipment of the troops sent against Pershing's men. With a view to improving the situation

[10] *For. Rel. U. S.*, 1916, pp. 480–491, 595–608; 1917, pp. 908–939.

with reference to the currency, Carranza promulgated, in April, 1916, a decree providing for the retirement of all paper money then in circulation and for the issue of 500,000,000 pesos of new currency " engraved on special paper in a manner impossible to counterfeit." Every peso of the new currency was guaranteed as having a value of twenty centavos in gold coin. The guarantee was not long maintained, for the reason that

> the government did not have sufficient gold reserve nor sufficient revenues in metallic money. . . . The disbursements of the government in metallic money continued to be made more urgent all the time, and the rise in the price of materials, munitions, equipment and provisions for the forces, which the government had to purchase in metallic money, made it necessary to expend from its revenues in gold. . . . The value of the paper continued to go down

until by the middle of September, 1916, the peso of the " infalsificable " issue was worth only five centavos in gold. Before the middle of December the paper money, though declared legal tender, had ceased to circulate. A general moratorium in favor of creditors was established by a decree of December 14, 1916.[11]

During this spectacular decline of the peso the possibility of arranging financial aid for the Carranza government was discussed in Washington. There were rumors of plans of the Carranza government to obtain a loan of 100,000,000 pesos or more in the United States for the reorganization of its finances. In banking circles in New York, however, it was pointed out that a loan was not likely to be made before the establishment of a stable government in Mexico, or without a guarantee by the government of the United States.[12] By the end of the year the country was reported to be exhausted by revolutionary struggles. Its very exhaustion, however, since it meant at least a temporary cessation of revolution, was said to afford encouragement to the

[11] Carranza's address, above cited. See also Antonio Manero, *El Banco de México* (New York, 1926), pp. 158–164. The " infalsificable " issue was liquidated after March 29, 1917, by means of a surcharge of one peso of that issue with every peso payable in gold on import duties and on the petroleum and metal production taxes.

[12] *Com. and Fin. Chron.*, August 5, 1916, p. 442, and September 9, 1916, p. 908.

United States and to American financiers to undertake the work of assisting in the reorganization of Mexican finances.[13]

Funds from the Banks of Issue

The possibility of financial assistance from sources other than the United States was indicated in reports which reached Washington in March, 1917. According to these reports the German bank at Mexico City and the German legation there were virtually guiding the financial and diplomatic affairs of Mexico, and a large quantity of German money had been furnished to the Carranza government. A denial of these reports was promptly made by Rafael Nieto, Acting Minister of Finance.[14] The suspicion that Mexico was receiving money from Germany was, however, so late as June 16, sufficiently prevalent in the United States to cause the termination by the Mexican government of an arrangement which had been made for the coinage in this country of $20,000,000 in gold bullion, declared by Nieto to have come entirely from Mexican sources.[15] The Mexican sources mentioned by Nieto probably included the Banco Nacional, the Banco de Londres y México, and other banks of issue whose metallic reserves were being taken by the government, following the cancellation of their concessions and the appointment of liquidating agencies. The reasons for the action of Carranza with reference to these banks appear to have included a belief that the banks had been too ready to lend financial assistance to Huerta and to profit by the privilege of issuing bank notes on the security of bonds delivered by Huerta.[16] The metallic reserves taken from the banks, to the total amount of more than fifty million pesos, were used chiefly in the establishment of specie as the only legal tender in transactions throughout the country.[17]

[13] *London Times Annual Financial Review*, January 19, 1917, quoted in *The Economist*, January 27, 1917, p. 137.

[14] *Com. and Fin. Chron.*, April 7, 1917, p. 1355.

[15] *Com. and Fin. Chron.*, July 28, 1917, p. 357.

[16] *Cf.* p. 254, *supra*.

[17] For the emphatic protests of the governments of the United States and France against the action of Carranza with reference to the banks, see *For. Rel. U. S.*, 1916, pp. 626–650; 1917, pp. 998–1017.

A Move toward Resumption of the Debt Service

On March 26, 1917, shortly after the denial of the exercise of undue influence by the German legation and of the receipt of money from German sources, the Carranza government announced that it was prepared to meet its bond obligations in the near future. The next Congress was to be asked to authorize the resumption of payments of interest on the foreign debt. The resumption, it was believed, would strengthen the relations of Mexico with France, England, the United States, and other countries in which Mexican bonds were held.[18] At the end of March, 1917, the Council of the Corporation of Foreign Bondholders at London informed the public that it had under consideration the question of forming a committee to represent the holders of various Mexican bonds with a view to the protection of their interests.[19] This statement was followed on April 3, 1917, by an announcement from the offices of Morgan, Grenfell and Company that the bankers responsible for the issue of the loans of 1899, 1910, and 1913 had, in conjunction with the representatives of their respective foreign offices, been making every endeavor to protect the interests of the bondholders. In October, 1915, when *de facto* recognition was given to Carranza, a general committee to represent all the holders of Mexican bonds and investors in Mexican enterprises had been formed in London. This committee had recently communicated with the interested French and American banking groups, and the various groups, after consultation through diplomatic channels, had decided that it was not then possible to take any active steps for the protection of the bondholders and investors. The committee was, however, carefully watching the course of events in Mexico, and at the proper time it would take appropriate action.[20]

Disquieting Elements in the Financial Situation

An event which had the indirect effect of creating further obstacles to financial recovery was the adoption by Mexico of a

[18] *New York Times*, March 26, 1917.

[19] *The Economist*, March 31, 1917, p. 610.

[20] *Ibid.*, April 7, 1917, p. 624.

new constitution, which came into effect on May 1, 1917. Certain provisions of this constitution, particularly those in Article 27, which among other things provided for the nationalization of the oil resources of the country, occasioned great solicitude among American and other foreign investors. It was apprehended that the application of these provisions would be virtually confiscatory.[21]

[21] Article 27 of the constitution of 1917 is in part as follows (H. N. Branch, *The Mexican Constitution of 1917 compared with the Constitution of 1857*, Washington, 1926, pp. 16–19):

"The Nation shall have at all times the right to impose on private property such limitations as the public interest may demand as well as the right to regulate the development of natural resources, which are susceptible of appropriation, in order to conserve them and equitably to distribute the public wealth. For this purpose necessary measures shall be taken to divide large landed estates; to develop small landed holdings; to establish new centers of rural population with such lands and waters as may be indispensable to them; to encourage agriculture and to prevent the destruction of natural resources, and to protect property from damage detrimental to society. Settlements, hamlets situated on private property and communes which lack lands or water or do not possess them in sufficient quantities for their needs shall have the right to be provided with them from the adjoining properties, always having due regard for small landed holdings. . . .

"In the Nation is vested direct ownership of all minerals or substances which in veins, layers, masses, or beds constitute deposits whose nature is different from the components of the land, such as minerals from which metals and metaloids used for industrial purposes are extracted; beds of precious stones, rock salt and salt lakes formed directly by marine waters, products derived from the decomposition of rocks, when their exploitation requires underground work; phosphates which may be used for fertilizers; solid mineral fuels; petroleum and all hydrocarbons — solid, liquid or gaseous. . . .

"The ownership of the Nation is inalienable and may not be lost by prescription; concessions shall be granted by the Federal Government to private parties or civil or commercial corporations organized under the laws of Mexico, only on condition that said resources be regularly developed, and on the further condition that the legal provisions be observed.

"Legal capacity to acquire ownership of lands and waters of the nation shall be governed by the following provisions:

"1. Only Mexicans by birth or naturalization and Mexican companies have the right to acquire ownership in lands, waters and their appurtenances, or to obtain concessions to develop mines, waters or mineral fuels in the Republic of Mexico. The Nation may grant the same right to foreigners, provided they agree before the Department of Foreign Affairs to be considered Mexicans in respect to such property, and accordingly not to invoke the protection of their Governments in respect to the same, under penalty, in case of breach, of for-

Towards the end of June, 1917, the Mexican Minister of Finance, Luis Cabrera, stated publicly that he intended to try to borrow money from American bankers but that he would not attempt to borrow from the government of the United States, because of the anti-American feeling in Mexico and of the Mexican desire to remain neutral in the war. The probability of the success of the Minister's negotiations with American bankers was reduced by the bankers' realization of the calls which were about to be made upon their investing public for war loans. Another factor militating against the success of such negotiations was the apprehension felt with respect to the application of the new constitution. This apprehension was felt as keenly in Europe as in the United States. The French government, for example, learning that "pressing applications for financial assistance" were likely to be made in Washington, expressed to Secretary Lansing on July 14, 1917, through Ambassador Jusserand, the opinion that

> it would be highly desirable, in the event of financial assistance being extended to President Carranza, to stipulate guaranties as to (*inter alia*) the provisions inconsistent with international law that are found in the new constitution.[22]

On July 20, 1917, the Mexican Chamber of Deputies passed a bill providing for the negotiation of a loan of 100,000,000 pesos for the purpose of establishing a bank with the exclusive right to issue currency.[23] On the same day it was reported that the government of the United States had through New York bankers offered a loan sufficient to reëstablish the credit of Mexico.[24] On the following day, however, the report was denied at the American Department of State, where it was declared that the question of financial assistance to Mexico had never been discussed between the American and Mexican authorities.[25]

Ten days later the question of financial assistance was in

---

feiture to the Nation of property so acquired. Within a zone of 100 kilometers from the frontiers, and 50 kilometers from the seacoast, no foreigner shall under any condition acquire direct ownership of lands and waters."

22 *For. Rel. U. S.*, 1917, p. 1011.

23 *Cf.* p. 268, *supra*.

24 *New York Times*, July 21, 1917.

25 *Ibid.*, July 22, 1917.

fact discussed between President Carranza and Henry P. Fletcher, the American Ambassador at Mexico City. Carranza stated that loans had been offered by two bankers and that he believed satisfactory terms could be made "if the United States Government did not veto such a loan." Fletcher explained the special interest which the government of the United States naturally had in foreign loans placed in the American market while the United States was at war. In his own opinion, however, he told Carranza, the government of the United States would not be disposed "to place any obstacles in the way of Mexico's securing financial assistance." In reporting his interview in a telegram of August 2, 1917, to Secretary Lansing, he said: [26]

> I suggest that I be authorized to say to President Carranza that the United States Government will not oppose his borrowing, if he can, in our market, up to the amount authorized by his Congress. I think it is important for me to be able to say this now, as there is some danger that the bankers, not finding the business attractive, may seek to place the responsibility for failure of the negotiations upon our Government. Personally, I do not believe he can secure loan from private sources but he intends to try and it is important that he should know that our Government does not oppose his effort so that if he fails he will know the real reason.

Lansing's reply, dated August 8, 1917, was as follows: [27]

> You may state to General Carranza that this Government will not veto loan from the bankers of the United States to the Mexican Government. It would be well, however, in discussing the matter with him to suggest as your opinion that the chances of the Mexican Government obtaining such a loan from any bankers are slight unless they are prepared to give some guaranty in regard to general financial reforms and recognition of valid vested interests, and also that there should be some distinct understanding that the money would be paid to Mexico in instalments.

Hopes for American Money

On August 18, 1917, the bill authorizing a loan of 100,000,000 pesos having meanwhile become a law, Dr. Alfredo Caturegli, agent of the Carranza government, who had just returned from the United States, stated at Mexico City that preliminary negotia-

[26] *For. Rel. U. S.*, 1917, p. 1013.
[27] *Ibid.*, p. 1014.

tions would soon be opened with several groups of American bankers.[28] Now that the Carranza government had "broken with its German advisers," it was thought by European observers that the loan might be approved by the government of the United States. There were various optimistic forecasts of improvements in the situation in Mexico. The reappearance of specie as a result of the repudiation of the paper currency had apparently revived the mining industry, and the needs of the war had stimulated the production of petroleum.[29]

The hopes of the Mexican government for immediate financial assistance from American bankers were raised by the publication, on August 21, of a news dispatch to the effect that the bankers had been assured at the White House that the Department of State would lend moral support to a Mexican loan. The exact character of the assurance given to the bankers was said not to have been revealed, but it was understood that if a Mexican loan were floated in the United States, President Carranza would accept advice as to its expenditure and would assent to a degree of supervision.[30]

The report was denied by Secretary Lansing and by the bankers in New York City. The latter stated that the only condition on which they would consider a loan to Mexico was that the United States government should guarantee the loan.[31]

Despite these denials in Washington and New York a representative of a New York banking house was reported, at the end of August, to have been negotiating with the Mexican government at Mexico City. This representative[32] left Mexico City for New York on September 1, accompanied by an agent of the Mexican government. The negotiations had not been successful up to the first of November, when Cabrera, in a published letter to a Mexican periodical,[33] indicated one of the possible reasons for the failure of the negotiations in his statement that the ques-

[28] *New York Times*, Sept. 1, 1917.
[29] *The Economist*, Aug. 18, 1917, p. 242.
[30] *New York Times*, August 21, 1917.
[31] *Ibid.*, August 22, 1917.
[32] T. W. Osterheld, of Lansburgh Brothers.
[33] *El Democrata.*

tion of a loan to Mexico should be independent of the question of the international attitude of the Mexican government. An alliance with the United States, said Cabrera, would doubtless facilitate a loan, but he knew of no incident of such a character as to compel Mexico to abandon her attitude of neutrality.

In January, 1918, the Mexican government was again reported to be prepared to solicit a loan in the United States. American financiers were apparently no more receptive to proposals for such a loan at this time than they had been in 1917. Reports of a projected loan from the United States government were denied by Secretary Lansing on February 15.[34]

Active negotiations for a loan from American capitalists were under way during April and May, 1918. The American bankers concerned in these negotiations were informally reminded by the State Department of the desire of the American government that Mexico should guarantee American vested property interests against the anticipated prejudicial effects of the application of the new constitution and that a responsible tribunal for the settlement of claims should be set up by the two governments. Their attention was also called to the fact that a loan to Mexico should be purely a banking operation and not a method of obtaining additional oil and mining concessions for American industries affiliated with the bankers. The policy of the American government, it was stated, was opposed to intervention in Mexico, and the official approval of a loan could not be used as an opening wedge to force intervention.[35]

That the considerations suggested by the State Department were borne in mind by the bankers and communicated by them to the Mexican government is indicated by the fact that President Carranza, at the end of May, freely expressed the opinion that the government of the United States was responsible for the failure of his negotiations with the bankers.[36]

The income of the Carranza government, it may be noted, was at this time apparently greater than that of the Díaz govern-

[34] *Com. and Fin. Chron.*, Feb. 23, 1918, p. 758.

[35] Information given Committee by State Department.

[36] C. F. B., *Forty-Sixth Annual Report,* 1918, pp. 231–236.

ment had been in its best years.[37] For the nine months ending May 1, 1918, the revenues were stated by Carranza to have amounted to 102,590,000 pesos.[38] For the year ending December 31, 1918, the revenues were given by the Minister of Finance as 149,141,373 pesos.[39] The budgeted expenditures for this year were, however, some 40,000,000 pesos in excess of the revenues. Of these expenditures 64.6 per cent, a total of 120,758,153 pesos, were allotted to the Ministry of War and Marine.[40]

On the sudden close of the World War, in November, 1918, there was an immediate revival of the hopes for financial assistance from the United States.[41] With a view to the discussion of a possible loan to Mexico, Nieto, the Acting Minister of Finance, left Mexico for New York in January, 1919. In extended conferences with J. P. Morgan and Company, Speyer and Company, and other New York banking houses, a plan was tentatively prepared for the refunding of the Mexican debt into a single comprehensive issue of bonds, the issuing of new bonds for internal development, and the pledging of the customs revenues as security under some form of international administration.[42] An alternative plan, suggested by T. W. Osterheld, of the New York firm of Lansburgh Brothers, who had been in negotiation with the Mexican government in 1917, provided for the transfer of oil, mining, and agricultural lands either to the National Railways of Mexico or to a new Commission, which would earn on these lands sufficient income to pay interest and amortization charges on both the national debt and the railway

[37] The enormous increase in the prices of raw materials during the World War enabled Carranza to obtain large sums in export taxes. The oil industry, which had been of slight importance under Díaz, was now yielding 12,000,000 pesos a year in duties. *Cf. Com. and Fin. Chron.*, Aug. 24, 1918, p. 744.

[38] C. F. B., *Forty-Sixth Annual Report*, 1918, pp. 231–236.

[39] C. F. B., *Forty-Seventh Annual Report*, 1919, p. 239.

[40] *Ibid.*

[41] *The Economist*, Nov. 23, 1918, p. 708.

[42] It was at first proposed to place the administration of the customs in the hands of a joint commission of representatives of the United States and Mexico. Later, the addition of British and French representatives was suggested. Nothing came of the plan. It was doubtless objectionable, in principle, to the Mexican government.

debt. Nieto returned to Mexico to lay these plans before his government.[43]

The International Committee of Bankers on Mexico

While Nieto was in New York, a project which had been under consideration for some months, in the Department of State at Washington and in the Foreign Offices at London and Paris as well as among American, English, and French bankers, was brought to maturity. The association of the United States with the Allied Powers during the World War had served to emphasize the community of interest among holders of Mexican securities in the United States, Great Britain, and France. It had also confirmed the disposition which the British and French governments had shown before the war to follow the lead of the United States in all matters affecting Mexico. During the month preceding the Armistice of November 11, 1918, New York bankers largely interested in Mexican securities had entered into discussions with bankers similarly interested in London and Paris. Conferences at the Department of State and at the British and French Foreign Offices had revealed that these organs of government would welcome the establishment of some concerted program of action, on the part of the bankers, with reference to government bonds and other Mexican securities. The American holdings of Mexican securities were considerably less than either the British or the French holdings. In view, however, of the special position of the United States in relation to Mexico, it had been readily acknowledged by the British and French bankers and their governments that, in any formal organization which might be effected, the American bankers should be accorded a predominant position in all questions of major policy.

The announcement of the organization effected by the bankers was made on February 23, 1919.[44] The organization was called the International Committee of Bankers on Mexico. Its purpose was

[43] *New York Times*, Feb. 11, Feb. 22, March 5, March 13, and March 20, 1919.

[44] The text of the announcement, as made in New York, was printed in the *Commercial and Financial Chronicle*, March 1, 1919, pp. 824–825.

declared to be the protection of the holders of "securities of the Mexican Republic and of the various railway systems of Mexico, and generally of such other enterprises as have their field of action in Mexico." The membership of the Committee was as follows:

J. P. Morgan, Chairman, of J. P. Morgan & Co.
John J. Mitchell, President Illinois Trust & Savings Bank, Chicago.
Walter T. Rosen of Ladenburg, Thalmann & Co., New York.
Charles H. Sabin, President Guaranty Trust Co., New York.
Mortimer L. Schiff of Kuhn, Loeb & Co., New York.
James A. Stillman, Chairman of the Board, National City Bank, New York.
James N. Wallace, President Central-Union Trust Co., New York.
Albert H. Wiggin, Chairman of the Board, Chase National Bank, New York.
Robert Winsor of Kidder, Peabody & Co., Boston.
Laurence Currie of Messrs. Glyn, Mills, Currie & Co., London.
Sir Clarendon Hyde of Messrs. S. Pearson & Sons, Ltd., London.
E. R. Peacock, Chairman of the bondholders committee of the Mexico Tramways and the Mexican Light & Power group of companies, London.
Vivian H. Smith of Messrs. Morgan, Grenfell & Co., London.
Vincent W. Yorke, Chairman of the Mexican Ry. Co., Ltd., London.
William d'Eichthal of Mirabaud & Co., Paris.
Georges Heine, director of the Banque de l'Union Parisienne.
André Honnorat, member of the Commission for the Protection of French Holders of Mexican Securities.
Jacques Kulp, Auditor of the Banque de Paris et des Pays-Bas, Paris.
Joseph Simon, Inspector of Finance, General Delegate of the Commission for the Protection of French Holders of Mexican Securities.

This Committee, it was stated, was "not yet prepared to announce a definite program of procedure." In general, however, the announcement continued,

its functions will be to inform itself as fully as possible as to existing conditions in Mexico with a view to such positive action as may be taken whenever circumstances permit. Especial care has been taken as to the composition of the committee upon a broad international basis, so as thereby to ensure so far as may be joint and united action by security holders in all three countries concerned, namely the United States, Great Britain and France.

The U. S. State Department at Washington, D. C., and the Foreign Offices respectively of the British and French Governments have been advised of the formation of this committee.

Upon T. W. Lamont's return to New York City from Paris, where, on behalf of the United States Treasury, he is in attendance upon the session of the American Commission to negotiate peace, and where he will have opportunity of conferring with the British and the French interests, he will, as originally planned, undertake the active duties of the Chairmanship of the committee.

The formation of the Committee was given the approval of President Carranza immediately after the announcement of February 23. Nieto also, after conferring with American members of the Committee, expressed his confidence that the Committee, considering the needs and problems of the Mexican people, could in conference with representatives of the Mexican government arrive at a plan of coöperation which would redound to the mutual advantage of Mexico and of the investors in Mexican securities.[45]

Further Moves toward Resumption of the Debt Service

An extraordinary session of the Mexican Congress was called for May 1, 1919. It was expected by observers interested in the financial situation of the country that the Congress would sanction the assignment of certain revenues for the service of the anticipated loan from American financiers and would pass legislation explaining and practically modifying the provisions of the constitution with respect to state ownership of oil lands.[46]

The expected action was not taken, and the possibility of a

[45] *New York Times*, Feb. 25, 1919; *Com. and Fin. Chron.*, March 1, 1919.

[46] *The Economist*, March 29, 1919, p. 515.

loan from American capitalists was rendered more remote by the persistence of armed opposition to the Carranza government, by raids of Villistas into the United States, and by the outbreak of a lively campaign in American journals and in the Congress at Washington with a view to bringing about American intervention for the abatement of the "international nuisance" across the border.[47] The chances of a loan in the United States were, moreover, seriously affected by the following declaration of Cabrera, the Mexican Minister of Finance, in November, 1919:

> If we had the cash in our treasury to resume payments on the national debt today we should prefer to wait. Our creditors have waited patiently and they will continue patient. We prefer to await the outcome of adjustments of problems of world-wide importance that may affect us directly. We must know what the world in general will do with its obligations, how many nations will repudiate their debts, and how many will trim their obligations to figures compatible with their income.[48]

An attitude more satisfactory to the bondholders was indicated at the end of the year 1919 by the dispatch of Nieto and General Candido Aguilar to Europe, with instructions to reorganize the Mexican financial agency in London and to prepare for the resumption of payments on the foreign debt. Consistent with this action was the announcement by the Mexican consulate in London on January 8, 1920, that the government intended to protect all vested interests, whether acquired before or after the adoption of the constitution. The satisfaction of the bondholders at these evidences of good intention was decidedly guarded. It was recalled that promises of financial reform had been made in 1917 and left unfulfiled, and a poet of ancient Rome was quoted to the effect that any one could be rich in promises.[49] The plan for resumption of payments on the foreign debt was in fact abandoned in April, 1920, in consequence of the extraordinary demands upon the treasury incident to the uprising led by General Obregón.[50]

[47] Rippy, *op. cit.*, pp. 352–355.

[48] *Investigation of Mexican Affairs, Preliminary Report and Hearings, Sen. Doc. No. 285*, 66th Cong., 2d Sess. (Fall Committee Report), p. 3301.

[49] *The Economist*, January 10, 1920, p. 57, and January 24, 1920, pp. 135–136.

[50] *Cf.* Rippy, *op. cit.*, p. 357.

Recommendations of American Senate Subcommittee

Shortly after the fall of the Carranza government in May, 1920, a subcommittee of the United States Senate Committee on Foreign Relations, which had been investigating Mexican affairs since the preceding summer, submitted its report and recommendations. After setting forth the conditions for the recognition of any government in Mexico — conditions which included guarantees for the preservation of order and the respect of acquired rights — the subcommittee urged that the government which might be recognized should be given not only the moral support of the United States but "financial aid without stint" for the refunding of the national debt and the rehabilitation and maintenance of all the Mexican railways. Such aid, said the subcommittee, should preferably be

> extended by the people of the United States as a national loan from them to the people of Mexico, upon long time and with moderate rates of interest, so that Mexico may not be compelled to refund her debt and finance her necessities through appeal to individuals and by granting special privileges or concessions to such individuals.[51]

Reassurances from Mexican Leaders

The importance of making provision for the settlement of the foreign debt was recognized by General Obregón, the leader of the successful uprising against Carranza.

> First [he declared], we will take care of Mexico's foreign obligations. . . . When that is done we will talk about borrowing money for the rehabilitation of railroads and the building of our ports and other public works which have been allowed to go to pieces. In other words, we propose to establish a credit in just the same way that the individual merchant establishes a credit, and that is by paying our debts.[52]

In the same spirit was the statement of the Provisional President, Adolfo de la Huerta, on October 22, 1920, to the effect that Mexico would pay all she justly owed "in conformity with all recognized principles of international law." It was not the inten-

[51] Fall Committee Report, *sup. cit.*, p. 3372.

[52] *Mexican Review*, September, 1920, p. 6.

tion of the Mexican government, the Provisional President continued, to give confiscatory effect to Mexican laws.[53]

So satisfactory did the attitude of the new government seem to the government at Washington that on the thirtieth of October Secretary of State Colby announced that recognition would be granted by the United States upon three conditions, which it was understood would occasion little or no difficulty. These were the establishment of a Mixed Claims Commission, the non-enforcement of the apparently retroactive provisions of the new constitution, and the recognition of the foreign debt.[54]

Overtures to the International Committee of Bankers

On February 7, 1921, Manuel C. Téllez, the Mexican chargé d'affaires at Washington, called at the office of James Speyer in New York by direction of General Obregón, who had become President of Mexico. Téllez explained to Speyer the wish of the Mexican government to discuss with Speyer and Company and the other creditors of the government a suitable way to reach a settlement of pending questions. He suggested that Speyer proceed to Mexico City for discussions of this matter. At the same time Téllez called on Thomas W. Lamont, Chairman of the International Committee of Bankers on Mexico, and made a similar suggestion to him.[55]

In a statement given out by Lamont on February 8, it was declared that inasmuch as the International Committee had been formed with the approval of the governments of the United States, Great Britain, and France, the decision of the American section of the Committee, with reference to acceptance of the invitation of the Mexican government, would of course be made only after consultation with the Department of State as well as with the foreign members of the Committee. The International Committee had always been and still was strongly desirous of assisting the Mexican government and people in any way possible in the adjustment of their financial situation. It was eager to

[53] *Com. and Fin. Chron.*, October 23, 1920.
[54] *New York Times*, Oct. 30, 1920.
[55] *Com. and Fin. Chron.*, February 12, 1921, pp. 603–604.

take any step which in the opinion of the Department of State might be helpful. The Department, it was added, would doubtless wish the Committee to confer with members of the incoming Harding administration.[56]

On March 29, 1921, Lamont announced that a representative of Belgian interests had been admitted to membership in the International Committee of Bankers. This step, he said, had been taken with the approval of the American Department of State and the British and French Foreign Offices. Representatives of Swiss and Dutch interests had previously been admitted with the approval of the Department of State and the Foreign Offices mentioned.[57]

Although it was apparently not desired by the Committee that its operations be given an official cast, it was evidently regarded as desirable that the composition of the Committee be officially approved. It was also considered important that the initiation of the discussions of the foreign debt proposed by President Obregón be similarly sanctioned. The delay in the acceptance of the invitation to engage in these discussions was the occasion for a complaint by President Obregón in June, 1921, to the effect that the acceptance had been "prevented by various governmental pressure." [58]

Acceptance of the Invitation for Conferences in Mexico

The considerations which may have caused the Department of State to delay approval of the acceptance of President Obregón's invitation may be inferred from the fact that Charles Evans Hughes, soon after his assumption of the office of Secretary of State, became convinced that the fundamental question in the relations of the United States with Mexico was that of safeguarding property rights against possible confiscation. It was obviously desirable that the discussions with reference to the financial rehabilitation of the country and the restoration of its credit be preceded by some understanding with reference to the security of

[56] *Com. and Fin. Chron.*, February 12, 1921, pp. 603–604.

[57] *Com. and Fin. Chron.*, April 9, 1921, p. 1463.

[58] *New York World*, June 27, 1921.

property rights in general. No such understanding had been reached when President Obregón's invitation was accepted by Lamont, with the approval of the Department of State, in September, 1921. The Department had, however, stated publicly that an agreement that Article 27 of the new constitution would not be given retroactive effect was a *sine qua non* of the establishment of relations between the two countries. The government of the United States, the Department had declared, did not peremptorily demand payment of the foreign debt nor of the claims for injuries caused by the revolution. On the contrary, it was ready to assist in the restoration of Mexico.[59]

The Bond Purchase Project

Another development of some importance which preceded Lamont's arrival in Mexico City, in October, for the financial discussions with the Mexican government, was a demonstration, which the American oil companies had begun in June, against a large increase of the oil export tax from which the government had hoped to obtain sufficient funds for the resumption of payments on the foreign debt in July. This demonstration had been so far effective that de la Huerta, the Minister of Finance, had before Lamont's arrival effected a compromise with representatives of the oil companies permitting the payment of the tax in Mexican government bonds, which could be bought in the market at less than forty per cent of their face value. The desire of the Minister of Finance to link this compromise with the agreement for the refunding of the debt was one of the causes for the failure of his negotiations with Lamont.[60]

The agreement with the oil companies contemplated the purchase of bonds by some banking syndicate which would be allowed a substantial profit on the bonds delivered to the oil companies for use in payment of the oil export tax. It was suggested to Lamont that the banking houses associated in the American section of the International Committee of Bankers coöperate in forming such a syndicate. The suggestion could

[59] State Department Press Release, Aug. 20, 1921.

[60] *Com. and Fin. Chron.*, February 25, 1922, pp. 802–803.

hardly have been expected to commend itself to banks which had participated in the sale of the bonds when they were floated in the United States. It would obviously have been embarrassing for such banks to make additional profits by purchasing at a low rate bonds which they had sold to their clients at par or thereabouts. The payment of the export tax in the manner contemplated was, moreover, open to question on legal grounds, since this tax constituted a part of the revenues pledged to the bondholders and ought therefore to be applied to the payment of interest or to the redemption of the bonds at par, rather than to the retirement of the bonds at rates which were low because of the long default in the payment of interest.[61]

The Minister of Finance maintained that there was no irregularity in the suggested plan, since under the various loan contracts the government had the right to buy its bonds at market rates. This right, however, Lamont believed, could be claimed and exercised only upon condition of the previous fulfilment by the government of its obligation to pay interest in due course. The fact that the United States Treasury was at this time purchasing Liberty Bonds of the United States at the current depreciated market price was said to furnish no analogy, inasmuch as the United States had regularly paid the interest on these bonds.[62]

Failure of the Negotiations in Mexico

Principally for the reasons here suggested, the negotiations at Mexico City broke down, and Lamont returned to New York on October 21, 1921. Disappointment at the failure of the negotiations was voiced strongly by bankers and business men, as well as by others who had hoped that a financial settlement would be a great factor in hastening the recognition of the Obregón government by the United States. The Minister of Finance, however, expressed confidence that an agreement would be reached later. His statement was characterized by the *New York Times* correspondent in Mexico City as so hopeful and poetical that it could almost have been set to music.[63]

[61] *New York Times*, October 25, 1921.

[62] *Ibid.*, October 29, 1921.

[63] *Ibid.*, October 25, 1921.

Negotiations in New York

The matter of the settlement of the debt was occupying most of the time of the Minister of Finance at the end of January, 1922, when a representative of his Ministry who had been conferring with bankers in New York returned to Mexico with new proposals from the bankers.[64] In pursuance of these proposals, President Obregón announced, on the eighteenth of March, that de la Huerta would go to New York for the purpose of negotiating with the bankers. On the twenty-second of the same month the President declared that the government was determined to fulfill its obligations and that its desire and promise to resume the payment of interest should conduce to recognition by the United States and to closer relations between the United States and Mexico.[65] About the same time, however, it became known that the important matter of the application of the apparently confiscatory provisions of the Mexican constitution, which had been the subject of decisions by the Mexican Supreme Court, was not regarded by the American Department of State as definitely settled in a sense sufficiently reassuring to the American interests involved.[66] It was believed by competent observers that a settlement of the question of the debt could not be made without a loan from American financiers.[67] The impossibility of such a loan being made before the recognition of the Obregón government was emphasized by the fact that the Secretary of State on March 3, 1922, had announced that in view of the possible national interests involved the Department of State should have the opportunity of indicating any objection which it might perceive to the flotation of any issue of the bonds of any foreign country in the United States.[68]

On May 22, 1922, de la Huerta was authorized by President Obregón to proceed to New York as the representative of his government in conferences to be held with the International Com-

[64] *Ibid.*, January 27, 1922.

[65] *New York Times*, March 23, 1922.

[66] *New York Times*, March 16, 1922; *cf.* Chargé d'Affaires Summerlin to Minister Pani, August 3, 1922 (Department of State Press Release, May 8, 1926).

[67] *The Economist*, April 8, 1922, p. 667.

[68] Press Release, March 3, 1922; *cf.* *United States Daily* (Washington), October 15, 1927.

mittee of Bankers "for the purpose of arriving at an agreement with the Committee in regard to the consolidation of the public debt" of Mexico. He was "further authorized to discuss the debts of the railroads and the Caja de Préstamos in order that these debts may be included in the consolidation."[69] He was reminded of the necessity for conducting the conferences "in the highest spirit of honor and showing always the sincere desire of Mexico to arrive with the least possible delay at a satisfactory settlement with all her creditors, which may permit her to face her obligations according to her financial capacity and in strictest equity."[70]

The conferences in New York began on June 2. They were attended by representatives of the American, British, Dutch, Swiss, and Belgian sections of the International Committee of Bankers and by a representative of the German bondholders, not yet admitted into formal membership of the Committee.[71] The views of the Mexican government and of the bankers appeared at first to be wholly irreconcilable. On the sixth of June, de la Huerta telegraphed his chief that the conferences were "in very critical situation."[72] President Obregón replied the same day that it would be better for the Minister of Finance to return to Mexico City without any definite agreement if the terms proposed by the Committee did not harmonize with the position of the

[69] The inclusion of the Caja de Préstamos bonds (*cf.* pp. 241–242, *supra*) was evidently appropriate inasmuch as the government had assumed control of the Caja in 1912. Among the reasons for the inclusion of all the obligations of the National Railways of Mexico, whether guaranteed by the government or not (*cf.* pp. 238–240), were (1) the government's interest, as majority stockholder, in the prevention of the foreclosure of mortgages upon the Railways' properties and (2) the existence of large claims by the National Railways for the use of their properties and for incidental damages since 1914. Similar claims, advanced by the Mexican Railway Company, which did not belong to the National Railways system, would have to be settled eventually by payments to that Company. The sums which the government might pay to the creditors of the National Railways could of course be deducted from the indemnities which might later be found to be due. *Cf.* Powell, *op. cit.*, pp. 25–35.

[70] *Documents relating to the de la Huerta-Lamont Agreement,* translated from *El Universal,* Mexico, April 23–May 13, 1924, Doc. No. 1.

[71] *Com. and Fin. Chron.*, June 3, 1922, p. 2416.

[72] *Documents relating to the de la Huerta-Lamont Agreement, sup. cit.*, No. 7.

Mexican government as previously indicated. "The only power in the hands of a weak people," he said, "is given them by their own dignity, and we should be very unwise if we renounced this power." [73]

The situation improved on the following day,[74] and by June 12 the bankers appeared to de la Huerta to be disposed to make a loan to Mexico to enable her to meet certain of her obligations.[75] On the thirteenth he assured the President that after the conclusion of the agreement with respect to the existing debt it would be very easy to negotiate a new loan. He would take up with the British group the matter of the Banco Único,[76] the establishment of which was proposed in a bill then pending in the Mexican Congress. He hoped to sell to the French group, in conjunction with an American banking house, forty-nine and one-half per cent of the stock of the Banco Único. Seeing that a loan could not be effected by direct means, in consequence of the lack of the recognition of the government, he had proposed that bonds be sold for the account of the government, through the existing Banco Nacional de México.[77]

Later in the same day, the thirteenth of June, the Minister's enthusiasm was checked by a statement of the bankers that there ought to be no question of a loan until after the definite acknowledgment of the debt by the government. The Minister then gave up the conferences as terminated, but in order to end the embarrassing situation he proposed to the Committee that he be furnished a written plan of agreement in order that he might give a written reply.[78]

The plan of agreement, as furnished to de la Huerta by the Committee, was believed by him to be acceptable.[79] Its general bases were declared by President Obregón, in a telegram of June 14, to be "convenient for the country," but the President feared that the economic condition of Mexico might not permit compliance with the engagements planned, unless the agreement in-

[73] *Ibid.*, No. 8.
[74] *Ibid.*, No. 9.
[75] *Ibid.*, No. 18.
[76] A bank with the exclusive right of issuing currency.
[77] *Ibid.*, No. 19.
[78] *Ibid.*, No. 20.
[79] *Ibid.*, No. 22.

cluded a supply of funds for the Banco Único and for irrigation work.[80]

On June 15 the President telegraphed de la Huerta that the economic condition of Mexico was beginning to alarm him seriously and that if funds for the Banco Único and for agricultural work and irrigation were not obtained he sincerely believed there was serious danger of failure in the proposed engagements.[81] De la Huerta replied that although the Committee had declined to insert in the agreement an undertaking of the bankers to lend money to Mexico, it was willing to insert in the preamble a statement of the constant interest of the individuals composing the Committee and their desire to coöperate in a useful manner in measures for insuring the prosperity of Mexico. Moreover, said the Minister, it would be a simple matter to arrange a loan on normal terms after the signature of the agreement. As soon as his position was assured by the agreement, he would initiate conferences with Jules Chevalier, Director of the Banque de Paris et des Pays-Bas, in regard to the sale of the stock of the Banco Único, and with Lamont, as representative of J. P. Morgan and Company, in regard to the flotation of a loan. He would not leave New York without settling the matter of the Banco Único and that of obtaining funds for irrigation work.[82]

The Agreement of June 16, 1922

The Minister's negotiations with the International Committee ended in the signature of an agreement, subject to ratification by the President, on June 16, 1922. The considerations on which the agreement was based were summarized in a preamble substantially as follows: [83]

1. The external obligations of the Mexican government held by foreign investors, together with the debts of the railways and certain internal loans held chiefly outside Mexico, approxi-

[80] *Documents relating to the de la Huerta-Lamont Agreement, sup. cit.*, No. 23.

[81] *Ibid.*, No. 25.

[82] *Ibid.*, Nos. 26 and 28.

[83] Slightly condensed. The full text of the agreement is printed as Appendix VII.

mate the sum of 1,000,000 pesos, as shown in the following schedule:[84]

	In pesos
3 per cent government bonds of 1886[a]	41,796,250
5 per cent City of Mexico bonds of 1889[b]	13,525,815
5 per cent government bonds of 1894[c]	94,298,200
5 per cent government bonds of 1899[d]	97,206,829
5 per cent State bonds of 1903–1907[e]	3,500,000
4 per cent government bonds of 1904[f]	74,312,800
4.5 per cent Caja de Préstamos bonds of 1908[g]	50,000,000
4 per cent government bonds of 1910[h]	101,898,810
6 per cent government bonds of 1913[i]	58,500,000
4 to 6 per cent Railway bonds and notes, 1893–1914[j]	502,077,441
Total	1,037,116,145

a *Supra*, pp. 203–211.
b *Supra*, 233.
c *Supra*, pp. 223–226.
d *Supra*, pp. 226–229.
e *Supra*, p. 232.
f *Supra*, pp. 234–236.
g *Supra*, pp. 241–242.
h *Supra*, pp. 243–244.
i *Supra*, pp. 249–251.
j *Cf.* pp. 237–240, 246, *supra*.

2. Upon this sum arrears of interest accumulated since 1913 amount to approximately 400,000,000 pesos.

3. Although, owing to successive revolutions since 1913, Mexico has as yet not regained her full economic stability, yet the present Government of Mexico declares its determination to meet faithfully and promptly its financial obligations to the utmost extent of its capacity.

4. The International Committee, recognizing the difficulties with which Mexico has had to contend and the limitations upon her capacity for the immediate payment of all her obligations, due or overdue, and earnestly desiring to find means of safeguarding the interests of the bondholders, and at the same time of co-operating with the Mexican Government in the solution of its problems and in the upbuilding of its credit, is prepared to this

[84] This schedule is condensed from the report of Alberto J. Pani, Minister of Finance, entitled *La Politica Hacendaria y la Revolución* (Mexico, 1926), p. 191. The schedule annexed to the agreement of 1922 was found to be inaccurate in detail.

end to recommend to the holders of Mexican Government obligations certain substantial diminutions and adjustments of their rights.

5. The Committee also recognizes that the Mexican Government has other obligations which it is important for it to meet, such as the restitution to the banks of the specie fund,[85] the agrarian debt,[86] and arrears of pay.

6. Taking into account the improvement which should result from the settlement of the debt question and the declared intention of the Government to maintain a sound administration, the Committee believes that, under prudent and economical management of its affairs, the Government is capable of providing for the service of its debt the sums which it agrees to provide.

7. The interests of the people and Government of Mexico, on the one hand, and of their external creditors, upon the other, being identical in that, for the benefit of both, the increasing prosperity of Mexico must be assured, . . . the individuals now composing the International Committee give assurance of their continued interest and desire for helpful coöperation.

It should be noted that the obligations enumerated in the schedule given above do not include the bonds of the unissued balance of the loan of 1913 which were delivered by Huerta to certain banks in Mexico, as security for funds advanced, nor the bonds of the same loan which were delivered by Huerta to John W. de Kay.[87] These bonds, it was represented to the Committee, could not be recognized except at the cost of the immediate overthrow of the government by an outraged Mexican public.[88]

The principal provisions of the plan of adjustment embodied in the agreement of June 16 were the following: [89]

1. Arrears of interest up to and including January 2, 1923, will be paid at par, but without interest on such arrears, over a period of 40 years beginning January 1, 1928.

2. For the payment of a part of the interest falling due from

[85] *Cf.* p. 268, *supra*.

[86] *Cf.* pp. 310, 320, 333, *infra*.

[87] *Cf.* pp. 258–260, *supra*.

[88] Memorial in behalf of John W. de Kay, *sup. cit.*, p. 456.

[89] Condensed. See full text in Appendix VII.

January 3, 1923, to December 31, 1927, the Government will provide and set aside a fund of not less than 30,000,000 gold pesos for 1923; 35,000,000 gold pesos for 1924; 40,000,000 for 1925; 45,000,000 for 1926; and 50,000,000 for 1927. The difference between the amounts thus provided and the amounts due shall be represented by Government "scrip" payable in 20 years and bearing interest at the rate of 3 per cent per annum after the first 5 years.

3. As a guarantee of the payment of the minimum fund to be provided during each of the five years 1923 to 1927, the entire oil export taxes established in 1921, together with any increases of such taxes, and a tax of 10 per cent on the gross receipts of the railways, together with the entire net operating revenues of the railways, if any, are to be delivered as collected to the International Committee or in accordance with its directions.

4. All sinking funds will be postponed for a period of not more than 5 years from January 1, 1923.

5. The service on the debt, including the sinking fund, will be fully resumed, in cash, on January 1, 1928.

6. The Government will make prompt return of the railways to private management and will, as soon as possible, restore them and their rolling stock to the same condition that they were in when they were taken over by the Government.

It was clear that the execution of this plan of adjustment would impose upon the Mexican government a heavy burden from which it had been free during the years of the suspension of payments on the debt. On the other hand, particularly in the postponement of the arrears of interest and in the reduction of the amount of current interest immediately payable, it involved, at least in theory, considerable sacrifices on the part of all the bondholders. The holders of the railway bonds, moreover, made a sacrifice which was said to be "of grave importance," in refraining from foreclosure on the railway properties.[90]

[90] *Cf.* telegram from Lamont to Minister Pani, March 26, 1925 (*Memoria de Hacienda,* 1923–1925, pp. 1080–1081).

Guarded Approval of the Agreement in Washington

The signature of the agreement of June 16 was characterized by officials in Washington as a step in the right direction. Failure to reach an agreement might, they conceded, have had an unfavorable effect upon the general attitude toward Mexico. The agreement, however, they noted, did not touch upon such vital questions as the retroactivity of Article 27 of the Mexican Constitution and did not contain guarantees for respect of rights legitimately acquired under Mexican laws. In view of the disposition which had been manifested by American banking groups to coöperate with the Department of State in Mexican financial matters, and in view of the frequent visits which Lamont had paid to the Department, there was little doubt that the negotiations had been conducted with the approval of the Department.[91]

And in Mexico

Equally guarded, but for different reasons, was the approval accorded to the agreement by President Obregón. The general bases for the agreement appeared to the President to be advantageous, but he was not certain that the agreement could be fulfiled with the resources at the disposal of the government. He therefore urged the Minister of Finance to return to Mexico City immediately for consultation. " In my interest," he said in a telegram of June 17 to the Minister, " return to this city, so that ratification may be authorized from here; obey." [92]

In response to this instruction the Minister of Finance stated on June 18 that he would return as soon as he had " handled all the phases of our financial problem, which will be during the coming week." [93] Nine days later, however, evidently in great excitement, the Minister telegraphed the President that he had suspended the negotiations because of the President's failure to ratify the agreement up to that time.[94] Replying on the same

[91] *New York Times*, June 17, 1922.
[92] *Documents relating to the de la Huerta-Lamont Agreement, sup. cit.*, No. 32.
[93] *Ibid.*, No. 38.
[94] *Ibid.*, No. 58.

date, the President urged the Minister to regain his usual serenity and to accept the assurance of the appreciation of his good work. He criticized the agreement of June 16, however, on certain points of detail, and he suggested that the provisions with respect to the railways might well be incorporated in a separate agreement.[95]

In a telegram of June 28, the Minister apologized for his excitement of the previous day. This excitement he attributed chiefly to pressure from members of the International Committee, who had understood from him that, in view of the definiteness of his instructions, no formal objection would be raised by the President. Many of the members of the Committee were, moreover, obliged to leave immediately for Europe. The realization of this fact, "the suffering of the millionaires from the extreme heat" of New York City, and the newspaper reports of assaults and crimes in Mexico had combined to upset the Minister completely. Although it had not been possible to bring the loan negotiations to the point of a signed contract, the establishment of the Banco Único, partly with funds to be subscribed by French bankers, must be considered as a fact.[96]

The separation of the provisions of the agreement relating to the railways from the other provisions of the agreement, as desired by the President, was impracticable, said de la Huerta, in a telegram of June 29, since the Committee had already dispersed. He would discuss with Lamont on the following day the matter of a loan for purposes of irrigation. Lamont had already stated that such a loan would be entirely agreeable to him, after the recognition of the Obregón government.[97]

The determination of the President to postpone the ratification of the agreement of June 16 occasioned deep regret to de la Huerta, who was pained to see how little confidence his old friend, the President, had in him. He had been assured, and he begged the President to note the word "assured," of funds for the establishment of the Banco Único. A loan for irrigation work had also been promised him. The President had nevertheless not had

[95] *Ibid.*, No. 59.
[96] *Ibid.*, No. 60.
[97] *Ibid.*, Nos. 61 and 62.

sufficient confidence in him to consider the matter definitely settled.[98]

President Obregón on July 3 expressed regret at the displeasure of his Minister of Finance. The Minister, he ironically owned, had been placed in the difficult position of having not only " to fight the Committee of International Bankers without weapons " but also " to contend with a chief whose lack of preparedness and lack of intelligence do not permit him to comprehend with all necessary clarity and in as brief a time as could be desired the details of the plan of agreement." The President unfortunately lacked also " the easy graciousness " which had led the Minister of Finance " to believe in the good faith and sincerity " of the International Committee. Having at length received " *in a concrete form* " the statement that the establishment of the Banco Único was " assured — a-se-gu-ra-do," he believed it advisable to give to the press of the United States and Mexico simultaneously, before the Minister's departure from New York, a declaration that the agreement was conceived " in a mutual and ample spirit of amity," but that since it required the sanction of Congress, official acceptance of it would be postponed until after the Minister's return to Mexico City.[99] A declaration in this sense was in fact given out at Mexico City on July 4.[100]

The Importance of Being Recognized

The ratification of the agreement of June 16 being thus postponed, de la Huerta was unable to make further progress in his negotiations for a new loan. An additional factor operating against the immediate success of these negotiations was the absence of recognition of the Obregón government by the United States. In de la Huerta's conversations with Lamont it had, indeed, been always understood that such recognition must of necessity precede a loan. It could not be otherwise, Lamont had intimated, inasmuch as " the American government during the past year often explained that it did not encourage its citizens to make loans to governments not recognized by the White

98 *Documents relating to the de la Huerta-Lamont Agreement, sup. cit.*, No. 72.

99 *Ibid.*, Nos. 73 and 74.

100 *Ibid.*, No. 77.

House." President Obregón had nevertheless decided that the adjustment of the debt should be "treated independently of the political question" and that the underwriting of a loan should likewise be "treated independently." If the President had not withheld approval of the agreement of June 16, de la Huerta would have been able, he said, to "work with all diligence toward a solution of the other aspects of our position, principally the international political situation." [101]

Balked in his negotiations for a loan, the Minister of Finance turned to "the other aspects" of his government's position. He conferred in New York with American oil producers, who sought to obtain assurances as to the protection of their holdings and the conditions under which they would be permitted to proceed to new developments. From New York he went to Washington, where he had a two-hour conference with Secretary Hughes on July 18. He had a briefer interview with President Harding. With neither the President nor the Secretary of State, however, did he discuss the question of the recognition of the Obregón government.[102] That question, it may be inferred from a development of the following day, was discussed at some length upon the occasion of the Minister's visit to the Capitol.

On July 19, Senator Ladd of North Dakota, speaking in the United States Senate, declared that the withholding of recognition of the Obregón government by the United States made it almost impossible for that government to borrow the funds urgently needed for the reëstablishment of transportation, commerce, and agriculture. The outbreaks of banditry (which had contributed to the agitation of de la Huerta in New York on June 27) had the appearance, the Senator said, of having been staged according to a prearranged plan, at the very moment best calculated to embarrass the Obregón government in its negotiations for the funding of its debt. It was evident that the Department of State was "using recognition as bait with which to fish for commercial advantages in the troubled waters of Latin America." [103]

The insinuations of Senator Ladd were indignantly repelled

[101] *Ibid.*, No. 70. [102] *Com. and Fin. Chron.*, July 8, 15, and 29, 1922.

[103] Edwin F. Ladd, *Our Duty to America* (*Congressional Record*, Vol. 62, Part 10, p. 10421).

by "a high official of the Department of State" [104] on July 20. The questions which had impeded and were still impeding the recognition of the Obregón government were said to be clearly understood by that government. The Obregón government, it was declared, had declined to accept any of the numerous opportunities it had had to demonstrate in a practical way its desire for the establishment of diplomatic relations with the United States. It had taken offense at the proposal made by Secretary Hughes, shortly after he came to the Department, that the United States and Mexico conclude a treaty of amity and commerce embodying an assurance with respect to the security of property rights. It had neglected to furnish the Department the texts of the reported decisions of the Mexican Supreme Court bearing on the question of the retroactivity of Article 27 of the Mexican Constitution, decisions which were alleged to be of such a character as to remove the difficulties on that score. It had executed agrarian laws in a manner which appeared to be confiscatory. It had withheld from the oil producers the assurances which they deemed indispensable for the continuance and extension of their activities in Mexico. Finally, President Obregón appeared to be indisposed to ratify the agreement of June 16 regarding the national debt.[105]

It was apparent that recognition of the Obregón government was as far off as ever, unless that government translated formal assurances into action and gave those definite and precise guarantees of security which were insisted upon by the United States.[106]

The statements attributed to the "high official" of the State Department having been brought to the attention of the Minister of Finance after his return to Mexico City, the Minister declared that he did not believe that the government of the United States had "authorized any public official to give out opinions so unjust to the President of Mexico." If some member of the United States Senate had made a speech which caused a bad impression, the Mexican government was not to blame for the speech, and

104 The consecrated journalistic designation of the Secretary of State.

105 *Com. and Fin. Chron.*, July 29, 1922, pp. 486–487.

106 *New York Times*, July 18, 1922.

should not be attacked in a form so much at variance with "the gentility, judgment, and intelligent discretion" which the Minister had found in President Harding and Secretary Hughes on his visit to Washington. With particular reference to the agreement of June 16, de la Huerta remarked that there was no foundation for the suggestion that President Obregón was unwilling to ratify this agreement.[107]

Substantially the same points reported to have been emphasized at the State Department on July 20 were made in an instruction which was sent by Secretary Hughes a few days later to George T. Summerlin, American chargé d'affaires at Mexico City, for communication to Alberto J. Pani, the Mexican Minister of Foreign Affairs. The points in controversy were summarized by Hughes as follows: [108]

"1. It appears that negotiations have been had looking to an adjustment of the claims of the holders of bonds representing the external debt of Mexico. While this Government has not been a party to these negotiations I have learned with satisfaction of a tentative agreement between the creditors of Mexico and the representative of the Mexican authorities who took part in these negotiations.

"It is understood, however, that no final agreement has yet been made and that the tentative agreement awaits the approval of General Obregón, who it has been publicly stated has said that it must also be ratified by the Mexican Congress.

"2. It is also understood that American citizens interested in oil properties in Mexico have been in negotiation with representatives of the Mexican authorities for the purpose of finding an agreed basis upon which they will be protected in their holdings and may be able to proceed to new developments of the properties, mutually satisfactory.

"This Government has not been a party to these negotiations and is not prepared to discuss the merits of particular proposals, but it has been gratified at the prospect of such an agreement. Again, however, it is understood that no agreement has yet been

[107] *Com. and Fin. Chron.*, July 29, 1922.

[108] Department of State Release, May 8, 1926.

concluded, and whatever has been done is subject to the approval of the Mexican authorities.

"3. No adequate action has yet been taken for the purpose of confirming, and assuring the protection of, valid titles acquired by American citizens prior to the adoption of the Constitution of 1917.

"Although it has been repeatedly said by Mr. Pani that the Mexican Congress is at liberty to regulate the interpretation of that constitution, and that it has exclusive authority for this purpose, no such action has yet been taken.

"4. I have not had opportunity as yet to examine the texts of the four decisions of the Supreme Court, but if, as seems to be implied, they follow the decision in the Texas case already announced, in order to form a precedent composed of five decisions upon the same point, they are inadequate to protect American rights against a retroactive and confiscatory application of the Mexican Constitution.

"5. Properties of American citizens have been seized and are threatened with seizure, under the guise of 'expropriation' without provision for just compensation."

The basis for the complaint as to the non-ratification of the agreement of June 16 was removed on September 29 by the promulgation of a decree by which that agreement was ratified.[109] The remaining obstacles to the recognition of the Obregón government were apparently considered to have been removed or overridden by the end of August of the following year, when the Commissioners of the United States and Mexico, who had been in conference at Mexico City for three months, agreed upon a basis for the renewal of diplomatic relations between the two countries.[110]

The Agreement in Operation

On December 7, 1923, the International Committee of Bankers on Mexico announced that the plan for the readjustment of

[109] *Diario Oficial*, Sept. 30, 1922, Vol. 22, p. 417.

[110] Department of State, *Proceedings of the United States-Mexican Commission convened in Mexico City, May 14, 1923* (Washington, 1925), p. iii.

the Mexican debt, adopted on June 16, 1922, had become operative, sufficient progress having been made under the agreement both in the deposit of bonds by the bondholders and in the deposit of funds by the Mexican government. The deposit of funds for 1923 was brought up to the minimum requirement of 30,000,000 pesos a few days before the end of the year.[111] The payment of this sum to the bondholders was delayed for nearly three months by the process of printing and distributing over thirty-five tons of receipts, cash warrants, and scrip.[112] The first disbursement of interest on the bonds deposited under the agreement was announced in New York on March 28, 1924. Ninety per cent of all the outstanding bonds were declared by Lamont to have been deposited with the International Committee.[113]

The Agreement Suspended

The completion of the deposit required for the first payment of interest under the agreement of 1922 was effected only with great difficulty. At the moment at which the deposit was completed the Mexican government was engaged in suppressing a revolt. The leader of the revolt was de la Huerta, the signer of the agreement on the part of Mexico. His " estrangement " from President Obregón had begun shortly after the signature of the agreement and was attributed by the President to the " various occasions " on which he was informed of the President's " displeasure " at having been made " individually and collectively responsible for an act of such transcendence by information which lacked veracity." [114] Before the end of September, 1923, relations between the President and his Minister of Finance had become so strained that the Minister had resigned his office.

The result of an initial survey of the condition of the federal treasury by Minister Pani, successor to de la Huerta, had been such as to contribute materially to the decision of de la Huerta to take up arms against the President. The obligations incurred

[111] *Com. and Fin. Chron.*, December 8, 1923.

[112] *Ibid.*, May 24, 1924.

[113] *Ibid.*, March 29, 1924.

[114] *El Universal* (Mexico City), May 12, 1924.

by the government during the first nine months of the year 1923, in addition to the obligations included in the agreement with the International Committee of Bankers, were found by Pani to have reached a total of nearly 235,000,000 pesos, for the satisfaction of which less than 200,000,000 pesos had been collected. The pay roll of public employees was declared to have been swelled with the names of individuals who "fulfilled no other mission than that of punctually collecting their pay." According to a later statement of President Obregón, there had been a "systematic pilferage" of the treasury. Under such conditions the treasury was believed by Pani to be "marching toward disaster."[115]

The revolt, which began in December, 1923, was quickly suppressed, largely by means of surplus army stores sold to Obregón by the government of the United States on deferred payment contracts.[116] The cost of the campaign against de la Huerta was, however, necessarily large. The cash expenditure for the campaign was reported by Minister Pani to have been in excess of 20,000,000 pesos; the floating debt was increased by nearly 8,000,000 pesos; more than 8,000,000 pesos of government funds were seized by de la Huerta; and government property valued at nearly 7,000,000 pesos was destroyed. It was estimated that other obligations incident to the campaign would bring the total cost to 60,000,000 pesos.[117]

Before the de la Huerta revolt the revenues for the year 1924 had been budgeted at 290,273,000 pesos, as against estimated expenditures of 297,982,472 pesos — including 72,374,261 pesos for the service of the public debt. The unanticipated expenditures occasioned by the revolt made it necessary for the government to seek additional funds. During the first three months of the year there were several reports to the effect that a substantial loan was about to be made by New York bankers. The sum of 20,000,000 pesos was in fact obtained from certain American oil producers, as an advance payment of

[115] *Memoria de Hacienda,* 1923–1925, pp. 14 *et seq.;* President Obregón's message to Congress, September 1, 1924.

[116] *New York Times,* January 1, 1924.

[117] *Memoria de Hacienda,* 1923–1925, p. 47.

taxes, but nothing came of the reported negotiations with the bankers.[118]

In April, 1924, the Mexican government addressed to the American members of the International Committee of Bankers tentative inquiries as to the possibility of a loan of $15,000,000.[119] The security proposed was a pledge of the tax on oil production, a new tax which had yielded 38,000,000 pesos in 1923 and over 54,000,000 pesos in 1922.[120] A loan on this security was refused. A factor in the refusal was doubtless the circumstance that the production of oil in Mexico had recently suffered a very considerable decline in consequence of the cessation of the operations of most of the American oil companies. These oil companies had not been completely reassured by the terms of the understanding effected between the governments of the United States and Mexico in August, 1923. In attempting to obtain more explicit and direct guarantees from the Mexican government, the American Association of Oil Producers in Mexico was declared by Mexican officials to have "evinced a sheer ignorance of our legislation and political conditions." It was to the influence of this Association that the same officials attributed the refusal of the bankers to "coöperate in a useful manner" in the measure proposed by the government "for insuring the prosperity of Mexico."[121]

In consequence of the bankers' refusal of a loan and because of several other considerations which were set forth at length by President Obregón, the execution of the debt agreement of 1922 was suspended by decree on June 30, 1924. The suspension, it was announced, would be terminated upon the restoration of the equilibrium of the federal treasury, by the application of revenues set apart for the service of the foreign debt or by the application of the proceeds of a loan to be contracted for the purpose.[122]

118 *New York Times*, January 17 and March 27, 1924.

119 *Com. and Fin. Chron.*, April 19, 1924.

120 C. F. B., *Fifty-Second Annual Report*, 1924, p. 281.

121 *New York Times*, July 2, 1924.

122 Text of decree given to press by Mexican Financial Agency, New York. The sum of 1,400,000 pesos had already been deposited with the International Committee on account of the 35,000,000 pesos due for 1924 under the agreement.

The Arlitt Loan Contract

In an effort to obtain the funds which were denied by the bankers in New York, Minister Pani, on September 20, 1924, signed a contract for a 6 per cent loan of $50,000,000 with J. L. Arlitt, of Austin, Texas. The objects of this loan were declared by Arlitt to be the payment of amounts which would be due up to April 1, 1925, under the agreement of 1922; the reduction of the floating debt; and the liquidation of the general expenses of the government. The security for the loan was to be the oil production tax which the members of the International Committee had been unwilling to accept as security. It was emphasized that in entering into this transaction the government had no desire or intention to oppose the International Committee. Lamont, the Chairman of the Committee, was quoted as having expressed the wish that the transaction might be successful. According to Arlitt, 65 per cent of the loan had been sold by October 13. Notwithstanding these auguries of success, Arlitt had up to December 20 failed to provide a guarantee bond of $100,000 and to deliver bonds of the loan to the Mexican Financial Agency at New York, as required by the contract. On the date mentioned, the contract was canceled by the Mexican government.[123]

An important factor in the result of the Arlitt transaction was believed to have been the absence of any indication of the attitude of the American Department of State with respect to it. The contract had not been submitted to the Department before the announcement of the loan, in accordance with the general request of March 3, 1922, and the Department did not deem it appropriate in the circumstances to make any statement of its attitude.

The Pani-Lamont Negotiations

Toward the end of January, 1925, Pani conferred with Lamont in New York with reference to the possibility of a loan of $60,000,000 and a revision of the agreement of 1922.

In a memorandum presented to Lamont on January 24,

[123] *Com. and Fin. Chron.*, October 4, 25, and 27, 1924.

1925,[124] Pani quoted from the preamble of the agreement of 1922 the paragraph (g) in which it was set forth

> That the interests of the people and Government of Mexico, on the one hand, and of their external creditors, upon the other, being identical in that, for the benefit of both, the increasing prosperity of Mexico must be assured, therefore, the individuals now composing the International Committee give assurance of their continued interest and desire for helpful coöperation.

He recalled further that President Obregón and the Mexican Congress had ratified the agreement in reliance upon assurances from de la Huerta, which were later found to be false, with respect to the negotiation of a foreign loan desired by Mexico and with respect to the actual condition of the public treasury. During the military uprising headed by de la Huerta and for several months after the failure of the uprising, the government and people of Mexico had made enormous sacrifices in order to comply faithfully with the agreement of 1922. The refusal of the International Committee to give its coöperation in the form of a small temporary loan of $20,000,000 on the security of the oil production tax in May, 1924, had made the sacrifices of the government and people seem wholly fruitless; and an intense public opinion, which could not be disregarded without danger to the stability of the national political institutions, had compelled the government to suspend the execution of the agreement.

Considering that the suspension of the agreement had been "imputable to both contracting parties," inasmuch as the agreement had been based on incorrect estimates of "the financial possibilities of the government of Mexico" and as the International Committee had been unable to grant the coöperation which it had been expected to grant under the agreement, Pani deduced

> with the strength of an incontrovertible logic, that in order to resume the service of the debt, on bases sufficiently strong to support the building which rests on them without danger of its crumbling down again, and strong enough to protect the credit of the government of Mexico as well as the interests of the holders of Bonds of the Mexican Exterior Debt, [it was] necessary to revise the Agreement mentioned, in order to limit the obligations

[124] Secretaría de Hacienda y Crédito Público, *La Deuda Exterior de Mexico* (Mexico, 1926), pp. 166–169.

that it imposes to the true fiscal capacity of the Government and to the co-operation that the International Committee of Bankers may be able or willing to lend.

The specific suggestions of Pani for the revision of the agreement of 1922 were that the debt of the railway companies be separated from the direct obligations of the republic; that the transition period of five years be increased or the amounts payable during that period reduced; and that the security for payment of interest and sinking fund be supplemented by the proceeds of the oil production tax, which was expected to yield more than $20,000,000 a year.

The loan of $60,000,000 desired by the government was to be applied, according to Pani's proposal, to the liquidation of a budgetary deficit of $25,000,000; to the payment of interest due under the agreement of 1922, in the amount of $17,500,000; and to the establishment of a Sole Bank of Issue (Banco Único).

In reply to Pani's memorandum the American section of the International Committee intimated that it felt bound toward the bondholders with respect to all the provisions of the agreement of 1922 and would not be inclined to change any of its terms. A loan of $60,000,000 was considered to be greatly in excess of the needs of the government. Payment of the $17,500,000 due under the agreement of 1922, could, it was suggested, be postponed until 1928. The Sole Bank of Issue, for the establishment of which $17,500,000 was desired, was not urgently needed. The actual necessities of the government could, in the opinion of the American section, be met with a loan of $20,000,000. A loan of this amount would be favored by the American section upon condition (a) that the railways be immediately restored to private management; [125] (b) that payment of interest for 1924 be made; and (c) that the necessary provisions be made for the payment of the oil production tax in New York.[126]

[125] The provision of the agreement of 1922 for the "prompt return" of the railways to private management had not yet been fulfiled.

[126] *La Deuda Exterior, sup. cit.*, pp. 169–174. The third stipulation was doubtless based on the consideration that a tax paid by importers in New York, through the Mexican Consulate General or some other agency of the Mexican government, was less likely to be taken by the government for purposes alien to the agreement.

A more detailed discussion occurred after the return of Pani to Mexico City. From that city on March 26, 1925, a representative of the International Committee, who had been in conference with Pani, telegraphed to Lamont definite proposals of the Mexican government with respect to the separation of the national debt from the railway debt, the postponement of interest for 1924 and 1925, and the deposit of allocated revenues in the Banco Nacional for remission to New York. The acceptance of these proposals, in principle, was indicated by the International Committee in June. It was stated, however, that the Committee had not found it possible to negotiate the loan desired by the government.[127]

In a memorandum communicated to a representative of the International Committee on August 20, Pani stated that, thanks to the economies of the administrative reorganization effected by the government, the immediate resumption of the service of the foreign debt was possible without recourse to the loan of $60,-000,000 which he had thought necessary at the beginning of the year. In the same memorandum he announced that the Sole Bank of Issue, which was considered by President Calles to be essential to a satisfactory arrangement for the renewal of the service of the foreign debt, was to be inaugurated on the first of September.[128]

The announcement as to the establishment of the bank of issue occasioned immediate protests from the Committee. In a message sent through a representative of the Committee at Mexico City, Lamont pointed out that the funds to be used in the inauguration of the bank would be in part the proceeds of revenues specifically allocated to the service of the 1922 agreement. In the past the government had declared (and the Committee had accepted the declaration in good faith) that only *force majeure* and an actual shortage of funds to meet pressing daily expenses of the government had prevented the fulfilment of that agreement. Now, however, it would appear that the government had simply taken revenues pledged to the bondholders and diverted them to a wholly new purpose. The Com-

[127] *Ibid.*, pp. 174–183.

[128] *Ibid.*, pp. 183–190.

mittee felt obliged to warn the Minister that should the plan for the establishment of the bank be carried out forthwith, as indicated, the bondholders, in the judgment of the Committee, would be bound to consider that the government had irrevocably broken faith with them and would call upon the Committee to declare the government finally in default, to release them from the agreement of 1922, and thus to enable them to seek through the Department of State and the various Foreign Offices such means of protest and satisfaction as might be open to them.[129]

A telegram to the same effect was sent to Pani at the same time through the medium of the Department of State at Washington and the American Embassy at Mexico City. The use of this channel of communication was noted with astonishment by Pani in his reply to Lamont on September 11. The Minister expressed astonishment also at the fact that the Committee had protested against an application of the funds in question to an object different from that stipulated in the agreement of 1922. The force of that agreement was, he said, "legally suspended,"[130] and the funds had been

> devoted to a national need that could not be postponed by any means, in accordance . . . with the financial plan adopted by the government precisely with a view to facilitating the resumption of the service of the foreign debt on bases of absolute security.[131]

The Agreement of October 23, 1925

The establishment of the Banco de México on September 1, 1925, did not so far estrange the International Committee as to make further negotiations impossible. Further negotiations were in fact commenced in New York at the beginning of October, and on the twenty-third of the month an agreement modifying and supplementing that of June, 1922, was signed by Pani and Lamont.[132]

129 *La Deuda Exterior, sup. cit.*, pp. 191–193.

130 By the decree of suspension of June 30, 1924.

131 *La Deuda Exterior, sup. cit.*, pp. 194–195. The funds for the inauguration of the Banco de México were obtained almost entirely by a transfer to the new institution of the government's interest in the Comisión Monetaria, S. A., which had been organized in April, 1916, and incorporated as a bank of discount and deposit in January, 1925.

132 See full text in Appendix IX.

The Pani-Lamont agreement recites that, according to statements of the government of Mexico,

1. The temporary suspension of the enforcement of the agreement of 1922 had been necessitated by the exceptional drain on the financial and economic resources of the government incident to the de la Huerta revolt;

2. The resumption of payments on the obligations scheduled in the agreement of 1922 would be unwise unless modifications of that agreement were made for the purpose of limiting those obligations to the actual financial capacity of the government;

3. The most effective and equitable way of accomplishing that purpose was to redefine the government's liability with respect to the railway obligations scheduled in the agreement of 1922 and to segregate those obligations from the obligations of the "Direct Debt"; and

4. The provisions of the agreement of 1922 with respect to the Caja de Préstamos bonds of 1908 required amendment.

The Committee, on the other hand, it was recited, "in order to reach a basis which in the expressed judgment of the government will enable the government to resume the service of the bonds deposited under the agreement (of 1922)," was prepared to recommend to the depositors the acceptance of the amendments urged in behalf of the government.

The important modifications of the agreement of 1922 which were embodied in the Pani-Lamont agreement were as follows:

1. The minimum funds which the government had undertaken to provide for the years 1924 and 1925 (35,000,000 gold pesos for 1924 and 40,000,000 for 1925) were to be deferred and liquidated, with interest at 3 per cent per annum, over a period of eight years beginning January 1, 1928.

2. The government ceased to be directly responsible for the obligations of the railways except in so far as it was bound by guarantees given with respect to those obligations prior to June 16, 1922. The receipts, aggregating $98,526,963, which had been issued under the agreement of 1922 for arrears of interest on the railway debt were to be retired by the railways by payments, out

of earnings in excess of fixed charges, of $2,463,174 a year, beginning January 1, 1928.

3. In addition to the entire oil export taxes which had been mentioned in the agreement of 1922, the Committee was to receive "the specific sum of $5,000,000 U. S. gold annually, payable in equal monthly instalments of $416,667 each out of the oil production taxes"; provided that any payments in excess of $12,192,845 United States gold in 1926 and $12,611,901 United States gold in 1927 should be returned by the Committee to the government. The funds received by the Committee were to be credited against the government's obligation for current interest on its Direct Debt of $267,000,000.

4. The railways were to be returned to private management on December 31, 1925, under conditions which would enable them under efficient management to earn their full fixed charges (approximately $11,276,695 a year). Beginning January 1, 1926, the entire net revenues of the railways were to be remitted each month to the International Committee for the payment of current interest on the railway debt.

5. The Caja de Préstamos bonds which had been deposited with the Committee were to be exchanged for direct obligations of the government. The trustee for the Caja de Préstamos bonds was to receive from the government non-interest bearing treasury notes for $5,000,000 United States gold, the proceeds of which were to be used in purchasing Caja de Préstamos bonds, or the new obligations issued in exchange therefor, at prices not to exceed 56 per cent of their par value.

Reversion to the Status Quo Ante

The agreement of October 23, 1925, was formally approved by the Mexican Congress in an act which was promulgated on January 25, 1926.[133] The railways had meanwhile been returned to private management on January 1. Meanwhile also, in December, 1925, the Mexican Congress had passed two laws for the purpose of giving effect to the provisions of Article 27 of the constitu-

[133] *Diario Oficial*, February 2, 1926.

tion of 1917 with reference to the ownership of land and of mineral deposits, including petroleum.[134] By the law of December 18, 1925, the ownership (*dominio directo*) of all deposits of petroleum was declared to be vested in the nation. Provision was made for the grant of concessions for exploitation of such deposits to Mexicans or Mexican companies and to foreigners, subject to the condition, which had been prescribed by the constitution, that such foreigners should formally agree to be considered Mexicans in respect of such concessions and "accordingly not to invoke the protection of their governments in respect to the same." The rights acquired by foreigners prior to the promulgation of the constitution of 1917 were to be confirmed, as a matter of course, by new concessions (which would presumably be subject to the condition above mentioned); provided that such rights arose from the actual commencement of exploitation before May 1, 1917, or from contracts made before that date for the express purpose of exploitation; and provided, further, that the confirmatory concessions should have a duration of not more than fifty years from the commencement of exploitation in the first class of cases and from the date of the contracts in the second class.[135] By the law of December 23, 1925, aliens were subjected to far-reaching restrictions with reference to the acquisition or ownership of land, particularly within one hundred kilometers from the frontiers or fifty kilometers from the coasts.[136] Both laws were denounced by interested foreigners as retroactive and confiscatory, and the correspondence between the Mexican Foreign Office and the Department of State at Washington became so heated as to give rise to apprehensions of a severance of diplomatic relations between the United States and Mexico.[137] The prospects for an amicable adjustment of the questions at issue were not improved by the publication in November, 1926, of a story, said to have

[134] *Cf.* p. 270, *supra*.

[135] *Diario Oficial*, December 31, 1925.

[136] *Diario Oficial*, January 21, 1926.

[137] *Cf.* J. Reuben Clark, Jr. (appointed Under-Secretary of State in August, 1928), "The Oil Settlement in Mexico," in *Foreign Affairs* (New York), July, 1928, pp. 600–614. The controversies with respect to oil and land rights of foreigners in Mexico will be fully discussed in a volume now in preparation under the auspices of the Research Committee on Latin America.

been inspired by an official of the Department of State, to the effect that the Mexican attitude toward vested property rights was attributable in large measure to Bolshevist influence.[138]

Besides the allegedly retroactive and confiscatory provisions of the law of December 23, 1925, foreign landowners in Mexico pressed upon the attention of their governments at this time the question of indemnities for appropriations which had recently begun to be effected on a large scale under various federal and state laws for agrarian reform.[139] Up to October 13, 1926, approximately 1,775,000 acres (2,775 square miles) of land had been taken from foreigners and given as *ejidos* (community lands) to Indian villages.[140] The land thus taken from foreigners con-

[138] *Cf.* Ernest Gruening, *Mexico and Its Heritage* (New York, 1928), pp. 611–612.

[139] The first definite measure for the satisfaction of the land-hunger of the dispossessed Indian population was Carranza's decree of January 6, 1915, which provided for the restitution or grant of *ejidos* (community lands) to the villages. The substance of this decree was incorporated in Article 27 of the Constitution of 1917. By this Article of the fundamental law, the state legislatures, as well as the Federal Congress, were directed to determine within their respective jurisdictions "those cases in which the occupation of private property shall be considered of public utility." The state legislatures were slow in passing the necessary laws, and the federal procedure for expropriation was not worked out in detail until January, 1922, when a law of January 10, 1920, providing for the issue of twenty-year five per cent bonds of the Agrarian Debt, in compensation for land taken, was supplemented by regulations. Up to the end of 1924, approximately 5,000,000 acres of land had been taken for *ejidos*. During the next two years the quantity of land so taken was nearly doubled. In all but a few cases the owners refused the tender of bonds and reserved their rights for future discussion. *Cf.* Gruening, *op. cit.*, pp. 143–167.

[140] *Boletín de la Secretaría de Educación Pública*, March, 1927, p. 34. The details as to nationality of foreign owners, number of estates affected, and number of *hectares* taken (1 *hectare* = approximately 2½ acres) are given as follows:

Nationality	Number of Estates	Hectares
Spanish	231	369,966
American	104	189,910
English	26	87,111
German	27	41,558
French	14	10,937
Others	19	11,286
Total	421	710,768

stituted about one-eighth of all the land distributed as *ejidos*,[141] and about one-forty-fifth of the total rural holdings of foreigners in Mexico.[142] It was alleged by the interested foreigners that, lacking favorable connections with local politicians, they had been subjected to discriminations in comparison with Mexicans. A more fundamental objection was made to the legal basis for the valuation of the land taken (the latest assessed value for taxation, plus ten per cent). The most serious grievance of the foreign landholders — a grievance which they shared with Mexicans — was the requirement that they accept, in payment for their land, bonds of the Agrarian Debt of a nominal value equal to that of the land, as fixed by law, but of an actual market value considerably less. The representations of the foreign landholders were considered by their governments to be well founded, and thus another political factor of disturbance was injected into the situation.

The situation was still further complicated as a result of the presidential decree of July 2, 1926, ordering the integral enforcement from August 1, 1926, of the provisions of Article 130 of the Constitution of 1917[143] with reference to "ministers of religious creeds" and "the religious institutions known as churches." In a pastoral letter of July 26, 1926, the government was charged

[141] *Ibid.*

[142] Frank Tannenbaum, *The Mexican Agrarian Revolution* (New York, 1929), p. 517. Foreign-owned rural lands valued at 5,000 pesos or over constituted, in 1923, one-fifth, in both value and area, of all privately owned rural lands in Mexico. *Ibid.*, p. 516.

[143] Among the provisions of this Article were the following:

The law recognizes no juridical personality in the religious institutions known as churches.

Ministers of religious creeds shall be considered as persons exercising a profession, and shall be directly subject to the laws enacted on the matter.

The State Legislatures shall have the exclusive power of determining the maximum number of ministers of religious creeds, according to the needs of each locality. Only a Mexican by birth may be a minister of any religious creed in Mexico.

No ministers of religious creeds shall, either in public or private meetings, or in acts of worship or religious propaganda, criticise the fundamental laws of the country, the authorities in particular or the government in general; they shall have no vote, nor be eligible to office, nor shall they be entitled to assemble for political purposes.

by the Catholic hierarchy in Mexico with persecution of the Church, and, by way of protest, the conduct of public worship by priests was ordered to be suspended. A *Liga de Resistencia,* supported by Catholic leaders, undertook to use economic pressure against the government by "calling upon the faithful to refrain from buying anything but absolute necessities." The church-state conflict has been declared to be "not unrelated to the unrest, banditry, and guerilla warfare" with which the government has had to contend in various parts of the country since 1926.

The prevailing conflicts and controversies were reflected in a real contraction of business as well as in what President Calles termed a "psychological depression." The taxes on the production and exportation of petroleum, which in 1922 had yielded 86,000,000 pesos, or nearly one-third of the total revenues, amounted to less than 35,000,000 pesos in 1926.[144] The loss on these taxes was partially offset by the proceeds of a new tax on incomes, which

[144] From 1920 (the first year in which Mexican petroleum production exceeded 90,000,000 barrels) to 1928 the figures for production, exportation, and taxes were as follows (in round numbers):

	Production (In barrels)	Exportation (In barrels)	Taxes (In pesos)
1920	157,000,000	146,000,000	45,000,000
1921	193,000,000	172,000,000	63,000,000
1922	182,000,000	181,000,000	86,000,000
1923	150,000,000	136,000,000	61,000,000
1924	140,000,000	130,000,000	55,000,000
1925	116,000,000	97,000,000	42,000,000
1926	90,000,000	81,000,000	35,000,000
1927	64,000,000	48,000,000	19,000,000
1928	50,000,000	....	11,000,000

The sharp decline in production was not due exclusively to the prevailing controversy with respect to Article 27 of the Constitution. Other factors were (1) the greatly increased cost of production, due chiefly to the exhaustion of most of the "gushers" near the coast and to the necessity of relying on wells of comparatively low yield in the interior; (2) the development of rival oil fields in Colombia and Venezuela; and (3) a dispute with the government as to the rate of taxation, which was declared by the operators to be excessive.

yielded 17,000,000 pesos. The total net revenues for the year were 322,000,000 pesos. The total expenditures, including approximately 27,000,000 pesos deposited with the International Committee of Bankers for current interest on the direct debt and on the railway bonds guaranteed by the government, were 329,000,000 pesos.[145]

The budgetary difficulties were considerably increased in 1927. The total net revenues dropped to 306,000,000 pesos. Of this sum only 19,000,000 pesos was derived from taxes on petroleum: 6,000,000 from the export taxes and 13,000,000 from the production taxes.[146] The deficiency to be made up from other sources for payment of interest due on the direct debt was thus about 6,000,000 pesos.[147] This deficiency was met by means of advances from the Banco de México and from the International Committee, which were repaid during 1928. Nothing was paid, however, either by the railways or by the government, on account of the interest due in 1927 on the guaranteed railway bonds.

The budget for the year 1928 was prepared with a full realization of the probable economic and fiscal effects of the continuing controversies, both internal and external. The net revenues were estimated by Minister of Finance Montes de Oca (who had succeeded Pani in February, 1927) at only 290,000,000 pesos, of which less than 19,000,000 pesos was expected to be derived from taxes on petroleum. The expenditures were estimated at 291,000,000 pesos — the largest items, besides payments on the

[145] Under the Pani-Lamont Agreement, it will be recalled, the entire oil export taxes and 10,000,000 pesos out of the oil production taxes were to be deposited, in each of the years 1926 and 1927, to the credit of the International Committee. If the oil export taxes plus 10,000,000 pesos from the oil production taxes proved insufficient for the payment of current interest on the direct debt to the extent required in the agreement of 1922 (21,219,000 pesos in 1926 and 21,848,000 pesos in 1927), the deficiency was to be made up from other sources. As the oil export taxes amounted to only 10,000,000 pesos in 1926, the revenues specified in the agreement of 1925 were more than 1,000,000 pesos short of the amount required for interest on the direct debt. From other sources, however, the government obtained funds with which it paid the full amount required for interest on the direct debt and, in addition, the sum of 5,350,000 pesos on railway bonds bearing its guarantee.

[146] *Cf.* note 144, p. 312, *supra*.

[147] *Cf.* note 145, *supra*.

public debt, being 97,600,000 pesos for Army, Navy, and Ordnance; 36,300,000 pesos for Communications, Public Works, and Road Construction; 31,500,000 pesos for Agriculture, Development, and Irrigation; and 27,000,000 pesos for Public Instruction. On the public debt, external and internal, it was proposed to pay 32,500,000 pesos, or about 11.3 per cent of the estimated revenues.

President Calles and Minister Montes de Oca were firmly of the opinion that it would be impossible for the Mexican government to pay during the year 1928 the sum of approximately 70,000,000 pesos due as interest and sinking fund on the direct debt included in the agreement of 1922. Accordingly, at the end of 1927, they sent delegates to New York to discuss with the International Committee the possibility of a new agreement which should be within the government's capacity to pay and in accordance with a comprehensive plan. After preliminary conferences it was decided that a new agreement could not profitably nor intelligently be made without more definite information than was then available in regard to the actual economic and fiscal condition of Mexico.

Two competent investigators, Messrs. Joseph E. Sterrett and Joseph S. Davis, went to Mexico in January, 1928, and spent approximately three months in collecting pertinent data at the original sources. Their report, presented to the International Committee toward the end of May, 1928,[148] tended to confirm the estimates of the Mexican government regarding its immediate capacity to make payments on its foreign debts. The investigators made it clear, however, that in their opinion Mexico's immediate capacity to pay was abnormally low. If — as they saw reason to hope — the various pending controversies, foreign and domestic, could be adjusted, and peaceful conditions could be assured throughout the country, the recuperative power of the Mexican people would, they believed, speedily assert itself and be shortly reflected in revenues ample for the satisfaction of both the external and the internal obligations of the government.

An event of good omen for the economic recovery of Mexico

[148] Not published.

occurred while the investigators were engaged in their task. This was the adjustment, to the satisfaction of the Department of State, of the questions at issue with respect to the application of the petroleum law to American properties.[149] The adjustment was due primarily to the conciliatory attitude of Ambassador Dwight W. Morrow, who had brought to his task, in October, 1927, an unusual equipment for the comprehension of the social, economic, and financial problems of Mexico. The relaxation of the former tension in the relations of the United States and Mexico was reflected in a more hospitable attitude in Mexico toward foreigners in general.[150] Controversies remained, notably regarding the expropriation of land for *ejidos*,[151] but the atmosphere in which these controversies were conducted was much more favorable to compromise.

In October, 1928, representatives of the International Committee, who had meanwhile digested the report of Messrs. Sterrett and Davis, went to Mexico, at the suggestion of the Mexican government, to discuss the basis for a new agreement regarding the foreign debt. At the conclusion of the discussions, in the first week of November, Minister Montes de Oca gave out a statement in part as follows:[152]

> The conferences were conducted with a mutual understanding of the difficulties to be overcome and of the necessity that the agreement which is to be signed shall be just to the bondholders and subject to Mexico's capacity to pay, as well as to the country's need for the recovery of its credit abroad. The Mexican Government has considered the problem of the Direct Debt [*i. e.*, the Direct Debt included in the agreements of 1922 and 1925] as an integral part of a larger general problem which includes obligations of another character, and it clearly expressed itself in this sense.
>
> The representatives of the Committee are returning to New York to report to the Committee and to the European sections. When their report has been studied, the necessary steps will be taken for the conclusion of a definitive convention in regard to the External Public Debt of Mexico — a convention which will be subject to the ratification of the Mexican Congress and to the approval of the bondholders represented by the International Committee.

[149] *Cf.* article of J. Reuben Clark, Jr., *sup. cit.*

[150] London *Times*, as quoted in *El Economista* (Mexico City), April 1, 1929.

[151] *Cf.* pp. 310–311, *supra.*

[152] *El Economista*, Nov. 16, 1928.

Toward the end of December the Minister of Finance submitted to the Congress a draft of a law which was designed to serve as a first step toward the settlement of the entire public debt. The draft was adopted without delay and was signed by the President on January 25, 1929.[153] It provides for the suspension of payments of principal or interest on all internal obligations, with certain exceptions,[154] pending the completion of a survey of these obligations by a Special Commission, which is to formulate a consistent plan for their settlement. The obligations of the direct debt included in the agreements of 1922 and 1925 are, according to this law, to be the subject of new arrangements with the bondholders, on the basis of a consolidation of all these obligations in a new issue of bonds bearing not more than five per cent interest per annum and redeemable in not less than forty-five years. The obligations of the National Railways, including those which bear the guarantee of the government, are not to be embraced in the new consolidated issue of government bonds but are to be the subject of direct negotiations between the Railways and their creditors. The claims of foreign governments now pending before Mixed Claims Commissions are, finally, in the discretion of the Executive, to be settled by lump sum payments under agreements with the respective governments.

The Special Commission provided for in the law of January 25, 1929, began its operations in the first week of February. At the same time, as a part of the general plan for "establishing a more significant and more stable basis for the entire problem of the public debt," the Federal Treasury began the payment, in cash or in certificates receivable for taxes, of old accounts for supplies

[153] See full text in Appendix X.

[154] The law is open to criticism on the score of the breadth of the exceptions allowed. The largest items on account of which payments may continue, despite the general suspension, are (1) the Agrarian Debt, for which bonds have been authorized to the amount of 50,000,000 pesos, and (2) the Banking Debt, which results from Carranza's seizure of the metallic reserves of the banks of issue to the amount of more than 50,000,000 pesos (*cf.* p. 268, *supra*). A decidedly questionable item is the payment of 55,000 pesos a month, under a contract of September 10, 1925, toward the redemption of the bonds for the liquidation of the Tehuantepec National Railway, which were not included in the agreements with the International Committee.

or personal services. The payment of these accounts was suspended as a result of the outbreak of a revolt on March 3, 1929. Up to that time approximately 5,000,000 pesos, in cash and certificates, had been paid on these accounts.[155]

The outbreak of the revolt had also the effect of preventing the resumption of discussions with representatives of the International Committee with a view to the conclusion of a new agreement regarding the direct debt included in the former agreements. The extraordinary expenditures occasioned by the revolt were met by transfers of appropriations that had been made for other objects, including the public debt. At the middle of April, although the victory of the government forces was then virtually assured, the fiscal dislocation resulting from the revolt was such that the Minister of Finance deemed it necessary to announce that a definitive agreement with the International Committee was not likely to be concluded during the year 1929.[156] Pending the conclusion of agreements with respect to the direct debt and the guaranteed railway debt, the arrears of interest on these debts continue to accumulate.

155 Treasury figures; *cf. El Economista,* March 1 and March 16, 1929.

156 *El Economista,* April 16, 1929.

CHAPTER IX

THE FOREIGN DEBT IN 1929

THE SIZE, CHARACTER AND DISTRIBUTION OF THE FOREIGN DEBT

THE bonded obligations of Mexico to foreigners, as of July 1, 1929, amount to approximately 1,100,000,000 pesos. In detail these obligations are as follows:

(In millions of pesos)

BONDED OBLIGATIONS TO FOREIGNERS	PRINCIPAL	INTEREST ACCRUED [a]	TOTAL
Customs secured government loans:			
5 per cent consolidated external gold loan of 1899	95.2	59.6	154.8
4 per cent external gold loan of 1910	101.9	53.0	154.9
6 per cent ten-year treasury notes of 1913, Series A	58.5	47.4	105.9
Unsecured government loan:			
4 per cent gold bonds of 1904	73.9	38.4	112.3
Internal government debts:			
3 per cent consolidated internal debt of 1885	35.0	15.3	48.3
5 per cent internal redeemable debt of 1895	89.0	63.5	152.5
5 per cent agrarian bonds of 1925 [b]	1.6	.4	2.0
Bonds for liquidation of Tehuantepec National Railway [c]	2.0	.....	2.0
Loans guaranteed by the government:			
5 per cent City of Mexico sterling loan of 1889	13.5	9.0	22.5
4.5 per cent Caja de Préstamos gold loan of 1908	44.6	28.6	75.2
5 per cent State loans of 1903–1907 [d]	3.5	2.4	5.9
5 per cent Tehuantepec National Railway gold loan of 1904 [e]	18.7	9.9	28.6
4.5 per cent Tehuantepec National Railway gold loan of 1909 [e]	3.7	1.8	5.5
4.5 per cent Vera Cruz and Pacific Railway gold loan of 1904	14.0	8.8	22.8
4 per cent National Railways of Mexico general mortgage gold bonds of 1907	101.4	55.8	157.2
Interest on debt of National Railways and subsidiaries, for period between January, 1923, and January, 1926, assumed by the government in agreement of 1922	.....	39.4	39.4
Totals	656.5	433.3	1,089.8

[a] The payments made for the years 1923 to 1927 have been deducted.
[b] The figures given here are a rough approximation.
[c] According to an agreement of September 10, 1925, between the government and

The distribution of the bonded obligations of Mexico in various foreign countries is roughly as follows:

(In millions of pesos)

Countries	Direct Debt [a]	Guaranteed Railway Debt [b]	Total
France	288.0	80.0	368.0
United States	204.0	28.5	232.5
Great Britain	176.5	77.8	254.3
Germany	60.5	.8	61.3
Netherlands	53.3	22.0	75.3
Belgium	51.5	4.4	55.9
Switzerland	35.6	5.9	41.5
Spain	1.0	.....	1.0
Totals	870.4	219.4	1089.8

[a] Including the Tehuantepec Railway loans and the State and Municipal loans for which responsibility has been assumed by the government.

[b] Exclusive of the Tehuantepec loans. *Cf.* note [a], *supra*.

In addition to the obligations represented by bonds Mexico has unliquidated obligations or liabilities to foreigners to an estimated amount of 305,000,000 pesos. These obligations or liabilities are distributed roughly as shown in the first table on page 320.

The total foreign debt of Mexico would thus appear to be approximately 1,400,000,000 pesos, distributed among various countries in the amounts and percentages as shown in the second table on page 320.

Foreign Governments and the Foreign Debt

As has been shown in detail in the preceding chapters of this study, the bonded foreign debt of Mexico had its origin almost wholly in loans made to the government by foreigners. Although

the Mexican Real Estate Company, an English concern, a cash payment of 55,000 pesos is to be made each month for the redemption of bonds of a nominal value of 67,000 pesos.

[d] States of Veracruz, Sinaloa, and Tamaulipas.

[e] The Tehuantepec National Railway is owned exclusively by the government, and under the terms of the loans of 1904 and 1909 these loans have become direct obligations of the government.

these loans appear to have been made in every instance without the participation of any foreign government,[1] the demands of the bondholders upon the Mexican government have on many occasions been seconded, usually in an unofficial manner, by the

(In millions of pesos)

	Foreign Claims Pending Before Mixed Commissions [a]	Indemnities for Agrarian Expropriations	Other Obligations or Liabilities	Total
United States	120.0	21.6	28.8	170.4
Spain	20.0	41.6	7.2	68.8
Great Britain	1.5	9.6	24.0	35.1
France	6.0	1.2	12.0	19.2
Germany	.8	4.8	1.2	6.8
Netherlands	.....	.4	1.2	1.6
Belgium	.2	.4	1.2	1.8
Switzerland	.....	.4	1.2	1.6
Totals	148.5	80.0	76.8	305.3

[a] The amounts given are based on the hypothesis that about ten per cent of the net amounts claimed of Mexico will be awarded by the Commissions. This hypothesis is supported by the history of arbitral awards. It may of course be inapplicable to one or more of the groups of claims now pending.

Countries	Amounts (In pesos)	Percentages
United States	402,900,000	28.9
France	387,200,000	27.8
Great Britain	289,400,000	20.7
Netherlands	76,900,000	5.5
Spain	69,800,000	5.0
Germany	68,100,000	4.9
Belgium	57,700,000	4.1
Switzerland	43,100,000	3.1
Totals	1,395,100,000	100.0

[1] The loans made to Maximilian in 1864 and 1865 were actively fostered by the government of France. These loans, however, were repudiated in 1867 and do not form the basis of any part of the present Mexican debt. *Cf.* pp. 171–173, *supra*.

governments to which the bondholders were entitled to look for protection. Under the rules of international law, these governments are at liberty to intervene, officially or unofficially, in behalf of their nationals who hold Mexican bonds.[2] The right of intervention is limited to some extent by the Hague convention of 1907 regarding the use of force for the collection of contract debts.[3] As has already been pointed out,[3] the signatories of that convention, including the United States, France, Great Britain, and Mexico, are prohibited by its terms from using force in behalf of bondholders until after efforts have been made without success to induce the debtor government to submit to an adjustment of the bondholders' rights by arbitration.[4] In actual practice, moreover, drastic intervention by governments in behalf of bondholders has been rare.[5] The considerations which have weighed against such intervention were well summarized by Lord Palmerston in the circular of 1848 to which reference has already been made.[6]

It has been hitherto [said Lord Palmerston] been thought by the successive Governments of Great Britain undesirable that British subjects should invest their capital in loans to foreign Governments instead of employing it in profitable undertakings at home; and with a view to discourage hazardous loans to foreign Governments, who may be either unable or unwilling to pay the stipulated interest thereupon, the British Government has hitherto thought

[2] "The right of interference on the part of a State, for the purpose of enforcing the performance of justice to its citizens from a foreign State, stands upon an unquestionable foundation, when the foreign State has become itself the debtor of these citizens." Phillimore, *International Law* (Third Edition, London, 1882), Vol. II, p. 8. *Cf.* Vattel, *Droit des gens,* Book II, Chapter XIV, Section 216; Hall, *International Law* (Eighth Edition, Oxford, 1924), p. 333; Fischer Williams, *op. cit.*, pp. 17–26. But see, *contra,* Westlake, *International Law* (Second Edition, Cambridge, 1910), Part I, pp. 331–334; *Revue de Droit International* (Paris), Vol. 35, pp. 603 *et seq.;* Luis N. Drago, *State Loans in their relation to International Policy* (*American Journal of International Law,* Vol. I, pp. 692–712).

[3] *Cf.* pp. 12, 257, *supra.*

[4] For an interesting discussion of the implications of this convention, to the effect that force may be used in the event of the failure of efforts to settle by arbitration, see *For. Rel. U. S.*, 1912, pp. 616–617.

[5] The cases in which "international controls" have been established in states which failed to pay their debts are reviewed by H. M. Alvares Correa in a treatise entitled *The International Controls of Public Finances* (Amsterdam, 1926).

[6] *Cf.* pp. 8, 94, *supra.*

it the best policy to abstain from taking up as International Questions the complaints made by British subjects against foreign Governments which have failed to make good their engagements in regard to such pecuniary transactions.

For the British Government has considered that the losses of imprudent men, who have placed mistaken confidence in the good faith of foreign Governments, would prove a salutary warning to others, and would prevent any other foreign loans from being raised in Great Britain, except by Governments of known good faith and of ascertained solvency.

It was recognized by Lord Palmerston in 1848, however, and it has been recognized since that time by other statesmen that, as the national holdings of foreign bonds increased in volume, the loss occasioned by the non-payment of interest on such bonds might become so great as to make the refusal of protection to the bondholders too high a price to pay for the salutary warning to speculators.

The question of intervention in behalf of holders of foreign bonds was reviewed by the French Minister of Foreign Affairs, Stephen Pichon, in 1907, shortly before the signature of the convention regarding the use of force for the collection of contract debts.[7] A government that is called upon to intervene in behalf of holders of foreign bonds, said the Minister, should give careful attention both to the circumstances of the acquisition of the bonds and to the circumstances of their issue. He continued:

Distinctions are to be made between controversies arising from usurious loans and those arising from regular loans; between States which sincerely desire to fulfil their obligations and those which refuse to do so; between governments which deliberately perpetrate denials of justice and those which respect the law; between those which show bad faith in meeting well-founded claims and those which, for reasons independent of their volition, may find themselves momentarily unable to accord legitimate satisfaction.

To the considerations suggested by Palmerston and Pichon it may be added that any government which is called upon to intervene in behalf of the holders of foreign bonds will naturally give due attention to the balance of interests as between the bondholders and its other nationals. The interests of the nationals of various countries in the various categories of the Mex-

[7] Fischer Williams, *op. cit.*, pp. 12–13.

ican debt have already been stated.[8] The balance of national interests, as between bondholders and other foreign creditors of Mexico, is perhaps more clearly indicated in the following table of percentages, which shows also the percentages of various categories of the debt held by Mexican citizens:

Creditors	Direct Debt in Agreement of 1922 (P885,000,000)	Guaranteed Railway (P225,000,000)	Foreign Claims (P150,000,000)	Agrarian Debt (P490,000,000)	Other Obligations (P250,000,000)	Total (P2,000,000,000)
American	22.9	12.5	80.9	4.50	12.0	20.2
British ..	19.6	35.9	1.0	2.00	10.0	14.1
French ..	32.4	36.4	4.0	.25	5.0	19.6
Dutch ..	6.0	10.0	...	.08	.5	3.9
Swiss ...	4.0	2.7	...	.08	.5	2.1
Belgian .	5.8	2.0	.1	.08	.5	2.9
German .	6.8	.3	.5	1.00	.5	3.5
Spanish .	...	...	13.5	8.67	3.0	4.0
Mexican.	2.5	.2	...	83.34	68.0	29.7

It is important to note that the interests of the foreign creditors of Mexico are by no means the only national interests which have to be considered in true perspective by each of the governments that may be called upon to intervene in behalf of the holders of Mexican bonds. Besides the foreign creditors, there are numerous foreigners who have invested large sums in property or in various kinds of enterprises (industrial, commercial, philanthropic, etc.) in Mexico. Foreign investments in Mexico, according to the most trustworthy estimate, amount to approximately 4,600,000,000 pesos, or well over three times as much as the total foreign debt. By nationalities, these investments are roughly as follows:

	(*In pesos*)
American	3,000,000,000
British	900,000,000
French	375,000,000
Others	325,000,000
Total	4,600,000,000

[8] *Cf.* pp. 318–320, *supra*.

It is obvious that no foreign government is likely to support the demands of bondholders or other creditors of Mexico in such a manner as to prejudice the security and prosperity of the investments of its nationals in Mexico.

The creditors of Mexico and the investors in Mexico are, finally, in every foreign country, only a small minority of the total population. No government can, of course, afford to support the interests of this small minority against the interests and the wishes of the great majority. Except in the improbable event that the Mexican government should deal with its foreign creditors in a manner clearly unjust and unfair, public opinion in the countries of which these creditors are nationals is not likely to approve drastic intervention by foreign governments.

On the whole, it would seem that, although friendly representations may be made by one or more foreign governments with a view to assuring a just and fair settlement between Mexico and her creditors, the actual arrangements with respect to the Mexican foreign debt, other than that growing out of claims referred to the Mixed Commissions, are likely to be made directly between the creditors and the debtor.

The Foreign Bondholders and the Mexican Government

During the last ten years the foreign holders of Mexican bonds have had over all other creditors of the Mexican government the advantage of being effectively organized under the leadership of the International Committee of Bankers on Mexico.[9] This advantage has been offset to only a limited extent by the fact that certain creditors residing in Mexico have been able, through persistency or influence, to make special arrangements with the government. The special arrangements which the government has made with individual creditors residing in Mexico have been, at most, in terms of millions of pesos. The arrangements between the government and the International Committee, to whose

[9] The English holders of Mexican bonds had acted as a unit, under a committee organized at London, as early as 1829 (*cf.* p. 58, *supra*). Since 1873 most of them had been affiliated with the Corporation of Foreign Bondholders in London. Similar organizations had been formed in Paris and Brussels in 1899.

economic power was added the formidable weight of the endorsement of its general aims by no less than seven foreign governments, have been in terms of hundreds of millions.

The agreement of 1922 between the International Committee and the Mexican government was not only an evidence of the effectiveness of the bondholders' instrument of self-help. It was also an evidence of the good will of both parties to the agreement. The Committee undertook to recommend to the bondholders the acceptance of the sacrifice involved in the distribution of arrears of interest over a period of forty years, without interest on such arrears. The members of the Committee formally expressed their desire to coöperate with the government in measures for the economic improvement of Mexico. The government, on the other hand, undertook to pay on account of its own debt and that of the National Railways amounts so large as to be clearly beyond its capacity to pay in the circumstances.

The agreement of 1925 was a further evidence of the good will of both the Committee and the government. Since the collapse of that agreement, the good will of both parties has been demonstrated in their coöperation in the economic and fiscal survey made by Messrs. Sterrett and Davis in 1928 and in the audit of the National Railways made by Price, Waterhouse and Company in 1929. The law of January 25, 1929, moreover, while envisaging the problem of the bonded foreign debt of 1,100,000,000 pesos as a part of the problem of the entire public debt of 2,000,000,000 pesos,[10] leaves the door open for an amicable adjustment of the bonded foreign debt upon the basis of the ascertained financial capacity of the government.

In view of these evidences of good will, it is to be expected that the problem of the bonded foreign debt will be settled in the near future in a just and reasonable manner. It should be recognized, however, that the settlement of this problem will have to be made in the face of considerable difficulties. Among these difficulties the following may be mentioned:

1. The impression, widely prevalent in Mexico, that the loans in which the foreign bonds had their origin were made

[10] *Cf.* p. 335, *infra.*

on oppressive terms and were of questionable benefit to the country.

2. The impression, widely prevalent abroad, that the Mexican government has almost uniformly evaded the payment of its bonded debts.

3. The fact that the problem of the bonded foreign debt is inextricably involved with the larger problem of the financial rehabilitation of the Mexican government.

In relation to the first of these difficulties it may be useful to consider the following tables:

CONDITIONS AND UTILIZATION OF EXTERNAL BOND ISSUES

1824 TO 1888 INCLUSIVE

(Amounts are in millions of dollars)

Year	1824	1825	1831	1837–1843	1846	1851	1888
Nominal amount	16.0	16.0	7.9	54.6	51.2	51.2	52.5
Contract price	8.8	13.9	...	...	...	...	41.9
Bankers' commission	.8	.8	...	5.4[c]	...	...	.7
Net proceeds	8.0	13.0	...	...	...	...	41.2
Interest on nominal amount	5%	6%	5.6%	2.6%	5%	3%	6%
Interest on amount obtained	11.6%	7.7%	...	...	...	...	8.01%
Annual carrying charges for external debt	1.0	2.0	.7	1.4	3.1	1.8	3.4
Income for year from revenues assigned for external debt	1.6	3.5	.6	1.0	3.0	.9	4.0
Total ordinary revenues for year	15.3[a]	9.8	13.4	18.4	13.0	6.2	27.1
Total expenditures for year	15.2	18.0	16.5	29.2	24.3	12.6	35.9
Utilization of bonds:							
Expenses of issue, discount on sale, interest, amortization, etc.	10.3	6.2[b]	...	5.4	...	...	12.9
Payment of preëxisting obligations	1.6	4.0	7.9	49.2	51.0	51.2	39.6
Purchase of military and naval equipment	.4	1.4	...	...	...	...	...
Current administration, etc.	3.7	4.4	...	...	.2	...	...

[a] Separate figures for ordinary and extraordinary revenues for 1824 not being available, the figure here given includes both.

[b] This figure includes the sum of $1,520,000 which was lost by the failure of the government's bankers.

[c] In bonds, not cash.

From these tables, supplemented by the discussions in preceding chapters, it would appear that the terms on which the various issues of foreign bonds were made by the Mexican government were, in general, as favorable as could have been expected under the circumstances. The most striking fact with respect to the utilization of the bonds issued is that some $410,000,000,

CONDITIONS AND UTILIZATION OF EXTERNAL BOND ISSUES
1889 TO 1913 INCLUSIVE
(Amounts are in millions of dollars)

YEAR	1889	1890	1893	1899	1904	1910	1913
Nominal amount	13.5	30.0	15.0	113.5	40.0	55.5	30.0
Contract price	...	26.6	9.6	...	35.6	52.6	27.0
Bankers' commission	...	.3	.2	1.1	...	...	...
Net proceeds	...	26.3	9.5	...	35.6	52.6	27.0
Interest on nominal amount	5%	6%	6%	5%	4%	4%	6%
Interest on amount obtained	...	6.95%	9.87%	5.32%	4.71%	4.41%	8.33%
Annual carrying charges for external debt	4.4	6.2	7.2	6.4	9.0	8.5	10.7
Income for year from revenues assigned for external debt	4.0	6.5	5.7	8.3	11.9	15.2	19.0
Total ordinary revenues for year	27.5	29.9	22.1	30.2	44.2	55.6	60.5
Total expenditures for year	44.8	53.8	26.8	27.4	51.8	100.8	76.7
Utilization of bonds:							
Expenses of issue, discount on sale, interest, amortization, etc	3.0	4.0	5.5	1.2	4.4	4.8	3.0
Payment or conversion of preëxisting obligations	...	...	4.0	108.4	22.7	50.7	21.0
Current administration, etc	...	...	5.5	3.9	...	...	6.0
Railway subsidies	10.5	26.0	...	...	7.5	...	...
Public works	...	...	...	....	5.4	...	...

or nearly four-fifths of the total, have been used in the payment or conversion of preëxisting obligations. The obligations thus paid or converted were in large part obligations of an internal character incurred in connection with the construction of public works or in the promotion of private railway enterprises. They were chiefly, however, obligations arising from previous issues of foreign bonds on which the service of interest and amortization had been neglected. The growth of the foreign debt through the process indicated was not "magical," as has been suggested by certain Mexican publicists; it was the natural result of the accumulation of arrears of interest and charges for amortization.

With respect to the difficulty constituted by the reflection on the record of the Mexican government in meeting its foreign obligations the following chronological summary of that record may be illuminating:

1824. Five per cent bonds for $16,000,000 issued in London net government $8,000,000.

1825. Six per cent bonds for $16,000,000 issued in London

net government $13,000,000, of which $3,000,000 is used in redemption of $5,000,000 of the bonds of 1824.

1831. Arrears of interest since October, 1828, amounting to $5,542,100, are capitalized in new bonds to the amount of $7,922,100.

1837–43. Outstanding bonds and unpaid coupons, to the total amount of $48,667,746, are funded in a new issue of bonds, of which half are "active," bearing interest at 5 per cent per annum, and half are "deferred," bearing no interest for ten years unless they are used during that time in the purchase of public lands at one dollar an acre. The bonds that had previously earned interest at the rate of 6 per cent per annum are funded at a premium of 12.5 per cent. The new issue, including bonds issued for commissions and debentures issued for interest unpaid from October, 1838, to October, 1842, amounts to $54,573,730.

1846. Outstanding bonds and unpaid coupons, to the total amount of $56,013,875, are converted into a new issue of bonds bearing five per cent interest per annum. The active bonds, with their coupons, are converted at 90 per cent of the face value of the bonds; the deferred bonds and the debentures at 60 per cent. The new issue totals $51,208,250.

1851. The bonds of 1846 are converted at par into new bonds bearing 3 per cent interest per annum. Arrears of interest amounting to $10,241,650 are liquidated by cash payments aggregating $3,800,000.

1865. Seven per cent bonds to the amount of $2,900,000 are issued in New York. (The bonds issued by Maximilian in Europe in 1864 and 1865 are omitted from this summary; *cf.* pp. 153–158, 171–173 *supra.*)

1886. Under an agreement with the London bondholders, arrears of interest amounting to $45,000,000 are capitalized in a new issue of 3 per cent internal bonds in the amount of 16,500,000 pesos, equivalent at the time to $13,300,000. Payment of interest on the outstanding bonds of 1851 is resumed at the rate of 1 per cent for 1886, 1.5 per cent for 1887, 2 per cent for 1888, 2.5 per cent for 1889, and 3 per cent for subsequent years.

1888. Six per cent bonds to the amount of $52,500,000 are issued in Berlin, London, and Amsterdam. The greater part of the proceeds of these bonds is applied to the redemption of the bonds of 1851 and 1886 at 40 per cent of their face value.

1889–1913. New bonds to the total amount of $300,000,000 are floated in various foreign markets at rates of interest, in some cases, but little above 4 per cent on the money actually obtained. The service on all the outstanding bonds is regularly maintained.

1922. Arrears of interest totaling $200,000,000 on the foreign debt (including the internal issues of 1885 and 1895, held chiefly by foreigners, and the obligations of the National Railways Company, for which the government assumes responsibility) are postponed, by agreement with the International Committee of Bankers, to the year 1928, when the first of forty equal annual payments is to be made on account of such arrears. A part of the interest for the years 1923 to 1927 is similarly postponed.

1925. The payments required under the agreement of 1922 having been suspended, the government is relieved of liability for future interest on the obligations of the National Railways Company except in so far as such liability results from guarantees antedating the agreement.

1928. The payment of interest and amortization on outstanding foreign bonds is suspended until it shall be possible to conclude new arrangements on the basis of the government's capacity to pay and in accordance with a comprehensive plan.

It is evident from this summary that the foreign obligations of the Mexican government have been met according to their terms during less than a third of the last century. It is evident also that the numerous compromises which the government has made with its foreign creditors have involved considerable sacrifices for those creditors. The actual sacrifices have, however, been less than the apparent sacrifices in consequence of the fact that the bonds affected by the various compromises were usually acquired by the holders at less than their face value.[11] On the basis of the contracts for the bonds of 1824 and 1825, for example, the holder of a one thousand dollar bond of each of those years should have received by the end of the year 1888 the face amount of each bond, with interest, aggregating the sums of $4,250 and $4,840, respectively. The cash returns (including redemption of

[11] *Cf.* charts of market quotations, on pages 330, 331.

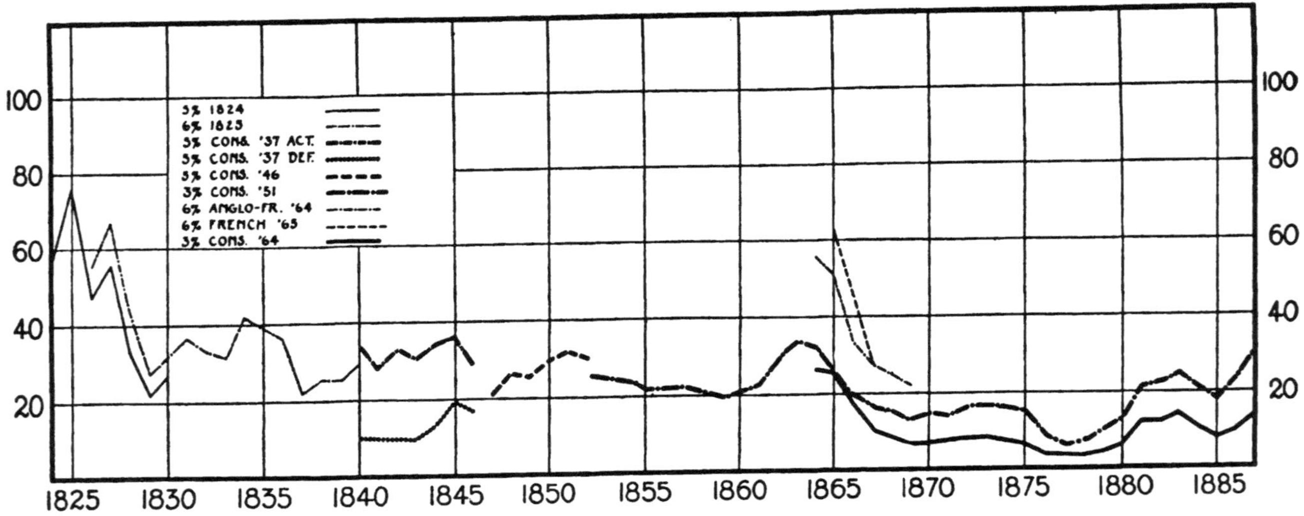

QUOTATIONS OF MEXICAN GOVERNMENT BONDS ON THE LONDON STOCK EXCHANGE 1824–1887

1824–1845 Yearly average of closing prices for the days January 1 and July 1.—*The Times*, London.

1846–1864 Yearly average of closing prices for the days January 27 and July 27.—*The Bankers' Magazine*, London. On 3 per cent Cons. '64 for 1864, only July 27 is shown.—*The Economist*, London. On 6 per cent Anglo-French '64 for 1864, price on Paris Bourse on July 1, is shown.

1865–1887 Yearly average of high and low prices for the year.—*The Investor's Monthly Manual*, London. On 6 per cent Anglo-French '64, price on London Stock market is shown; for the year 1869, low only is shown.

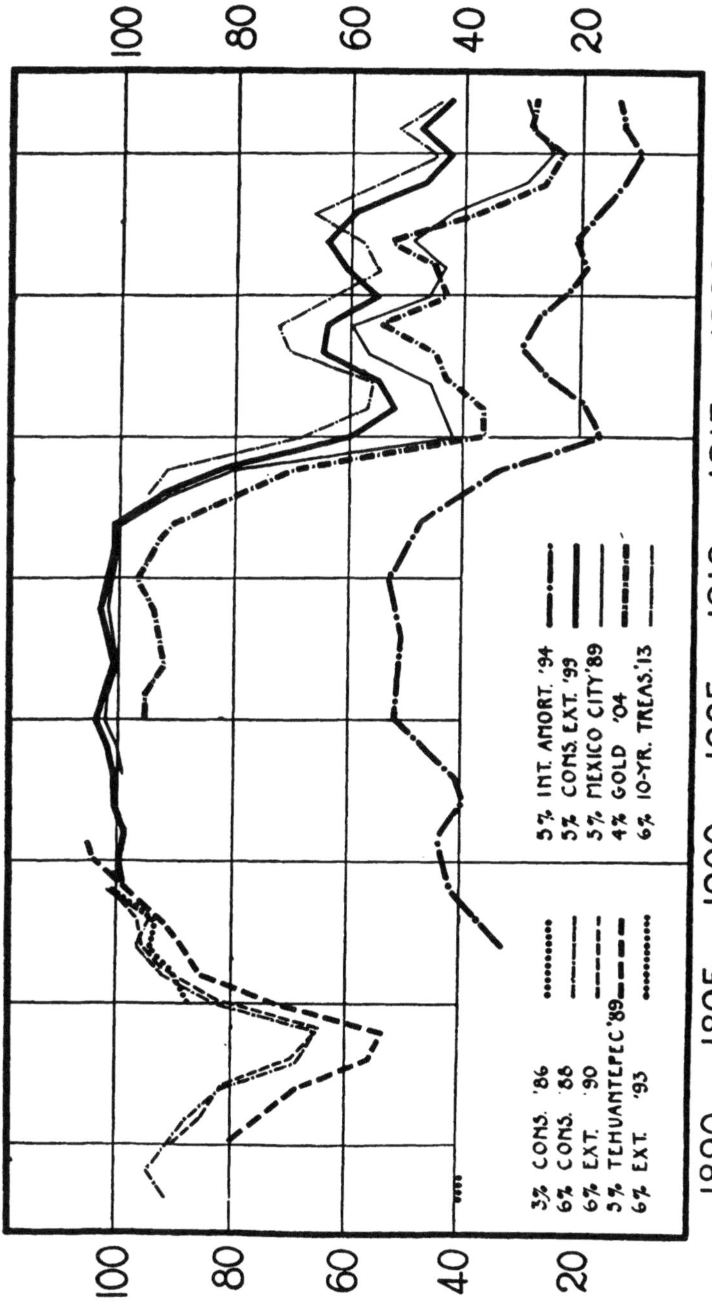

QUOTATIONS OF MEXICAN GOVERNMENT BONDS ON THE LONDON STOCK EXCHANGE 1887–1927

Yearly average of high and low prices.—*The Investor's Monthly Manual*, London.

principal) actually received to the end of 1888 by an investor who purchased at the issue price a one thousand dollar bond of each of the years mentioned were as follows:

Year	On $1,000 5 Per Cent Bond of 1824, Purchased at Issue Price of $580	On $1,000 6 Per Cent Bond of 1825, Purchased at Issue Price of $867.50
1824	$ 50.00	......
1825–27	137.50	$ 150.00
1831	6.25	7.50
1832	25.00	30.00
1839–43	138.95	144.80
1846	40.40	42.00
1851–54	219.00	230.00
1864–67	134.50	152.00
1886	14.00	15.50
1887	25.00	26.00
1888	659.00	682.00
Totals	$1,449.60	$1,479.80

The investor who bought the bonds at the issue price was thus eventually able, despite numerous defaults and partial repudiations in the meantime, to recover the whole of his capital with interest averaging about 2.25 per cent a year on the bond of 1824 and about 1.1 per cent a year on the bond of 1825. The investor who paid from 20 to 30 per cent of the face value of the bonds obviously fared much better.

The last of the three difficulties mentioned above is of such importance as to justify its discussion in some detail under the head of

The Problem of the Foreign Debt as a Part of a Larger Problem

Besides the debt of 1,400,000,000 pesos to foreigners and foreign governments,[12] the Mexican government has a debt, estimated at 600,000,000 pesos, to its own citizens. The internal obligations of the Mexican government, other than those included

[12] *Cf.* pp. 318–320, *supra.*

in the agreements of 1922 and 1925 with the International Committee of Bankers, were estimated by a special commission of the Ministry of Finance in November, 1928, at approximately 773,000,000 pesos.[13] These obligations, however, especially in so far as they arise from expropriations of land for *ejidos*,[14] from damages to railroads, or from the seizure of the metallic reserves of the banks of issue,[15] are held to a very considerable extent by foreigners. The obligations of the Mexican government held by Mexican citizens would appear to be approximately as shown in the table on page 334.

The largest of the items shown above, namely, the debt arising from the expropriation of lands for *ejidos*,[16] is of great importance in connection with the question of the revival of agriculture, the dominant occupation of the country. Until some satisfactory provision is made for the payment of indemnities to those who have been deprived of their lands, the present landholders who are liable to further expropriations, under the agrarian laws, cannot be expected to raise the normal crops upon which the country largely depends. The railways and banks cannot operate efficiently until they receive the payments that are due them from the government. The business houses from which the government has bought large supplies will continue to be embarrassed until their accounts are paid. In short, the economic life of the country is considerably handicapped by the failure of the government to pay its debts to local creditors. The conclusion of agreements with respect to the foreign debt would doubtless improve the credit of the country abroad, but unless the terms of the agreements are such as to leave to the government the means of providing in due measure for its debts to local creditors, the agreements will be doomed to failure. The Mexican government, to paraphrase a famous declaration, cannot endure half-solvent and half-insolvent.

The government, according to its own account of its situation, is at present unable to pay all that is due and payable either to its local creditors or to its foreign creditors. It may be worth

[13] *Cf.* report of the commission, as published in *El Economista*, January 1, 1929. [14] *Cf.* pp. 310–311, *supra*. [15] *Cf.* p. 268, *supra*. [16] *Cf.* pp. 310–311, *supra*.

OBLIGATIONS OF GOVERNMENT TO CITIZENS

		(*In pesos*)
Bonds of the debt included in the agreements of 1922 and 1925		22,000,000
Bonds for salaries of federal employees		6,000,000
Bonds for expropriations under the agrarian laws		8,000,000
Verified obligations not represented by bonds		80,000,000
To former banks of issue for metallic reserves taken by Carranza	25,000,000	
To Bank of Mexico for advances	6,000,000	
To States and Municipalities for legal participation in revenues collected by federal government	5,000,000	
To railroads for damages	2,500,000	
To various parties under contracts	20,000,000	
Other accounts	21,500,000	
Unverified obligations		484,000,000
Claims pending before National Claims Commission [a]	45,000,000	
Claims of railways for subventions, accounts, and damages [b]	15,000,000	
Arrears of salaries to federal employees	12,000,000	
Various accounts payable	12,000,000	
Agrarian debt (including interest) [c]	400,000,000	
Total		600,000,000

a Reduced by one-half from amount stated in report of the special commission.

b The amount here given includes a rough estimate of the loss resulting to Mexican shareholders from damage done to the railways during the revolt of March and April, 1929.

c In the report of the special commission, claims for definite expropriations to the amount of 106,000,000 pesos were listed as pending a decision as to their lapse. The interest due at the rate of five per cent since the taking of each parcel of land was, however, not included. This interest would appear to have run on an average of five years, on all the land expropriated. Upon the assumption that most of the claims pending decision as to their lapse will be disallowed, the total of the agrarian debt to Mexicans, including interest to July 1, 1929, will be about as shown above.

while to consider for a moment whether the government has not underestimated its present capacity to pay. The following data and observations appear to be pertinent to this question:

1. The total Mexican debt of 2,000,000,000 pesos represents a debt of about 133 pesos for each of the 15,000,000 inhabitants of the country. These figures may be compared with the following in regard to the debts of various other countries:[17]

Country	Amount of Debt (In pesos)	Debt per Capita
Argentina	2,180,000,000	218
Belgium	4,278,500,000	549
Brazil	2,681,400,000	88
Chile	831,000,000	208
France	37,742,000,000	902
Great Britain	76,337,000,000	1,608
Italy	5,172,100,000	127
Netherlands	2,405,440,000	324
Norway	730,760,000	261
Peru	224,300,000	49
Spain	5,050,000,000	230
United States	39,300,000,000	340

Country	Annual Debt Service (In pesos)	Percentages of Normal Revenues
Argentina	156,000,000	29.8
Belgium	238,000,000	41.2
Brazil	96,000,000	34.6
Chile	60,000,000	24.2
France	1,253,000,000	39.5
Great Britain	3,114,000,000	40.4
Italy	308,000,000	35.5
Netherlands	106,000,000	19.9
Norway	40,000,000	29.2
Peru	18,000,000	20.8
Spain	226,000,000	30.1
United States	1,500,000,000	19.2

[17] The data for Argentina, Chile, and Peru were obtained from the latest available records at the United States Department of Commerce. Those for other countries, principally as of 1925 or 1926, are from League of Nations, *Memorandum on Public Finance*, 1922–1926 (Geneva, 1927).

2. The amount required annually for the service of the existing debt of the Mexican government, if that debt were funded upon reasonable terms, would not be in excess of 100,000,000 pesos, or one-third of the present annual revenues. These figures compare with the corresponding figures in regard to the debt services of various other governments as shown in the second table on page 335.[18]
The comparison with Mexican figures of the period 1895–1911, when the service of the debt was uniformly maintained, is as follows:

YEAR	DEBT SERVICE (In pesos)	PERCENTAGES OF NORMAL REVENUES
1895–96	17,000,000	38.0
1898–99	20,000,000	37.5
1902–03	22,000,000	30.0
1905–06	27,000,000	26.1
1908–09	26,000,000	26.6
1910–11	26,000,000	23.7

3. The comparison of the debt and debt services of Mexico with those of other countries cannot fairly be made without reference to the fact that the present productive capacity of the Mexican people is considerably below that of many other peoples. There is, moreover, a minimum sum below which the Mexican government could not be expected to go in the maintenance of essential administrative services. In view of the urgent social and economic needs of the Mexican people, following a long period of neglect, it may not be reasonable to expect the present government to apply as large a proportion of its revenues as was applied in former years to the service of its debt. It should be borne in mind, however, that the present program of education, sanitation, irrigation, highway construction, and agrarian reform might be greatly accelerated by the use of foreign capital that would be placed at the disposal of the government as soon as a satisfactory adjustment of the existing debt was assured. The accomplishment of these projects and the increase of foreign trade that

[18] From sources cited in note immediately preceding.

would almost certainly coincide with the restoration of Mexican credit would, in turn, result in the enhancement of the national revenues.

4. In addition to its annual revenues the Mexican government possesses realizable assets of considerable value which might not unreasonably be used in the reduction of the existing debt. Among these assets are 95 per cent of the outstanding stock of the Banco de México; about 51 per cent of the stock of the National Railways Company; and real estate, not specially adapted to government use, to the value of over 100,000,000 pesos. One of the principal objections to the use of these assets toward the payment of the public debt could be overcome by a provision that they should be sold only to Mexican citizens. To prevent the control of the bank and of the railways from passing into foreign hands, it might be provided that stock of the bank or of the railways when held by foreigners should carry no voting rights.

Apart from data and observations such as the foregoing and upon the assumption that the Mexican government is in fact unable to meet all its financial engagements at the present time, it is pertinent to inquire what line of conduct may reasonably be expected of the government in the circumstances. According to standards of conduct generally recognized as applicable in relations between debtor and creditor, the Mexican government, it is believed, might reasonably be expected, in consideration of the forbearance of its creditors:

1. To reduce its current expenditures to the lowest point compatible with efficient administration.

2. To refrain from incurring new debts.

3. To devote to the payment of its debts all ordinary revenues in excess of the minimum required for efficient administration and all such sums as may be realized through the sale of liquid assets not used for administrative purposes.

4. To refrain from making payments to individual creditors or classes of creditors in preference to other individuals or classes except in so far as preferential payments may be generally admitted to be proper.

On the score of the reduction of current expenditures, the creditors of the Mexican government can find little to criticize in the recent record of the government. The budget of expenditures for 1928 was carefully calculated and was substantially adhered to; the supplementary appropriation of 5,000,000 pesos at the end of the year being in favorable contrast with the supplementary appropriations of 21,000,000 pesos in 1927, 50,000,000 pesos in 1926, and 90,000,000 pesos in 1925. During the first half of the year 1929, as already noted, the budgeted expenditures have not been exceeded, despite the unusual calls upon the treasury in connection with the revolt of March and April. The amounts allotted in the budgets of 1928 and 1929 to such items as education, sanitation, irrigation, and highway construction are probably as low as could be expected in view of the program of social betterment to which the government is committed.

On the score of refraining from the contraction of new debt, the recent record of the government is highly vulnerable. Salaries and supply bills, which were formerly allowed to fall into arrears, have, indeed, been paid in cash since the beginning of 1928. The government has, however, continued the policy of expropriating lands for *ejidos*, without paying cash for them, and has thus greatly increased the agrarian debt, the present or future amount of which it is impossible for anyone to state or predict with confidence. So long as the government continues to increase the agrarian debt without regard for the possibility of paying it, there can of course be no real balancing of the budget and no definite settlement of other categories of debt.

Considering the record of payments on the debt over the period since the beginning of 1923, one cannot well find fault with the government in regard to the amounts paid on the debt out of ordinary revenues. The fact that larger payments were not made out of these revenues was due in part to the unexpected decline of the revenues [19] and in part to the extraordinary expenditures required in connection with the de la Huerta revolt

[19] *Cf.* p. 312, *supra.*

of 1923–1924. No sums of consequence appear to have been realized through the sale of liquid assets.

Considering the record over the same period from the point of view of preferences accorded to individual creditors or classes of creditors, the local creditors would doubtless regard as unjustified the preferences accorded to the holders of some of the bonds included in the agreements of 1922 and 1925. The bondholders represented by the International Committee would, on the other hand, have some grounds for objection to such settlements as those made in 1925 with various banks and railway companies and with the holders of the Tehuantepec Railway liquidation bonds. The relatively small payments made in 1928 and 1929 on account of the debt for arrears of salaries and for supplies furnished to the government in previous years appear to have been generally admitted to be just and proper. The government has lately, in the law of January 25, 1929, foreshadowed what is undoubtedly the soundest and most equitable procedure with reference to future payments on account of the debt. This procedure is based upon the recognition of the fact that the problem of the Mexican debt cannot be definitely and permanently settled unless all the outstanding obligations are comprised in the settlement.

Counsels of Expediency

The problem of the foreign debt of Mexico is, of course, primarily a Mexican problem to be solved by the Mexican government to the best of its ability. Upon purely domestic considerations — political, social, and economic — the Mexican government might possibly justify the complete neglect of this debt for such period as may be required for the accomplishment of its projects of education, sanitation, irrigation, highway construction, and agrarian reform. As a member of the family of nations, however, unable to subsist without commercial and economic intercourse with other nations or without a measure of good will from them, Mexico may be, apart from all questions of law or justice, under the practical necessity of making reasonable provision for the payment of her foreign obligations. The payments required on account of these obligations may absorb funds for lack of which the immediate projects of social betterment will be greatly retarded, but as the history of Mexico herself clearly indicates,[20] such payments, if accompanied by other evidences of consideration for the opinions of the outside world, are almost certain to be followed in due time by an immense acceleration of the national progress in the direction desired.

If the Mexican government is under the practical necessity of giving due consideration to its foreign creditors, these creditors are no less truly under the practical necessity of giving due consideration to the Mexican government. In the interest of all the creditors, as well as of the Mexican people, the government must be maintained as a "going concern." The restoration of the economic health of the country may require the payment of certain classes of unsecured debts on a parity with, or even in preference to, debts which have been secured by solemn pledges of customs duties. The exigencies of the political situation, which any government disregards at its peril, may, moreover, require expenditures that cannot be justified on economic or social grounds. There can be no doubt that the foreign creditors of Mexico will, in the end, get a larger proportion of what is due them if they will show an appreciation of the peculiar difficulties with which the Mexican government is confronted in its efforts to consolidate the social gains of the revolution of 1910–1920 and at the same time to achieve the reconquest of its former high credit abroad.

In 1885, after the failure of several attempts to settle the foreign debt of Mexico apart from the domestic debt, President Díaz appointed a Mexican commission to draw up a plan for the settlement of the entire debt of the republic. In pursuance of the recommendations of the commission, the Congress passed a law prescribing the bases on which it was believed that all the obligations of the republic could be met, "provided that such bases were accepted freely and spontaneously by those interested."[21] The bases laid down in this law were accepted, with certain modifications, by both the foreign and the domestic creditors, and within the next few years these creditors were rewarded

[20] *Cf.* pp. 203 *et seq.*, *supra*. [21] Casasús, *op. cit.*, p. 469; *cf.* p. 203, *supra*.

by a considerable enhancement of the value of their securities, while the Mexican government saw its credit rise to a parity with that of the foremost governments of the world.

At the present time history seems to be ready to repeat itself. The requirements of the situation appear to be, first, a reasonable and well considered plan for the settlement of the entire debt, and, second, a disposition on the part of the creditors to accept immediate sacrifices of theoretical values in return for an assurance that the plan adopted will actually be followed over a period of years. It must be realized, of course, that the best laid schemes for the financial rehabilitation of Mexico may be wrecked either by the recrudescence of civil strife or by heedless persistence in projects of social betterment that are beyond the means of the government. Unless there is moral certainty that peace will be preserved and that restraint will be exercised with respect to the agrarian and other reforms, the creditors of Mexico will hardly consider it worth their while to conclude any arrangement whatever with the government.[22]

[22] On July 25, 1930, after this volume had been sent to the press, the signature of a new agreement between Mexico and the International Committee of Bankers was announced. This agreement is of course subject to the approval of the bondholders. See note on page 15, *supra*.

APPENDICES

	1824	1825	1830	1837
	(5 Per Cent Loan)	(6 Per Cent Loan)	(Capitalization of Interest)	(Convers[ion] Begun[)]
EXTERNAL LOANS				
Nominal Amount.......	£ 3,200,000	£ 3,200,000	....	....
Contract Price..........	£ 1,760,000	£ 2,776,000	....	....
Bankers' Commission [a]..	£ 160,000	£ 166,560	....	£ 231,200 pai[d] 50,000 " £ 281,200 "
Net Proceeds...........	£ 1,600,000	£ 2,609,440	....	....
Real Interest...........	11.6%	7.7%	....	....
Annual Carrying Charges [b]	£ 160,000 Interest 32,000 Amortization £ 192,000 or P 960,000	£ 192,000 Interest 32,000 Amortization £ 224,000 or P 1,120,000	....	....
Income from Revenues Specially Assigned....	P 1,622,092	P 1,835,443	....	....
TOTAL EXTERNAL DEBT				
Amount...............	£ 3,200,000	£ 6,294,600	£ 6,865,820	£ 9,247,37[illegible]
Annual Carrying Charges	£ 160,000 Interest 32,000 Amortization £ 192,000 or P 960,000	£ 352,000 Interest 64,000 Amortization £ 416,000 or P 2,080,000	£ 147,790 Interest or P 738,950	£ 231,184 [illegible] or P 1,155,920
Income from Revenues Specially Assigned....	P 1,622,092	P 3,457,533	P 638,099	P 498,380
FOREIGN TRADE........	....	P 24,178,951	....	....
Exports................	....	P 5,080,235	....	....
Imports...............	....	P 19,093,716	(P 15,067,423) [e]	P (7,959,235)
REVENUES AND EXPENDITURES [c]............	1824 [d]	1825 [d]	1830–31	1836–3[7]
Revenues..............	P 15,254,601	P 9,770,372	P 16,952,555	P 17,279,027
Ordinary.............	....	....	13,386,438	9,606,135
Extraordinary.........	....	....	3,566,117	7,672,892
Foreign Loans......	....	....	....	....
Other Sources......	....	....	....	....
Expenditures...........	P 15,165,875	P 17,986,674	P 16,466,038	P 17,610,730
Legislative Power.....	.... }	P 301,268	462,109	352,538
Executive Power......	.... }		25,363	59,403
Ministry of Relations..	....	105,737	608,746	724,224
Ministry of Justice ...	....	77,220	299,172	468,599
Ministry of War......	....	12,000,000	8,186,549	6,193,391
Ministry of Marine...	....	2,934,533	154,110	238,148
Ministry of Treasury..	....	2,567,916	6,729,989	9,574,427

[a] The bankers' commissions listed in this table are the commissions given, according to the contracts, for issuing interest as the case may be. In addition, the following commissions for interest and amortization payments were a[llowed]

1824 — 1.5 per cent on interest and amortization payments
1825 — 1 per cent on amortization payments and 1.5 per cent on interest payments
1830 — 0.5 per cent to depositaries who receive funds assigned, and 1 per cent to commissioners for expe[nse] payments
1837 — 0.2 per cent to depositaries who receive funds assigned
1846 — To agents in Mexico 1 per cent on remittances in bills of exchange, 0.5 per cent on those in specie
To agents in London 1 per cent on cash payments
1888 — 0.25 per cent on interest and amortization payments
1889 — " " " " " " " "
1890 — " " " " " " " "
1893 — " " " " " " " "
1899 — " " " " " " " "
1904 — " " " " " " " "

THE BURDEN OF THE EXTERNAL DEBT OF MEXICO (NOT INCLUDI

43	1846	1850	1864 [h]	
ERSION LETED)	(CONVERSION)	(CONVERSION)	(CAPITALIZATION OF INTEREST)	
.....	....	....	....	....
.....	....	....	....	....
,023 bonds	....	....	....	....
,000 "				
,032 "				
.....	....	....	....	....
.....	....	....	....	....
.....	....	....	....	....
.....	....	....	....	....
.....	....	....	....	....
.....	....	....	....	....
.....	....	....	....	....
14,746 89,583 r 47,915	£ 10,241,650 £ 512,082 Interest 100,000 Amortization £ 612,082 or P 3,060,410	£ 10,241,650 £ 307,250 Interest 50,000 Amortization £ 357,250 or P 1,786,250	£ 15,106,450 £ 453,194 Interest P 2,044,100	....
09,215	P 3,000,000 [f]	P 930,680	Guaranty inoperative	....
50,820	....	....	....	....
09,262	....	....	....	....
41,558	P (12,268,968) [e]	(9,703,761) [e]	(P 12,456,476) [e]	....
43	1846 [g]	1850–51	1865 [g]	
19,083	P 25,905,348	P 12,625,111	P 43,073,611	
21,384	13,000,000	6,158,744	20,873,611	....
97,699	12,905,348	6,466,367	....	....
.....	....	....	22,200,000 [i]	....
.....	....	....	....	....
20,119	P 24,310,031 [g]	P 12,635,217	P 48,263,871 [g]	....
35,608	710,657	380,202	....	Legislative Power
57,628	110,700	41,181	....	Executive "
74,843	529,649	707,880	....	Judicial "
54,178	394,853	203,209	....	Ministry of Relations
07,323	21,815,635	3,384,854	....	" " Interior
59,005		67,275	....	" " Justice and Pub Education
31,534	1,158,537	1,273,778 (Extraordinary)	....	Ministry of Communic tions
		6,576,838		Ministry of Development
				" " Treasury
				" " War and Marine
				Extraordinary

oans, or capitalizing

mption and interest

1910 — 0.25 per cent on interest payments, 0.125 per cent on amortiz
1913 — 0.25 per cent on interest and amortization payments
1922 — For expenses and compensation, 1 per cent of the principal required for expenses and obligations of International Commi

[b] Interest and amortization payments as listed in the loan contracts. The co subsequently, at the average annual rate of exchange on London for the fiscal y

[c] Revenues and expenditures in this table are actual revenues and expenditure

[d] Budgeted.

[e] Calculated from revenues reported.

[f] Approximated.

[g] Estimated.

[h] Loans of Maximilian and Juárez are not included in the table. See pages 1

[i] Income from Imperial Loans. See pages 153–158.

[j] The outstanding bonds of the London debt were redeemed with the proceed

[k] These bonds were given as payment for the construction of the Tehuantepec

DIX I

NG FOREIGN INTEREST IN INTERNAL DEBT) AT VARIOUS EPOCHS

	1888	1889	1890	1893	
	(6 Per Cent Loan)	(5 % Per Cent Loan)	(6 Per Cent Loan)		(5 Per
	£ 10,500,000	£ 2,700,000 [k]	£ 6,000,000	£ 3,000,000	£ 22,70c
	8,370,000	....	5,325,000	1,927,569	21,913
	131,250	....	60,000	37,500	227
	8,238,750	....	5,265,000	1,890,069	21,686
	8.01%	....	6.95%	9.87%	
	£ 630,000 Interest 52,500 Amortization £ 682,500 or P 4,372,664	£ 135,000 Interest [l] 54,000 Amortization £ 189,000 or P 1,250,620	£ 360,000 Interest 15,000 Amortization £ 375,000 or P 2,208,589	£ 180,000 Interest 7,500 Amortizat'n £ 187,500 or P 1,618,705	£ 1,135 140 £ 1,275 P 13,157
	P 4,980,765	.... [m]	P 2,542,224	P 2,046,961	P 17,713
	£ 10,500,000 [i] £ 630,000 Interest 52,500 Amortization £ 682,500 or P 4,372,664	£ 13,200,000 £ 765,000 Interest 106,500 Amortization £ 871,500 or P 5,766,749	£ 19,200,000 £ 1,125,000 Interest 121,500 Amortization £ 1,246,500 or P 7,341,350	£ 22,037,660 £ 1,305,000 Interest 129,000 Amortizat'n £ 1,434,000 or P 12,379,856	£ 22,70c £ 1,135 140 £ 1,275 P 13,157
	P 4,982,765	P 5,048,873 [n]	P 8,065,552 [n]	P 10,290,353 [n]	P 17,713
	P 85,500,346	P 100,183,317	....	P 109,630,776	P 287,044
	48,885,908	60,158,423	P 63,276,395	79,343,287	158,247
	36,614,438	40,024,894	....	30,287,489	128,796
	1887–1888	1888–1889	1890–1891	1893–1894	1
	P 46,885,309	P 59,954,992	P 67,366,753	P 48,319,766	P 64,61c
	33,932,227	34,374,783	37,391,805	40,211,747	64,261
	....	....	....	....	355
	11,445,813	20,228,738	26,625,000	4,950,000	..
	1,507,269	5,351,470	3,349,948	3,158,019	..
	P 44,914,256	P 56,040,840	P 67,288,518	P 48,644,525	P 58,30
	975,579	976,162	978,561	953,038	97
	41,725	41,187	43,930	40,081	74
	448,094	451,365	458,719	455,306	44
	440,612	391,764	518,533	405,271	53
lic	3,099,463	3,232,521	3,506,900	2,423,072	3,91
a-	1,238,453	1,281,338	1,376,883	1,504,125	2,88
	....	....	....	5,512,176	6,73
	3,975,564	5,317,290	23,919,035	558,241	1,15
	16,872,819	25,819,477	14,418,537	19,881,339	28,19
e	11,569,737	11,814,006	11,707,178	9,789,513	13,40
	6,252,210	6,715,730	10,360,242	7,092,363	.

ation payments

amount of the bonds deposited. This may be increased to 1.5 per cent if ttee of Bankers.

nversion into pesos is made at the rate of 5 pesos to a pound through 1864; year in which the loan is issued.

es in cash for the fiscal year in which they are listed.

53–159.

s of the Bleichroeder loan.

Railroad and were placed on the market by the contractors.

[l] Until July 1, 1899, wh amortizations were made. beginning July 1, 1890, c

[m] The revenues assigne revenues would amount t

[n] Does not include reve

[o] The outstanding bonds total amounts of the debt

[p] No commission was st

[q] The Municipal Loan f

[r] No commission. The

[s] No commission. The

[t] No provision was mad about five and a half milli

[u] Includes Treasury Obl

1904	1910	1913	1922	1925
(4 Per Cent Loan)	(4 Per Cent Loan)	(6 Per Cent Loan)	(Agreement)	(Agreement)
$ 40,000,000	£ 11,100,000	£ 6,000,000	……	……
35,600,000	10,517,250	5,400,000	……	……
……[p]	……[r]	……[s]	……	……
35,600,000	10,517,250	5,400,000	……	……
4.71%	4.41%	8.33%	……	……
$ 1,600,000 Interest	£ 444,000 Interest	£ 360,000 Interest [t]	……	……
260,000 Amortization	152,070 Amortization	or	……	……
$ 1,860,000 or	£ 596,070 or	P 3,966,942	……	……
P 3,852,527	P 5,829,535	……	……	……
No special guaranty	P 15,216,241	P 7,214,339	……	……
£ 32,072,115 [q]	£ 31,018,921	£ 31,757,613	£ 145,173,759	£ 89,020,189
£ 1,583,539 Interest [q]	£ 1,414,639 Interest	£ 1,846,680 Interest	£ 3,000,000	£ 2,138,569
218,161 Amortization	294,231 Amortization	292,698 Amortization	or	or
£ 1,801,700 or [f]	£ 1,708,870 or	£ 2,139,378 or	P 30,000,000	P 21,385,690
P 18,260,473	P 16,712,665	P 23,574,413		(1926)
P 24,698,252	P 30,432,482	P 37,937,471	P 30,000,000	……
P 386,725,413	P 499,627,914	P 492,698,014	883,579,640	1,073,481,004
208,520,451	293,753,640	300,405,552	568,471,114	682,484,832
178,204,962	205,874,274	192,292,462	315,108,526	390,996,172
1904–1905	1910–1911	1912–1913	1923	1925
P 130,406,194	P 211,846,347	P 163,509,618	265,664,880	336,717,470
92,083,887	111,142,402	120,958,902	……	……
……	……	……	……	……
33,583,368	100,703,945	42,550,716 [u]	……	……
4,738,939	……	……		
P 107,967,010	P 201,617,869	P 153,332,587	334,826,457	333,201,136
1,121,277	1,749,236	1,801,474		
275,260	228,695	278,861	……	……
431,254	585,731	691,276	……	……
1,395,622	2,388,409	2,046,047	……	……
11,508,910	12,564,029	14,690,078	……	……
	1,532,276 Justice	1,929,180	……	……
4,934,041	7,277,389 Education	7,705,632	……	……
1,791,801	13,498,866	12,991,296	……	……
9,041,811	3,283,043	3,567,681	……	……
33,717,033	37,372,094	36,377,536	……	……
14,935,787	20,434,156	28,702,810	……	……
28,814,214	100,703,943	42,550,715	……	……

ayments were to begin, interest payments were to be £135,000 a year. After that payments were to decrease as
s would, therefore, average £68,175 a year over the entire life of the loan. The government was to pay interest
uction was finished.
of the gross products of the railroad, telegraph, and pier. It was not possible to tell at this time what these

ehuantepec Railroad Loan. See note [m].
t were converted by this loan. The small amounts of unconverted bonds of the old loans are not included in the

nkers bought the bonds outright at 89 and sold them at 94, thus realizing a profit of 5 per cent.
ico is included. See page 233.
94.75 and the issue price 97.625, giving a profit of 2.875 per cent.
s 90 and the issue price 96, giving a profit of 6 per cent.
r amortization payments. The loan was to be redeemed at the end of ten years, however, which would require
amortization.
See page 247.

APPENDIX II

PRINCIPAL PROVISIONS OF CONTRACT OF FEBRUARY 7, 1824, AS AMENDED[1]

1. This loan is negotiated under the guaranty of a general mortgage and shall be divided into bonds or special obligations as follows:

A.	8,000	Special bonds of £100	£800,000
B.	16,000	" " " 150	2,400,000
	24,000	Special bonds amounting to	£3,200,000

These shall be issued with interest at 5% beginning October 1, 1823, and shall be paid in London to bearer quarterly with no deduction, the first payment being made for two quarters on April 1, 1824, and the subsequent payments on July 1, October 1, January 1, and April 1 of each year.

2. For the general mortgage, to secure payment of both capital and interest of the loan, there shall be hypothecated all the revenues of the Mexican nation in addition to the tax which shall be imposed and destined especially for the payment of interest and amortization according to article 5 of the act of the Congress of May 1, 1823.

3. The general treasurers of Mexico shall be authorized and obliged, by a formal and irrevocable decree of the Congress and of the Executive Power, to collect and reserve separately the proceeds from the stated tax, in such a way that they may not be applied to any other public need and that the sum for the payment of the half-yearly interest and amortization may be complete and ready for remission to London; if it happens that the amount of these revenues shall not be sufficient for this payment, these general treasurers shall be obliged to make up the deficit from the

[1] Alamán, *Liquidación General, sup. cit.*, pp. 4–6, 9; Casasús, *op. cit.*, pp. 36–44; Ortiz de Montellano, *op. cit.*, p. 5.

general revenues of the nation, and shall not be permitted to apply any part of the general revenues to any other need or object until this payment is made; to provide for the amortization of the principal of the loan, there shall be set aside the sum of £64,000 in the first year, beginning October 1, 1823, and there shall be remitted to England the sum of £32,000 in each one of the following years in equal half-yearly payments, to serve as a fund for amortizations, the first of which is to be made on April 1, 1824; the general treasurers are to be especially charged with the execution of this article in all its details, and with the remission of the funds under the direction and at the expense, account, and risk of the Mexican Government, to the agents in London for the payment of interest and the establishment of the amortization fund, the remission of which shall always be made from Mexico at least four months previous to the time at which payment should be made in London.

4. The sum set aside for amortization shall be employed in the first period of its establishment in the purchase of bonds. With the same object the sums remitted for amortization during subsequent half-years shall be supplemented by the amount of the interest saved on all the bonds amortized to date, and shall be applied with the latter sum to new amortizations of the existing bonds within the half-year immediately following that in which the shipments of money are made and in which interest has been saved. If at any time these bonds are held at more than par, excluding the dividend due, then in order that the amortization fund shall continue its operation, the agents in London, together with the envoy who resides there, or another person or other persons duly authorized by him or by the Government of Mexico, shall determine by lot which of the existing bonds shall be redeemed at par with the unapplied amortization fund of the current half-year. There shall be published in the Gazette of London the numbers of the bonds drawn and to be paid, and they shall be paid immediately, with interest for the current half-year to the time of the announcement, all other interest on the same bonds ceasing. All the bonds amortized and paid shall be cancelled and deposited in the Bank of England, in the presence of

a public actuary, of B. A. Goldschmidt and Company, and of the envoy of Mexico who resides in London, or of the person authorized for this object, by him or by the Government of Mexico; there being published in the Gazette of London the numbers of the bonds amortized in each half-year. The bonds shall remain deposited in the Bank of England until the whole loan is amortized, at which time all the special bonds and the general bond shall be delivered and placed at the disposal of the Government of Mexico; provided that if at the expiration of the term of thirty years, reckoned from October 1, 1823, any of the special bonds shall not have been amortized, the Government of Mexico shall pay for them and amortize them at par.

5. The bond or obligation of general mortgage, together with the special power conferred upon D. Francisco de Borja Migoni, shall be deposited in the Bank of England in the presence of Migoni, of B. A. Goldschmidt and Company, of a notary public of London, and shall also be cancelled when the entire loan is amortized and repaid on the stated terms.

6. Payment of interest on the loan and its amortization by funds destined therefor shall be carried out in time of war as in peace, without any distinction being made between the holders or owners of the bonds as to whether they belong to a friendly or an enemy nation, and if any alien holder or owner of any one of the special bonds dies intestate, such bond shall pass to his representatives in the order of succession established by the laws of the country of which they are subject, and shall be exempt from all kinds of sequestration at the demand of public authorities or of individuals.

7. B. A. Goldschmidt and Company undertake to place at the disposal of the Mexican Government within one year the sum of £600,000 in return for special bonds of the nominal value of £1,200,000. They reserve the option to take the remainder of the special bonds at the same rate within fifteen months. They have the right to act as agents of the Mexican Government for the payment of interest and amortization of bonds during a period of ten years. Their commission for this service is fixed at 1.5 per cent.

8. The Government undertakes to refrain from contracting any further loan within one year. If it contracts a second loan before the completion of the operations of the first loan, one-fourth of the proceeds of the second loan are to be applied to the redemption of bonds of the first loan at the market price.

APPENDIX III

PRINCIPAL PROVISIONS OF CONTRACT OF AUGUST 25, 1824, FOR THE LOAN OF 1825[1]

1. Messrs. Barclay, Herring, Richardson and Company, after the lapse of one year, stipulated as one of the conditions of the loan contract made by D. F. de B. Migoni with Messrs. B. A. Goldschmidt and Company, during which period no other loan can be made by the Republic, are to proceed to put on sale at the most favorable price a new loan for the value of £3,200,000; the Minister of Hacienda concurring.

2. There are to be printed and drawn up in London 24,000 bonds in the following form:

With the initial C	16,000	at £150	£2,400,000
" " " D	8,000	at £100	800,000
Total	24,000		£3,200,000

3. Interest on these bonds shall be six per cent and shall start with the quarter in which they are put in circulation.

4. The sale shall take place on the London Exchange in one, two, or more series, but in such a manner that from the beginning of April the contracting house shall have for the Government's disposal £200,000 monthly.

5. One-fourth of the proceeds of the loan shall be destined for the purchase of bonds of the loan negotiated by Migoni; for which purpose there shall be delivered to the house of Goldschmidt and Company, from the month of April, above mentioned, £50,000 monthly of the £200,000 which is to be placed at the disposal of the Government.

6. The P500,000 advanced by Mr. Vigors Richards is to be repaid in the first five months, £20,000 being repaid each month

[1] Casasús, *op. cit.*, pp. 68–69.

with interest at six per cent per annum from May 31, 1824; the peso being considered as 48d.

7. From the last funds of the loan there shall be repaid to the firm the costs of the arms and ships contracted for.

8. There shall be paid to the firm commissions of six per cent on the net proceeds of the sale of the loan; one per cent for the payment of amortization; and 1.5 per cent for the payment of interest which should be made quarterly.

9. From the proceeds of the loan there shall be reserved the amount necessary for the payment of the first six interest coupons and for the amortization, amounting to £32,000 annually, which should be paid quarterly at the same time as the interest.

APPENDIX IV

THE DOYLE CONVENTION OF DECEMBER 4, 1851[1]

The Government of the Mexican Republic having made known its inability to comply with certain conventions and arrangements now existing between the Mexican Government and various British subjects, made under the guarantee of H. B. M.'s Legation, because the penurious state of the Federal Exchequer has obliged the said Government to suspend the payment of the quotas to which it was bound by such conventions and arrangements; after long and repeated conferences, in which were discussed the state of the revenues of the Republic, the numerous liabilities to which these are subject, and the common convenience of establishing an arrangement upon practicable conditions, and not upon those of difficult or uncertain fulfilment, which, besides the injury they would cause to the creditors, might compromise the harmony that now exists between both countries; Mexico wishing to do justice to the demands of her creditors as far as her resources and the obligation and right of self preservation will permit her to do so, and the creditors agreeing to make a sacrifice in their claims, upon the basis of as equitable an adjustment as the pecuniary situation of the Government may permit, and relying upon the exact fulfilment of the guarantee and security stipulated; the undersigned Minister of Relations of the United Mexican States, authorized by the decree of the 17th of October of the present year, and Her Britannic Majesty's Chargé d'Affaires, having met in diplomatic conference, have agreed upon the following articles:

Article 1st. The claimants interested in the existing conventions and arrangements bearing the names of Martinez del Rio Brothers and of Montgomery, Nicod & Company, represented by the house of Jecker & Company, and the Pakenham Convention, signed on the 15th of October 1842, shall present themselves

[1] Payno, *op. cit.*, App., pp. 85–87.

at the General Treasury for the adjustment of their credits in conformity with this Convention, and the said office shall effect the same in the peremptory term of thirty days from the date hereof.

Article 2nd. The Mexican Government binds itself to pay annually five per cent for the redemption of this consolidated fund, and three per cent per annum for interest, calculated according to the progressive decrease occasioned by the redemption.

Article 3rd. The payment of the annual sums destined for the redemption of the credits comprised in the present Convention and for the payment of interest thereon shall be made at the end of every half-year to the agent who may be named for this purpose by the creditors. In order that the stipulations contained in the preceding article may be made effective, the Mexican Government obliges itself to assign a certain percentage of the products of the import duties that may be collected in the ports of the Republic, sufficient to cover the five per cent for redemption and the three per cent for interest dedicated to the credits comprised in the present Convention. In order that the payment of this five and three per cent shall not at any time be deferred or suspended, the Mexican Government promises to pass an order to the Administrators of the said revenue, stating the quota of the said duties which they should remit in separate drafts on the Treasury General in favor of the said Agent; the said drafts shall be paid as soon as received by the Treasury.

If at the end of the year, the interest and the five per cent redemption should not have been covered, the General Treasury, without any further orders, shall pay the deficit from the first bills that may be received from the Maritime Customs Houses; and the Agent on his part, should he have received a greater sum than the said annual interest and redemption amount to, shall return the surplus to the said Treasury.

Article 4th. The Minister of Relations of the Republic shall pass to H. B. M.'s Chargé d'Affaires a copy of the order which the Minister of Finance communicates to the administrators of the Customs Houses in compliance with the foregoing article, which shall be considered as herein inserted and shall form a part of the present Convention.

Article 5th. The Mexican Government, desiring to give unequivocal proofs of the justice and equity with which it proposes to proceed in this arrangement, binds itself to better the condition of the creditors, after the fifth year from this date, by increasing the amount assigned for interest on the capital and for redemption. Consequently the Government binds itself to pay, after the conclusion of the fifth year, four per cent per annum for interest and six per cent for redemption, so that this increase may commence from the sixth year.

Article 6th. As the Mexican Congress is occupied in forming a law for the payment of the internal debt, the persons comprised in the present Convention are at liberty, each one of them, to transfer their credits to the fund which, in virtue of such law, may be created, by making their decision known to the Minister of Relations, who will communicate the same to H. B. M.'s Legation.

Article 7th. It is expressly stipulated and agreed, that in case any of the obligations contracted by the present Convention are broken, suspended, or deferred by the Mexican Treasury, this Convention shall by this fact be annulled, and the creditors shall be reinstated in the enjoyment of the rights acquired by the agreements and conventions now existing.

In witness whereof, the aforesaid Minister of Relations and H. B. M.'s Chargé d'Affaires have hereunto set their seals and affixed their signatures in the City of Mexico this 4th of December 1851. — Percy W. Doyle. — José F. Ramirez.

APPENDIX V

THE CARBAJAL–CORLIES CONTRACT[1]

To all whom it may concern:

As appears from various decrees or supreme orders of different dates, it is consistent with the policy of the Republic of Mexico, of which Citizen Benito Juárez is now President, to encourage immigration and the colonization of the States of Mexico.

And following this policy the said Citizen President issued supreme orders in the city of Chihuahua, then the seat of the Government, one dated November 8, the other November 12, 1864, giving to General Carbajal, at that time and at present civil and military Governor of the States of Tamaulipas and San Luis Potosí, among other powers and commissions, authority "to devise the ways and means necessary" for certain purposes specified therein and "to promote the said policy." Extracts from these supreme orders containing such authorizations have been copied in the English and Spanish languages and have been delivered to the persons hereinafter designated as the second contracting party.

Therefore, it is hereby recorded that, in accordance with the said policy, and in conformity with the supreme authorization above mentioned and with the terms of an arrangement and agreement between the respective parties through letters dated, in New York City, August 25, 26, and 29, 1865, respectively, the said General José M. J. Carbajal has undertaken and agreed and by this instrument, drawn up in the City and State of New York, on the eleventh day of September, 1865, binds and obligates the Government of the United Mexican States, of which he is herein shown to be the authorized agent, constituting the first contracting party, and the mercantile firm of John W. Corlies and Company (composed of John W. Corlies and Jonathan N. Tifft) of the

[1] *Contratos hechos en los Estados-Unidos, etc., sup. cit.*, pp. 443–447.

aforementioned city of New York, constituting the second contracting party, at the same time undertakes and agrees to be bound by the following terms and figures, to-wit:

I

The first contracting party, in order to accomplish the ends mentioned above, and in consideration of the money hereinafter mentioned, has conceded and by the present instrument does concede to the second contracting party, its successors and representatives, one hundred square Mexican leagues, equivalent to some four hundred forty thousand English acres, of vacant lands, suitable for pasture and cultivation, situated in the States of Tamaulipas and San Luis Potosí [Mexico], and likewise fifty vacant mines each consisting of seven pertenencias of which each contains two hundred square "varas," or some fifty acres, more or less, to each mine.

II

The foregoing concessions are, however, subject to the following conditions and stipulations:

First. — That the second contracting party, its successors or representatives, pay or cause to be paid to the party of the first part, in the place or places designated by the latter, the sum of one peso per acre for the grazing or farm lands above mentioned.

Second. — That all the said grazing, farm and mining lands shall be selected and denounced by the party of the second part or its agents, successors or representatives, and shall be colonized and worked in accordance with the laws of the Mexican Republic and of the aforementioned States, after permission to work them has been asked of the Government of the State or States in which the lands or mines are situated.

Third. — That the price or prices fixed for the said grazing, farm or mining lands must be paid and the said lands or mines must be selected and denounced by the party of the second part within two years from this date, in case it has been decided, within that period, to take them.

Fourth. — In case the said party of the second part, its successors or representatives neglect or fail to select and denounce the said lands and mines within two years from this date, then and in such case this concession shall cease and be null and void with regard to the lands and mines which have not been denounced and selected, and with regard to those for which payment has not been made before the expiration of this period. But, as stated, the concession shall hold good with regard to the lands and mines actually selected and denounced and with regard to those for which payment has been made as required herein, at the expiration of the prescribed period.

III

And the first contracting party agrees, also, to deliver to the party of the second part, for negotiation and sale, bonds of the Government of the United Mexican States and of the States of Tamaulipas and San Luis Potosí up to the sum of thirty million pesos, which are to be delivered as soon as they are completed for this purpose and duly issued and ready for sale, bearing the same interest, and secured and redeemable in substantially the same manner, as the bonds, destined for a like purpose, which at the present are being prepared by the Company known as the "United States Bank Note Company of New York," which was at one time authorized to negotiate these bonds in accordance with a contract (now null) with the United States, European and West Virginia Land and Mining Company. This delivery shall be made under the following conditions:

First. — That the party of the second part, without unnecessary delay, shall make as diligent and strenuous efforts as possible to arrange for the sale of the said bonds with the greatest promptness. But in no case, unless it be so decided by the party of the first part, may all the bonds or a part of them be sold for a sum less than sixty cents in lawful money of the United States for each peso. And the proceeds of the said sale shall be held subject to the order of the said José M. J. Carbajal, or of the Minister of Finance of the Republic of Mexico. In the latter case, the order or draft must be certified by the Minister Plenipotentiary of the said Government in Washington, or by the Consul General of Mexico resident in that city, or by Jesus Fuentes y Muñiz, general agent in this country of the said Carbajal.

Second. — That the party of the second part shall give a duly written receipt for the said bonds as soon as they are delivered for sale.

Third. — That the party of the second part shall open suitable account books in which shall be noted the amount of the bonds received for sale, the date on which they are received and the inclusive numbers of each denomination; it shall likewise keep an exact account of debit and credit containing the entry of all the bonds sold by the party of the first part, delivered for sale, the date of the respective sales, the inclusive numbers and denominations, and the amounts received for them respectively; the sums paid to the party of the first part, the date and amount of each payment and the name of the person to whom the payment is made. This account or register shall always be kept in writing by the party of the second part, and the party of the first part, through its duly authorized agents, shall have free access to such register whenever it deems it expedient, with the right to take copies and extracts. And the party of the second part, as frequently as may reasonably be required, shall give accurate and exact reports and accounts of all the money realized by the sale of the bonds for the account of the party of the first part and of all the bonds received from the said party of the first part for sale.

Fourth. — That nothing but cash may be received in payment for such bonds as shall be delivered for sale, unless the party of the second part receive express orders from the party of the first part, or its authorized agents, to negotiate the bonds in another way; in which case the party of the second part shall act in accordance with the said instructions in so far as may be practicable without prejudice to its rights or commission.

Fifth. — That all the costs and expenditures for engraving and stamping the said bonds shall be deducted and kept by the party of the first part from the commission which is to be paid to the party of the second part for the negotiation and sale of the said bonds, provided the amount does not exceed $25,000.

Sixth. — And that all the other expenditures or costs connected with the introduction, negotiation and sale of the said bonds, printing, publicity, announcements, clerks, and servants, so far as may be deemed necessary by the party of the second part for the mutual advantage and benefit of both contracting parties, shall be made and paid by the party of the second part out of the special fund hereinafter indicated.

IV

As a special fund to defray the expenses and costs connected with the negotiation of the said loan above mentioned, and for the commission and remuneration to be received for the consummation of the negotiation and for the sale of the said bonds, the party of the first part agrees to deliver to the party of the second part bonds of Mexico, similar to those already described, up to the sum of seven and one-half millions of pesos, which are to become the property of the party of the second part on condition, however, that the total loan of thirty millions above mentioned is negotiated, it being the true meaning and intention that the said seven and one-half million pesos of bonds shall be delivered to the party of the second part when, and in such sum and proportion as, the sales of the loan of thirty millions are made and not before.

V

That as a contingent fund to reimburse and indemnify the party of the second part for the undertaking, for the expenses and losses which may arise, result or occur in consequence of fruitless efforts to place the aforementioned loan or any considerable part thereof, the party of the first part agrees to deliver and place in the hands of the party of the second part one million pesos of the aforementioned bonds, making this delivery from the first issue of the said bonds, which bonds the party of the second part shall use in the manner it considers to be most expedient and best adapted to promote the mutual interest of the contracting parties in bringing to a prompt and satisfactory conclusion the placing of the said loan. It is mutually understood that the object and purpose of this arrangement is to enable the party of the second part to make the considerable expenditures necessary to test the market, and at the same time to protect and indemnify the party of the second part in case the said loan is not obtained. But in case the party of the second part succeeds in negotiating the said loan to the extent of four millions, then the said one million pesos of the contingent fund is to be deducted from the commission received from the aforementioned special fund and shall not be an addition thereto.

VI

The said party of the second part, in consideration of the foregoing and of the promises therein contained, hereby firmly binds itself, in return, to undertake by the greatest possible efforts and without delay the placing and negotiation of the loan of thirty million pesos herein referred to, and to observe, maintain and faithfully fulfil the conditions, stipulations and rules fixed above, with all the limitations and reservations contained herein.

VII

The contracting parties mutually agree, one with the other, that in case the party of the second part shall faithfully comply with the arrangements contained in this agreement, no other loan or negotiation for such loan shall be placed on the market by the party of the first part or by any one of its component parts in competition with the above mentioned loan, as long as the negotiations for the said loan continue and until the party of the second part decides to abandon these negotiations.

VIII

That in case the party of the first part or any one of its members desires to place another loan on the market and wishes to place its negotiation in the hands of the party of the second part, said party of the second part hereby agrees to delay [undertake ?] the negotiation of the same as soon as possible in return for a fixed commission of three per cent on the bonds of such loan negotiated and sold by it.

IX

And it is also agreed and understood by both contracting parties, as a condition absolutely necessary for the validity of the concession of the lands and mines hereby granted by the party of the first part, that nothing contained therein shall be interpreted in such a way as to attack the sovereignty or integrity of the Republic of Mexico; that the representatives employed by the party of the second part shall pay all the legal contributions and taxes levied on their property in the said Republic; that those whom the said party of the second part shall establish on the lands or mines hereby conceded shall conform to the laws of the Republic and of the States thereof, and shall become citizens thereof with all the privileges of such citizens and subject to all the obligations of such citizens with respect to compliance with all the laws; that the said party of the second part and its agents or employees shall never, under any circumstances, give aid or assistance directly or indirectly to any plan of revolution or separation against the constitutional Government of Mexico and its free institutions. At the same time, the party of the second part shall not be responsible for the illegal or unauthorized conduct of its emigrants, employees, representatives, or other persons, nor from such conduct shall there result any loss to the said party of the second part, unless it shall be proved to have taken part therein voluntarily, being cognizant of and encouraging such unlawful acts. And it is also expressly understood that the concession of lands and mines herein contained shall remain in full force and validity so long as the laws of the Republic and of the said States are observed by the interested parties, the said emigrants or residents being obliged to become citizens, as has been herein determined.

X

It is likewise agreed that as soon as the said party of the second part shall have caused a sufficient number of emigrants or colonists to be assembled at the places designated for their residence, the government of the State in which they are assembled, upon the presentation of the petition of the said emigrants or colonists, shall incorporate them in towns, and grant them free community lands, provided the said petitioners have become citizens of the Republic of Mexico and have submitted their petition for municipal rights in conformity with the law of the State. Once incorporated, the citizens of the said town shall have the privilege of electing their municipal authorities and of administering their community affairs, particularly as regards local taxes and public schools.

XI

If the party of the second part shall fail to effect the sale of ten millions of the bonds, within three months from the date on which they are put on the market, the said party of the second part agrees to return the amount of the bonds remaining unsold (which shall be retired), for an equal sum of bonds which the party of the first part is ready to issue and which shall carry other acceptable guarantees and securities.

XII

The aforesaid general agent (Jesus Fuentes Muñiz) shall deliver to the said party of the second part the bonds duly prepared for sale, in the amounts required to supply the purchasers, provided that not more than one million pesos of the said bonds be delivered at one time, and that the deliveries follow each other in succession, due account being kept of the deliveries and of the proceeds of the sales of the former deliveries, in accordance with the instructions of the party of the first part and to the satisfaction of the said agent; it being understood that there shall be kept an appropriate account of the disposition of all the bonds which the party of the second part has assigned for sale to the banks or bankers.

In faith of which we have signed and sealed the present instrument on September 11, 1865.

J. M. J. CARBAJAL.
JOHN W. CORLIES AND COMPANY.

A true copy. New York, September 11, 1865.

F. D. MACIN.

APPENDIX VI

CONTRACT FOR MEXICAN EXTERNAL FOUR PER CENT GOLD DEBT OF 1910[1]

The contract concluded between the Federal Executive Power of the United Mexican States, represented by Sr. M. de Zamacona, Financial Agent of the Mexican Government in London, and the Banco Nacional de México; the firm of S. Bleichroeder, Berlin; the Deutsche Bank, Berlin; the Dresdner Bank, Berlin; Messrs. Morgan, Grenfell and Company, London; Messrs. J. P. Morgan and Company, New York; the Banque de Paris et des Pays Bas, Paris; the Crédit Lyonnais, Paris; the Société Générale pour favoriser le Développement du Commerce et de l'Industrie en France, Paris, and the Comptoir National d'Escompte de Paris, Paris, who in the following articles are briefly called "the contracting banks."

WHEREAS, (1) The Federal Executive Power of the United Mexican States was authorized by the law of the Congress of the Union promulgated May 31, 1910, in the *Diario Oficial* of the Government of the United Mexican States, and annexed to the present contract, to convert or repay the External Consolidated Five Per Cent Mexican Debt of 1899 and to substitute for it another on similar conditions, with interest at 4 per cent, the service for the amortization and interest of which requires smaller sums than those which are needed at present for this purpose;

AND WHEREAS, (2) The Federal Executive Power of the United Mexican States, for the purpose of satisfying the stipulations of the law previously mentioned, will be bound by this contract to use the amount of the loan, which forms the object of the present contract, for the refunding of the Mexican External Consolidated Five Per Cent Debt of 1899, and for the costs

[1] Ernesto Madero, *Memoria de Hacienda y Crédito Público*, July 1, 1910, to June 30, 1911, pp. 311–318.

of the present loan and of the conversion charged to the Mexican Government, according to the stipulations of the present contract;

Between the parties mentioned there has been concluded a contract which includes the following articles:

Art. 1. The Federal Executive Power of the United Mexican States issues, in accordance with the authorization conferred by the above mentioned law, a loan of:

Two hundred sixteen million, four hundred fifty thousand Mexican pesos, nominal value ($ Mex. 216, 450,000);

Or five hundred sixty million, five hundred fifty thousand francs, nominal value (Frs. 560,550,000);

Or twenty-two million, two hundred thousand pounds, sterling, nominal value (£22,200,000);

Or four hundred fifty-two million, eight hundred eighty thousand German marks, nominal value (Rm. 452,880,000);

Or one hundred seven million, six hundred seventy thousand dollars of the United States of North America, of the present weight and fineness, nominal value ($107,670,000 United States gold).

This loan shall be called the "Mexican External Four Per Cent Gold Debt of 1910."

The capital and interest of this loan shall be paid in gold and shall be exempt at all times from all Mexican duties or taxes existing or to be established for any reason whatsoever.

Art. 2. The nominal capital of the loan shall be represented by bonds of the following nominal value: ($ Mex. 195, Frs. 505, £20, Rm. 480, $97 U. S. gold).

The Mexican Government agrees to prepare the definitive bonds, as the contracting banks ask for them, as a unit or in groups; the declarations relating to the bonds which represent the part of the loan taken outright, as shall be stated later, must be communicated to the Mexican Government by the contracting banks not later than July 31, 1910.

The bonds of the loan are to be payable to bearer and are to be drawn up in Spanish, German, English and French. They shall be numbered in sequence and shall contain in the text the recognition on the part of the United Mexican States of the obligation to pay the sum mentioned in each one of the bonds; the obligation to repay the capital and to pay the interest in the form and in the places determined by this contract; the designation of the special guaranties of the loan which are fixed according to Article 5; and finally, the declaration that these bonds are exempt forever from all duties and all taxes of the Mexican Government.

The bonds of the loan shall bear the facsimile signature of the Treasurer of the Federation of the United Mexican States and the autographed signature of one or various special delegates named for this purpose by the Minister of the Treasury. They shall contain the text of the law previously cited and an extract of the stipulations of Articles 1 to 6 of this contract.

Art. 3. The Mexican Government shall pay on this loan, on January 1 and July 1 of each year, interest at the rate of 4 per cent per annum, at the contracting banks in Mexico, Paris, Berlin, London, and New York, and also at the firms in Frankfort on Main, in Amsterdam and in other cities designated by the contracting banks.

Each of the bonds of the loan shall be provided with a sheet of sixty-nine coupons the first of which shall be due January 1, 1911.

The value of each coupon shall be stated in Mexican pesos, francs, pounds sterling, marks, and gold dollars of the United States, and shall correspond to the nominal amount of the bonds of the loan, that is: $ Mex. 3.90; Frs. 10.10; £0. 8s od; Rm. 816; $ gold U. S. $1.94.

The coupons shall bear the promise of the United Mexican States to pay at maturity the sum corresponding to each category of bonds, at the option of the bearers, in Mexico, Paris, Berlin, London or New York, at the contracting banks; in Frankfort on Main or in Amsterdam or in any other place, at the firms designated; in Amsterdam the payment shall be made in Dutch florins, figuring the Reichmark according to the rate of exchange, at sight, on Berlin. (See Article 8 of the present contract concerning interest on provisional certificates.)

The contracting banks shall cancel the interest coupons

paid and the bonds of the loan redeemed, and shall keep them thereafter in each place at the disposal of the Mexican Government.

Interest coupons shall be barred from payment after five years from maturity. Coupons lost, stolen, or destroyed are to be governed by the Mexican law.

The Banco Nacional de México, to whom according to its concession contract there was given the service on the debt of the United Mexican States and on loans contracted by the Government, shall transfer this service irrevocably to the Banque de Paris et des Pays Bas and to the firm of S. Bleichroeder in all that relates to the service in Europe and in the United States of America.

Differences in exchange in connection with the payment of interest coupons and the amortization of bonds of the loan (see Article 4) in Paris, Berlin, London, New York, Frankfort on Main, and Amsterdam, from the amounts remitted by the Banco Nacional for the account of the Government, shall be borne by the Banque de Paris et des Pays Bas and the firm of S. Bleichroeder. The coupons and bonds paid in Frankfort on Main and in Amsterdam shall be considered, as regards the matter of the difference in exchange, as though they had been paid in Berlin.

The Mexican Government concedes to the contracting banks, for the payment of interest, a commission of one-quarter of one per cent ($\frac{1}{4}$ per cent) and for the payment of bonds amortized by purchase or drawings, by reimbursements or conversions, a commission of one-eighth of one per cent ($\frac{1}{8}$ per cent). These commissions shall be paid in the manner indicated in Article 6 of this contract.

Art. 4. The loan shall be reimbursed by means of regular amortizations, from January 1, 1911, to the completion of the reimbursement, which shall occur not later than January 1, 1945.

For this purpose, as provided in Article 6, the Mexican Government shall deliver to the Banco Nacional de México each half-year during the existence of the loan, 2.685 per cent of the nominal amount of the loan; and this semiannual payment shall be applied to the service of the interest and amortization of the loan. The first semester shall begin July 1, 1910.

Until the loan is completely issued, the Government shall provide for service only on the part issued. The amortization of the part of the loan not issued shall be assured by the Government's destruction of a proportional part of the bonds remaining in its hands so that the complete amortization of the total loan shall not extend beyond January 1, 1945, whatever may be the time at which the remainder of the loan is issued.

The amortizations shall be effected at the end of each half-year, for the first time in December, 1910, and after that at the end of the months of June and December of each year.

If the price of the loan is par or above, the amortization of the loan shall be by drawings. These drawings shall be made in London, upon the request of the Banco Nacional de México, by Messrs. Morgan, Grenfell and Company for the Mexican Government with the aid of its Financial Agent in London and in the presence of a Notary Public. The drawings shall be made not later than June 15 and December 15 of each year.

When the drawings are made, the list of the bonds amortized shall be published in Mexico in the *Diario Oficial,* and the Financial Agent of the Mexican Government in London shall publish it in two newspapers in Paris, two in Berlin, two in London, two in New York, one in Frankfort on Main, and one in Amsterdam.

Payment of the bonds called for redemption shall be made at the same time and on the same conditions as that of the next corresponding coupon, and such payment shall be made at the option of the holders in Mexico, Paris, Berlin, London, or New York at the contracting banks, in Frankfort on Main, in Amsterdam, or in any other place at the firms designated; in Amsterdam the payment shall be made in Dutch florins, the amount of which in marks shall be calculated at the sight rate of exchange on Berlin.

The bonds of the loan which are called for redemption shall be presented for payment with all the coupons which mature after the time of redemption and shall cease to bear interest from the date fixed for redemption; if, however, the quotation of the bonds of the loan shall be less than par at the time of amortization, the amortization shall be made by means of purchases.

Until the delivery of the definitive bonds in exchange for the provisional certificates or for the bonds held in place of these, the amortizations shall be made by means of purchases. The total sum provided for the half-yearly amortization by means of drawings shall be used for these purchases.

The amounts of the bonds purchased which exceed the provision for the amortization by drawing shall be deducted from future amortizations, starting with the last.

The purchases shall be made jointly by the firm of S. Bleichroeder and the Banque de Paris et des Pays Bas, who shall give an account of these purchases to the Banco Nacional de México. The latter shall inform the Mexican Government in due course of the purchases made. The numbers of the bonds purchased shall be published under the same conditions as those of the bonds amortized by drawings.

Both the bonds amortized by drawings and those amortized by purchase shall be canceled and kept in each place at the disposal of the Mexican Government.

The Mexican Government has the right, beginning July 1, 1925, to increase the amortization fund at will or to redeem at one time the whole of the loan; in the latter case a previous notice of three months shall be necessary; this notice shall be given to the bearers of the bonds in the said newspapers through the Banco Nacional de México and at the expense of the Government. The redemption of the bonds amortized or denounced in this manner shall be effected by the contracting banks and by the offices of payment designated by them in Frankfort on Main, Amsterdam, and other places.

The redeemed bonds of this loan shall be barred from payment after twenty years from the day on which they are eligible for redemption. Substitution for bonds lost, stolen, or partially or totally destroyed shall be governed by the Mexican law.

Art. 5. As a special guaranty for the strict execution of the stipulations of this contract concerning the payment of interest and amortization of the loan, the Mexican Government assigns and charges in favor of the holders of the bonds, in a manner uniform for all and with preference to none, for all the time in which these bonds are not completely amortized, sixty-two per cent (62 per cent) of the total product of the taxes which the law of revenues calls duties on imports and exports, whatever may be the special denomination of these taxes or the place in which the customs formalities are performed.

These taxes assigned as a guaranty should in each fiscal year exceed by at least ten per cent (10 per cent) the amount necessary for the payment of interest and amortization. In case the product in a fiscal year is insufficient to cover this margin of ten per cent, the Mexican Government is obliged by this contract to raise proportionally, in the first quarter of the following fiscal year, the part allocated from the taxes assigned to the holders of bonds of the loan. The increase shall be maintained during the time necessary to assure this margin for a whole fiscal year. Aside from this case, the fixed guaranty, which represents an inalienable security in favor of the holders of the bonds of this loan, shall not be modified in any manner.

Art. 6. In order that the guaranty stipulated in Article 5 may be made effective, the Government shall immediately make the necessary arrangements for the offices of the maritime and frontier customs of the country to deliver to the Banco Nacional de México, for the semimonthly payment due, the product of the taxes assigned, and it shall maintain these arrangements in full force during the continuance of the present loan. The delivery of the taxes for the semimonthly payment is to be effected before July 15, 1910; for the second payment, on the first of August; and thereafter on the first and fifteenth days of each month.

Such portion of the sums derived from the assignment mentioned in Article 5 as may be required for the payment of interest and amortization of the loan shall be remitted by the Banco Nacional de México, five-eighths to the Banque de Paris et des Pays Bas, of Paris, and three-eighths to the firm of S. Bleichroeder, of Berlin.

The Banco Nacional de México shall take the measures necessary to insure that on the fifteenth of each month the Banque de Paris et des Pays Bas, of Paris, and the firm of S. Bleichroeder, of Berlin, shall be in effective possession of the sum necessary to form a sixth part of the amount of interest and amortization for a half-year, and also the corresponding commissions, etc.

For the first semiannual payment the remittances shall be a fifth part, and the first shall reach the Banque de Paris et des Pays Bas, of Paris, and the firm of S. Bleichroeder, of Berlin, before August 15, 1910.

The Mexican Government has at all times the right to make through the Banco Nacional de México deliveries larger than those now fixed and to dispose of the surplus arising from the taxes assigned after the amount of the interest due the first of the months of January and July following and the amount of the amortization for a semester have been completed.

The depositaries for the funds remitted to them for the service of the loan, that is, the Banque de Paris et des Pays Bas and the firm of S. Bleichroeder, shall credit the Mexican Government with these funds from the day following their actual receipt in Paris and Berlin, respectively, with interest fixed at 1.5 per cent less than the discount rate of the Bank of France, for the funds deposited in Paris, and at one per cent less than the discount rate of the Imperial Bank of Germany, for the funds deposited in Berlin, when this rate does not exceed 3 per cent a year. Interest shall cease the fifteenth day of June and the fifteenth day of December, that is, fifteen days before each semiannual maturity of the service of the loan.

At all times when the sum necessary for the payment of interest, amortization and commission for collection is not covered by the revenues of the customs assigned as guaranty, the Mexican Government is obliged, by this contract, to deliver from its other sources to the Banco Nacional de México the amount necessary to complete it, in order that the firm of S. Bleichroeder and the Banque de Paris et des Pays Bas shall be not later than fifteen days before each maturity in possession of the funds necessary for the service of this loan.

Until the 5 per cent loan of 1899 is entirely redeemed, the 62 per cent of the proceeds of the customs duties assigned for the services of the 5 per cent loan of 1899 and the present 4 per cent loan of 1910 shall be collected by the Banco Nacional de México, according to Article 6 of the contract of the loan of 1899 and according to the present article.

Of the sums thus collected, the Banco Nacional de México shall form two parts: one which it shall remit at the proper time to the firm of S. Bleichroeder, charged with the service on the 5 per cent loan of 1899 remaining in circulation, in conformity with Article 6 of the contract of the loan of 1899; and the other which shall be remitted at the proper time to the Banque de Paris et des Pays Bas and to the firm of S. Bleichroeder, charged with the service of the bonds of the 4 per cent loan of 1910 in circulation in conformity with the present article.

As soon as all the bonds of the 5 per cent loan of 1899 have been converted or called for redemption, Articles 5 and 6 of the present contract shall be in full force.

Art. 7. The present loan shall be destined exclusively to supplying the funds necessary for the conversion or redemption of the Mexican consolidated external 5 per cent loan of 1899.

Art. 8. Of the total of the present loan, or:

Two hundred sixteen million, four hundred fifty thousand Mexican pesos ($ Mex. 216,450,000), or

Five hundred sixty million, five hundred fifty thousand francs (Frs. 560,550,000), or

Twenty-two million, two hundred thousand pounds sterling (£22,200,000), or

Four hundred fifty-two million, eight hundred eighty thousand German marks (Rm. 452,880,000), or

One hundred seven million, six hundred seventy thousand gold dollars of the United States of America ($ gold U. S. A. 107,-670,000), nominal value,

The contracting banks take outright and the Mexican Government allows them

$ Mex.	108,225,000	or
Frs.	280,275,000	or
£	11,100,000	or
Rm.	226,440,000	or
$ U. S. A.	53,835,000	

under the following conditions:

The purchase price is fixed at 94.75 per cent of the expressed nominal amount of the bonds of the loan taken outright, beginning July 1, 1910.

Consequently, the purchasing banks shall have to pay Frs. 280,275,000 at 94.75 per cent, that is to say, they shall by the terms of Article 11 of this contract credit the Mexican Government with Frs. 265,560,562.50 on July 1, 1910, in French money, in Paris, against previous delivery of a general obligation, beginning July 1, 1910.

While waiting for the delivery of the definitive bonds, the contracting banks may issue provisional certificates, the distribution of which may be in series, may be in each one of the places, or may be in one or in several of the places in which they shall issue the part of the loan taken outright.

The contracting banks shall determine the conditions under which they shall pay, on the provisional certificates, the interest due January 1 and July 1, 1911.

All the expenses incident to the delivery and issue of the definitive bonds, which ought to take place not later than September 1, 1911, shall be charged to the Mexican Government.

The Mexican Government shall bear all the costs for stamps which are placed on the provisional certificates as well as those placed on the definitive bonds of the loan, according to the laws of the countries in which the contractors make the issue. In a current account, which shall be begun according to the terms of Article 11, the Banco Nacional de México shall charge the Mexican Government with the amounts expended for stamps by the contracting banks.

The contracting banks shall after the conclusion of the present contract draw up the prospectus necessary for the introduction of the new loan on the exchanges of Paris, Berlin, Frankfort on Main, Amsterdam, London, New York, and Mexico. The Mexican Government is obliged to examine and, after its approval, to sign the prospectus which the commissions on admission of the exchanges mentioned may demand.

Art. 10. The contracting banks may issue the part of the loan taken outright through subscription or by allotment.

They shall have the right to fix the rate at which they shall issue the new loan and also the methods of payment and the date from which interest will be paid.

Art. 11. The Banco Nacional de México shall open for the Mexican Government, in the name of the contracting banks, a current account for the bonds taken outright in accordance with the present contract.

The Government shall be credited in this account in francs, as of July 1, 1910, with the value of the bonds taken outright.

There being charged to this account:

1. The amount in francs expended for stamps by the contracting banks up to the day of the payment.

2. The sums transferred to the firm of S. Bleichroeder. These sums are to be transferred not later than December 15, 1910, from the credit of the Mexican Government, to the firm of S. Bleichroeder, of Berlin, to be applied, according to irrevocable orders, to the redemption of obligations of the 5 per cent loan of 1899.

The transfer of the funds of the loan of 1910 to Berlin for the custody of the contracting banks shall be on the terms most favorable to the Mexican Government between June 30 and December 15, the firm of S. Bleichroeder deciding as to the opportune time for the delivery and notifying the Banco Nacional de México thereof.

For the next semiannual drawing, which shall take place in December, 1910, the Mexican Government shall increase the normal amortization by a supplementary amortization for an amount corresponding to the bonds of the 5 per cent loan of 1899 to be redeemed January 1, 1911.

From July 1 to December 15, 1910, all the funds mentioned in the paragraph (of this article) numbered 2, above, shall produce for the Mexican Government interest at the rate of 1.75 per cent a year; and from September 16 to December 15 they shall yield interest at the rate of 2.25 per cent a year.

Art. 12. The Government concedes to the contracting banks an option to take the balance of the loan, that is to say:

$ Mex.	108,225,000	Nominal value
Frs.	280,275,000	
£	11,100,000	
Rm.	226,440,000	
$ U. S. A.	53,835,000	

between the date of this contract and April 1, 1911, at the rate of 94.75 per cent of the nominal amount of the bonds of the loan increased by the amount of the current coupon.

The Banco Nacional de México, on the application of the Banque de Paris et des Pays Bas and of the firm of S. Bleichroeder, shall be authorized to exercise this right of option in the name of all the contracting banks until the expiration of the time mentioned, and this for the total amount of the option or for partial amounts, which, in any case, ought not to be less than 50,000,000 francs, nominal value.

To exercise each option, total or partial, the Banco Nacional de México, through its Committee in Paris, must make a declaration by registered letter addressed to the Financial Agent of the Mexican Government in London.

The stipulations of Articles 8, 9, and 10 of the present contract shall be applied equally to the bonds on which the option is exercised.

It shall be likewise agreed that the proceeds of the bonds on which the option is exercised shall be destined exclusively to the redemption of the balance of the 5 per cent loan of 1899, whether this redemption shall be effected as a whole, at one time only, or shall be effected by increasing the sum of the semiannual amortization. The proceeds shall be credited to the Mexican Government as of the day on which the right of option is exercised; on these proceeds the Government shall be credited with interest at 2.25 per cent a year up to December 15, 1910, or June 15, 1911, respectively, the dates on which the amount shall be employed for supplementary amortizations.

The bonds on which the contracting banks have exercised their option may be issued by public subscription or by allotment, or may be offered by the banks for their own account and risk and at their own expense, in the places which seem to them suitable, for the conversion of the bonds of the 5 per cent loan of 1899 not yet amortized.

The banks have complete liberty to fix the rate at which they shall issue these bonds as well as the manner of payment, the date for commencement of interest, and the rates at which the conversion of the old bonds can be made. Likewise, it shall be for them to decide the manner and the proportion in which they desire to use the new bonds, either to exchange them for old bonds, or to sell them for money; the right being likewise reserved to leave in circulation in the places mentioned the bonds of the loan of 1899 whose bearers have accepted the conversion. These bonds, provided with a stamp, shall serve as provisional certificates while waiting to be exchanged for definitive bonds.

The Mexican Government is obliged to call for redemption, on the conditions previously fixed by the contract of the loan of 1899, the amount of the bonds not already amortized from this loan, if the contracting banks exercise at one time the right of option conceded to them.

In the account for the converted bonds, the Banco Nacional de México will charge to the Mexican Government:

1. The value in francs of the nominal amount of the 5 per cent obligations presented for conversion, the pound sterling being calculated at the rate of 25.25.

2. The difference in francs between 4 per cent and 5 per cent interest for three months on the 5 per cent bonds of 1899 accepted for conversion.

Art. 13. The Mexican Government is obliged not to conclude nor issue up to December 31, 1911, any loan of the external public debt without the previous consent of the contracting banks.

Art. 14. If, up to the day which the contracting banks have fixed for the public subscription or the allotment of the bonds taken outright according to Article 8, incidents shall arise or disorder shall be shown in any of the markets charged with the operation;

or if the quotation on the 3 per cent loan falls below 97 per cent in Paris;

or the quotation on the 4 per cent bonds of the National Railways of Mexico falls to less than 482 in Paris;

or the quotation on the English consolidated debt falls to less than 81 per cent in London;

or the quotation on the Mexican 5 per cent loan of 1899 falls to less than 100 per cent in Berlin;

or the quotation on the 4.5 per cent first mortgage bonds of the National Railways of Mexico falls to less than 92 per cent in New York;

the contracting banks shall have the right to decline the execution of the present contract.

Art. 15. For the execution of this contract and for the operations relative to the same, the Mexican Government is represented by its Financial Agent in London, who ought to be in agreement on all points with the Banque de Paris et des Pays Bas and the firm of S. Bleichroeder, acting for themselves or for the contracting banks.

Art. 16. 1. The Banco Nacional de México participates in the operation which is the object of the present contract for its own account and for the houses and the persons which it represents in the operation to the amount of 15.00 per cent.

2. S. Bleichroeder, Deutsche Bank, Dresdner Bank, Morgan, Grenfell & Company, J. P. Morgan & Company, to the amount of 42.50 per cent.

3. The Banque de Paris et des Pays Bas to the amount of 12.75 per cent.

4. The Crédit Lyonnais to the amount of 10.20 per cent.

5. The Société Générale to the amount of 10.20 per cent.

6. The Comptoir National d'Escompte de Paris to the amount of 9.35 per cent.

The group of banks indicated in paragraph 2 and each of the banks indicated in paragraphs 1, 3, 4, 5, and 6 are, moreover, agreed among themselves on all matters relating to the portion of the loan taken outright or to the rights and obligations incident to the purchase of this portion of the loan or the exercise of the option for the remainder of the loan.

This contract has been signed in eleven copies, in Paris, July 2, 1910.

Read and approved: The Financial Agent of the Mexican Government, M. Zamacona; Banque de Paris et des Pays Bas, Ed. Noetzlin, Albert Turretini; Crédit Lyonnais, Ed. Fabre-Luce; Comptoir National d'Escompte de Paris, Ullman; Société Générale pour Favoriser le Développement du Commerce et de l'Industrie en France, Le Directeur, Minvielle; Banco Nacional de México, Ed. Noetzlin. Read and approved: Attorney for S. Bleichroeder, Deutsche Bank, Dresdner Bank, Morgan, Grenfell & Company, J. P. Morgan & Company, Arthur Guttmann.

London, July 20, 1910. Secretary, P. M. del Paso. (Signed.)

(This is translated from the original in French)

Mexico, May 24, 1911. The Official Mayor, R. G. Revuelta.

APPENDIX VII

AGREEMENT BETWEEN THE MEXICAN GOVERNMENT AND THE INTERNATIONAL COMMITTEE OF BANKERS ON MEXICO

It having been made clear in the discussions between the Finance Minister and the International Committee of Bankers on Mexico:

(*a*) That the external obligations of the Mexican Government held by foreign investors approximate, together with the National Railways debt, and certain internal loans shown on the list attached, the sum of 1,000,000,000 pesos;

(*b*) That upon such sum, interest accumulated and unpaid since 1913 approximates the sum of 400,000,000 pesos;

(*c*) That although, owing to successive revolutions since 1913, Mexico has as yet not regained her full economic stability, yet the present Government of Mexico declares its determination to meet faithfully and promptly its financial obligations to the utmost extent of its capacity;

(*d*) That the International Committee, recognizing the difficulties with which Mexico has had to contend and the limitations upon her capacity for the immediate payment of all her obligations, due or overdue, and earnestly desiring to find means of safeguarding the interests of the bondholders, and at the same time of co-operating with the Mexican Government in the solution of its problems and in the upbuilding of its credit, is prepared to this end to recommend to the holders of Mexican Government obligations certain substantial diminutions and adjustments of their rights;

(*e*) That they also recognize that the Mexican Government has other obligations which it is important for it to meet, such as the restitution to the banks of the specie fund, the agrarian debt and arrears of pay, which may have to be cared for by the issue of internal bonds or in some other manner later to be considered;

(*f*) That, as to the minimum sums to be set aside by the Mexican Government for the service of its debt for the year 1923, and for the succeeding four years, the International Committee, after examination of the situation, believes that, under prudent and economical management of its affairs by the Mexican Government, the providing of such sums and the carrying out of this plan is within the capacity of Mexico, taking into account the improvement which should result from the settlement of the debt question and the declared intention of the Government to maintain a sound administration; and the fact that the plan itself, if adopted, may readily result in greatly improving the economic situation of Mexico;

(*g*) That the interests of the people and Government of Mexico, on the one hand, and of their external creditors, upon the other, being identical in that, for the benefit of both, the increasing prosperity of Mexico must be assured, therefore, the individuals now composing the International Committee give assurance of their continued interest and desire for helpful co-operation;

Therefore, in accordance with the foregoing, the following plan for the adjustment of the external obligations of the Mexican Government and of the National Railway System and of certain internal obligations appearing on the schedule annexed has been agreed to by the Mexican Minister of Finance and by the International Committee, which will do its utmost to arrange for its acceptance by the holders of the obligations listed in the schedule annexed.

1 — Arrears of Interest

The payment in cash of all interest due and payable on or before January 2, 1923, on both the government and the railway obligations, is to be waived by the bondholders.

The payment of interest upon all arrears of interest due and payable on or before January 2, 1923, on both the Government and railway obligations is to be waived by the bondholders.

The coupons for interest attached to the bonds are to be detached (if permitted by the various mortgages and indentures) and deposited with some trustee satisfactory to the International Committee who will issue receipts or certificates to the bondholders for the face amount of coupons so detached. The government will set aside annually, beginning on January 1, 1928, substantially equal annual sums sufficient to retire at par in proportionate annuities all said receipts or certificates within a period of forty years ending January 1, 1968. The annual amounts to be paid by the Mexican Government shall be paid by it through the financial agency of the Mexican Government in New York to the agencies that the Committee may designate and the Committee will determine the method of retirement. If for any reason the coupons cannot be detached from the bonds, some other plan for effecting the above arrangement satisfactory to the Committee shall be adopted. If there are any bonds to which coupons representing any back interest have never been attached the Mexican Government will supply such coupons for the purposes of these bonds so that the bondholders may be able to deposit them.

2 — Sinking Funds

All sinking funds to be postponed for a period not to exceed five years, from January 1, 1923.

3 — Matured Government Obligations

All Government notes which have matured or are about to mature will be extended for a reasonable length of time. (*See addendum, Exhibits A. and B.*)

4 — Current Interest

Payment of current interest to be resumed as follows:

(*a*) The Government will provide and set aside a fund which, for the first year, shall amount to 30,000,000 gold pesos present standard and shall be increased each year for a period of four years by not less than 5,000,000 pesos, so that the payment for the fifth year shall be at least 50,000,000 pesos. (*See addendum, Exhibit C.*)

(*b*) If, during the five year period, the funds provided for do not in any one year reach the guaranteed minimum amount, the Mexican Government will provide out of its other sources of revenue a sum sufficient to bring the amounts up to the guaranteed minimum and at such time and in such amounts as are required to meet current interest payments according to the schedule to be submitted to the Minister by the Committee.

(*c*) The entire oil export taxes (which the decree of June 7, 1921, provides for) and any increases thereof and the tax of 10% on the gross railway revenues hereafter provided for and the net operating railway revenues, if any, shall be paid as collected, in a manner to be agreed on with the International Committee, which will make arrangements for distribution of the sums so received among the holders of the obligations listed in the schedule attached, to which may be added such other issues as the Minister and the Committee may jointly agree should be included in the Government's external debt and railway debt. Part of such fund may be used in the discretion of the Committee in buying or retiring scrip for current interest. The Committee may retain and distribute the entire amounts received on account of the taxes specified in this section (*c*) although they may be in excess of the guaranteed minimum annual payments.

(*d*) Any difference between the amounts of cash paid on account of current interest (in accordance with the arrangements for distribution of current interest according to the schedule to be submitted by the Committee) and the full amount due therefor during a period of five years, beginning January 2, 1923, is to be dealt with in scrip. Such scrip shall be issued by the Mexican Government for the full amount of such difference and delivered through the Committee for distribution to the holders of obligations in such form as the Committee may determine. This scrip will become due and payable in 20 years. It will not bear any interest during the first 5 years but, for the balance of 15 years, it will bear interest at the rate of 3%, payable half-yearly. The Government will have the option to buy this Scrip in the market for cancellation, in a manner to be arranged with the Committee, or to call all or any part thereof at 105 and interest, accrued and unpaid to date of call, at any time before maturity thereof. During the first 5 years any surplus of the current interest fund, after paying current interest, shall be applied towards the purchase and cancellation of this Scrip as provided above.

(*e*) The payment of current interest in cash on the scale to be submitted to the Minister by the Committee will begin for interest becoming due and payable after January 2, 1923. Full resumption in cash of the service on the debt including full sinking fund payments will be resumed for payments becoming due and payable on and after January 1, 1928.

(*f*) The proceeds of the oil export taxes, which since January 31, 1922, have been paid or accumulated under the agreement of September 3, 1921, shall be paid over to the fund forthwith and all future proceeds of such tax shall be paid over from the date hereof; and the proceeds of the tax of 10% on the gross railway revenues shall be currently paid over as soon as the tax is created. Payments will be made in a manner to be agreed on with the International Committee.

(*g*) During the period prior to the full resumption of the service on the debt the Government will continue the export taxes on oil and will not diminish the rate of such taxes payable in cash as the same has been applied since September 3, 1921.

(*h*) After the expiration of the period of five years at the end of which the Mexican Government will resume the full service of the debt the special provisions made for this period in this paragraph 4 will be at an end except for the obligation of the Mexican Government contained in the current interest scrip and except that if there is then still outstanding any current interest scrip the tax of ten per cent (10%) on the gross railway revenues will be continued and applied through the Committee, for redemption of the current interest scrip in a manner to be arranged with the Committee.

5 — National Railway System

The holders of outstanding railway bonds and notes shall present their existing securities to be stamped with the agreement of the Mexican Government assuming the payment of principal, interest and sinking fund of the securities. For all amounts paid by the Mexican Government on account of the railroads for such interest, principal and sinking fund the Government will be a creditor of the Railways in the same manner as is provided in the Executive Decree and Plan of Readjustment and Union of the Mexican Central Railway Co., Ltd., and National Railroad Company of Mexico with respect to payments made on account of its guarantee of the General Mortgage 4% bonds of the National Railways of Mexico.

The liens created on the railway properties by the present mortgages and indentures in favor of the railway securities now outstanding are to be held by a trustee or trustees satisfactory to the International Committee and are not to be enforced unless the government is in default in its obligations under this plan when they may be enforced in favor of the holders of railway securities.

The government will make prompt return of the railways to private management, details of which are to be arranged. (*See addendum, Exhibit D.*)

Ten per cent (10%) annually of the gross receipts of the railways is to be set aside and paid over currently as herein provided towards the government debt service including the railway debt, and proper provision is to be made therefor in the rates by surcharge or otherwise.

Until the full cash payment of current interest on the bonds is resumed the net operating revenues of the railways are to be added to the fund provided for the government debt service and thereafter are to be applied to the service of the railway securities.

The Mexican Government recognizes the obligation to restore the railroads, including rolling stock, to the same condition that they were in when the Government took them over and will make every effort to do it (viz., such restoration) as soon as possible.

Railway notes that have matured or are about to mature will be extended for a reasonable length of time.

6 — Recognition of Obligations

The Mexican Government recognizes all obligations assumed by it, either direct or by way of guarantee and all provisions of the contracts and pledges under which the several bonds were issued, these provisions to be in full operation at the end of five years and prior thereto will be subject to the modifications herein provided for.

7 — Resumption of Rights

The bondholders will resume all their contractual rights if for any reason this plan is not fully carried out during the period of five years.

8 — Commission

Any difficulties that may arise in connection with the execution of this agreement will be settled by a special commission nominated by both parties.

9 — Ratification

This agreement is subject to the ratification of the President of Mexico. (*See addendum, Exhibit E.*)

(Signed) Adolfo de la Huerta

International Committee of Bankers on Mexico
by
(Signed) Thomas W. Lamont, Chairman.
(Signed) Ira H. Patchin, Asst. Secy.

June 16th, 1922.

SCHEDULE OF OBLIGATIONS

$48,635,000.	Mexican Government 5s, 1899.
50,949,000.	Mexican Government 4s, 1910.
29,100,000.	(£6,000,000) Mexican Government 6s, 1913.
$128,684,000.	Total Secured Debt.

6,769,000.	5% Municipal Loan.
37,037,000.	Mexican Government 4s, 1904.
25,000,000.	Caja de Prestamos 4½s.
$68,806,000.	TOTAL UNSECURED DEBT.
21,151,000.	Mexican Government 3s, 1886.
46,455,000.	Mexican Government 5s, 1894.
$67,606,000.	TOTAL INTERIOR DEBT.
50,748,575.	National Railways Guaranteed 4s.
7,000,000.	Vera Cruz and Pacific 4½s.
84,804,115.	National Railways Prior Lien 4½s.
23,000,000.	National Railroad Prior Lien 4½s.
24,740,000.	National Railroad 4s, 1951.
5,850,000.	Mexican International Prior Lien 4½s.
4,206,500.	Mexican International Prior Lien 4s, 1977.
2,003,000.	Pan American 5s, 1934.
1,484,000.	Pan American 5s, 1937.
1,374,000.	Mexican Central Priority 5%.
1,112,456.	National Railways Equipment 5s.
33,662,131.	National Railways Notes.
2,000,000.	Tehuantepec Second Mortgage 4½s.
1,750,000.	Miscellaneous.
$243,734,777.	TOTAL RAILWAY DEBT.
$508,830,777.	TOTAL OF DEBT.

NOTE.—In the foregoing schedule provision has not been made for (1) such bonds of the Huerta issues (following so-called issue "A") which are held by banks as collateral; nor (2) for the bonds of the so-called DeKay issue which the Government does not recognize.

To the above may be added such other issues as may be agreed on by the Minister and the International Committee as provided in the agreement. Amounts are stated according to latest available information and are given in gold dollars.

APPENDIX VIII

DEPOSIT AGREEMENT

FOR

BONDS, NOTES AND OTHER SECURITIES

included in

PLAN AND AGREEMENT

Dated June 16, 1922,

Executed by

His Excellency ADOLFO de la HUERTA

Minister of Finance of the United States of Mexico

AND

INTERNATIONAL COMMITTEE OF BANKERS ON MEXICO

and ratified September 29, 1922 by

His Excellency ALVARO OBREGON, President,

AND THE

CONGRESS OF THE UNITED STATES OF MEXICO

Agreement dated July 1, 1922, by and between such holders of the bonds, notes and other securities, hereinafter set forth and described, affected by the Plan and Agreement hereinafter mentioned and of the coupons or other evidences of indebtedness for or rights to unpaid interest thereon due and payable on and before January 2, 1923, as shall become parties to this Agreement in the manner hereinafter provided (hereinafter termed the Depositors), parties of the first part, and International Committee of Bankers on Mexico composed of individuals hereinafter named (hereinafter termed the Committee), parties of the second part:

WHEREAS the International Committee of Bankers on Mexico

was formed for the purpose among other things of negotiating with the Governmental authorities of Mexico in the interests of the holders of various obligations of the Mexican Government and other securities relating to Mexico, and for the purpose of protecting the interests of holders of said securities and the said Committee is composed of, AMERICAN SECTION: Thomas W. Lamont, Chairman; Mortimer L. Schiff, Vice-Chairman; George W. Davison, Jesse Hirschman, R. G. Hutchins, Jr., Charles E. Mitchell, John J. Mitchell, Walter T. Rosen, Charles H. Sabin, Albert H. Wiggin, and Robert Winsor. BRITISH SECTION: Vivian H. Smith, Chairman; Laurence Currie, Sir Clarendon Hyde, E. R. Peacock, Frank C. Tiarks, Vincent W. Yorke. FRENCH SECTION: G. Griolet, Chairman; Jules Chevalier, Paul Cretenier, William D'Eichthal, George Heine, Jacques Kulp. SWITZERLAND: G. Pictet. THE NETHERLANDS: C. E. ter Meulen. BELGIUM: Auguste Dupont; and

WHEREAS the Committee, after extended negotiations with His Excellency Adolfo de la Huerta, Minister of Finance, acting under authority of His Excellency Alvaro Obregon, President of the United States of Mexico, has devised a Plan and Agreement for the readjustment of the debt upon the following bonds, notes and other securities:

(1) Republic of Mexico 5 per cent Consolidated External Gold Loan of 1899
(2) Republic of Mexico 4 per cent External Gold Loan of 1910
(3) Republic of Mexico 6 per cent 10-year Treasury Notes of 1913 (Series A £6,000,000)
(4) City of Mexico 5 per cent Sterling Loan of 1889
(5) Institution for Encouragement of Irrigation Works and Development of Agriculture (S. A.) Thirty-Five-Year 4½ per cent Sinking Fund Gold Bonds due November 1, 1943 (Caja de Prestamos, etc.)
(6) United States of Mexico 4 per cent Gold Bonds of 1904
(7) Republic of Mexico Consolidated 3 per cent Internal Debt of 1885

(8) United States of Mexico 5 per cent Internal Redeemable Bonds of 1895
(9) State of Vera Cruz 5 per cent Bonds due April 1, 1927
(10) State of Vera Cruz 5 per cent Bonds dated January 1, 1907
(11) State of Tamaulipas 5 per cent Bonds dated July 1, 1903
(12) State of Tamaulipas 5 per cent Bonds dated January 1, 1907
(13) State of Sinaloa 5 per cent Bonds dated January 1, 1907
(14) National Railways of Mexico Guaranteed General Mortgage 4 per cent Seventy-year Sinking Fund Redeemable Gold Bonds due October 1, 1977
(15) Vera Cruz & Pacific Railroad Company 1st Mortgage 4½ per cent Gold Bonds due July 1, 1934
(16) National Railways of Mexico Prior Lien 4½ per cent Fifty-year Sinking Fund Redeemable Gold Bonds due July 1, 1957
(17) National Railroad Company of Mexico Prior Lien 4½ per cent Gold Bonds due October 1, 1926
(18) National Railroad Company of Mexico 1st Consolidated Mortgage 4 per cent Gold Bonds due October 1, 1951
(19) The Mexican International Railroad Company 4½ per cent Prior Lien Sterling Bonds due September 1, 1947
(20) The Mexican International Railroad Company 1st Consolidated Mortgage 4 per cent Gold Bonds due September 1, 1977
(21) Pan American Railroad Company 1st Mortgage 5 per cent Gold Bonds due January 1, 1934
(22) Pan American Railroad Company General Mortgage 5 per cent Gold Bonds due January 1, 1937
(23) Mexican Central Railway Company, Limited, 5 per cent Priority Bonds due July 1, 1939
(24) Mexican Central Railway Company, Limited, 5 per cent Equipment Notes and Certificates:
  (a) First Series dated April 1, 1897
  (b) Second Series dated October 2, 1899
  (c) Series No. 8 dated August 17, 1906

(d) Series No. 10 dated January 1, 1907
(e) Series No. 11 dated March 22, 1907

(25) National Railways of Mexico 6 per cent Secured Gold Notes, maturing up to January 1, 1917:
(a) Series " B " dated April 1, 1914
(b) Three-months Secured dated December 1, 1913
(c) Three-year Secured dated January 1, 1914
(d) Series " C " dated June 1, 1914

(26) National Railways of Mexico 6 per cent Secured Notes, maturing up to July 1, 1916
(a) Two-year, due June 1, 1915
(b) Two-year, due July 1, 1916

(27) Tehuantepec National Railway 5 per cent Gold Loan due June 30, 1953

(28) Tehuantepec National Railway 4½ per cent Gold Loan due June 30, 1953.

(hereinafter termed Bonds), which Plan and Agreement has been executed by His Excellency Adolfo de la Huerta, Minister of Finance under date of June 16, 1922 and has been ratified by His Excellency Alvaro Obregon, President of the United States of Mexico, and by the Congress of the United States of Mexico, under date of September 29, 1922 and

WHEREAS the Committee has agreed to recommend for acceptance by the holders of the said Bonds the said Plan and Agreement, a copy of which is hereto annexed and is herein termed the " Plan and Agreement "; and

WHEREAS the parties hereto desire to provide a method for the acceptance of and joining in the Plan and Agreement by the holders of the said Bonds and of coupons or other evidences of indebtedness for or rights to unpaid interest maturing on said Bonds on and prior to January 2, 1923 (hereinafter termed " Interest in Arrears ");

NOW, THEREFORE, THIS AGREEMENT WITNESSETH.

The parties hereto for and in consideration of the premises and of the advantages which will accrue from the union of interests and the above action, and all other good and valuable considerations, each for himself, his successors and assigns, and not for any of the others do agree as hereinafter set forth and provided:

FIRST

Parties to Deposit Agreement

The Depositors hereby make, constitute and appoint Thomas W. Lamont, Mortimer L. Schiff, George W. Davison, Jesse Hirschman, R. G. Hutchins, Jr., Charles E. Mitchell, John J. Mitchell, Walter T. Rosen, Charles H. Sabin, Albert H. Wiggin, Robert Winsor, Vivian H. Smith, Laurence Currie, Sir Clarendon Hyde, E. R. Peacock, Frank C. Tiarks, Vincent W. Yorke, G. Griolet, Jules Chevalier, Paul Cretenier, William D'Eichthal, George Heine, Jacques Kulp, G. Pictet, C. E. ter Meulen, Auguste Dupont, parties of the second part hereto, and their respective successors and associates as a Committee under this Agreement with all the rights, privileges and powers given to and vested in the Committee by this Agreement. Holders of the Bonds hereinabove set forth and affected by the said Plan and Agreement and of due and unpaid coupons or rights to Interest in Arrears thereon may become parties to this Agreement by depositing their Bonds with all unmatured coupons and all due and unpaid coupons or rights to Interest in Arrears for the marking or stamping of the Bonds and detaching of coupons as provided herein, under and in the manner provided in this Agreement, with the respective depositaries therefor set forth in the schedule hereto annexed following page 36 and made a part hereof and marked " Schedule " which are hereby appointed depositaries under this Agreement, or with an agent or agents designated for such purpose by the respective depositaries or with such other depositaries as may be appointed hereunder by the Committee as in its discretion it may determine to be advisable (all of which collectively are hereinafter termed Depositaries). All such Bonds, if in negotiable form with coupons thereto attached, shall be deposited with all coupons thereto appertaining maturing January 3, 1923 and thereafter and shall be accompanied by all unpaid coupons thereto appertaining due prior to January 3, 1923 unless the Committee shall otherwise permit or the depositing bondholder is not the owner or holder of such coupons, and, if registered Bonds or Bonds without coupons thereto attached, shall be accompanied by properly executed instruments of transfer and assignments in blank of all interest due and unpaid and to become due and payable thereon. Interest in Arrears held by persons who do not hold the Bonds relative thereto may be deposited separately from such Bonds when the Plan has been declared operative and shall be deposited under the same terms and conditions in so far as appropriate, as the relative Bonds are deposited.

The Committee in its discretion with or without prior publication or notice may at any time fix a date or limit of time after which holders of any of the said Bonds or Interest in Arrears shall not be entitled to deposit the same hereunder, and any holder who may fail to make deposit hereunder on or before the date so fixed or within such limit shall not be entitled to deposit the same or become a party to this Agreement or to share the benefits hereof and shall claim no rights hereunder, but the Committee in its discretion, either generally or in special instances and upon such terms and conditions as it shall prescribe, may extend the time for receiving deposits or authorize the deposit at a later date or waive a default and may permit the holders or owners of any of said Bonds or Interest in Arrears to become parties to this Agreement and depositors hereunder otherwise than as herein specifically provided.

SECOND

Deposited or Assenting Bonds and Coupons and Interest in Arrears

As soon as practicable after the Committee shall have declared the Plan and Agreement operative with respect to any issue of the deposited Bonds, the respective Depositaries for the Bonds with respect to which the Plan and Agreement shall have been declared operative shall mark or stamp each of such Bonds or cause the same to be marked or stamped with a notation or legend to the effect that the owner or holder thereof has assented to and is bound by this Agreement and all the terms and conditions hereof and has accepted and joined in the Plan and Agreement and that all rights on such Bond are subject to the provisions of and are modified as provided in the Plan and Agreement, and this agreement; such notation or legend to be in such form as may be approved by the Committee and its counsel and to contain such further provisions as may be determined by the Committee.

At the time of the marking or stamping of any Bond the Depositary therefor shall detach therefrom all of the appurtenant coupons or rights to interest thereon with maturity dates during the period after January 2, 1923 and prior to January 1, 1928 (hereinafter termed " the five-year period ") all of which coupons shall, unless the rights of the Mexican Government under the Plan and Agreement be declared terminated prior to January 1, 1928, be retained and held on deposit and in escrow by the Bankers Trust Company, New York, as special depositary, or its successor as appointed by the Committee, until January 1, 1928, or the same shall have been paid, cancelled, and surrendered as provided herein and in the Plan and Agreement.

The depositary for such Bond shall also detach therefrom all the appurtenant coupons or rights to interest maturing on or prior to January 2, 1923, all of which coupons or rights to interest shall, unless the rights of the Mexican Government become terminated as herein provided, be retained and held on deposit and in escrow by Guaranty Trust Company of New York until the retirement of the relative receipts as provided herein.

The Bonds, Current Interest and Interest in Arrears deposited with or delivered to the depositary or depositaries therefor shall at all times be held in escrow by such depositary or depositaries and, except as hereinafter provided, title thereto shall not pass to the Committee but shall remain in the respective depositors. After the deposit or delivery of Bonds and Coupons or Interest in Arrears, no separate action shall be taken by any depositor with respect to the deposited Bonds or any of the coupons or rights thereto appertaining or the Interest in Arrears or otherwise so long as this Agreement shall continue in effect. The Committee may, however, at any time in its uncontrolled discretion take title to the detached deposited coupons or rights to interest, or any part thereof by filing with the respective depositary or depositaries for such coupons or rights to interest as to which it determines to take title, a certified copy of the resolution of the Committee duly adopted, that it has determined to accept transfer of title to it of detached coupons or rights to interest or any part thereof deposited with such depositary; and immediately upon the filing of such resolution the title to the coupons or rights to interest specified therein and all assignments relating to such coupons or rights to interest shall forthwith pass from the depositors to and vest in the Committee as trustees of an express trust with all the rights and powers of the owners thereof.

THIRD

Issue of Receipts, Cash Warrants, Scrip Receipts and Receipts for Interest in Arrears

Each depositor shall be entitled upon the deposit or delivery hereunder of his Bond or Interest in Arrears to receive from the depositary with whom such deposit is made, one or more appropriate receipts executed by or on behalf of such depositary transferable as the Committee may determine and in such form as the Committee may approve representing the assenting or deposited Bond and coupons or interest thereto appertaining or deposited Interest in Arrears as the case may be; which receipt shall be exchangeable for the Bond when marked or stamped as hereinafter provided and the coupons thereon maturing on and after January 1, 1928 and Cash Warrants, Scrip Receipts and Receipts for Interest in Arrears as hereinafter set forth.

As soon as practicable after the Plan and Agreement has been declared operative with respect to any issue of Bonds and each deposited Bond of such issue has been marked or stamped and all the appurtenant coupons thereon with maturity dates prior to January 1, 1928 detached and Current Interest Cash Warrants, Current Interest Scrip Receipts and Receipts for Interest in Arrears as hereinafter described representing such detached coupons have been prepared and are ready for delivery, there shall be delivered to the depositor against the surrender of the receipt (1) The Bond, with all deposited appurtenant coupons with maturity dates on and subsequent to January 1, 1928, represented by such receipt marked or stamped as herein provided, and instruments in such form as approved by the Committee as follows:

(*a*) *A Current Interest Cash Warrant* for each of the detached and deposited coupons or instalments of interest or rights to interest maturing on the assenting Bond affected by the plan during the five-year period, each of which Cash Warrants shall represent the right of the Bondholder to receive on the maturity date of the coupon described therein, and if, when and as received by Bankers Trust Company, New York as Depositary, the amount of cash then payable on such coupon under the terms of the Plan and Agreement and this Agreement. In the event the rights of the Mexican Government under the Plan and Agreement be terminated as therein provided prior to January 1, 1928, the coupons maturing during such five-year period will be returnable (stamped to indicate the cash payments made thereon, if any) to the then holder of the receipts for such coupons (the Current Interest Scrip Receipts) except that in case no Current Interest Scrip Receipt has been issued in respect to a coupon but only a Cash Warrant has been issued, then return of such coupon shall be made to the holder of the Cash Warrant relating thereto.

The bearer of the last maturing Cash Warrant, or, if the Committee shall so determine, the bearer of the marked or stamped Bond, shall be entitled to receive a pro rata share of the balance, if any, of the fund for expenses provided in Article Eighth of this Agreement remaining upon the termination of this Agreement.

(*b*) *A Current Interest Scrip Receipt* for each of the current interest coupons, or instalments of interest or rights to interest in respect to which Mexican Government Scrip is deliverable, constituting a receipt for the coupon or interest instalment therein described and representing the right to receive after June 1, 1928, if, when, and as received by the Bankers Trust Company, New York, for delivery and upon surrender thereof at the office of

Bankers Trust Company, Mexican Government Twenty-year Scrip. This Scrip will not bear any interest during the first five years but, for the following fifteen years, it will bear interest at the rate of 3% per annum, payable half-yearly, and is to be issued in an amount equal to the difference between the face amount of the deposited coupons maturing during the five-year period and the amount payable in cash thereon under the terms of this Agreement and the Plan and Agreement. Each Scrip Receipt will provide that the bearer thereof, at his option, provided the rights of the Mexican Government under the Plan and Agreement shall have been declared terminated prior to January 1, 1928, in the manner in this Agreement and in said Plan and Agreement provided, upon presentation thereof at the office of the Bankers Trust Company, New York, and upon payment of such sum or sums if any, as may be imposed by the Bankers Trust Company to cover expenses of such delivery, and by the Fiscal Authorities having jurisdiction, instead of such Mexican Government Scrip, may receive the coupon in respect of which such Current Interest Scrip Receipt has been issued, having marked or stamped thereon a notation of the cash payment, if any, made thereon.

All Mexican Government Scrip deliverable against matured Current Interest Scrip Receipts is to be deposited with the Bankers Trust Company, New York, as Depositary and will be delivered by such Depositary or its agents against the surrender of such matured Current Interest Scrip Receipts after June 1, 1928, or earlier at the option of the holder of matured Scrip Receipts in the event of the termination of the rights of the Mexican Government in the manner herein provided, but only upon the presentation and surrender thereof in the principal amounts aggregating $100 or multiples thereof, or in other appropriate currencies in cases in which the deposited coupons make no provisions for payment in United States of America gold dollars.

Current Interest Scrip Receipts so delivered may be purchased in the market, or, if not so purchaseable, may be redeemed in accordance with the terms of the Plan and Agreement at 105 and interest out of the excess, if any, available for distribution to the Bondholders under the terms of the Plan and Agreement, of the revenues allocated by the Mexican Government for current interest payments over and above the amount necessary to make the cash payments required to be made on the Current Interest Cash Warrants as provided in the Plan and Agreement and the schedule hereto annexed.

The acceptance by the holder of any such matured Current Interest Scrip Receipt, of the Mexican Government Scrip to which he is entitled, shall constitute a waiver by such holder of the right to the return of the coupon in respect to which such Current Interest Scrip Receipt shall have been issued and a satisfaction and discharge of all his right title and interest in and to such coupon and in and to the obligation represented thereby and such acceptance shall constitute and evidence his irrevocable assent to its cancellation or such other disposition as the Committee may determine; and

(2) A Receipt or Receipts for Interest in Arrears for such of the detached and deposited coupons or rights to interest as shall have matured on and prior to January 2, 1923. Receipts for Interest in Arrears will be issued by Guaranty Trust Company of New York as depositary and shall be of two classes, designated, respectively, Class A and Class B. There shall be delivered, in respect to each deposit, Receipts either wholly Class A or wholly Class B, or partly Class A and partly Class B, which in their aggregate shall equal the face amount of Interest in Arrears deposited. Class A Receipts shall represent either the entire amount of Interest in Arrears, or when not representing the entire amount, shall represent interest which shall have matured on the earlier payment dates, and similarly, Class B Receipts, when not issued in respect to the entire amount of Interest in Arrears, will be issued in respect to the interest which shall have matured on the later payment dates. The matured interest payment dates of each issue in respect to which Class A and Class B Receipts will be issued, are set forth in the schedule hereto annexed. All Receipts for Interest in Arrears, Class A, shall be entitled to be retired out of the annual payments to be made on account of Interest in Arrears under the Plan and Agreement by the Mexican

Government over the forty-year period — January 1, 1928, to January 1, 1968 — before any Receipts for Interest in Arrears Class B may be retired. As and when such funds are so set aside by the Mexican Government, the said Receipts to the extent that such funds are available, are to be purchased in the market, if the same may be purchased at less than the face amount thereof, or, if purchase at less than the face amount of such Receipts cannot be effected, are to be redeemed at the face amount thereof. In the event (a) that the rights of the Mexican Government under the Plan and Agreement are declared terminated prior to January 1, 1928, or (b) that thereafter while any Receipts for Interest in Arrears are outstanding and unprovided for the Mexican Government shall fail to set aside annually beginning in 1928, substantially equal sums sufficient to retire at par all said receipts by January 1, 1968, and such failure shall have continued for a period of six months, then upon surrender thereof to Guaranty Trust Company of New York and upon payment of such sum or sums, if any, as may be imposed by Guaranty Trust Company of New York to cover expenses of the delivery to be made in respect to such surrender, and by the Fiscal Authorities having jurisdiction, the holder of a Receipt for Interest in Arrears at his option may receive from Guaranty Trust Company of New York the deposited coupons, or assignments of rights to interest, represented thereby. The retirement of any Receipt for Interest in Arrears issued hereunder, by the sums to be set aside annually by the Mexican Government during the forty-year period — January 1, 1928, to January 1, 1968 — or otherwise by the Mexican Government shall to that extent constitute full satisfaction and payment of the amount due on the coupons or rights to interest represented by the Receipt so retired, and the coupons or other evidences representing the amount so satisfied and discharged shall be cancelled; all coupons fully so discharged or paid shall be surrendered to the Mexican Government.

FOURTH

Acceptance of Plan and Agreement, Deposit Agreement and Schedule

The Plan and Agreement, a copy of which is hereto annexed, and the schedule of priorities and method of disbursement of moneys received in connection with the payment of current interest and method of distribution of Receipts for Interest in Arrears under and pursuant to the said Plan and Agreement, a copy of which schedule is hereto annexed following page 36 hereof and herein termed the "Schedule," are hereby adopted and approved and assented to by the Depositors with the same force and effect as though each and every statement of the said Plan and Agreement and the said Schedule had been embodied and repeated herein, and the said Plan and Agreement and the said Schedule and this Agreement shall be read as one and the same instrument; but no estimate, statement, explanation or suggestion contained in the said Plan and Agreement, the said Schedule or this Agreement or in any letter, circular or notice issued or which hereafter may be issued by or on behalf of the Committee is intended or is to be taken as a representation or warranty or as an inducement or a condition of assent under or to the said Plan and Agreement, the said Schedule or this Agreement, and no defect, error or omission therein shall release any party hereto except by written consent of the Committee.

FIFTH

Certain Special Powers of Committee

Each Depositor hereby constitutes and appoints the Committee as from time to time constituted, attorney in fact irrevocable with full power of substitution in his name and on his behalf and in respect of the Bonds and Interest in Arrears deposited by him to consent to the Plan and Agreement and to make and do any and all things necessary in the uncontrolled discretion of the Committee to carry out and make effective the said Plan and Agreement and this Agreement and the Schedule in accordance with the true intent and meaning thereof as interpreted by the Committee. Each Depositor does further likewise grant to the Committee full power and authority to make and negotiate with the Mexican Government or otherwise such changes or modifications in the said Plan and Agreement as are or may be found necessary to carry out the intent thereof.

The Committee is fully authorised and empowered to do any and all of the following acts on behalf of all or any of the Depositors, the enumeration whereof is not to be construed in any way as by way of limitation of the powers of the Committee hereby conferred or intended so to be, the purpose and intent of this Agreement being to grant to the Committee full power and authority to do any and all things for and on behalf of the Depositors necessary, proper or advisable in the opinion of the Committee fully to perform and carry out the terms and conditions of the said Plan and Agreement hereto annexed, and this Agreement in accordance with the true intent and meaning thereof, that is to say:

(1) To waive during the five-year period, any and all rights to enforce any security for any of the Bonds or Interest in Arrears deposited hereunder where such waiver is required by the Plan and Agreement or is necessary, proper or advisable in the opinion of the Committee for the performance by or the carrying out of the obligations of the Depositors under the said Plan and Agreement.

(2) To waive any and all rights to sinking-fund payments required to be made in respect to any of the Bonds deposited hereunder, under the terms thereof or of the Indentures or Deeds of Trust under which such Bonds are issued, or otherwise, over a period of five years after January 2, 1923, to and including December 31, 1927.

(3) To agree to the extension of and to extend the time of payment of the principal of the Notes of the National Railways of Mexico secured by Bonds of the Railway Company (No. 26 of the Schedule) until January 1, 1933, with interest at 5 per cent per annum for the first five years beginning in 1923 and thereafter at 6 per cent per annum and to that end to enter into

any and all necessary or proper agreements on behalf of the holders of such Notes and do any and all other things or acts necessary and proper in the premises.

(4) To agree to the extension of and to extend the time of payment of the principal of the 6 per cent Notes of the Mexican Government (No. 3 of the Schedule) and the National Railways Notes secured by 6 per cent Mexican Government Notes of 1913 (No. 25 of the Schedule) until January 1, 1933 with interest at the rate of 6 per cent per annum.

(5) To agree to the extension of and to extend the time of payment of the principal of State of Vera Cruz 5% Bonds, (No. 9 of the Schedule), National Railroad Company of Mexico Prior Lien 4½% Gold Bonds, (No. 17 of the Schedule), and Mexican Central Railway Co., Ltd., 5% Equipment Notes and Certificates (No. 24 of the Schedule), with interest at the rate of 6% per annum from the respective dates on which they were originally due until the date to which they are to be extended, viz: January 1, 1933.

(6) To demand, sue for, collect and receive during the said five-year period, the funds in cash, scrip or otherwise constituted, in any way to become due under the said Plan and Agreement or otherwise with respect to the deposited Bonds or deposited coupons or rights to interest detached and to disburse the same among the Depositors against the Current Interest Cash Warrants and Current Interest Scrip Receipts under and in accordance with the terms and provisions thereof and of this Agreement, the Schedule and the said Plan and Agreement as the same now exist, or hereafter may exist with such modifications thereof as the Committee may make as herein provided.

(7) To declare the said Plan and Agreement operative as to any issue of Bonds at any time at which the Committee in its opinion shall deem a sufficient number of Bonds of such issue to have been deposited hereunder. Thereupon the Committee shall file such declaration with the Depositary or Depositaries for the respective issues concerning which the Plan and Agreement is declared operative. The Committee shall not be required to publish notice thereof.

The Committee shall be the sole and final judge as to when and whether the assent of a sufficient number of holders of Bonds shall have been obtained to warrant the Committee in declaring the Plan and Agreement operative as to any or all issues involved.

(8) To deal, negotiate and contract with the Mexican Government or its representatives in respect to any modification or change in or interpretation of the Plan and Agreement deemed by the Committee necessary or advisable and to bind the Depositors by such modification, change or interpretation.

(9) To waive during the said five-year period, any default or to agree to the change or waiver during such period of any of the contract rights of bondholders under any of the Bonds or the agreements, indentures or mortgages, relative thereto where such waiver or change is necessary, proper or advisable, in the opinion of the Committee, for the carrying out or performance by the depositors of their obligations under the said Plan and Agreement, and on behalf of the particular Bonds affected to enter into any agreement with the Trustee in the indenture securing the same and to mark or stamp such Bonds or cause the same to be marked or stamped to indicate any such waiver of default, the payment of any Sinking Fund or the right to enforce any provisions of said indenture securing said Bonds.

(10) To agree and on behalf of the particular Bonds affected to enter into any agreements with the Mexican Government whereby the Mexican Government shall, in accordance with the said Plan and Agreement, assume the payment of any Bonds and interest thereon and Sinking Fund, if any, payable in respect thereto, not at the time of the deposit of such Bonds assumed by or representing an obligation of the Mexican Government; to mark or stamp such Bonds or cause the same to be marked or stamped with a notation or inscription in such form as the Committee may determine and as may be agreed upon by the Mexican Government, to evidence the assumption by the Mexican Government of payment of such Bonds and the interest thereon and the Sinking Fund, if any, payable in respect thereto, in place of the obligation of assumption or guaranty included in the said Plan and Agreement and referred to in the marking or stamp evi-

dencing the assent of the depositor to the terms of said Plan and Agreement and this Agreement.

(11) To negotiate and agree with the Mexican Government on steps to be taken to make effective the collection and payment by the Mexican Government of the oil export taxes and the 10% gross revenues and the net operating revenues of the National Railways of Mexico, in the said Plan and Agreement provided to be paid as a part of the fund to meet current interest during the said five-year period on deposited Bonds.

(12) To negotiate, contract and agree on behalf of any and all the depositors on the basis, method and generally with respect to the returning to private management of the properties of the National Railways of Mexico and any other railway properties affected by the Bonds deposited hereunder.

(13) With the consent of the Mexican Government to include or add to the securities affected by the Plan and Agreement, other issues of securities and to allow and provide that the holders of such other securities may become parties to this Agreement, all in such manner as the Committee may deem advisable.

(14) Anything to the contrary in this Agreement contained notwithstanding, the Committee shall have full power and authority whenever in its sole discretion and judgment it shall deem it for the benefit of the bondholders to modify the Plan and Agreement in such manner as the Committee may determine, without notice to the depositors, to provide that to the extent that the proceeds of the allocated revenues payable to the interest fund for 1923 exceed the specified minimum amounts payable in that year, the Mexican Government may be relieved, in whole or in part, from its obligations under the Plan and Agreement to pay such excess into the fund; or, to provide that any or all of such excess may be applied on account of the amounts required to be paid under the terms of the Plan and Agreement in any one or more of the respective years succeeding 1923 in which case and to the extent that such excess is so applied, the Mexican Government will be relieved of its obligations in such succeeding years.

(15) The Committee shall further have the sole right on behalf of all of the Depositors during the said five-year period to

determine whether or not there has been a failure of the Mexican Government to perform its obligations under the said Plan and Agreement and whether the Depositors shall be, in accordance with the said Plan and Agreement, entitled to the resumption of their rights, except in so far as the extent to which the Plan and Agreement shall have been carried out renders that impracticable, by contract or otherwise existing under the said Bonds and the agreements under and to which the said Bonds may relate as of the date of this Agreement. Unless and until the Committee shall have declared that there has been a default by the Mexican Government under the said Plan and Agreement, the Depositors shall have such and only such rights during the five-year period as are provided in this Agreement and are set forth in the Schedule and arise out of the said Plan and Agreement and any modifications thereof as herein provided.

SIXTH

Constitution and Action of Committee

The Committee, as at any time constituted, and notwithstanding any vacancy, shall have all the powers, rights and interests of the Committee as originally formed and hereby appointed. The Committee may from time to time add to its number by electing an additional member or additional members, and the member or members so elected shall have all the rights, powers and authority of members of the Committee, and, together with those herein named or their successors, shall constitute the Committee under this Agreement, with the like force and effect as if they were specifically herein named as parties of the second part. Any member of the Committee may resign by filing written notice of his resignation with the secretary of the Committee.

In case at any time a vacancy shall occur in the Committee by death, resignation or otherwise, such vacancy may, but need not, be filled by the affirmative vote or concurrent action of a majority of the remaining members of the section (as shown in the preambles hereof) of the Committee in which such vacancy shall exist, by the selection and appointment of a successor to fill such vacancy, and such successor shall have and may exercise all the rights, powers and authority under this Agreement previously possessed by the person in whose place he shall have been elected or appointed, and to the same extent and effect as if he were herein named as one of the Committee.

Except as otherwise provided the action of a majority of the members of the Committee, as from time to time constituted and notwithstanding any vacancy, expressed from time to time at a meeting or by writing without a meeting shall, for all purposes, constitute the action of the Committtee and have the same effect as if assented to by all. It may adopt its own rules of procedure. It may appoint sub-committees with such powers as it may determine and which may be discretionary. Any member of the Committee may vote or act by proxy (who may, but need not, be another member of the Committee), and the vote or act of such proxy shall be as effective as the vote or act of the member appointing such proxy.

The Committee shall have power to employ such depositaries, counsel, attorneys, accountants, experts, agents and employees as in its judgment shall be necessary or useful, and may fix the compensation for their services and its own reasonable compensation and may make or authorize such other expenditures as it shall deem necessary or appropriate for any of the purposes of this Agreement and it may procure the performance of any of the matters herein provided for by agents, trustees or substitutes. Neither the Committee nor any of its members nor the Depositaries shall be personally liable for any act or omission of any agent, attorney or employee selected in good faith, nor for any error of judgment or mistake of law, nor for anything other than its or his own wilful malfeasance.

The Depositaries shall incur no liability for anything done or permitted to be done at the request or direction of the Committee, the deposited or assenting Bonds and Interest in Arrears being intended and agreed to be wholly subject to the order and under the control of the Committee. Depositaries or any of them may resign by giving to the Chairman of the Committee or to any other two members of the Committee and the Secretary of the

Committee a notice of resignation, at least thirty days before such resignation becomes effective, unless the Committee shall waive such notice. Any of the Depositaries may at any time be removed by a majority vote of the Committee. A successor to any Depositary may be appointed by the Committee in the event of the resignation or removal or inability or incapacity from any cause to act of such Depositary. Such successor shall be vested with all the powers, rights, duties and obligations of the original Depositary appointed hereunder with the same effect as if a successor Depositary so appointed had been originally named in the Schedule. Any Depositary who shall resign or be removed or otherwise be incapable of acting, upon the payment of all charges and moneys due to it, shall deliver to the new Depositary who may be appointed in its place and stead, the securities or property deposited with it by the depositors or the securities or property deposited with it by the Committee, or held for account of the Committee or the Depositors, and such Depositary for the time being shall comply with the obligations of any predecessor Depositary which shall have issued Receipts, Cash Warrants, Scrip Receipts or any other instrument as herein provided with the same effect as if the same had been issued by such new Depositary.

The term " Depositaries " wherever used in this instrument shall refer in every instance to the Depositaries which may at the time be acting as such under this agreement.

Any member of the Committee and any firm, association or corporation of which he may be a member, officer, director or stockholder or in which he may be otherwise interested, and the Depositaries, their officers and agents and the members of their boards of directors, may be or become pecuniarily interested in any property or matter which is or may become the subject of this Agreement, and may contract with the Committee or be a member or manager of any other committee or of any syndicate which may contract with the Committee or be formed in contemplation of or in connection with the Plan and Agreement or any Plan and Agreement prepared or approved and adopted by the Committee under this Agreement or modifications thereof, made as herein provided.

SEVENTH

Right and Power of Committee to Borrow and Pledge

The Committee may, subject only to the limitations in this Article Seventh hereof contained, borrow from any person, firm or corporation, including its own members or any of them, for such period and upon such terms and conditions as it may determine, such sums of money as in its judgment may be required to meet its expenses or liabilities or generally for any of the purposes of this Agreement, and it may, subject to the limitations hereinafter in this Article Seventh set forth, charge or pledge for the payment of any sums borrowed the detached and deposited coupons or rights to interest and any property of any character other than the deposited Bonds and coupons thereto appertaining maturing on and subsequent to January 1, 1928, held by or on behalf of the Committee under authority conferred by any of the provisions of this Agreement, or any part of the said coupons or rights to interest or property, subject always to the limitation that the Committee shall not and may not at any time borrow for the purposes of this Agreement amounts which in the aggregate exceed the amount or the part thereof then not set aside and paid as hereinafter in Article Eighth of this Agreement provided to be set aside for use by the Committee for its expenses, obligations and indebtedness under this Agreement.

The Committee shall apply the sum hereinafter provided to be set aside and used by the Committee for its expenses, obligations, liabilities and indebtedness under this Agreement or such part thereof as may (subject to the provisions of Article Eighth hereof) be necessary, to the payment of any sum or sums of money borrowed by or procured to be advanced to it and to the payment of sums of money heretofore advanced or borrowed by the members of the Committee in connection with the negotiations and investigations incident to the Plan and Agreement and this Agreement and to the payment of its compensation and its expenses, indebtedness, obligations and liabilities, whether such expenses, indebtedness, obligations or liabilities shall have been incurred before or after the appointment of the Committee under this Agreement.

Upon borrowing money, whether upon pledge or not, the Committee may give to the lender its promissory note or notes executed by any of its members duly authorized for the sums borrowed.

The Committee in charging or pledging the coupons or rights to interest or other property held hereunder as aforesaid or as may be necessary, to the payment of any sum or sums of money may in writing direct any of the Depositaries to hold the deposited coupons or rights to interest and other property or any designated part thereof as security for the repayment of any moneys advanced or to be advanced to the Committee, in which case such coupons or rights to interest or other property shall be held by such Depositaries as security for such advances with the same effect as if actually deposited with the person making such advances for the security of the payment thereof, provided, however, that none of the deposited coupons or rights to interest relating to any one Bond shall be held as security for or pledged in connection with any such advances where the proportion of the security therefor furnished by such deposited coupons or rights to interest is greater than one and one-half per centum (1½%) of the face principal amount of such Bond.

EIGHTH

Fund for Expenses and Compensation

The Committee shall be entitled to receive and shall receive and retain as a fund for the payment of its expenses, (which expression includes any expenditure the making of which the Committee may consider desirable to facilitate the adoption generally or by any body of Bondholders and the carrying out of this Agreement and the Plan and Agreement), indebtedness, compensation, obligations and liabilities incurred hereunder and prior to appointment hereunder, a sum equal to one per centum (1%) of the principal amount of the Bonds deposited hereunder, and such additional amount, if any, as may be required to satisfy the expenses and obligations of the Committee; such additional amount, however, shall not in any event exceed one half of one per centum (½%) of the principal amount of the Bonds deposited. The said fund (to the extent of one per centum (1%) of the principal amount of the deposited Bonds) shall be made up from the first amounts received in cash from the Mexican Government and the equivalent thereof shall be deducted from the amounts to be paid in cash upon the earliest maturing Current Interest Cash Warrants upon said Bonds, and the additional fund (to the extent of one half of one per centum (½%) of the principal amount of said Bonds) shall be made up from such later maturing Current Interest Cash Warrants at such time as the Committee in its sole discretion shall determine, provided that in no event shall there be deducted in any one year from the amounts received in cash from the Mexican Government and from the amounts distributable on account of the payments of current interest upon the Bonds an amount in excess of one half of one per centum (½%) of the principal amount of the Bonds. The balance of such fund and additional fund, if any, not required for the purposes above mentioned, and remaining upon the termination of this Agreement, shall be returned to the bearers of the last maturing Cash Warrants, or, if the Committee so determine, to the bearers of the marked or stamped Bonds pro rata and in accordance with their rights.

Such fund shall be used as the Committee in its sole discretion may determine to be necessary or advisable in paying the expenses, indebtedness, compensation, obligations and liabilities of the Committee. Provided that the Committee shall have received such fund for the payment of the said expenses, indebtedness, compensation, obligations and liabilities as aforesaid, it shall not be entitled to receive from the bondholders in any other manner, payment for expenses or compensation hereunder, but nothing herein contained shall limit amounts payable to the Committee and the Depositaries by way of indemnity or otherwise necessary to meet or pay liabilities and obligations incurred by virtue of acting hereunder.

NINTH

Interpretation, Construction and Modification of Deposit Agreement, Plan and Agreement and Schedule

The Committee may and hereby is authorized and empowered to construe this Agreement and the Plan and Agreement and its construction of the same or action thereunder in good faith shall be final, conclusive and binding upon all depositing or assenting Bondholders and upon all holders of Current Interest Cash Warrants, Current Interest Scrip Receipts and Receipts for Interest in Arrears issued hereunder. It may supply any defects or omissions herein or in the said Plan and Agreement or may make such modifications herein or in the said Plan and Agreement as in its judgment may be expedient effectively to carry out this Agreement and the said Plan and Agreement and to such extent as shall be deemed by the Committee necessary, proper or advisable to carry out this Agreement and the said Plan and Agreement properly and effectively, and the Committee shall be the sole judge of such necessity, propriety or advisability.

In particular, but not by way of limitation of the general powers hereby granted to the Committee to make changes and modifications in the Plan and Agreement and in this Agreement, the Committee shall have power to make such modifications, as in its judgment it deems necessary, provided that no change of the percentages of current interest to be paid in cash as provided in the Schedule shall be made except upon the unanimous consent of the members of the Committee.

It shall have power whenever it shall deem proper at any time, and whether or not the Plan and Agreement shall have been declared operative, to alter, modify, depart from or abandon any part thereof. It may at any time or times after any such partial abandonment restore to the plan any abandoned part or parts and may seek to carry such part into effect as if such part or parts had not been abandoned. Any change or modification made by the Committee shall thereupon become part of the Plan and Agreement and of this Agreement and all provisions concerning the present Plan and Agreement and this Agreement shall apply to the Plan and Agreement and this Agreement as so changed and modified and the term "Plan and Agreement" wherever used in this Agreement shall include any change or modified plan adopted as herein provided.

In case of any change or modification of the Plan and Agreement or of this Agreement in the Committee's judgment materially and adversely affecting any class of depositing bondholders, the Committee shall file a statement of such proposed change or modification with each of the then acting Depositaries named in the Schedule, and with the successors of those of the Depositaries therein named not then acting, and give notice of the fact of such filing as hereinafter provided in Article Thirteenth. At any time within two weeks after final publication of such notice, any depositor materially and adversely affected by any change or modification may withdraw his assent to this Agreement so modified and his Bonds, coupons or rights to interest or other securities theretofore deposited and then under the control of the Committee, upon surrender to the respective Depositary therefor in transferable form of any and all temporary Receipts, Cash Warrants, Scrip Receipts and Receipts for Interest in Arrears issued to him and then outstanding. Further, upon presentation to the Depositary of the marked or stamped assenting Bond the Depositor shall be entitled to have such marking or stamping cancelled upon the payment of any stamp tax or other governmental charge payable in respect of such withdrawal or re-delivery and at the election of the Committee upon the payment of such amount as the Committee shall in its discretion fix as the fair contribution towards the compensation and expenses of the Committee, not exceeding a sum equal to one and one-half per centum (1½%) of the principal amount of Bonds to be withdrawn, provided that the Committee shall not have theretofore received for its compensation and expenses the one and one-half per centum (1½%) of the principal amount of the Bonds provided for in Article Eighth hereof.

Every depositor entitled to withdraw and surrender as aforesaid who shall not within two weeks after final publication or the giving of said notice surrender, withdraw and make payment as aforesaid, if any, shall be deemed to have assented to the proposed change or modification and whether or not otherwise objecting shall be bound thereby as fully and effectively as if actually assenting thereto.

The Depositors so withdrawing shall upon withdrawal as aforesaid, without any further act, be fully relieved from the obligations of this Agreement and shall cease to have any rights hereunder.

The Committee shall have the sole and exclusive right to determine whether any change or modification of the Plan and Agreement or of this Agreement materially or adversely affects any depositor or holder of a certificate or receipt issued hereunder and the determination of the Committee shall be final and conclusive on all parties hereto.

In case the Committee shall finally abandon the entire Plan and Agreement either on account of failure of the Mexican Government to perform thereunder as in the said Plan and Agreement provided or otherwise, as it may do in its uncontrolled discretion, it shall give notice of such abandonment as hereinafter provided, and the Bonds and coupons or rights to interest of any of the parties hereto which shall have been transferred and assigned to and then be under the control of the Committee shall be delivered to the respective parties entitled thereto in accordance with their respective rights upon the surrender of Receipts, Current Interest Cash Warrants, Current Interest Scrip Receipts and Receipts for Interest in Arrears, as the case may be, and upon the payment of any stamp tax or other governmental charge payable in respect to the re-delivery thereof and upon the further payment at the election of the Committee of such sum as the Committee shall in its discretion fix as a fair contribution toward the compensation and expenses of the Committee in the manner and subject to the limitations hereinabove provided for delivery and withdrawal of bonds upon modifications hereof materially and adversely affecting depositors.

No party hereto shall be entitled to withdraw from this Agreement or to receive Bonds or coupons or rights to interest transferred or assigned to the Committee, except as in this Agreement expressly provided, but the Committee may at any time require the surrender of any of the instruments issued in respect of any Bonds deposited hereunder and require the holder thereof to accept the Bonds, Coupons or Rights to Interest and Interest in Arrears represented thereby.

TENTH

Duties of Committee and Depositaries

The Committee undertakes to endeavor to carry out the Plan and Agreement and this Agreement, but neither the Committee nor any member thereof, nor any of the Depositaries appointed hereunder, assumes any individual responsibility either for the execution of the Plan and Agreement or this Agreement or any part thereof or for the result of any steps taken or acts done in good faith for the purposes thereof. None of the Depositaries nor the Committee assumes any responsibility or liability as to the genuineness, validity, enforceability or regularity of or title of the Depositor to any of the Bonds or Coupons, Rights to Interest or Interest in Arrears deposited hereunder or subject hereto. None of the Depositaries nor the Committee nor any member thereof shall be liable for any action taken in good faith in the belief that any of the Bonds or any other documents or any signatures are genuine, nor shall the Committee or any member thereof or any of the Depositaries be individually liable for any act or omission of any agent or employee selected in good faith nor for any error of judgment or mistake in fact or law nor in any case except for his, its or their own individual wilful malfeasance or neglect; nor shall the Committee or any member thereof or any of the Depositaries be liable for the acts or defaults of each other.

It is expressly understood and agreed that the Committee shall be under no duty or obligation of any kind to exercise any of the powers or authority hereby granted to it and it shall in no way be responsible to any Bondholder party hereto or otherwise for its failure, refusal or neglect to exercise such powers or authority.

This Agreement shall be terminated on July 1, 1928, unless earlier terminated as herein provided or otherwise. After the termination hereof the Committee shall be discharged of all further duty and obligations to Depositors under this Agreement or otherwise and subsequent to December 31, 1927 shall be under no duty of any kind in event of a failure of the Mexican Government to perform any duties required under the Plan and Agreement to be performed subsequent to December 31, 1927.

ELEVENTH

Committee May at Any Time Terminate Representation of Any Issue

The Committee may in its absolute discretion at any time decline further to represent the depositors of any class or issue of Bonds and the coupons or rights to interest relating thereto, which it has theretofore represented, while continuing to represent the depositors of the remaining classes or issues of Bonds. In such event, the Committee shall publish in the manner prescribed hereinafter a notice specifying the issue of Bonds the depositors of which the Committee declines further to represent and giving to depositors thereof an opportunity of withdrawing them on the terms named in Article Ninth hereof, and at the expiration of four weeks from the first publication of such notice such depositors shall cease to be parties to this Agreement provided however that they may not withdraw their Bonds except on said terms and the Committee will cease to be under any responsibility to represent the deposited Bonds or coupons or rights to interest of the issue so specified in such notice.

TWELFTH

Miscellaneous

(1) *Enumeration of Specific Powers not to Limit General Powers.* The enumeration of specific powers herein conferred shall not be construed to limit or restrict the general powers herein conferred or intended so to be. It is hereby distinctly

declared that it is intended to confer on the Committee in respect to all Bonds and coupons or rights to interest deposited and in all respects any and all powers which the Committee may deem necessary or expedient towards carrying out or promoting the purposes of the Plan and Agreement and of this Agreement in any respect as now existing or as the same may be modified or amended, even though such power be apparently of a character not now contemplated and the Committee may exercise any and every such power as fully and effectively as if the same were herein distinctly specified and as often as for any cause or reason it may deem expedient.

(2) *Powers of Committee Irrevocable.* All powers and authority by this Agreement conferred upon the Committee are hereby declared to be irrevocable and coupled with an interest.

(3) *Invalidity of Part shall not affect Validity of Remainder of Agreement.* The invalidity of one or more phrases, sentences, clauses or paragraphs contained in this Agreement or in the said Plan and Agreement shall not affect the remaining portion of this Agreement or the Plan and Agreement or any part thereof, all the phrases, sentences, clauses or paragraphs of this Agreement and of the Plan and Agreement being inserted conditional on their being held valid and lawful and in the event that any one or more of the phrases, sentences, clauses or paragraphs contained in this Agreement or in the Plan and Agreement should be invalid, this Agreement and the Plan and Agreement shall be construed as if such invalid phrases, sentences, clauses or paragraphs had not been inserted.

(4) *Deposited Securities not Merged or Discharged.* All Bonds and coupons or rights to interest deposited hereunder or subject hereto, shall remain in full force and effect for all purposes not inconsistent with the terms of this Agreement and the Plan and Agreement, and shall not be deemed merged, satisfied, released or discharged by any delivery of Deposit Receipts or Cash Warrants, Scrip Receipts, or Receipts for Interest in Arrears thereagainst, except to the extent that payments may be made thereon or otherwise satisfied as provided in this Agreement.

(5) *Agreement only for Benefit of Parties hereto.* This Agree-

ment shall be construed strictly as among the parties hereto only and as solely affecting and relating to them, and no other person, firm or corporation shall have any right or obligation hereunder. The Plan and Agreement and this Agreement shall bind and benefit the several parties and their and each of their surviving heirs, executors, administrators, successors and assigns.

(6) *Further Assurances by Depositors.* Each depositor for himself and for each and every of his successors in interest in respect of any and all Bonds or coupons or rights to interest to which he has title agrees, at any time and from time to time on demand of the Committee, to execute all such further transfers and assignments and all other instruments as may be required for further evidence of vesting in the Committee or its nominees all the powers herein conferred upon the Committee in respect thereof and agrees to deposit all such transfers and assignments and other instruments with the respective and appropriate Depositaries in the manner and at the time the Committee may designate.

Each Depositor for himself and for each and every of his successors in interest agrees, on demand of the Committee, to execute such releases with respect to the deposited coupons or other rights to interest maturing during the five-year period or for Interest in Arrears as the Committee may require.

In case any Depositor shall at any time fail to execute any instrument or make any delivery or deposit on demand of the Committee within such period of time as the Committee may prescribe, he shall at the election of the Committee forfeit all rights and cease to be entitled to any benefits under the Plan and Agreement or this Agreement.

(7) *Depositors.* The terms Depositor or Depositors as herein used shall mean and include any and all holders of Bonds and coupons or rights to interest or Interest in Arrears who have become parties to this Agreement and their successors in interest including any and all holders of Deposit Receipts, Bonds marked or stamped hereunder, and of Cash Warrants, Scrip Receipts and Receipts for Interest in Arrears issued hereunder.

THIRTEENTH

Publication of Notices and Calls

All calls or notices required to be given hereunder shall be inserted for publication if practicable in one daily newspaper in the City of Mexico, one daily newspaper in the City of New York, one daily newspaper in the City of London, England, one daily newspaper in the City of Paris, France, one daily newspaper in the City of Geneva, Switzerland, one daily newspaper in the City of Brussels, Belgium, and one daily newspaper in the City of Amsterdam, Holland, or any of them, and in such other place or places as the Committee shall determine and shall be published once in each week for four successive weeks beginning on any day of the week. Such calls or notices are not required to be published in the same newspaper, but may be published in different newspapers, provided publication is had in at least one daily newspaper once in each week for four successive weeks. Any call or notice whatsoever when so published by the Committee shall be taken and considered as though personally served on all the holders of Deposit Receipts, marked or stamped Bonds, Cash Warrants, Scrip Receipts and Receipts for Interest in Arrears as of the date of the first publication thereof and such publication shall be the only notice required to be given under any provision of this Agreement. When a call or notice shall have been advertised as above specified, publication shall be complete as regards all parties hereto and no further publication or notice shall be required. The Committee may, however, in its discretion, cause additional publication to be given of any notice in any other newspaper or journal published in said cities or elsewhere than as above specified, as the Committee may determine.

In event that this Agreement or any of the relative Certificates, Receipts, Warrants, or instruments of any nature, or any announcements provided for or contemplated herein shall be printed in any other language or languages than the English language the text of the original of this Agreement or of the relative Certificates, Receipts, Warrants or other instruments in

English as interpreted by the Committee shall govern in all respects.

FOURTEENTH

Execution of Deposit Agreement

It is understood that for convenience this Agreement may be signed by the Committee in several counterparts with like force and effect as though all signatures were upon one part thereof.

Original counterparts of this Agreement shall be signed by the Committee and filed with Bankers Trust Company and Guaranty Trust Company of New York at their respective principal offices in New York City.

By receiving a Deposit Receipt or Cash Warrant, Scrip Receipt or Receipt for Interest in Arrears executed by or on behalf of any of the Depositaries, or any Bond marked or stamped as herein provided, any recipient or holder thereof shall thereby become and be a party to this Agreement and be bound by its provisions with the same force and effect as though actually executing and delivering the same.

The Committee by the execution and delivery of this Agreement is not under any obligation, legal or equitable, expressed or implied, to any person or persons whomsoever other than the holders of Bonds marked or stamped hereunder, Deposit Receipts, Cash Warrants, Scrip Receipts and Receipts for Interest in Arrears issued in accordance with the terms of this Agreement.

In witness whereof, the members of the Committee have subscribed this Agreement and the parties of the first part have deposited their Bonds or Interest in Arrears, all as of the day and year above written.

Executed at New York City, New York, this second day of July, 1923.

		AMOUNTS OUTSTANDING AND TITLES OF ISSUES INCLUDED IN THE PLAN.	First Coupon or unpaid interest included in plan	Se Cla Represen interest ma on the da first defau on and pri
No. 1	£ 9,957,260	Republic of Mexico 5% Consolidated External Gold Loan of 1899	July 1, 1914	Jan. 1,
No. 2	£10,451,160	Republic of Mexico 4% External Gold Loan of 1910..........	July 1, 1914	Jan. 1,
*No. 3	£ 6,000,000	Republic of Mexico 6% 10-year Treasury Notes of 1913........ (Series A £6,000,000)............................	Jan. 1, 1915	Jan. 1,
No. 4	£ 1,385,500	City of Mexico 5% Sterling Loan of 1889.................	Apr. 1, 1914	April 1,
No. 5	$25,000,000	Institution for Encouragement of Irrigation Works and Development of Agriculture (S. A.) 35-year 4½% Sinking Fund Gold Bonds due November 1, 1943 (Caja de Prestamos, etc.).......	May 1, 1914	Nov. 1,
No. 6	$37,037,500	United States of Mexico 4% Gold Bonds of 1904............	June 1, 1914	Dec. 1,
No. 7	P42,383,850	Republic of Mexico Consolidated 3% Internal Debt of 1885.....	June 30, 1914	
No. 8	P92,911,700	United States of Mexico 5% Internal Redeemable Bonds of 1895.	Apr. 1, 1914	
*No. 9	P 831,200	State of Vera Cruz 5% Bonds due April 1, 1927.............	Mar. 31, 1914	Mar. 31,
No. 10	P 664,000	State of Vera Cruz 5% Bonds dated January 1, 1907.........	June 30, 1914	Dec. 31,
No. 11	P 741,500	State of Tamaulipas 5% Bonds dated July 1, 1903...........	Mar. 31, 1914	Mar. 31,
No. 12	P 796,600	State of Tamaulipas 5% Bonds dated January 1, 1907........	June 30, 1914	Dec. 31,
No. 13	P 466,700	State of Sinaloa 5% Bonds dated January 1, 1907............	July 1, 1914	Jan. 1,
No. 14	$50,748,575	National Railways of Mexico Guaranteed General Mortgage 4% 70-year Sinking Fund Redeemable Gold Bonds, due October 1, 1977..	Oct. 1, 1914	April 1,
No. 15	$ 7,000,000	Vera Cruz & Pacific R. R. Co. 1st Mortgage 4½% Gold Bonds due July 1, 1934..	July 1, 1914	Jan. 1,
No. 16	$84,804,115	National Railways of Mexico Prior Lien 4½% 50-year Sinking Fund Redeemable Gold Bonds due July 1, 1957...........	July 1, 1914	Jan. 1,
*No. 17	$23,000,000	National Railroad Co. of Mexico Prior Lien 4½% Gold Bonds due October 1, 1926..	July 1, 1914	Jan. 1,
No. 18	$24,740,000	National Railroad Co. of Mexico 1st Consolidated Mortgage 4% Gold Bonds due October 1, 1951......................	Oct. 1, 1914	April 1,
No. 19	£ 1,200,000	The Mexican International R. R. Co. 4½% Prior Lien Sterling Bonds due September 1, 1947..........................	Sept. 1, 1914	Mar. 1,
No. 20	$ 4,206,500	The Mexican International R. R. Co. 1st Consolidated Mortgage 4% Gold Bonds due September 1, 1977.................	Sept. 1, 1914	Mar. 1,
No. 21	$ 2,003,000	Pan American R. R. Co. 1st Mortgage 5% Gold Bonds due January 1, 1934...	July 1, 1914	Jan. 1,
No. 22	$ 1,484,000	Pan American R. R. Co. General Mortgage 5% Gold Bonds due January 1, 1937.......................................	July 1, 1914	Jan. 1,
No. 23	$ 1,374,000	Mexican Central Railway Co. Ltd., 5% Priority Bonds due July 1, 1939..	July 1, 1914	Jan. 1,
*No. 24		Mexican Central Railway Co. Ltd., 5% Equipment Notes and Certificates:		
	$ 150,000	(A) First Series dated Apr. 1, 1897.....................	Oct. 1, 1914	April 1,
	$ 300,000	(B) Second Series dated Oct. 2, 1899....................	Oct. 1, 1914	April 1,
	$ 109,345	(C) Series No. 8 dated Aug. 17, 1906...................	†	Aug. 17,
	$ 342,000	(D) Series No. 10 dated Jan. 1, 1907..................	July 1, 1914	Jan. 1,
	$ 162,000	(E) Series No. 11 dated Mar. 22, 1907..................	Sept. 22, 1914	Mar. 22,
*No. 25		National Railways of Mexico 6% Secured Gold Notes, maturing up to January 1, 1917:		
	$ 1,509,752	(A) Series "B" dated April 1, 1914....................	Jan. 1, 1917	Jan. 1,
	$ 746,000	(B) 3-months Secured dated Dec. 1, 1913...............	June 1, 1915	Dec. 1,
	$ 2,460,325	(C) 3-year Secured dated Jan. 1, 1914..................	July 1, 1914	Jan. 1,
††	$ 813,055	(D) Series "C" dated June 1, 1914......................	Jan. 1, 1917	Jan. 1,
**No. 26		National Railways of Mexico 6% Secured Notes, maturing up to July 1, 1916:		
†††	$26,730,000	(A) 2-year, due June 1, 1915........................	Dec. 1, 1914	June 1,
	$ 1,403,000	(B) 2-year, due July 1, 1916..........................	July 1, 1916	July 1,
No. 27	£ 1,955,300	Tehuantepec National Railway 5% Gold Loan, due June 30, 1953	July 1, 1918	July 1,
No. 28	£ 385,540	Tehuantepec National Railway 4½% Gold Loan, due June 30, 1953	July 1, 1918	July 1,

*To be extended as provided until January 1, 1933.
**To be extended until January 1, 1933 with interest at 5% per annum during the five year period and 6% per an
†Each August 17 and February 17, from August 17, 1914 to August 17, 1916 inclusive.

SCHED

...st in Arrears — ...PTS — Class "B" — ...epresenting ...erest matured ...ior to Jan. 3, ...3 and on and ...bsequent to	Approximate per cent of total interest in arrears	Percentages of Current Annual Interest to be paid in cash during the Five-Year Period (See Note) — YEAR — First %	Second %	Third %	Fourth %	Fifth %	Depositaries in United States — New York	Depositaries in England — London	De...
...	...	100	100	100	100	100	Chase National Bank	Morgan Grenfell & Co.	Banquede]
...	...	100	100	100	100	100	National City Bank	Morgan Grenfell & Co.	Banquede]
...	...	100	100	100	100	100	U.S. Mortgage & Trust Co.	Morgan Grenfell & Co.	Banquede]
ly 1, 1917	65	50	70	90	100	100	New York Trust Co.	Trustees Corporation Ltd.	
ay 1, 1917	65	60	75	90	100	100	New York Trust Co.	Westminster Bank Ltd.	
ne 1, 1917	65	50	70	90	100	100	Equitable Trust Co.	Westminster Bank Ltd.	Crédit Lyo
ne 30, 1914	100	20	25	35	50	60	Chase National Bank	Glyn, Mills, Currie, Holt & Co.	Crédit Lyo
ril 1, 1914	100	20	25	35	50	60	National City Bank	Glyn, Mills, Currie, Holt & Co.	Crédit Lyo
ne 30, 1917	65	20	25	35	80	100	Equitable Trust Co.	Morgan Grenfell & Co.	
ne 30, 1917	65	20	25	35	80	100	Equitable Trust Co.	Morgan Grenfell & Co.	
ne 30, 1917	65	20	25	35	80	100	Equitable Trust Co.	Morgan Grenfell & Co.	
ne 30, 1917	65	20	25	35	80	100	Equitable Trust Co.	Morgan Grenfell & Co.	
ly 1, 1917	65	20	25	35	80	100	Equitable Trust Co.	Morgan Grenfell & Co.	
t. 1, 1917	65	50	70	90	100	100	New York Trust Co.	Glyn, Mills, Currie, Holt & Co.	BanquedeI
y 1, 1917	65	60	75	90	100	100	Title Guarantee & Trust Co.	Glyn, Mills, Currie, Holt & Co.	
y 1, 1917	65	60	75	90	100	100	Central Union Trust Co.	Glyn, Mills, Currie, Holt & Co.	
y 1, 1917	65	65	85	100	100	100	Central Union Trust Co.	Glyn, Mills, Currie, Holt & Co.	
t. 1, 1917	65	60	75	90	100	100	Central Union Trust Co.	Glyn, Mills, Currie, Holt & Co.	
t. 1, 1917	65	60	75	90	100	100	Central Union Trust Co.	Glyn, Mills, Currie, Holt & Co.	
t. 1, 1917	65	60	75	90	100	100	Metropolitan Trust Co.	Glyn, Mills, Currie, Holt & Co.	
y 1, 1917	65	50	70	90	100	100	Chase National Bank	Glyn, Mills, Currie, Holt & Co.	
y 1, 1917	65	50	70	90	100	100	Chase National Bank	Glyn, Mills, Currie, Holt & Co.	
y 1, 1917	65	65	75	90	100	100	National City Bank	Glyn, Mills, Currie, Holt & Co.	
t. 1, 1917	65	50	65	90	100	100	National City Bank	Glyn, Mills, Currie, Holt & Co.	
t. 1, 1917	65	50	65	90	100	100	National City Bank	Glyn, Mills, Currie, Holt & Co.	
). 17, 1913	65	50	65	90	100	100	National City Bank	Glyn, Mills, Currie, Holt & Co.	
y 1, 1917	65	50	65	90	100	100	National City Bank	Glyn, Mills, Currie, Holt & Co.	
t. 22, 1917	65	50	65	90	100	100	National City Bank	Glyn, Mills, Currie, Holt & Co.	
...	...	100	100	100	100	100	Chase National Bank	Glyn, Mills, Currie, Holt & Co.	
...	...	100	100	100	100	100	Chase National Bank	Glyn, Mills, Currie, Holt & Co.	
...	...	100	100	100	100	100	Chase National Bank	Glyn, Mills, Currie, Holt & Co.	
...	...	100	100	100	100	100	Chase National Bank	Glyn, Mills, Currie, Holt & Co.	
c. 1, 1917	65	60	75	90	100	100	Central Union Trust Co.	Glyn, Mills, Currie, Holt & Co.	
n. 1, 1918	65	60	75	90	100	100	National City Bank	Glyn, Mills, Currie, Holt & Co.	
n. 1, 1920	65	30	40	50	60	70	New York Trust Co.	Glyn, Mills, Currie, Holt & Co.	
n. 1, 1920	65	30	40	50	60	70	New York Trust Co.	Glyn, Mills, Currie, Holt & Co.	

*Face amount of the Notes actually $158,456 wl
††Equivalent of $4,083.29 + £4,062,000 at 4.86
†††Equivalent of $160,694.05 + £121,860 at 4.86

ULE

epositaries in France	Depositaries in Holland	Depositaries in Switzerland		
Paris	Amsterdam	Geneva	Zurich	Basle
Paris et des Pays-Bas	Lippmann, Rosenthal & Co.	Banque de Paris et des Pays-Bas	Credit Suisse	Société de Banq
Paris et des Pays-Bas	Amsterdamsche Succursale der Banque de Paris et des Pays-Bas	Banque de Paris et des Pays-Bas	Crédit Suisse	Société de Banq
Paris et des Pays-Bas	Lippmann, Rosenthal & Co.	Banque de Paris et des Pays-Bas	Crédit Suisse	Société de Banq
None	Hope & Co.	Banque de Paris et des Pays-Bas	Crédit Suisse	Sociéte de Banq
None	Teixeira de Mattos Bros.	Crédit Suisse	Crédit Suisse	Société de Banq
nnais	Teixeira de Mattos Bros.	Crédit Suisse	Crédit Suisse	Sociéte de Banq
nnais	Alsberg, Goldberg & Co.	Crédit Lyonnais	Crédit Suisse	Société de Banq
nnais	Alsberg, Goldberg & Co.	Crédit Lyonnais	Crédit Suisse	Société de Banq
None	Alsberg, Goldberg & Co.	Banque de Paris et des Pays-Bas	Crédit Suisse	Société de Banq
None	Hope & Co.	Banque de Paris et des Pays-Bas	Crédit Suisse	Société de Banq
None	Hope & Co.	Banque de Paris et des Pays-Bas	Crédit Suisse	Société de Banq
None	Hope & Co.	Banque de Paris et des Pays-Bas	Crédit Suisse	Société de Banq
None	Alsberg, Goldberg & Co.	Banque de Paris et des Pays-Bas	Crédit Suisse	Société de Banq
Paris et des Pays-Bas	Hope & Co.	G. Pictet & Co.	Crédit Suisse	Société de Banq
None	Teixeira de Mattos Bros.	G. Pictet & Co.	Crédit Suisse	Société de Banq
None	Hope & Co.	G. Pictet & Co.	Crédit Suisse	Société de Banq
None	Teixeira de Mattos Bros.	G. Pictet & Co.	Crédit Suisse	Société de Banq
None	Teixeira de Mattos Bros.	G. Pictet & Co.	Crédit Suisse	Société de Banq
None	Teixeira de Mattos Bros.	G. Pictet & Co.	Crédit Suisse	Société de Banq
None	Hope & Co.	G. Pictet & Co.	Crédit Suisse	Société de Banq
None	Hope & Co.	G. Pictet & Co.	Crédit Suisse	Société de Banq
None	Hope & Co.	G. Pictet & Co.	Crédit Suisse	Société de Banq
None	Hope & Co.	G. Pictet & Co.	Crédit Suisse	Société de Banq
None	Hope & Co.	G. Pictet & Co.	Crédit Suisse	Société de Banq
None	Hope & Co.	G. Pictet & Co.	Crédit Suisse	Société de Banq
None	Hope & Co.	G. Pictet & Co.	Crédit Suisse	Société de Banq
None	Hope & Co.	G. Pictet & Co.	Crédit Suisse	Société de Banq
None	Hope & Co.	G. Pictet & Co.	Crédit Suisse	Société de Banq
None	Hope & Co.	G. Pictet & Co.	Crédit Suisse	Société de Banq
None	Hope & Co.	G. Pictet & Co.	Crédit Suisse	Société de Banq
None	Hope & Co.	G. Pictet & Co.	Crédit Suisse	Société de Banq
None	Hope & Co.	G. Pictet & Co.	Crédit Suisse	Société de Banq
None	Hope & Co.	G. Pictet & Co.	Crédit Suisse	Société de Banq
None	Hope & Co.	G. Pictet & Co.	Crédit Suisse	Société de Banq
None	Hope & Co.	G. Pictet & Co.	Crédit Suisse	Société de Banq
None	Hope & Co.	G. Pictet & Co.	Crédit Suisse	Société de Banq

hich includes $49,111 interest.
+ M. 8,416,938 at 20.40 to the £ Sterling.
+ M. 252,508.14 at 4.20 to the Dollar.

NOTE: The
dealt with in sc

Depositaries in Belgium		Depositaries in Germany	
Brussels	Antwerp	Berlin	Frankfort-on-the-Main
é Générale de Belgique	Banque d'Anvers	S. Bleichroder	None
é Générale de Belgique	Banque d'Anvers	S. Bleichroder	None
Anversois	Crédit Anversois	S. Bleichroder	None
e de Bruxelles	Banque Centrale Anversoise	None	None
Anversois	Crédit Anversois	Deutsche Bank	Lazard Speyer-Ellissen
Anversois	Crédit Anversois	Deutsche Bank	Lazard Speyer-Ellissen
e de Bruxelles	Banque Centrale Anversoise	None	Deutsche Effecten und Wechsel Bank
e de Bruxelles	Banque Centrale Anversoise	None	Deutsche Effecten und Wechsel Bank
Anversois	Crédit Anversois	None	None
Anversois	Crédit Anversois	None	None
e de Bruxelles	Banque Centrale Anversoise	None	Deutsche Effecten und Wechsel Bank
e de Bruxelles	Banque Centrale Anversoise	None	Deutsche Effecten und Wechsel Bank
e de Bruxelles	Banque Centrale Anversoise	None	None
é Générale de Belgique	Banque d'Anvers	Berliner Handelsgesellschaft	None
e de Bruxelles	Banque Centrale Anversoise	None	Lazard Speyer-Ellissen
é Générale de Belgique	Banque d'Anvers	Berliner Handelsgesellschaft	None
é Générale de Beligque	Banque d'Anvers	Deutsche Bank	Lazard Speyer-Ellissen
é Générale de Belgique	Banque d'Anvers	None	Lazard Speyer-Ellissen
e de Bruxelles	Banque Centrale Anversoise	None	Lazard Speyer-Ellissen
e de Bruxelles	Banque Centrale Anversoise	None	Lazard Speyer-Ellissen
Anversois	Crédit Anversois	Berliner Handelsgesellschaft	None
Anversois	Crédit Anversois	Berliner Handelsgesellschaft	None
e de Bruxelles	Banque Centrale Anversoise	Berliner Handelsgesellschaft	None
e de Bruxelles	Banque Centrale Anversoise	Berliner Handelsgesellschaft	None
e de Bruxelles	Banque Centrale Anversoise	Berliner Handelsgesellschaft	None
e de Bruxelles	Banque Centrale Anversoise	Berliner Handelsgesellschaft	None
e de Bruxelles	Banque Centrale Anversoise	Berliner Handelsgesellschaft	None
e de Bruxelles	Banque Centrale Anversoise	Berliner Handelsgesellschaft	None
é Génerale de Belgique	Banque d'Anvers	None	Lazard Speyer-Ellissen
é Générale de Belgique	Banque d'Anvers	None	Lazard Speyer-Ellissen
é Générale de Belgique	Banque d'Anvers	None	Lazard Speyer-Ellissen
é Générale de Belgique	Banque d'Anvers	None	Lazard Speyer-Ellissen
é Générale de Belgique	Banque d'Anvers	Berliner Handelsgesellschaft	None
é Générale de Belgique	Banque d'Anvers	Berliner Handelsgesellschaft	None
Anversois	Crédit Anversois	Dresdner Bank	None
Anversois	Crédit Anversois	Dresdner Bank	None

en the face amounts of interest due and the percentages shown herein to be paid in cash on the various issues, are to be
).)

APPENDIX IX

AGREEMENT BETWEEN THE MEXICAN GOVERNMENT
AND THE
INTERNATIONAL COMMITTEE OF BANKERS ON MEXICO

Modifying and Supplementing
the Agreement dated June 16, 1922

AGREEMENT, between the Government of the United States of Mexico, (hereinafter called the Government), and the International Committee of Bankers on Mexico, (hereinafter called the Committee), in modification of and supplemental to the Plan and Agreement dated June 16, 1922, (hereinafter called the Agreement).

WHEREAS the Government states that because of the exceptional drain on its financial and economic resources caused by the outbreak of a revolt subsequent to the execution and ratification of the Agreement, it has found itself obliged to suspend temporarily the enforcement of the Agreement;

AND WHEREAS the Government also states that for the further security of the Bondholders it deems it unwise to resume payments upon its obligations, due or overdue, as scheduled in the Agreement, unless modification of the Agreement is made as hereinafter set forth, with the purpose of limiting the said obligations to the actual financial capacity of the Government to make provision for them;

AND WHEREAS the Government further states that the most effective and equitable way of accomplishing that purpose is to amend the provision in said Agreement with regard to the return of the National Railways of Mexico, (hereinafter called the Railways), to private management by defining the Government's liability with respect to such Railways' obligations, (Schedule "A" hereto attached), guaranteed by the terms of the Agreement as hereinafter set forth, and by segregating them as provided herein from the other obligations, hereinafter referred to as the Direct

Debt, (Schedule " B " hereto attached), mentioned in the schedule attached to and made a part of the Agreement;

AND WHEREAS the Government further states that it is necessary that the terms of the Caja de Prestamos Bonds, dated November 2, 1908, and the provisions of the Agreement in regard thereto, be amended as hereinafter set forth;

AND WHEREAS the Committee, in order to reach a basis which in the expressed judgment of the Government will enable the Government to resume the service on the bonds deposited under the Agreement, is prepared to recommend to the depositors under the Agreement and the Deposit Agreement of July 1, 1922, that they accept the following amendments of the Agreement which have been urged by His Excellency, the Minister of Finance, in behalf of the Government;

THEREFORE, the following amendments of the Agreement have been agreed to by the Minister of Finance and by the Committee, (subject to approval by its European Sections), and immediately upon ratification of this amended Agreement by the President and Congress of the United States of Mexico, the Committee will endeavor to obtain acceptance thereof by the Depositors under the Agreement and the Deposit Agreement of July 1, 1922.

SECTION 1 — ARREARS OF INTEREST, Third Paragraph is amended to read as follows:

1. The coupons for interest attached to the bonds are to be detached (if permitted by the various mortgages and indentures) and deposited with some trustee satisfactory to the Committee who will issue receipts or certificates to the bondholders for the face amount of coupons so detached. If for any reason the coupons cannot be detached from the bonds, some other plan for effecting the above arrangement satisfactory to the Committee shall be adopted. If there are any bonds to which coupons representing any back interest have never been attached the Mexican Government will supply such coupons for the purposes of these bonds so that the bondholders may be able to deposit them.

2. The Government is to provide for the retirement of the Arrears of Interest Receipts or Certificates issued with respect to the Direct Debt, such Interest in Arrears Receipts aggregating $108,346,230. Discharge of this liability is to be made by payments beginning January 1, 1928, of $2,708,656 annually which payments shall continue until the complete retirement of such Receipts or until provision has been made therefor.

3. The Railways are to provide for the retirement of the Arrears of Interest Receipts or Certificates issued with respect to the Railways' Debt, such interest in Arrears Receipts or Certificates aggregating $98,526,963. Discharge of this liability is to be made by payments out of earnings in excess of fixed charges beginning January 1, 1928 of $2,463,174 annually which payments shall continue until the complete retirement of such Receipts or until provision has been made therefor.

4. Nevertheless, such payments by the Government and by the Railways will be used by the Depositary designated by the Committee, for the retirement of any of the Arrears of Interest Receipts or Certificates issued under the Agreement, but nothing herein contained shall be construed as in any way affecting the separate obligations of the Government and the Railways, as above stated. Such Receipts shall be cancelled upon payment. As soon as practical after complete retirement of all Arrears of Interest Receipts or Certificates, such depositary will surrender the coupons held by the Guaranty Trust Company of New York, as custodian of Arrears of Interest coupons, in cancelled form, to the Government and to the Railways, respectively.

SECTION 4 — CURRENT INTEREST.

Paragraph (a) is amended by adding at the end thereof the following:

The 1924 and 1925 minimum funds are to be deferred and liquidated with interest at the rate of 3% per annum from January 1, 1928 to the respective dates of payment, in accordance with Schedule "C" attached hereto.

Paragraph (c) is amended to read as follows:

1. The entire oil export taxes as provided for in the Decree of June 7, 1921 and any increases thereof, and the specific sum of $5,000,000 U. S. gold annually, payable in equal monthly instalments of $416,667 each out of the oil production taxes, are to be paid to the Financial Agency of the Mexican Government in the City of New York, for account of the Committee, and immediately upon receipt by such Financial Agency are to be remitted to the depositary designated by the Committee, to the credit of the Committee.

2. Payments of the said oil export and oil production taxes shall begin with all collections made on and after January 1, 1926. All such payments in excess of the following amounts:

$10,692,845 U. S. gold and the additional sum of
$1,500,000 U. S. gold in 1926
$11,011,901 U. S. gold and the additional sum of
$1,500,000 U. S. gold in 1927

shall be returned by the Committee to the Government.

3. All such funds received by the Committee are to be credited against the Government's obligation for current interest on its Direct Debt under the Agreement as herein modified, and are to be distributed to assenting bondholders in accordance with the schedule provided for in the Agreement, or, if not required for that purpose, used as provided in paragraph 5 of Section 4 below, in such manner and at such times as the Committee may determine.

4. In the event of a deficiency in any six months' period in the gold equivalent received by the Committee from the sum of (*a*) the oil export tax plus (*b*) the $416,667 U. S. gold monthly payable out of the production tax in respect of the amount required for the service on the Direct Debt during such six months' period according to such schedule provided for in the Agreement, the Government hereby covenants that such deficiency is to be paid by the Government at the end of each six months' period, out of production taxes, or if necessary other Government revenues or resources.

5. Any sums received by the Committee for current interest in excess of the requirements for interest on the bonds included in the schedule attached to the Agreement, (whether such excess over interest requirements according to such schedule arises: (*a*) out of receipts from the oil taxes in excess of such requirements of the Direct Debt, or (*b*) from the net earnings of the Railways, as provided in Section 5, paragraph 3, in excess of such requirements of the obligations of the Railways), may be utilized in the discretion of the Committee, in paying overdue Cash Warrants or in retiring any of the Current Interest Scrip.

Paragraph (f) is eliminated.

Paragraph (g) is amended to read as follows:

If during the period prior to the full resumption of the service on the Debt, *i. e.*, January 1, 1928, the Government diminishes the rates of export and production taxes on oil so that the revenues from these sources are less than the amounts agreed to be remitted for the service of the Direct Debt as set forth in sub-paragraph 2 of paragraph (*c*) hereinabove, the Government will forthwith make up any deficiency.

Paragraph (h) is amended to read as follows:

After the expiration of the period of five years, *i. e.*, on January 1, 1928, the Government will resume the full service of the Direct Debt according to the original contracts.

SECTION 5—NATIONAL RAILWAYS SYSTEM.

Nothing herein contained shall be construed as in any way modifying the guarantees of the Government existing prior to June 16, 1922, with respect to the Railways' Debt included in the Agreement.

Section 5 is amended to read as follows:

1. The Government agrees to return the Railways on December 31, 1925, to private management under conditions which under efficient operation will enable the Railways to earn their

full fixed charges (which are now approximately $11,279,695 U. S. gold annually), in accordance with the expressed judgment of the Executive President-elect of the Railways, prior to the date of such return. The rates in force on the date the Railways are returned to private management, shall not be reduced unless and until modified by recommendation of the Tariff Commission hereinafter mentioned.

2. Any revenues received by the Railways in respect of transactions on or prior to December 31, 1925 shall be remitted to the Government. The Government assumes the responsibility for payment of all salaries and wages due or accrued in respect of any period ending on or prior to December 31, 1925.

3. Beginning January 1, 1926, the entire net revenues of the Railways as available shall be remitted each month by the Executive President of the Railways directly to the Committee, at its office in New York, for the purpose of satisfying Cash Warrants issued in respect of the Railways' Debt subject to the Agreement, and any surplus over the amount thus required shall be utilized, as provided in sub-paragraph 5 of paragraph (*c*) of Section 4, as herein amended, in the discretion of the Committee in paying overdue Cash Warrants or in retiring Current Interest Scrip issued under the Agreement.

4. Beginning January 1, 1928, the Railways will set aside, out of earnings in excess of fixed charges, the sum of $2,463,174 U. S. gold per annum, toward the fund to retire Interest in Arrears Receipts or Certificates as hereinabove specified in Section 1 as amended.

5. A Commission of three members, to be known as Commission of Efficiency, shall be appointed as follows: one member by the Government, one by the Board of Directors of the Railways and the third by agreement between the Government and the Board of Directors. The member of the Commission nominated by the Government to be compensated by the Government and the member nominated by the Board of Directors to be compensated by the Railways. The compensation of the third member to be paid equally by the Government and the Railways. This Commission shall decide within the period between Janu-

ary 1, 1926 and December 31, 1928 what adjustments with respect to wages, expenses or tariffs, if any, are necessary, in order to enable the Railways to efficiently earn fixed charges, and before January 1, 1928, the additional amount required to retire Interest in Arrears Receipts as provided in Section 1.

6. A Tariff Commission composed of three members shall be appointed and compensated in a similar way to the Commission of Efficiency, in order to adjust Tariff Schedules for the Railways. Upon the submission of such schedules by this Commission they shall be immediately made effective by the Government. Pending the report of such Tariff Commission no reduction in tariff rates shall be made which, in the judgment of the Executive President, will adversely affect the Railways' ability to meet their full fixed charges plus their contribution to the fund to retire Interest in Arrears Receipts.

7. If any act of the Government during the period ending November 30, 1928 adversely affects the earning capacity of the Railways the Government agrees to permit the Railways to increase their rates to an amount sufficient to insure the Railways earning the sums above specified in paragraph 1, or to pay to the Railways at the end of each six months' period any amount by which the Railways' net earnings are less than their full fixed charges during that period.

8. Notwithstanding the provisions in paragraph (*c*) of Section 4, sub-paragraph 5 of the Agreement, as amended, the Committee will return to the Government any excess, (up to the amount so paid by the Government under paragraph 7 of this Section 5), by which the sum of (*a*) the amount so paid, plus (*b*) the Railways' net earnings, exceeds the Railways' fixed charges for the calendar year in respect of which the payment was made.

9. A Valuation of Damages Commission of three experts shall determine the amount of damages suffered by the Railways during the period of Government control and operation. This commission shall be appointed as follows: one member by the Government, one by the Committee and the third by agreement between the Government and the Committee. The member of the Commission nominated by the Government shall be compensated

by the Government and the member nominated by the Committee shall be compensated by the Railways. The compensation of the third member shall be paid equally by the Government and the Railways. Such claim for damages is to be gradually liquidated by the use of part of the 10% Railways' tax on gross revenues as hereinafter set forth in paragraph 10.

10. The 10% tax on gross revenues of the Railways shall continue and shall be used by the Executive President for the following purposes:

(*a*) pursuant to agreement with the creditors of the Railways for the gradual liquidation of the floating debt of the Railways (which shall continue as a liability of the Government);

(*b*) for the rehabilitation of the Railways up to the amount of damages as determined by the commission of experts, provided for in paragraph 9; and

(*c*) for the gradual liquidation of any debts of the character of loss or damage claims or claims for refunds of charges accrued or accruing on December 31, 1925, which claims shall be a liability of the Government.

11. When the proceeds of said 10% tax are no longer required for the purposes stipulated above in 10, they shall be applied, as provided in sub-paragraph 5 of paragraph (*c*) of Section 4, toward the retirement of the Current Interest Scrip issued under the Agreement, and the said 10% tax shall continue until all such Current Interest Scrip has been retired or provision made therefor.

12. Until after December 31, 1928, the liens created on the properties of the Railways by the present mortgages and indentures in favor of the Railways' securities now outstanding are not to be enforced, nor are any rights of action arising from defaults thereunder to be exercised or other notice taken of such defaults unless the Government is in default in its obligations under the Agreement as herein amended.

13. For all amounts paid or provided to be paid by the Mexican Government on account of the Railways' obligations under this Agreement as amended the Government will be a creditor of the Railways in the same manner as is provided in the Executive

Decree and Plan of Readjustment and Union of the Mexican Central Railway Co., Ltd., and National Railroad Company of Mexico with respect of payments made on account of its guarantee of the General Mortgage 4% bonds of the National Railways of Mexico.

A new section is added to the Agreement as follows:

10 — CAJA DE PRESTAMOS BONDS.

The Government shall create a new issue of its direct obligations having a maturity and provisions for interest payments and sinking fund identical with those of Caja de Prestamos Bonds dated November 2, 1908. The Government shall deposit such obligations with the Committee for the purpose of exchange for the Caja de Prestamos Bonds deposited with the Committee and listed as No. 5 on the schedule attached to the said June 16, 1922 Agreement, and the Government shall issue to the New York Trust Co., New York, the Trustee for the Caja de Prestamos Bonds, $5,000,000 (U. S. gold) Mexican Government non-interest bearing Treasury Notes maturing $50,000 monthly, beginning February 1, 1926, the proceeds of such Treasury Notes to be used in buying in the open market, on behalf and for the benefit of the Government, the Caja de Prestamos Bonds or the new obligations issued in exchange therefor at a price which, except pursuant to a subsequent understanding between the Government and Messrs. Speyer & Co., shall be not in excess of 56% of their par value and interest. All Caja de Prestamos Bonds or the new obligations of the Government so purchased are to be cancelled forthwith as acquired. In consideration of such exchange and upon the delivery of the new obligations and the Treasury Notes as provided above, the Caja de Prestamos is to surrender to the Government its holdings of lands, mortgages and all other properties as of October 13, 1925, and shall execute such contracts of transfer as shall make such plan effective. Such new obligations issued in exchange for the Caja de Prestamos Bonds shall participate in the benefits of and shall be subject to the Agreement as hereby modified in lieu of the Bonds for which they are to be exchanged.

Except as herein modified, the Agreement remains in full force and effect.

This Agreement in modification of and supplemental to the Agreement ratified by the President and the Congress of the United States of Mexico as set forth in the Decree of the President, dated September 29, 1922, is subject to similar ratification by the President and the Congress of the United States of Mexico.

Dated October 23, 1925.

THE GOVERNMENT OF THE UNITED STATES OF MEXICO
by
(Signed) A. J. PANI,
Minister of Finance.

INTERNATIONAL COMMITTEE OF BANKERS ON MEXICO
by
(Signed) THOMAS W. LAMONT,
Chairman.

(Signed) IRA H. PATCHIN,
Secretary.

SCHEDULE "A"

$50,748,575 National Railways of Mexico Guaranteed General Mortgage 4% 70 Year Sinking Fund Redeemable Gold Bonds, due October 1, 1977

$7,000,000 Vera Cruz & Pacific R. R. Co. 1st Mortgage 4½% Gold Bonds due July 1, 1934

$84,804,115 National Railways of Mexico Prior Lien 4½% 50 Year Sinking Fund Redeemable Gold Bonds due July 1, 1957

$23,000,000 National Railroad Co. of Mexico Prior Lien 4½% Gold Bonds due October 1, 1926

$24,740,000 National Railroad Co. of Mexico 1st Consolidated Mortgage 4% Gold Bonds due October 1, 1951

£1,200,000 The Mexican International R. R. Co. 4½% Prior Lien Sterling Bonds due September 1, 1947

$4,206,500 The Mexican International R. R. Co. 1st Consolidated Mortgage 4% Gold Bonds due September 1, 1977

$2,003,000 Pan American R. R. Co. 1st Mortgage 5% Gold Bonds due January 1, 1934

$1,484,000 Pan American R. R. Co. General Mortgage 5% Gold Bonds due January 1, 1937

$1,374,000 Mexican Central Railway Co. Ltd., 5% Priority Bonds due July 1, 1939

Mexican Central Railway Co. Ltd., 5% Equipment Notes and Certificates:

$150,000	(A) First Series dated April 1, 1897
$300,000	(B) Second Series dated Oct. 2, 1899
$55,434*	(C) Series No. 8 dated Aug. 17, 1906
$342,000	(D) Series No. 10 dated Jan. 1, 1907
$58,590*	(E) Series No. 11 dated Mar. 22, 1907

National Railways of Mexico 6% Secured Gold Notes, maturing up to January 1, 1917:

$1,509,752	(A) Series "B" dated April 1, 1914
$746,000	(B) 3 Months Secured dated Dec. 1, 1913
$2,460,325	(C) 3 Year Secured dated Jan. 1, 1914
$813,055	(D) Series "C" dated June 1, 1914

National Railways of Mexico 6% Secured Notes, maturing up to July 1, 1916:

$26,730,000	(A) 2 Year, due June 1, 1915
$1,403,000	(B) 2 Year, due July 1, 1916

£1,918,600 Tehuantepec National Railway 5% Gold Loan, due June 30, 1953

£381,800 Tehuantepec National Railway 4½% Gold Loan, due June 30, 1953

* Represents unpaid interest on Notes.

SCHEDULE "B"

£9,957,260 Republic of Mexico 5% Consolidated External Gold Loan of 1899

£10,451,160 Republic of Mexico 4% External Gold Loan of 1910

£6,000,000 Republic of Mexico 6% 10 Year Treasury Notes of 1913, (Series A £6,000,000)

£1,385,500 City of Mexico 5% Sterling Loan of 1889
$25,000,000 Institution for Encouragement of Irrigation Works and Development of Agriculture (S. A.) 35 Year 4½% Sinking Fund Gold Bonds due November 1, 1943 (Caja de Prestamos, etc.)
$37,037,500 United States of Mexico 4% Gold Bonds of 1904
P41,796,250 Republic of Mexico Consolidated 3% Internal Debt of 1885
P94,298,200 United States of Mexico 5% Internal Redeemable Bonds of 1895
P831,200 State of Vera Cruz 5% Bonds due April 1, 1927
P664,000 State of Vera Cruz 5% Bonds dated January 1, 1907
P741,500 State of Tamaulipas 5% Bonds dated July 1, 1903
P796,600 State of Tamaulipas 5% Bonds dated January 1, 1907
P466,700 State of Sinaloa 5% Bonds dated January 1, 1907

SCHEDULE "C"

Year	Last day of	Principal outstanding	Principal payable	Interest @ 3% per Annum payable	Total payable
1928	January	$37,500,000.	$312,500.	$93,750.	$406,250.
	February ...	37,187,500.	312,500.	92,969.	405,469.
	March	36,875,000.	312,500.	92,187.	404,687.
	April	36,562,500.	312,500.	91,406.	403,906.
	May	36,250,000.	312,500.	90,625.	403,125.
	June	35,937,500.	312,500.	89,844.	402,344.
	July	35,625,000.	312,500.	89,062.	401,562.
	August	35,312,500.	312,500.	88,281.	400,781.
	September ..	35,000,000.	312,500.	87,500.	400,000.
	October	34,687,500.	312,500.	86,718.	399,218.
	November ..	34,375,000.	312,500.	85,937.	398,437.
	December ..	34,062,500.	312,500.	85,156.	397,656.
			$3,750,000.	$1,073,435.	$4,823,435.
1929	January	$33,750,000.	$312,500.	$84,375.	$396,875.
	February ...	33,437,500.	312,500.	83,594.	396,094.
	March	33,125,000.	312,500.	82,813.	395,313.
	April	32,812,500.	312,500.	82,031.	394,531.
	May	32,500,000.	312,500.	81,250.	393,750.
	June	32,187,500.	312,500.	80,469.	392,969.
	July	31,875,000.	312,500.	79,687.	392,187.
	August	31,562,500.	312,500.	78,906.	391,406.

FORWARD

Year	Last day of	Principal outstanding	Principal payable	Interest @ 3% per Annum payable	Total payable
	September ..	31,250,000.	312,500.	78,125.	390,625.
	October	30,937,500.	312,500.	77,344.	389,844.
	November ..	30,625,000.	312,500.	76,562.	389,062.
	December ..	30,312,500.	312,500.	75,781.	388,281.
			$3,750,000.	$960,937.	$4,710,937.
1930	January	$30,000,000.	$312,500.	$75,000.	$387,500.
	February ...	29,687,500.	312,500.	74,219.	386,719.
	March	29,375,000.	312,500.	73,438.	385,938.
	April	29,062,500.	312,500.	72,656.	385,156.
	May	28,750,000.	312,500.	71,875.	384,375.
	June	28,437,500.	312,500.	71,094.	383,594.
	July	28,125,000.	312,500.	70,312.	382,812.
	August	27,812,500.	312,500.	69,531.	382,031.
	September ..	27,500,000.	312,500.	68,750.	381,250.
	October	27,187,500.	312,500.	67,969.	380,469.
	November ..	26,875,000.	312,500.	67,187.	379,687.
	December ..	26,562,500.	312,500.	66,406.	378,906.
			$3,750,000.	$848,437.	$4,598,437.
1931	January	$26,250,000.	$390,625.	$65,625.	$456,250.
	February ...	25,859,375.	390,625.	64,648.	455,273.
	March	25,468,750.	390,625.	63,672.	454,297.
	April	25,078,125.	390,625.	62,695.	453,320.
	May	24,687,500.	390,625.	61,719.	452,344.
	June	24,296,875.	390,625.	60,742.	451,367.
	July	23,906,250.	390,625.	59,766.	450,391.
	August	23,515,625.	390,625.	58,789.	449,414.
	September ..	23,125,000.	390,625.	57,812.	448,437.
	October	22,734,375.	390,625.	56,836.	447,461.
	November ..	22,343,750.	390,625.	55,859.	446,484.
	December ..	21,953,125.	390,625.	54,883.	445,508.
			$4,687,500.	$723,046.	$5,410,546.
1932	January	$21,562,500.	$390,625.	$53,906.	$444,531.
	February ...	21,171,875.	390,625.	52,930.	443,555.
	March	20,781,250.	390,625.	51,953.	442,578.
	April	20,390,625.	390,625.	50,977.	441,602.
	May	20,000,000.	390,625.	50,000.	440,625.
	June	19,609,375.	390,625.	49,023.	439,648.
	July	19,218,750.	390,625.	48,047.	438,672.
	August	18,828,125.	390,625.	47,070.	437,695.
	September ..	18,437,500.	390,625.	46,094.	436,719.
	October	18,046,875.	390,625.	45,117.	435,742.

FORWARD

Year	day of Last	Principal outstanding	Principal payable	Interest @ 3% per Annum payable	Total payable
	November ..	17,656,250.	390,625.	44,141.	434,766.
	December ..	17,265,625.	390,625.	43,164.	433,789.
			$4,687,500.	$582,422.	$5,269,922.
1933	January	$16,875,000.	$390,625.	$42,188.	$432,813.
	February ...	16,484,375.	390,625.	41,211.	431,836.
	March	16,093,750.	390,625.	40,234.	430,859.
	April	15,703,125.	390,625.	39,258.	429,883.
	May	15,312,500.	390,625.	38,281.	482,906.
	June	14,921,875.	390,625.	37,305.	427,930.
	July	14,531,250.	390,625.	36,328.	426,953.
	August	14,140,625.	390,625.	35,352.	425,977.
	September ..	13,750,000.	390,625.	34,375.	425,000.
	October	13,359,375.	390,625.	33,398.	424,023.
	November ..	12,968,750.	390,625.	32,422.	423,047.
	December ..	12,578,125.	390,625.	31,445.	422,070.
			$4,687,500.	$441,797.	$5,129,297.
1934	January	$12,187,500.	$468,750.	$30,469.	$499,219.
	February ...	11,718,750.	468,750.	29,297.	498,047.
	March	11,250,000.	468,750.	28,125.	496,875.
	April	10,781,250.	468,750.	26,953.	495,703.
	May	10,312,500.	468,750.	25,781.	494,531.
	June	9,843,750.	468,750.	24,609.	493,359.
	July	9,375,000.	468,750.	23,438.	492,188.
	August	8,906,250.	468,750.	22,265.	491,015.
	September ..	8,437,500.	468,750.	21,094.	489,844.
	October	7,968,750.	468,750.	19,922.	488,672.
	November ..	7,500,000.	468,750.	18,750.	487,500.
	December ..	7,031,250.	468,750.	17,578.	486,328.
			$5,625,000.	$288,281.	$5,913,281.
1935	January	$6,562,500.	$546,875.	$16,406.	$563,281.
	February ...	6,015,625.	546,875.	15,039.	561,914.
	March	5,468,750.	546,875.	13,672.	560,547.
	April	4,921,875.	546,875.	12,305.	559,180.
	May	4,375,000.	546,875.	10,937.	557,812.
	June	3,828,125.	546,875.	9,570.	556,445.
	July	3,281,250.	546,875.	8,203.	555,078.
	August	2,734,375.	546,875.	6,836.	553,711.
	September ..	2,187,500.	546,875.	5,469.	552,344.
	October	1,640,625.	546,875.	4,102.	550,977.
	November ..	1,093,750.	546,875.	2,734.	549,609.
	December ..	546,875.	546,875.	1,367.	548,242.
			$6,562,500.	$106,640.	$6,669,140.

SCHEDULE "C" *Continued.*

RECAPITULATION

Year	Principal payable	Interest payable	Total payable
1928........	$3,750,000.	$1,073,435.	$4,823,435.
1929........	3,750,000.	960,937.	4,710,937.
1930........	3,750,000.	848,437.	4,598,437.
1931........	4,687,500.	723,046.	5,410,546.
1932........	4,687,500.	582,422.	5,269,922.
1933........	4,687,500.	441,797.	5,129,297.
1934........	5,625,000.	288,281.	5,913,281.
1935........	6,562,500.	106,640.	6,669,140.
	$37,500,000.	$5,024,995.	$42,524,995.

APPENDIX X

THE LAW OF JANUARY 25, 1929[1]

Article I. The Federal Executive shall proceed to the settlement of the obligations of an internal character which the Mexican Government may have on the date of the present law in accordance with the following bases:

1. A Commission shall be established to verify all the obligations against the Nation presented under the terms fixed by the respective Regulations, and, when the nature and amount of such obligations shall have been determined, the Executive, in view of the draft which the Commission shall present him to this end, shall submit to the Honorable Federal Congress a bill providing for the payment of the aforesaid obligations. The Commission shall be composed of a President, who shall be the Minister of Finance, and three members appointed by the same official.

The Executive shall issue the laws and regulations necessary to carry out the verification of the obligations submitted to the Commission and to fix the periods within which they must be presented or shall be prescribed.

With the exception of the Mixed Commissions, all Claims Commissions functioning shall be suppressed.

2. From the date of the promulgation of this law, payments shall be suspended on the aforesaid obligations of an internal nature with the exception of those mentioned below, upon which payments shall continue in accordance with the respective laws or contracts, with only such changes as, in the judgment of the Executive, may be imposed by the paying capacity of the Republic:

(1) Obligations contracted within the respective budget allotment but not covered in the corresponding fiscal year.

[1] *Diario Oficial,* February 4, 1929, pp. 1–3.

(2) Participations in imposts, duties and collections which the Federal Government effects.

(3) Revenues unduly received.

(4) Advances on account of imposts and short term banking loans.

(5) Public Agrarian Debt created by law of January 10, 1920, to the amount authorized by the same law.

(6) Banking Debt, providing the creditor institutions agree that the respective conventions shall be modified to meet the paying capacity.

(7) Obligations derived from contracts for irrigation works under construction.

(8) Obligations derived from the contract of September 10, 1925.[2]

Payments made in contravention of this provision shall entail the responsibility, according to the laws which may be issued by the Executive, of the official authorizing them and of the officials and employees executing them.

Article II. Indemnities for agrarian expropriations declared to have been lawful under the existing laws and not covered by bonds of the issue authorized by the law of January 10, 1920, shall be covered in the manner prescribed by the law which the Congress will issue at the suggestion of the Executive and in accordance with the report of the Commission charged with the settlement of the Internal Debt.

Article III. To the end of unifying the obligations included in and derived from the Conventions of June 16, 1922, and October 23, 1925, the Executive shall proceed immediately to conclude arrangements with the holders of the respective bonds, according to the following bases:

1. The obligations shall be consolidated in a single issue the annuity of which shall be within the capacity to pay of the Government of the Republic, the refunding period not less than forty-five years, and the rate of interest not more than five per cent per annum.

2. There shall not be included in the consolidation the obliga-

[2] *Cf.* note 154, p. 316, *supra.*

tions arising from the Debt of the National Railways of Mexico Company, which shall be paid in accordance with arrangements which the Company may make directly with its creditors.

3. As specific guarantee of the payment of the principal and interests of the new debt, the Executive may pledge the revenues from such imposts and duties as he may consider suitable.

4. Payments made in accordance with any agreement or agreements that may be signed shall have only the character of deposits until such agreement or agreements are ratified by the Honorable Congress of the Union and accepted by a majority of the creditors.

5. The Executive shall submit for the approval of the Honorable Federal Congress any convention or conventions which he may conclude in the exercise of the powers vested in him by the present article.

Article IV. The Executive is authorized to conclude with foreign governments conventions for the settlement *en bloc* of the claims presented by the subjects of each country before the respective Commissions, when, in the judgment of the Executive, such a procedure is advantageous to the national interests.

INDEX

INDEX

References to citations of books, periodicals, etc., are to first citations.

Aberdeen, Earl of, 13, 34, 59
Adams, Charles Francis, 137–139, 153, 183
Adams, E. D., *British Interests and Activities in Texas 1838–1846*, cited, 87
Agrarian reform, 310, 311, 341. *See also* Debt of Mexico, agrarian
Agreements, *see* Bondholders, agreements of Mexico with
Aguascalientes, Military Convention of, 264
Alamán, Lucas, 25, 29; *Historia de Méjico*, cited, 17
Alcabala, 19
Aldham, Captain, 123, 124, 129, 131–133, 194
Almonte, Juan N., 115, 127, 148, 152
Alvares Correa, H. M., *The International Controls of Public Finances*, cited, 321
American Academy of Political and Social Science, *International Relations of the United States*, 1914, cited, 258
American Journal of International Law, cited, 321
American republics, conference of, 264; mediation by, 266
Amortization, *see* Bonds, amortization provided for
Antoine y Zayas, Juan, 101–104
Anuario Estadístico, cited, 198
Argentina, 261, 335
Arlitt, J. L., contract for loan by, 302
Arrillaga, Francisco de, 25
Association Nationale des Porteurs Français de Valeurs Mobilières, 11

Banco Central Mexicano, 242
Banco de Londres y México, 237, 242, 268
Banco de México, 313, 333, 337. *See also* Banco Único
Banco Mexicano de Comercio é Industria, 242
Banco Nacional de México, 196, 212, 219, 220, 228, 236, 237, 242–244, 249, 250, 258, 261, 268, 287, 305
Banco Nacional Mexicano, *see* Banco Nacional de México
Banco Único, 271, 287, 288, 293, 304, 305
Bancroft, Hubert Howe, *History of Mexico*, cited, 16
Bankers, International Committee of, on Mexico, 3–4, 12, 276–278, 281–291, 293, 294, 301–308, 313–317, 324–325, 339
Bank für Handel und Industrie, 240
Banks, advances by, 113, 220, 253, 254, 258, 268, 290; commissions to, 36–37, 43, 75–77, 154, 156, 162–164, 213, 222, 236, 344; participation of, in loans to Mexico, 29–45, 50, 51, 58, 73, 153, 154, 157, 162–163, 212–216, 218–220, 227, 228, 236, 237, 240, 242–244, 249, 250, 259, 326, 327, 344; profits of, on bonds, 36, 93, 214, 219, 236, 244, 250, 344; seizure of metallic reserves of, 268
Banque de l'Union Parisienne, 249
Banque de Paris et des Pays-Bas, 243, 249, 259, 288
Barclay, Herring, Richardson and Company, 29, 30, 41–45, 50
Baring Brothers, 51, 58, 73
Barra, Francisco León de la, 246
Barra, Luis L. de la, 249
Barragán, Miguel, 67, 70
Barron, Forbes, and Company, 113
Barry, James, 22, 23, 26, 40, 41
Belgium, agrarian debt, interest of, in, 320; association of foreign bondholders formed in, 11; bonds held in, 1, 10, 319; bonds sold in, 10; debt and debt service of, 335; International Committee of Bankers, representation on, 282
Berliner Handelsgesellschaft, 240
Bleichroeder, house of, 212–215, 218, 227, 228
Boletín de la Secretaría de Educación Pública, cited, 310
Bondholders, agents of, in Mexico, 58, 60, 96, 97, 146, 181, 183, 184, 187, 283, 305, 314, 315; agreements of Mexico

with, 3–4, 12–13, 61, 72, 75, 91, 96–98, 153, 192, 197, 202, 208, 288, 292, 301, 305–307, 313–317, 324, 325, 341, 379–386, 421–436; committees representing, 11–13, 58–61, 75, 89, 91, 96, 179, 197, 202, 203, 208, 269, 276–278, *see also* Bankers, International Committee of; Corporation of Foreign, *see* Corporation of Foreign Bondholders; funds of, seized, 117–119, 130, 131; interests of, not necessarily coinciding with those of committees representing them, 203; opposed to hostile interposition, 186; organized action by, 3–4, 11–13, 57–61, 73, 75, 91, 96, 97, 118, 130, 131, 183, 188, 196–197, 207–208 (*see also* Bankers, International Committee of; Bondholders, committees representing; Corporation of Foreign Bondholders); sacrifices made by, 4–6, 62, 75, 93, 97, 207–210, 289–291, 307, 325, 329

Bonds, "active," 72, 76–79, 91, 209; amortization provided for, 36, 43, 213, 215, 222, 225, 236, 244, 344, 348, 352; arrears of interest on, 51, 53, 58, 62, 65, 93, 97, 130, 154, 187, 191, 193, 209, 256, 289, 290, 314, 318; auction of, 176–179, 190; Caja de Prestamos, 241, 286, 307, 308; Carbajal-Corlies, 162–166, 187, 190–195, 206, 214; conversions of, 70–78, 91–93, 98, 154, 157, 205–211, 228–229, 243–244; "deferred," 72, 76–79, 90, 91, 209; de Kay, *see* de Kay, John W.; distribution of, 1, 319; Huerta, 248–251, 259; interest funded on, 60–62, 93, 154, 209, 291, 307; issues of: 1824, 4–5, 35, 326, 327; 1825, 4–5, 43, 326–328; 1831, 60–62, 326, 328; 1837–1843, 70–78, 326, 328; 1846, 93, 209, 326, 328; 1851, 98, 209, 212, 326, 328; 1864, 153–156, 209; 1865, 158–166, 328; 1886, 6, 10–11, 208, 246, 289, 318, 328; 1888, 5, 6, 10–11, 214, 229, 246, 262, 326, 328; 1889, 215, 246, 262, 289, 318, 327, 329; 1890, 218, 229, 246, 262, 327, 329; 1893, 221, 222, 229, 246, 262, 327, 329; 1894, 223–226, 246, 289, 318; 1899, 226–229, 246, 262, 289, 318, 327, 329; 1904, 234, 246, 262, 289, 318, 327, 329; 1908, 241–242, 289, 318, 327, 329; 1910, 242–244, 247, 262, 289, 318, 327, 329; 1912, 247, 262; 1913, 248, 254, 262, 289, 318, 327, 329; market price of, 5, 42, 50, 55, 76, 218, 330–331; Maximilian, 4–5, 153–156, 320; municipal, 233; Peza, 116, 117; proposed purchase of, by syndicate, 283, 284; railway, *see* Debt of Mexico, guaranteed railway; redemption of, 5, 36, 43–44, 213, 243; repudiation of, 4–5, 155–156, 171–173, 249, 320; Sanchez Ochoa, *see* Sanchez Ochoa, General Gaspar; San Luis Potosí, 206; Series "C," 259; State, 232, 246, 289, 318; utilization of, 40, 43, 61, 78, 93, 98, 154–158, 164–166, 209, 213–215, 218, 222–224, 229, 235, 243, 247, 250, 326, 327, 344; Woodhouse, *see* Woodhouse, Daniel

Branch, H. N., *The Mexican Constitution of 1917 compared with the Constitution of 1857*, cited, 270

Bravo, Nicolás, 25, 91

Brazil, 261, 335

British and Foreign State Papers, cited, 33

Broughton, Charles R., 31, 32

Bryan, William J., 251, 254

Buchanan, James, 88, 108, 112, 121

Budgets, *see* Revenues and expenditures

Bustamante, Anastasio, 57, 62, 67, 69, 70

Butler, Anthony, 65, 66

Cabrera, Luis, 271, 273, 274, 279

Calero, Manuel, 248; *The Mexican Policy of President Wilson*, cited, 248

California, Lower, desired by United States, 121–123

Callahan, J. M., *Evolution of Seward's Mexican Policy*, cited, 115

Calles, Plutarco Elias, 305, 312, 314

Canning, George, 28, 32, 34, 40, 42

Capacity to pay, *see* Debt of Mexico, burden of

Carbajal, Francisco, 261

Carbajal, General José María, 158–164. *See also* Bonds, Carbajal-Corlies

Carlotta, Empress of Mexico, 169

Carranza, Venustiano, 10, 249, 260, 261, 263–269, 272–275, 278, 280

Casasús, Joaquin D., *La deuda contraida en Londres*, cited, 20

Cass, Lewis, 108, 112, 113, 121, 126

Catholic Church, *see* Church, Catholic

Caturegli, Alfredo, 272

Certificates of 1851, 98, 209; of 1866, 209

Chile, 31, 38, 261, 335

Church, Catholic, 20, 86, 93, 113–115, 122, 125, 131, 134, 135, 140, 143, 311, 312

Churchwell, William M., 121
Claims, pecuniary, of foreign governments, 316, 320, 323. *See also* Belgium, France, Germany, Great Britain, Spain, United States
Clark, J. Reuben, Jr., 9, 309
Colby, Bainbridge, 281
Colombia, 22, 31, 37, 38, 43, 44, 312
Commerce, U. S. Department of, *Railways of Mexico*, cited, 197
Commercial and Financial Chronicle, cited, 246
Committees representing bondholders, *see* Bondholders, committees representing
Comonfort, Ignacio, 104, 112, 113
Comptoir National d'Escompte de Paris, 243, 249
Congress, United States, Executive Documents of: House, 351, 25th Congr., 2d session, cited, 67; House, 100, 37th Congr., 2d session, cited, 138; House, 73, 39th Congr., 1st session, cited, 160; Senate, 20, 40th Congr., 1st session, cited, 171
Constitution, Mexican, of 1824, 39, 48; of 1836 (*siete leyes*), 71; of 1857, 113; of 1917, 12, 270, 271, 310, 311
Contratos hechos en los Estados Unidos por los comisionados del gobierno de México durante los años de 1865 y 1866, cited, 162
Conventions, diplomatic, concerning debts, 6, 7, 9, 83, 100–103, 107, 110, 114, 124, 134–135, 138, 143–147, 173, 174, 176, 177, 179, 187, 190, 200, 201, 205, 208–210, 214, 215, 223
Conversions of bonds, *see* Bonds, conversions of
Convoys, seizure of, 24, 35
Coolidge, Calvin, 13
Corlies, John W., and Company, 162–164. *See also* Bonds, Carbajal-Corlies
Corporation of Foreign Bondholders, activities of, 11, 186–188, 269; annual reports of, cited, 36
Corwin, Thomas, 127, 133–137, 142–144, 149–151
Cowley, Earl, 137
Crédit Lyonnais, 243
Crédit Mobilier, 154
"Credits," 35, 67, 82
Cuenta del Tesoro, cited, 216
Currency, fluctuation of, 220, 222, 233, 247, 267; issue of, 24, 263, 264, 267; reform of, 233–236
Customs duties, assignments of, 7, 36, 43, 53, 54, 65, 69–70, 72, 75, 82, 83, 91, 96, 97, 99, 101–104, 119, 124, 130, 135, 152, 154, 169, 173–175, 184, 185, 203–204, 213, 216–219, 222, 228, 244, 249; certificates redeemable for, 51, 52, 69, 71, 75, 117

Davis, Joseph S., 314, 315, 325
Dayton, William L., 137, 138
Debentures, 75
Debt of Mexico, amount of, at various epochs: 1822, 17–18, 26; 1823, 25; 1838, 81; 1850, 99; 1860, 124; 1861, 7, 133; 1873, 187; 1885, 214; 1888, 262; 1889, 215; 1890, 262; 1893, 220, 221, 262; 1894, 226; 1895, 226; 1897, 226; 1899, 226, 262; 1900, 229, 230; 1901, 226; 1903, 226, 262; 1904, 262; 1910, 242–243, 262; 1911, 246, 262; 1913, 226, 262; 1914, 262; 1929, 1, 318; 1824–1925, 344; burden of, 1, 4, 79–80, 230, 233, 243, 286–289, 291, 307, 335–337, 344; distribution of, 1, 319, 320, 323; kinds of: agrarian, 316, 323, 333; consolidated, 205–207, 221; direct, 1, 305, 307, 315, 323; floating, 1, 212, 213, 221, 319; guaranteed railway, 1, 239–240, 246–247, 286, 289, 305, 307, 323; guaranteed State, 232, 246, 289, 318; redeemable internal, 224-226; repudiation of, *see* Bonds, repudiation of. *See also* Bonds, Conventions
Decrees, laws and orders relating to finance: June 25, 1822, 22, 26; May 1, 1823, 26; May 14, 1824, 36; June 28, 1824, 18, 223; November 16, 1827, 52, 53; November 21, 1827, 52; May 23, 1828, 54, 58; October 28, 1828, 54; October 2, 1830, 60, 62; May 20, 1831, 61; January 20, 1836, 69; April 4, 1837, 70; April 12, 1837, 70; May 6, 1837, 69; June 1, 1839, 74; July 29, 1839, 74; December 13, 1843, 77; April –, 1845, 90; July 19, 1847, 92, 96; October 14, 1850, 97, 98, 205; November 30, 1850, 98, 205, 206, 223; January 23, 1857, 146; January 17, 1861, 205; May 29, 1861, 130; July 17, 1861, 134, 146; April 10, 1864, 154; June 14, 1883, 198–200, 202, 222; June 22, 1885, 205–211, 222; December 13, 1887, 212; May 27, 1889, 223. May 29, 1893, 222; September 6, 1894;

209, 211, 223, 224; December –, 1904, 234; May 30, 1913, 249; December 23, 1913, 256; December 24, 1917, 263; December 18, 1925, 309; December 23, 1925, 309; January 25, 1926, 308; January 25, 1929, 316
de Kay, John W., 249, 258–260, 290
Department of State, Press releases of, cited, 285; *Proceedings of the United States-Mexican Commission convened in Mexico City, May 14, 1923*, cited, 298
Deutsche Bank, 228, 242, 249
Dewey, Davis R., *Financial History of the United States*, cited, 165
Diario Oficial, cited, 154
Díaz, General Porfirio, 2–3, 171, 186, 188–190, 196, 202, 216, 221, 226, 244, 340
Díaz Dufoo, Carlos, *Limantour*, cited, 234; *Una Victoria Financiera*, cited, 240
Dictamen de la Mayoria de Crédito Público, cited, 99
Diplomacia Mexicana, cited, 21
Diplomatic Correspondence of the United States, cited, 68
Doblado, Mexican Minister of Foreign Affairs, 148, 151, 152
Documentos relativos de la Deuda Interior, cited, 99
Documents relating to the de la Huerta-Lamont Agreement, cited, 286
Doyle, Percy, 96, 101, 103
Drago, Luis N., *State Loans in their relation to International Law*, cited, 321
Dresdner Bank, 216, 228, 249
Dublán, Manuel, 203–211, 216, 340; *Cuenta del uso de la autorización para consolidar y convertir las deudas ferrocarriles*, cited, 216; *Informe . . . sobre el emprestito contratado en Europa de £10,500,000*, cited, 209
——— and José María Lozano, *see Legislación Mexicana*
Ducoing, Magua and Atocha, 81, 82, 84, 85
Dunlop, Captain, 119–120, 123, 124, 129, 194

Economist, The, cited, 173
Economista, El, cited, 315
Ejidos, 311, 338
Ellis, Powhatan, 84
Encyclopedia, Catholic, cited, 20
Encyclopédie, La Grande, cited, 128
Escobar y Armendariz, Jesús, 155, 156
Esteva, Minister of Finance, 45, 50
Expenditures of Mexico at various epochs, *see* Revenues and expenditures

Fall Committee, 280. *See also Investigation of Mexican Affairs*
Federal District, bonds of municipalities of, 233
Ferrocarriles Nacionales de México, *Third Annual Report*, cited, 247
Ferrocarril Nacional del Istmo de Tehuantepec, cited, 216
Finance Committee, Mexican, established by Maximilian, 153, 154, 156
Fischer Williams, Sir John, *International Law and International Financial Obligations Arising from Contract*, cited, 14
Fletcher, Henry P., 272
Foreign Relations of United States, cited, 184
Forsyth, John, 104–113, 121
Fort, Serment P., and Company, 103
Foster, John W., 187–195
France, bondholders supported by, 257; bonds of Mexico floated in, 10, 154, 173, 218, 228, 243, 249; bonds of Mexico held in, 1, 9–10, 12, 319; Corwin treaty, attitude of, toward, 137–139, 149; debt and debt service of, 335; direct lenders to Mexico supported by, 7, 69, 128, 133; Huerta, attitude of, toward, 251, 254, 255; International Committee of Bankers, attitude of, toward, 12, 276; intervention by, 2, 73, 80, 134, 137–142, 147–149, 152, 169; Maximilian bonds delivered to, 155; Maximilian loans encouraged by, 154, 173, 217, 320; "pastry war" of, with Mexico, 73, 80; pecuniary claims of, 138, 155, 320; relations of, with Mexico in general, 68, 115, 123, 134, 173, 180, 186, 196, 217, 268, 271; treaties and conventions negotiated by, with Mexico, 7, 100–103
Fuente, A. de la, 129

Gamboa, Frederico, 252, 253
Germany, bonds of Mexico held in, 1, 10, 319; Huerta, attitude of, toward, 251, 254, 255; International Committee of Bankers, representation on, 286; loans of Mexico floated in, 10, 212–216, 218, 228, 236, 240, 242, 244, 250; relations

of, with Mexico in general, 123, 186, 215, 268, 269, 273
Germiny, Count de, 153, 156
Gibbs, Antony, and Sons, 212
Glyn, Mills and Company, 153, 157
Goldschmidt and Company, 31, 32, 35–45
Gómez Farías, Valentin, 67, 69
Gómez Pedraza, President, 55, 62–65, 69
González, Manuel, 199, 200, 207
González, Minister of Foreign Affairs, 63
Great Britain, bondholders, representations of, in behalf of, 7–9, 11, 57–60, 63–65, 73–76, 87, 92–97, 117–119, 129, 131, 133, 145–146, 172, 194–195, 201; bonds of Mexico held in, 1, 9–10, 12, 319; Corwin treaty, attitude of, toward, 137–139, 143, 149, 151–152; debt and debt service of, 335; direct lenders to Mexico supported by, 7, 69, 82, 83, 100–103, 110, 114, 119–120, 123–124, 134, 146, 194–195; Huerta, attitude of, toward, 251, 254, 255; International Committee of Bankers, attitude of, toward, 12, 276; intervention by, 2, 7–9, 134, 137–142, 147–149; loans of Mexico floated in, 8, 10, 35–45, 154, 156, 157, 213, 216, 218, 228, 233, 236, 240, 242, 244, 250; pecuniary claims of, 151, 320; relations of, with Mexico in general, 8, 28, 29, 40, 47, 87, 89, 115, 129, 131, 134, 173–175, 180, 186, 200–202; treaties and conventions negotiated by, with Mexico, 7, 46–47, 83, 100–103, 114, 143–147, 151, 152, 174, 194–195, 200, 205
Gruening, Ernest, *Mexico and Its Heritage*, cited, 310
Guerrero, General, 55, 57

Hacienda, Memorias de, see Memorias de Hacienda
Hague Convention on use of force for recovery of contract debts, 9, 11, 12, 257, 321
Hall, *International Law*, cited, 321
Hallgarten and Company, 240
Harding, Warren G., 294, 297
Heffter, *Europäische Völkerrecht*, cited, 172
Herrera, José Joaquin, 88
Hervey, Lionel, 32–34, 46
Holy Alliance, 37, 38, 40
Honduras, 9
Huerta, Adolfo de la, 280, 283, 284–288, 292–297, 299, 300
Huerta, Victoriano, 10, 248–261
Hughes, Charles E., 282, 295–298

International Committee of Bankers on Mexico, *see* Bankers, International Committee of
Investigation of Mexican affairs, Preliminary Report and Hearings, cited, 279
Irrigation, plans for, 242, 288, 293
Italy, debt and debt service of, 335; relations of, with Mexico, 186
Iturbide, Agustin de, 16, 17, 20, 21, 25, 31

Jackson, Andrew, 65, 66, 70
Jackson, Henry R., 202, 207
Jecker, J. B., and Company, bonds purchased by, 4–5, 116, 117, 128, 133, 158
Jecker, Torre and Company, advances made by, 102, 103
Juárez, Benito Pablo. 113, 118–128, 151, 152, 171–175, 186
Justo Corro, José, 67, 70

Kératry, Émile de, *La Créance Jecker, les Indemnités Françaises et les Emprunts Mexicains*, cited, 117
Kinder, Thomas, Jr., house of, 28, 30
Kuhn, Loeb and Company, 240, 249

Ladd, Edwin F., *Our Duty to America*, cited, 295
Ladenburg, Thalmann and Company, 240
Laguna Seca, funds seized at, 123, 130, 138, 145
Lamont, Thomas W., 278, 281, 283–288, 292, 302–308
Lansing, Robert, 272, 273
Latané, John H., *The United States and Latin America*, cited, 147
Lazard Speyer-Ellison, 236, 242
League of Nations, *Memorandum on Public Finance*, cited, 335
Lebrija, Minister of Finance, 80, 81
Lefêvre, Eugène, *Intervention Française au Mexique*, cited, 104
Legislación Mexicana, cited, 18
Lerdo de Tejada, Miguel, 44, 105, 106, 122
Lerdo de Tejada, Sebastián, 182, 184, 186–189
Letcher, R. T., 98, 100
Lill, Thomas R., *National Debt of Mexico*, cited, 128
Lillienthal, Jesse W., 217–218
Limantour, José Yves, 221–243; reports of, cited, 222

Lincoln, Abraham, 135, 136
Lind, John, 252, 253
Livingston, Edward, 66
Lizardi, F. de, and Company, 73–77, 93
Loans, external, *see* Bonds, issues of
Loans, forced, 17, 18, 20, 21, 56, 67–69, 87, 170
Loans, internal, 17–18, 20, 21, 53, 54, 63, 67–68, 81–82, 87, 93, 101–103, 113, 115–117, 171, 189, 210, 222, 226, 230, 235, 253, 256, 263, 268. *See also* Loans, forced
Loans, railway, *see* Debt of Mexico, guaranteed railway; Railways in Mexico
Loans, unsuccessful negotiations for, 22, 23, 55, 105–111, 115, 136, 143, 149–151, 159–161, 164, 167, 199, 256, 271–275, 287–288, 293–295, 301–305
Lobato, General José María, 33, 39
London Times Annual Financial Review, cited, 268
Lozano, José María, *see Legislación Mexicana*
Lyons, Lord, 137

McCaleb, Walter F., *The Public Finances of Mexico*, cited, 17
Macedo, Pablo, *Tres Monografías*, cited, 100, 125
Mackie, P., 28, 29, 30, 32
McLane, Robert M., 121–123, 126
Madero, Francisco, 245–247
Manero, Antonio, *El Banco de México*, cited, 267
Maniau, Joaquin, *Compendio de la historia de la real hacienda de Nueva España*, cited, 19
Manning, William R., *Early Diplomatic Relations between the United States and Mexico*, cited, 33
Manuscript Despatches of the United States, cited, 28
Manuscript Instructions of the United States, cited, 84
Mariscal, Ignacio, 201, 203
Marshall, John, 58–60
Martinez del Rio Brothers, internal bonds held by, 101
Masonic orders, conflict of, 51
Mathew, George B., 118
Maximilian, Emperor of Mexico, 2, 4–5, 148, 153–158, 166, 167, 169, 170, 172–173. *See also* Bonds, Maximilian
Mayer, Brantz, 86
Memorias de Hacienda, cited, 17
Mendoza, Tomás, 193
Mesilla, purchase of by United States, 104
Mexican Review, cited, 263
Mexico, A Weekly, cited, 253
Mexico, bonds of City of, *see* Federal District
Mexico, Financial Documents, cited, 236
Michelena, José Mariano, 38
Migoni, Francisco de Borja, 21, 22, 26–39
Miramón, Miguel, 4–5, 114–118, 127, 158
Mon, Alejandro, 115, 127
Mon-Almonte treaty, 115, 127
Monroe, James, 21, 40, 42, 47, 111; doctrine of, 110, 138, 140, 245
Montes de Oca, Luis, 313–317
Montgomery, Nicod and Company, 81, 83
Moody, *Analyses of Investments*, cited, 232
Mora, José María Luis, *Méjico y Sus Revoluciones*, cited, 17
Morán, Padre, 100, 102, 124
Moratorium, 256, 267
Morgan, Grenfell and Company, 243, 249, 269
Morgan, Harjes and Company, 249
Morgan, J. P., and Company, 228, 243, 249, 275, 288
Morgan, J. S., and Company, 228
Morgan, Philip H., 198
Morier, James, 46
Morny, Duc de, interest in Jecker bonds, 128, 168
Morrow, Dwight W., 315
Muzquiz, Melchor, 62

Napoleon III, 2, 5, 134, 166–169
Negrete, Pedro Celestino, 25
Nelson, Thomas H., 184
Netherlands, The, bondholders, activities of, 11, 98, 202, 282; bonds of Mexico held in, 1, 9, 10, 319; bonds of Mexico sold in, 10, 213, 218, 228; debt and debt service of, 335; International Committee of Bankers, representation on, 282; pecuniary claims of, 320
New York Times, cited, 248
Nieto, Rafael, 268, 275–279
Noetzlin, Edward, 196, 202

Obregón, Alvaro, 10, 263, 264, 279–288, 292–301
Ocampo, Melchor, 120
O'Donojú, Juan, 16
O'Gorman, Charles, 32–34

Oil companies, assurances sought by, 295–297, 301; taxes, dispute regarding, 283; taxes paid in advance by, 300
Ortega, Jesús González, 167
Ortiz de Montellano, Mariano, *Apuntes para la liquidación de la deuda contraida en Londres*, cited, 23
O'Shaughnessy, Nelson, 254
Osterheld, T. W., 273, 275
Otterbourg, Marcus, 171
Otway, L. C., 114

Pacheco, Juan B., 127
Packing Company, Mexican National, Limited, 259
Pakenham, British Chargé d'Affaires, 60, 63, 64
Palmer, William J., 192
Palmerston, Viscount, 8, 73, 89, 94, 95, 173, 321, 322
Pani, Alberto J., 297–300, 302–308; *La Politica Hacendaria y la Revolución*, cited, 289
Paredes, Mariano, 88, 91
Parliamentary Session Papers, cited, 201
Paxson, F. L., *Independence of the South American Republics*, cited, 33
Payno y Flores, Manuel, *Cuentas, Gastos, Acreedores y Otros Asuntos del Tiempo de la Intervención Francesa y del Imperio*, cited, 154; *México y Sus Cuestiones Financieras con la Inglaterra, la España, y la Francia*, cited, 18
Peat and Company, 260
Pedido de los acreedores del erario nacional, cited, 81
Penaud, Admiral, 120
Pérez Verdía, L., *Compendio de la historia Mexicana*, cited, 128
Perigny, Maurice de, *Les États Unis du Mexique*, cited, 234
Pershing, General John J., 266
Peru, 31, 37, 38, 335
Petroleum, ownership of, 309; production of, 273, 275, 302, 312; taxes on, 283, 300, 308, 312. *See also* Oil companies
Peza bonds, 116, 117
Phillimore, *International Law*, cited, 321
Pichon, Stephen, 322
Pierce, Franklin, 108
Plumb, Edward L., 177–179
Poinsett, Joel R., 28, 44, 46, 47, 50–56; *Notes on Mexico*, cited, 33
Ports, works at, 221, 224–225, 232, 235, 236, 246, 256
Powell, Fred Wilbur, *The Railways of Mexico*, cited, 239
Préstamos, Caja de, *see* Bonds
Priestley, Herbert Ingram, *The Mexican Nation, a History*, cited, 16
Prim, Spanish Commissioner, 147–149

Railways in Mexico, in general, 183, 188, 192, 193, 213, 216–218, 221, 224, 235, 237–240, 246–247, 256, 286, 291, 308, 327, 333; in particular, Chiapas, 221; International 185, 238; Interoceanic, 213, 219, 234, 238; Mexican, 185, 188, 218, 235; Mexican Central, 185, 218, 235, 238–240; Mexican National, 192, 197, 219, 221, 235, 238–240; Mexican Southern, 235; Michoacán, 221; Monterrey and Gulf, 221, 235; National, 239–240, 247, 275, 286, 291, 304, 307, 308, 325, 337; Tehuantepec, 1, 184, 185, 213, 215, 228, 229, 235, 247, 316, 318, 339; Veracruz and Pacific, 235, 247. *See also* Debt of Mexico, guaranteed railway
Ramirez, José F., 100, 101
Research Committee on Latin America, 309
Revenues and expenditures of Mexico at various epochs: 1789 (New Spain), 17–18; 1823, 24; 1825, 39, 47; 1826, 49; 1836–1837, 68; 1837–1838, 80; 1843, 79; 1846, 88; 1847–1848, 94; 1866, 169; 1878, 191–192; 1882–1885, 197, 199; 1894–1900, 231; 1906–1907, 240; 1907–1908, 240; 1908–1909, 241; 1909–1910, 241; 1918, 275; 1922, 312 (*see* tables, 326, 327, 344)
Revolutions and revolts: 1822–1823 (Santa Anna), 25; 1828 (Guerrero), 55; 1829 (Bustamante), 56, 57; 1832 (Santa Anna) 62; 1844 (Herrera), 88; 1845 (Paredes), 88; 1846 (Santa Anna), 92; 1854 (Comonfort), 104; 1858 (Zuloaga) 113; 1858 (Miramón), 114; 1871 (Lerdo, Díaz), 186; 1876 (Díaz), 188–189; 1910 (Madero), 3, 245; 1913 (Carranza), 260; 1920 (Obregón), 279; 1923 (de la Huerta), 300; 1929, 4, 13, 37
Revue de Droit International, cited, 321
Rippy, J. Fred, *The United States and Mexico*, cited, 88, 89, 123, 126
Robertson, William P., 96

Romero, Matías, 158–161, 164–166, 175–179, 186; *Memoria de Hacienda y Crédito Público*, cited, 17; *Mexico and the United States*, cited, 49
Rosecrans, General W. S., 175, 181–184
Rothschild, house of, 113, 115
Russell, Lord John, 117, 118, 128–131, 137–141, 143, 152
Russia, attitude of, toward Huerta, 254; influence of, on Mexico, 310
Ryan, Thomas, 217–219

St. John, Sir Spenser, 201
Saligny, Count de, 128, 147–149
Sanchez Ochoa, General Gaspar, bonds issued by, 164, 187
Santa Anna, Antonio Lopez de, 25, 62, 67, 69, 70, 80, 88, 92, 96, 104, 167
Schurz, Carl, 139
Scott, James Brown, *The Hague Conventions and Declarations of 1899 and 1907*, cited, 257
Secretaría de Hacienda y Crédito Público, *La Deuda Exterior de México*, cited, 303
Seligman, Henry, 217–218
Seligmann Brothers, 216
Senate, United States: McLane treaty rejected by, 123; Corwin treaty rejected by, 142, 150–151
Seward, William H., 2, 3, 135–137, 141, 142, 160, 166–168, 178
Siglo XIX, cited, 181
Sinaloa, bonds of, guaranteed by Mexico, 232, 318
Sinking funds, *see* Bonds, amortization provided for
Slidell, James M., 88, 89
Smith, Dennis A., 23, 26, 41
Société Générale pour Favoriser le Developpement du Commerce et de l'Industrie en France, 243, 249
South American Journal, cited, 220
Spain, Corwin treaty, attitude of, toward, 137–140, 149; debt and debt service of, 335; exploitation policy of, in New Spain, 17; Huerta, attitude of, toward, 251, 254; intervention by, 2, 138–142, 147–149; pecuniary claims of, 127, 320; protests by, 123, 200; relations of, with Mexico in general, 21–24, 26, 39, 40, 47, 51, 56, 115, 127, 134, 173, 180, 186; treaties and conventions negotiated by, with Mexico, 7, 16, 21, 100–104, 115, 127, 174, 205
Speyer and Company, 236, 238, 240, 242, 247, 250, 275, 281
Speyer Brothers, 236, 240, 242
Spitzer, A., and Company, 249
Stabilization of peso, *see* Currency, reform of
Staples, Robert P., 27, 29, 30–35, 40, 41
States, bonds of, *see* Bonds, State
Statist, The, cited, 220
Sterrett, Joseph E., 314, 315, 325
Stevens, Thaddeus, 166
Sturm, General Herman, 165–167; *The Republic of Mexico and Its American Creditors*, cited, 167
Summerlin, George T., 297
Switzerland, bonds of Mexico held in, 1, 10, 319; International Committee of Bankers, representation on, 282

Taft, William H., 245; *Opinion and Award* in arbitration between Great Britain and Costa Rica, cited, 172
Tamaulipas, bonds of, guaranteed by Mexico, 232, 318
Tampico, arrest of Americans at, 260
Tannenbaum, Frank, *The Mexican Agrarian Revolution*, cited, 311
Tehuantepec, proposed ship canal across, 184; railroad company, 184. *See also* Railways in Mexico
Teixeira de Mattos Brothers, 236, 242
Tellez, Manuel C., 281
Texas, desired by the United States, 66; Mexican struggle for recovery of, 70, 80, 87, 89; plan for colonization of, 70–72, 89; plan for payment of 5,000,000 pesos to bondholders by, in consideration of Mexican recognition of independence, 87
Thompson, Waddy, 82, 84, 85
Thouvenel, French Minister of Foreign Affairs, 137, 138
Treasury obligations, *see* Bonds, issues of
Treaties and conventions of Mexico with other countries: Colombia, 44; France, 74, 100–103, 120; Great Britain, 46, 47, 83, 100–103, 114, 120, 123, 145–147, 151, 152, 174, 200; Spain, 16, 21, 100–104, 115, 127, 174; the United States, 86, 95, 106–108, 122, 123, 149–151, 178
Treaties, Conventions, International Acts, Protocols and Agreements between the United States and other Powers, 1776–1909, cited, 84

United States, The, bonds of Mexico held in, 1, 3, 10, 12; bonds of Mexico sold or offered in, 9–11, 23–24, 65–67, 105, 160–164, 189, 198, 217, 228, 271, 272, 274, 285, 304; debt and debt service of, 335; debt of Mexico, guarantee by, proposed, 181–183, 189, 273; debt of Mexico, purchase by, proposed, 183; debt of Mexico, recognition of, by Mexico, demanded, 281, 292, 296–298, 306; direct lenders to Mexico denied support by, 85; direct lenders to Mexico supported by, 82, 84, 100; European intervention in Mexico, attitude of, toward, 2, 40, 126, 141, 166–168; Huerta, opposition of, to, 248, 251–255, 257, 260–261; International Committee of Bankers, attitude of, toward, 12, 276, 283, 292; intervention by, apprehended, 247; official loan desired from, 65, 106, 133–140, 166–167; pecuniary claims of, against Mexico, 85–87, 98, 178, 190, 274, 281, 283, 320; relations of, with Mexico in general, 21, 89–92, 95, 104, 181, 190, 193, 265, 298; revolutions, attitude of, toward, 2, 10, 112, 121, 126, 171, 189, 219, 265, 274; territory of Mexico acquired by, 66, 95–96, 104; treaties and conventions negotiated by, with Mexico, 84, 95, 106–108, 121–123, 137, 142–143, 149–151, 178; vested rights of, insisted on, 274, 281, 282, 285, 296–298, 309; war of, with Mexico, 88–89, 94–96, 101
United States Daily, cited, 285
United States, European and West Virginia Land and Mining Company, *see* Woodhouse, Daniel
Universal, El, cited, 286
Vattel, *Droit des gens*, cited, 321
Venezuela, 22, 312
Veracruz: bonds of, guaranteed by Mexico, 232, 318; occupation of, by the United States, 261
Victoria, Guadalupe, 25, 28, 29, 47, 50, 53, 54
Villa, Francisco, 263, 264, 266

Wallace, General Lewis, 158–159, 161
Ward, H. G., 32–34, 47; *Mexico*, cited, 49
Warrants for vacant lands, 70–72
Webster, Daniel, 84
Westlake, *International Law*, cited, 321
Wilson, Henry Lane, 251
Wilson, Woodrow, 10, 248, 251–255, 257, 260–261
Woodhouse, Daniel, secretary and financial agent of United States, European and West Virginia Land and Mining Company, 159–162, 167
Wyke, Sir Charles, 128, 129, 131–133, 143–149, 151–152
Wyllie, Robert Crichton: *The Present State and Prospects of the Spanish American Loans*, cited, 89; *México: Noticia sobre su hacienda pública bajo el gobierno español y despues de la independencia*, cited, 90

Yearbook, Mexican, cited, 238

Zamacona, Manuel María, 135, 143–147
Zamora, Governor, 119
Zarco, Francisco, 180, 181
Zavala, Lorenzo de, 55; *Ensayo Historico de las Revoluciones de México*, cited, 17
Zozaya, Manuel, 23, 24
Zuloaga, Felix, 113, 114

MEXICO

IN

INTERNATIONAL FINANCE AND DIPLOMACY

VOL. I. *Mexico and Her Foreign Creditors.* By EDGAR TURLINGTON. 8vo cloth, pp. x + 449. $6.00 net.

VOL. II. *In preparation.* By FREDERICK S. DUNN. An analysis of the diplomatic policies and legal questions relative to the protection of American lives and property in Mexico.

VOL. III. *In preparation.* By HERBERT FEIS. A study of the foreign financing of the railroads of Mexico.

COLUMBIA UNIVERSITY PRESS
COLUMBIA UNIVERSITY
NEW YORK

FOREIGN AGENT
OXFORD UNIVERSITY PRESS
HUMPHREY MILFORD
AMEN HOUSE, LONDON, E.C.

Bei Fragen zur Produktsicherheit wenden Sie sich bitte an:
If you have any questions regarding product safety,
please contact:

Walter de Gruyter GmbH
Genthiner Straße 13
10785 Berlin
productsafety@degruyterbrill.com